DARYL CHAMPION

The Paradoxical Kingdom

Saudi Arabia and the
Momentum of Reform

D0204360

Columbia University Press
New York

Columbia University Press
Publishers since 1893
New York
Copyright © 2003 Columbia University Press
All rights reserved

Library of Congress Cataloging-in-Publication Data
Champion, Daryl.
  The paradoxical kingdom: Saudi Arabia and the momentum of
reform/by Daryl Champion.
    p. cm.
  Includes bibliographical references and index.
  ISBN 0–231–12814–2 (cloth: alk. paper)
  1. Saudi Arabia—Economic conditions—20th century. 2. Saudi
Arabia—Social conditions—20th century. 3. Globalization—Economic
aspects—Saudi Arabia. 4. Social structure—Economic aspects—Saudi
Arabia. I. Title.
HC415.33.C475   2003
330.9538—dc21   2002073706

c 10 9 8 7 6 5 4 3 2 1

ACKNOWLEDGEMENTS

There are a number of people who must be thanked above all others, for without their assistance and support beyond the call of duty, this book could not have been completed. These people are the Director of the Centre for Arab and Islamic Studies (CAIS) at The Australian National University (ANU), Professor Amin Saikal; my parents Yvonne and Bruce; Christine Champion and George Paton. They are all aware of the nature of their varied, vital contributions.

Dr Fiona Hill displayed generosity above the call of duty; her proof-reading, editing and advice on an earlier version of this text was professional, timely and supportive. I also thank Dr Tony Gorman for his vital and painstaking feedback on chapter 1. Tony's contribution was admirable in that it was volunteered in the midst of his own preparations to begin teaching at the American University in Cairo. Dr Andrew Vincent of Macquarie University deserves thanks for his nurturing of my interest in Saudi Arabia during my undergraduate years; without his early encouragement, this book might never have been written.

I would like to thank Professors Bob Springborg and James Piscatori, who offered sound advice and insights whenever they were able. Jim was an exceptionally warm host and valuable adviser during my time at Oxford in 1998. Dr Felix Patrikeeff of the Politics Department at the University of Adelaide displayed great kindness in discussing with me some basic concerns when just such a discussion was required. Hans-Heino Kopietz must be thanked for his extremely valuable support and advice during my time in London and in regular communication thereafter. I also extend my appreciation to Michael Dwyer of Hurst & Co., the publishers, for patience and understanding he has consistently displayed while my personal circumstances have been difficult. I hope the wait will prove to have been worthwhile.

I would like to acknowledge the source of my inspiration for the concept of '*asabiyya* capitalism', which became such a central component of this study. This inspiration sprang from a single, albeit lengthy discussion of my research in June 1999 with Dr Deb Mitchell of the Economics Program at the Research School of Social Sciences at the ANU. It was she who suggested that the development of a Saudi- or Arab-relevant equivalent of the Asian economic crisis-spawned term, 'crony capitalism', might be of use. Dr Mitchell also put me on the track to tackle economic internationalisation as the only currently tangible aspect of 'globalisation'. As far as economic affairs are concerned, I am indebted to my friend Rob Ackland in the Faculty of Economics at the ANU, who assisted me many times whenever I had queries of an economic nature. It was also he who suggested that I contact Dr Mitchell.

There are many others who must be acknowledged for their varied contributions to my work and overall disposition over more than four years. These people include Minerva Nasser-Eddine for her support and companionship in Adelaide, and Aileen Keating, Dr Kirill Nourzhanov, Michael Merrick and Bruce Koepke at the CAIS. Carol Laslett and Chris Kertesz at the CAIS were pillars of support of a very practical kind.

To his Excellency Ambassador Mohammad I. Al Hejailan and First Secretary Abdullah M. Al Rashoud of the Royal Embassy of Saudi Arabia, Canberra I owe a great debt of thanks and appreciation. In Saudi Arabia itself, I wish to express my warm regard and respect for Shaikh Hamad Abu-Nasr al-Shubaili, for Saudi hospitality, and for the Saudi people in general. There are, of course, many others both inside and outside the kingdom whom, for various reasons, I cannot thank publicly; I can only hope that these words will serve as a clear indication of my gratitude for their sometimes extraordinary input.

At this point I should say that I know this book may not be viewed in an entirely positive light in Riyadh. It is, and always has been, my intention not to offend but to conduct research diligently and to present my conclusions as openly as possible. The 'Magic Kingdom' has indeed come a long way in a short time, and on occasion when I pause to reflect on the significance of this remarkable journey I confess to having experienced a feeling approaching awe. Perhaps the kingdom did not quite reach the twenty-first century ahead of time, but I for one would like to see it consolidated there soon without losing what makes the country unique.

Finally I must pay tribute to the sublimity of the offerings of Jean-Philippe Rameau, Christoph Willibald Gluck, Johann Sebastian Bach, Franz Schubert, Johannes Brahms, Erik Satie, Astrud Gilberto, Drew Neumann, Portishead and the noble coffee bean, without which I would surely now be residing in a rubber cell.

Beirut, January 2003 D. C.

CONTENTS

ix

TABLES AND DIAGRAMS

NOTE ON ARABIC TRANSLITERATION
AND CONCEPTS

The late Marshall Hodgson, when introducing his monumental three-volume work *The Venture of Islam* (Hodgson: 1974), lamented that there was no universally accepted system for the transliteration of the Arabic language into English. I, along with many other scholars in the field, can only echo his lament. Though tempted to adopt the system of transliteration employed by the *International Journal of Middle East Studies*, I decided to opt for a more familiar, no-frills system with which the educated general reader would feel comfortable. Even so, no system of transliteration is set in stone, and many augmentative decisions must necessarily be exercised. Such decisions have been made in this book; many of them will displease purists, but few decisions would please all scholars in any case. Hence, some clarification of the system employed here is necessary.

In the interests of simplicity and readability for a non-specialised readership, representation of the Arabic guttural letter *'ain* has been dispensed with. This letter is normally represented by the standard opening inverted comma (') and while scholars may miss it in words such as *'ulama, da'wa* and *'asabiyya*, and in names such as Dir'iyya, 'Abd al-'Aziz, Sa'd, Musa'id, 'Auda and, indeed, Sa'udi, most readers may well be thankful. For this reason, Shi'a and Shi'i have been totally Anglicised and are rendered as Shiite/Shiites. The same policy, however, has not been adopted with the medial *hamza* represented by the closing inverted comma ('), because its absence will lead English-speaking readers to totally incorrect pronunciations. Thus, for example, Ha'il, Ta'if and (Prince) Na'if presented as Hail, Taif and Naif would create an unnecessary barrier to a more nuanced grasp of the subject matter. The diphthong formed by *fatha–ya* has been rendered as *'ai'* (thus, for example: shaikh rather than shaykh or sheikh, Bahrain rather than Bahrayn). The diphthong formed by *fatha–wow* has been rendered as *'au'* (thus, for example, *tauhid* rather than *tawhid*, Auda rather than Awda).

Where Arabic words have entered English usage or are widely recognised by a particular form, they are presented in the familiar form and not italicised (such as Mecca, Jedda, Khobar, Maghreb, Hussein, shaikh, amir).

xiii

Less familiar Arabic words are either italicised throughout, or are presented in italics only at the first occurrence if, like *ulama* and *imam* for example, the word is in frequent use in the book. When quoting directly, or when following the preference of better-known personalities or published authors in the English transliteration of their names, the decision has been taken to use the presented/preferred form. Two important examples illustrate this policy. First, the 'correctly' transliterated name of a relatively well-known Saudi dissident, Saad al-Fagih, is *Faqih*. However, Fagih is the pronounced form in Gulf dialect and is the form preferred by Fagih himself. This is the result of the pronunciation of the guttural letter *qaf* as a 'g'. By the same token, *Qusaibi* becomes Gosaibi for one of Saudi Arabia's better-known ambassadors, Ghazi al-Gosaibi, the kingdom's colourful former ambassador to Britain. Thus, Fagih and Gosaibi, respectively, are the forms presented in this book. On the other hand, in some cases the rendering of the names of individuals had to be assessed in light of whether they would be known outside a small circle of contacts or scholars. If the individual concerned was unlikely to be well known, the transliteration of the name on his business card, for example, was changed to a standardised form. 'Muhammad' is a good example: the various romanised forms of the name must be dealt with cohesively one way or another. Thus an individual who is likely to remain obscure to anyone but myself and who presents his name as Mohamed, would find his name rendered as Muhammad in this book. Likewise, the technically rendered 'Abd Allah has been presented here in the familiar form, Abdullah.

After introduction with full name, an Arabic personage is usually referred to by the main name only, except in referencing, where the definite article *al* is retained (thus, for example, Muhammad al-Masari is generally referred to as Masari). Arabic names with *al* have been listed in the bibliography alphabetically according to the first letter of the name proper. Thus, Fouad al-Farsy would be listed under 'F' for Farsy, although the entry would be: al-Farsy, Fouad (1990). Some Arabic place-names beginning with the definite article have been presented in full at first mention, but have 'al' omitted where used subsequently (e.g. al-Khobar is presented subsequently as Khobar). Except for the names of some Arabic publications, such as *Al-Hawadith* and *Al-Quds al-Arabi* (which are also listed under 'A' in the bibliography), the definite article in Arabic names has been rendered with a lower-case 'a'; the exception is when referring to an extended family as a whole, such as the Al Saud, where the 'Al', the conventional shortened form for *ahl* (people), denotes 'House of Saud' (see glossary). When employed as part of the full name of a (royal) Saudi *individual*, however, the *al* in the al-Saud is rendered in lower case (for example: Abdullah bin Abd al-Aziz al-Saud).

'Arabian' is the term I use in this work to denote a native of the Arabian peninsula—and, in a more specific sense as far as this book is concerned, to citizens of the Saudi state—as opposed to 'Arab', which may be used to refer to any citizen of the Arab world. Alexander Bligh (1984: 3–4) insists on the linguistically accurate term of 'heir designate' to refer to the official Saudi king-in-waiting; however, I have employed the universal form of 'Crown Prince'. Although Christine Moss Helms (1981: 14; but cf. Lacey, 1981: 59–60) argues against using the name Ibn Saud to refer to the founder of the modern kingdom, Abd al-Aziz bin Abd al-Rahman al-Saud, I have often used 'Ibn Saud' to differentiate clearly between the greatest Abd al-Aziz of the Al Saud and the many other Saudis of the same name, including his direct descendants, who are variously featured throughout the book.

A glossary has been compiled which contains the most important, useful and common Saudi-related, Arabic and Islamic terms and concepts employed in the book. It is not meant to be comprehensive, but has been specifically designed to augment this book. Its inclusion has left little need for explanations or definitions in the main text of the book; but, where warranted in incidental cases, some terms are defined in the text. The reader is advised to peruse the glossary before beginning to read the book.

GLOSSARY

The compilation of this glossary owes no debt to any pre-existing one; however, the assistance of the Hans Wehr, *Dictionary of Modern Written Arabic*, New York, 1976, is acknowledged.

ahl/Al: 'family' or 'people'. Conventionally written in its contracted form 'Al' (the Arabic letter *alif* with the sound-lengthening *madda*) when used in the context of referring to an extended family group—in this way, for example, the House of Saud is often referred to as the Al Saud. 'Al' in this sense is not the definite article 'al-'.

alim (pl. *ulama*): a man learned in religion. See *ulama* below.

amir: (also 'emir') especially in the Arabian peninsula: a prince, a provincial or district governor, a tribal shaikh or village chief.

asabiyya: 'group feeling' or 'tribal/group solidarity', emanating from kinship and real or imagined common descent. From the verbal root *'asaba* (to tie, bind, wrap…). A key concept developed by the fourteenth century Maghrebi Arab scholar, Ibn Khaldun (1332–1406). Fuller contextual definition is provided in chapter 2, in the section 'Tribalism, *asabiyya* and the contemporary Saudi regime'. (*Asabiyya*, like other Arabic words and names containing the letter *'ain*, is rendered in this book without the symbol (') representing *'ain*—see 'Note on Arabic transliteration and concepts'.)

bida: 'innovation' or, in a religious sense, 'heretical doctrine' a 'heresy'. From the verbal root *bada'a* (to introduce, originate, contrive). A potentially very serious offence.

bin: see *ibn*, below.

bint: daughter/'daughter of…'

dawa: 'invitation'—a call to Islam, or 'missionary activity'.

eid: festival. The two main festivals in Islam mark the beginning of the Islamic new year at the end of the annual *hajj*, and mark the conclusion of the month of fasting at the end of Ramadan.

fatwa (pl. *fatawa*): a non-binding religious-legal opinion or edict that may, from time to time, be issued by a religious scholar or group of ulama.

five pillars of Islam: the essential elements of Muslim faith,

(1) *shahada*: profession of faith (in the One-ness of Allah and affirmation of Muhammad as the messenger of Allah);

(2) *salat*: prayer;

(3) *zakat*: charity/the giving of alms;

(4) *hajj*: pilgrimage (to Mecca);

(5) *saum*: fasting (from dawn to sunset in the month of Ramadan).

GCC: Gulf Cooperation Council. The GCC was formed in 1981; its members are Saudi Arabia, Kuwait, Bahrain, Qatar, the United Arab Emirates and Oman. The bloc's principal goals are to foster economic, political and military coordination and cooperation.

hadith: traditional reports of the deeds and sayings of the Prophet. The second most important source, after the Quran, of Muslim knowledge and of Islamic law. Various collections are extant, some including historical reports of considerable reliability, others mere folktales.

hajj: one of the 'Pillars of Islam'—the duty of pilgrimage to Mecca incumbent on every Muslim at least once in a lifetime if he/she is able to perform it. The *hajj* is an annual event.

al-Hasa: the original name of the region that is now the Eastern Province of Saudi Arabia; it is the province that incorporates Saudi Arabia's Gulf coastline (see map).

Hashim: the family line of the Prophet Muhammad.

al-Hijaz: the Hijaz—the central western strip of territory in the Arabian peninsula that borders the Red Sea, roughly corresponding to the modern Saudi provinces of Mecca and Madina (see map). The Hijaz contains the two holy cities of Mecca and Madina and, therefore, the birthplace of the Prophet, the Quran and of Muslim society and civilisation; it is the single most important territory in the Islamic world. Natives of the region are referred to as 'Hijazis'.

al-hijra: 'the migration'. One of the most significant events in early Islamic history was the *hijra* of the Prophet and his companions from Mecca to Madina, where they established the first Muslim society. The Muslim lunar calendar begins from the *hijra*.

hijra (pl. *hijar*): a tribally based agricultural colony of the Ikhwan—the former bedouin tribespeople who undertook the symbolic *hijra* from a nomadic lifestyle to a settled one in the interests of greater piety.

ibn/bin: son/'son of...' Sometimes shortened to 'b.'.

ijtihad: in Islamic law, to formulate an independent opinion on a legal or theological question using disciplined reason and a knowledge of Quran, hadith and legal precedents. The word comes from the root JHD, 'to strive, endeavour'—the same root as *jihad*.

Ikhwan: 'brothers'—bedouin followers of the *muwahhidi*–Hanbali ideology of Muhammad bin Abd al-Wahhab who, during the first decades of the twentieth century, acted as the core strike force for Ibn Saud's conquest of central Arabia. Ibn Saud encouraged the spread of *muwahhidi* doctrine among the bedouin to facilitate their allegiance to him. Not to be confused with *al-ikhwan al-muslimun* (the Muslim Brotherhood), founded in Egypt in 1928.

imam: in the strictly religious sense, the leader of a session of prayer. 'Imam' has, in certain historical instances, been the title given to a political leader who also enjoys a special religious status.

jahiliyya: the state of pagan ignorance which existed in the Arabian peninsula before the Quran was revealed to Muhammad.

jihad: 'holy war' or 'endeavour' (from the Arabic verbal root JHD, 'to strive, endeavour'). At first, it was a duty to wage war, of expansion or defence, on those who threatened the community from without or within. Like the English word 'crusade', it has taken on a range of meanings, such as: a just war; a political struggle for social justice; the private, inner struggle for spiritual perfection.

kafir (pl. *kafirun*): a generally derogatory term for an unbeliever or 'infidel'. In extreme cases of prejudice the term can be used to refer to all non-Muslims, and even to other Muslims who follow a different school of Islamic thought.

khutba: 'sermon'. Usually refers to the message delivered by the imam of a mosque during the midday Friday congregational prayer.

madhhab: a school of Muslim jurisprudence founded by one of a number of early and venerated scholars of Islam. The four surviving, 'orthodox' Sunni schools are: Hanafi (after the thought of Abu Hanifa, *c.* 699–767), Maliki (after the thought of Malik bin Anas, *c.* 715–95), Shafi (after the thought of Muhammad bin Idris al-Shafi, *c.* 767–820) and Hanbali (after the thought of Ahmad bin Hanbal, *c.* 780–855).

majlis: 'assembly'. Specifically, in pre-Islamic and early Islamic custom, a body of eminent men from the society who met to discuss issues and advise the caliph or other leader. The leader is expected to seriously consider the advice of the *majlis*, but is not legally required to abide by it. The custom of a leader being accessible to his people through his *majlis* is an honourable tradition in Arabia. The custom has been likened to a form of 'democracy'.

majlis al-shura: the assembly of consultation, or 'consultative council' (see also *shura*, below).

malik: the Arabic word for 'king'.

mujaddid: a reformer or renewer—from the verbal root JDD, 'to be new'. In Islamic application, a strong religious personality with historical significance who is regarded as a reformer or renewer of Islam at a time of decline or decadence. Such charismatic personalities have been a periodic phenomenon in Islam, and have taken on an air of semi-legend. Aya-tollah Khomeini is thought by many to be a modern *mujaddid*.

muwahhidun: 'professors of the unity of *Allah*', or 'unitarians'—the fol-lowers of the teachings of the eighteenth century central Arabian reli-gious reformer, Muhammad bin Abd al-Wahhab (1703–92), who preached as his central doctrine the Islamic concept of *tauhid*. Also known by the unflattering and pejorative, but ubiquitous, term 'Wahhabis', after Ibn Abd al-Wahhab.[1] In Sunni Islam, a school of thought within the Hanbali *madhhab*, it is the dominant interpretation of Islam in Saudi Arabia. See chapter 2, the sections 'The original Saudi–Wahhabi 'religiopolitical' relationship' and 'The first Saudi realm, *c.* 1744–1819' (and notes) for further discussion and definition.

Najd: the central region of the Arabian peninsula, roughly corresponding to the modern Saudi provinces of Riyadh, Qasim and Ha'il (see map). Najd is the home territory of the Al Saud. Natives of this region are referred to as 'Najdis'.

nasab: the Arabic term for family lineage and descent which, in Arabian tradition, takes on a hereditary quality and then commands a status akin to 'pedigree'.

OPEC: the Organisation of Petroleum Exporting Countries. OPEC was formed in 1960 by Iran, Iraq, Kuwait, Saudi Arabia and Venezuela. Qatar, Indonesia, Libya, the United Arab Emirates, Algeria and Nigeria joined the organisation over the following 11 years. OPEC's stated objective is to coordinate petroleum policies among member states, 'in order to secure fair and stable prices for petroleum producers; an efficient, eco-nomic and regular supply of petroleum to consuming nations; and a fair return on capital to those investing in the industry'. The OPEC Con-ference of Ministers meets in ordinary session twice a year at the organisation's headquarters in Vienna.

salaf (pl. *aslaf*): 'predecessor, forebear, ancestor, forefather', derived from *salafa*, the Arabic verb 'to be over, be past…to precede'. In the Islamic context, the *aslaf* are the first generation of Muslims and the great theo-logians of the first Islamic centuries. They are traditionally regarded as the rightly-guided 'forefathers' of the Muslim community, the Muslims of a perfect society and developers and guardians of the pivotal tradition of Sunni Islam.

salafi/al-salafiyyat: a Sunni Muslim movement which looks back to re-vered early Muslims for inspiration, founded from the thought of the Egyptian intellectual and *alim*, Muhammad Abduh (1849–1905). Applied

---

[1] I have attempted to avoid the term 'Wahhabi' since it is regarded by many Saudi citizens as insulting.

generally to conservative Muslims who identify with the earliest Muslims as the best examples of Islamic practice, and who attempt to imitate them in every aspect of life (see *salaf*, above). It is a more common term of reference which is preferred by most *muwahhidun*. *Muwahhidi* and *salafi* basically equate in the Saudi Arabian context and are interchangeable.

sharia: 'way of life'. Often called 'Islamic law'. The product of jurisprudence (*fiqh*), the science of law and social morality, based on the Quran, *hadith* and *ijtihad* (judgement by analogy). A normative code of all human actions, it includes private acts (of worship, manners), personal status (marriage, divorce, inheritance), and much of criminal law. All human actions are classified as either obligatory, recommended, morally neutral, reprehensible, or forbidden. Each *madhhab* has drawn up its own code of human conduct, although differences between them are minor. The *sharia* grew up by a slow process of interaction between the norms of the Quran and *hadith* and local community customs and laws.

sharif: the name given to a family which traces descent from the Prophet Muhammad, and a title of noble leadership.

shura: consultation, advice, the taking of counsel. A traditional and important ideal of leadership in Arabia.

sultan: in Arabic, an abstract term for 'authority, dominion, ruling power'. From the tenth century onward it came to be used as a title of secular power.

sunna: noble deeds and practices which may accumulate and become attached to a family. The term is now synonymous with the life and deeds of the Prophet Muhammad; the *sunna* of the Prophet is the *sunna* par excellence, held in reverence by most mainstream Muslims.

sura: a 'chapter' of the Quran.

tauhid: 'unification'—in the Islamic application the term means the fact of, and belief in, the unity or 'oneness' of *Allah*, a concept extended to the whole of 'creation' in Islamic mysticism. From the verbal root WHD, 'to be alone, unique, incomparable', which is also the root of the numeral 'one'.

ulama (sing. *alim*—'learned'): men learned in the Quran, *hadith* and law and who can interpret these. In Sunni doctrine, the sources of inspiration (Quran and *hadith*) are regarded as eternal, but must be continually reinterpreted for individual and changing circumstances, by those with authority to perform this task: the ulama. The sources of Islamic knowledge do not specify how the ulama are to be composed. The term may refer to the informal group of scholars who are widely recognised by reputation, or to the body appointed and/or recognised officially by a particular state.

umma: the community of believers, regardless of tribal, ethnic or other origin, who are united by belief in Islam. The term is feminine, from the

Arabic word *umm*, meaning 'mother'. The sense of belonging to this universal community is expressed in the belief that it is the duty of all members to care for each other's temporal and spiritual well-being, and to protect the community.

Wahhabi: see *muwahhidun* above.

wasta: the word for the informal system of personal relations based on the mutual granting of favours that is prevalent in the Arab world. Derived from the verbal root 'to be in the middle', a person in a position to intercede on behalf of a relative, friend or business associate extends *wasta* to help secure whatever the latter's goal may be. Examples of such intercession include the obtaining of an audience with an influential third person; the granting of an exclusive agency, permit, licence, financial grant or scholarship; the provision of financial, legal, educational, personal or other official documents whether authentic or forged; the provision of employment regardless of suitability; and official or unofficial legal or physical protection. Such favours are granted on the understanding that at some time in the future, roles may be reversed and the patron extending *wasta* today may tomorrow need to call on a return favour from his erstwhile client. Providing favours for family members is in particular regarded as a duty. Loyalty to family, friends and the informal favour mechanism generally overrides institutional loyalty and loyalty to the state and to broader society.

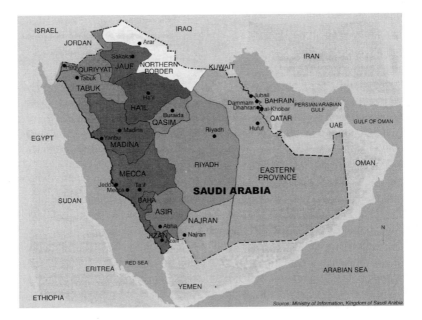

1

INTRODUCTION

One thing was swiftly and forcefully demonstrated after Iraq's 1990 invasion of Kuwait: the economic and strategic importance to the West of the Kingdom of Saudi Arabia. This importance has not diminished.

Economically, Saudi Arabia possesses around a quarter of the globe's known and accessible reserves of petroleum. It is the major player in the international oil industry cartel, the Organisation of Petroleum Exporting Countries (OPEC), and is able to bring considerable influence to bear on the other producers to sway the fortunes of the world economy, as witnessed in the important OPEC meetings of 1999 and 2000. Geostrategically, it lies at or near the junction of the Middle East, Central Asia and Africa, and the vital sea lanes of the Persian (or 'Arabian') Gulf, Horn of Africa, Red Sea and Suez Canal: the stability of the kingdom cannot but be at the heart of concern in Western centres of power.[1]

This economic and geostrategic significance is betrayed by the relative paucity of research on the latest developments in the country. What happens there is of vital consequence, and will have significant long-term ramifications not only for the economies and sociopolitical structures of the kingdom's smaller Gulf Arab neighbours, but for the broader Gulf region and the Middle East generally, and for the West and the global economy.

---

[1] It is not the place of this book to settle any argument over the name of the Persian/Arabian Gulf. While it is acknowledged that Gulf Arabs recognise 'Arabian Gulf' as the 'correct' name of that important body of water, 'Persian Gulf' is more widely recognised (see Sick and Potter, 1997: 9n. 1, for a brief discussion of this issue). The abbreviated form of the name—simply, 'Gulf'—is in general usage and is the main term employed here.

1

Only a few years ago, in the immediate aftermath of the 1991 Gulf War, a similar study to this one might well have been entitled 'Twilight of a Dynasty: Saudi Arabia and the Critical Mass of Reform'. Certainly, a number of treatises did bear titles similar to this, reflecting a view at the time that the Al Saud were stretching their legitimacy to breaking point, with potential consequences like those that befell the Shah's Iran. References to a 'storm' of socio-political upheaval and other serious problems became almost commonplace. The play on words captured everything associated with the kingdom in the 1990s: the harsh physical environment—which of course is also associated with oil—and the 1991 Gulf War, code-named 'Desert Storm', in turn associated with oil in a political context.[2] In the wake of the Gulf War the posited domestic 'storm' did indeed appear to be brewing, with hitherto unheard of open criticism of the Saudi rulers and their policies, the formation of loosely organised bodies for the articulation of grievances against the regime, widespread repression as the regime responded to these developments, and the counter-response of dissident radicalisation, which culminated in the Khobar bombing of June 1996.

However, to the non-Saudi onlooker the kingdom appears calm and stable. Certainly the image projected by the Saudi royal family is one of unshakeable power. More recently, other images have also been proudly fostered: for example, that the desert can be made to bloom, and that by the early 1990s the country had already entered the twenty-first century in terms of development and modernisation. In fact, almost anything seemed within the reach of this oil-rich kingdom. But the rising political dissent of the early- and mid-1990s led to speculation about the ultimate security of the Saudi regime. The first and most fundamental aspect of its image, Saudi stability, appeared under threat. During the late 1990s, however, it began to be apparent that economic rather than political security was going to be the main determinant of the kingdom's immediate

---

[2] Examples of titles playing on 'storm' and 'Desert Storm' include the following: 'Eye of the storm' (Armstrong, 1991); *Arabia after the Storm* (Hardy, 1992); *Saudi Arabia: The Coming Storm* (Wilson and Graham, 1994); 'Desert shock: Saudis are cash-poor' (Chandler, 1994); 'The storm and the citadel' (Viorst, 1996). Even the finance industry journal, *The Banker* (1999, 'Riding the storm'), could not resist the analogy when it came to banking in the Middle East.

and medium-term fortunes. Yet another aspect of its image, that of wealth and prosperity, is under assault.

The answers to many questions regarding what is really happening in the land of the two holy mosques lie in the story of the directions and choices facing the Al Saud today. Their roots go back a quarter of a century to when, transformed by the oil boom of 1973–4, the reincarnated Saudi oil state was faced with the task of feeding (or 'distributing') petroleum revenues into the economy and society. The Arabian equivalent of Asia's infamous 'crony capitalism', called '*asabiyya* capitalism' in this work, ran rampant in tandem with socially-disruptive modernisation and development programmes as Saudi Arabia locked itself into the mould of a welfare state—wealthy, but entirely dependent on the income (or 'rent') received from the extraction and export of oil. Technically, the kingdom became a 'rentier–distributive' state.[3] When the boom times turned sour in the early 1980s, it was unable and unwilling to restructure. Today, the uneasy dichotomy between tradition and modernity in the kingdom is being exacerbated by the postmodern phenomenon of 'globalisation' and the tensions between the two are shifting to the Al Saud mode of managing the economy, doing business, and governing.

The Saudi rentier–distributive state has, in fact, been dysfunctional for many years. Now, in the era of the global village and economic internationalisation, pressure is mounting for economic restructuring. The reforms that must be made to the kingdom's socioeconomic structure and that need to accompany the formal end of the Saudi distributive–welfare state carry with them the potential to increase pressure for political reform and to destabilise the regime if all does not go well. Socioeconomics—that is, those areas where economy and society converge, such as employment patterns, income and wealth distribution, inflation, and state subsidies and welfare—are set to play a greater role in the political life of the kingdom. From the Al Saud point of view, this is a negative and potentially threatening development.

---

[3] The terms 'rentier state' and '*asabiyya* capitalism' are introduced in more depth later in this chapter. *Asabiyya* capitalism in particular is treated as a localised political–economic system with organic roots in Arabian society, and is a recurring reference point in this work. See the Glossary for a brief definition of the Arabic word.

Despite these challenges, the power of the Al Saud is indeed firmly entrenched, and domestic policies aimed at addressing a plethora of extensive and interrelated economic, social and political problems have been initiated. These policies are aimed at pleasing both the advocates of a global economy—powerful supranational organisations such as the International Monetary Fund (IMF), the World Bank, and the World Trade Organisation (WTO)—and the bulk of the domestic population with its religiocultural roots deep in proud tradition. Managing the forces of domestic sociopolitics has strained the House of Saud on a number of occasions, from the Ikhwan revolt of 1927–30 to the 1979 siege of the Great Mosque of Mecca, and from the rise of popular dissent associated with the 1990–1 Gulf Crisis to the Khobar bombing of 1996 and the extensive fallout from the 11 September 2001 airliner hijacking-suicide attacks against New York and Washington. However, with its various mechanisms of state and royal power, the regime has dealt with all such points of strain in what has overall been a continuum of relative stability. The 'storm' has not materialised, but Gary Sick's assessment of 1997, namely that a drawn out 'crisis in slow motion' is actually well under way—for all the Gulf Arab states—remains as valid today as when the term was first coined (Sick, 1997: 12–14).

Thus, despite the persistence of political opposition and the coming crunch of major economic restructuring with all its social consequences, we are unlikely to witness serious political instability in Saudi Arabia; to this extent, the projections of the regime's image-makers are not far removed from reality. While the present work will demonstrate that all in the kingdom is not as calm or as stable as these image-makers would have the world believe, it also posits, in the context of an analysis of the regime's 'survivability' (my chosen term), that the Al Saud ruling dynasty is not likely to lose its grip on the kingdom in the foreseeable future.

Major themes and the structure of the book

This book develops and deals with five principal, interrelated themes. The first concerns what very soon becomes apparent to any serious observer of Saudi Arabia, namely the unique nature of the historical connections between religion, tradition, society, economy, politics, and the state. Saudi Arabia is the land of the Prophet Muhammad and the revelation of the Quran, the site of the first Muslim community from which Islam spread to the world, and where the most sacred Islamic sites are located, in and around the cities of Mecca and Madina. The Saudi king is also the custodian and protector of the holy places and the kingdom is the core of the Muslim religious world. These clear links between history and religion have fused with Arabian traditions and found social expression in more than one form, among which the central Najd, 'Wahhabi' interpretation of Islam is the most prominent example.

The modern state's roots in these historical, religious and conservative social foundations are inevitably reflected in the politics and economic structure of the kingdom. More precisely, the ways in which a historically and religiously unique society interact with the kingdom's politics and economy places the emphasis of analysis in the composite fields of sociopolitics, political economy and socioeconomics. The underlying principles of these organic connections must be addressed by any study of the kingdom. Thus, Chapter 2 provides a selective and concise account of the history of the modern kingdom: the origins of 'Wahhabism', the evolution of the successive Al Saud political entities, and the essential background to modern Saudi Arabian society and politics, relating historical events to contemporary political realities. The chapter also deals with Islam and tribalism in their specifically Saudi contexts and their relationship with the political structure established by the Al Saud, thus laying the foundations for the introduction of the concept of *asabiyya* capitalism. No attempt has been made to present a complete history of the Saudi dynasty. For more comprehensive historical studies, the work of R. Bayly Winder (1965), Gary Troeller (1976), Christine Moss Helms (1981) and Joseph Kostiner (1993), for example, should be consulted.

The three next main themes are dealt with in Chapters 3 and 4. The first of these is the gathering momentum of economic and socioeconomic reform in the kingdom, and the potential of change in these spheres to contribute to pressure for political reform. The momentum of reform has been building up for many years, but the Al Saud have managed to keep serious changes at bay thanks to the financial leeway provided by the wealth generated from the production and export of oil. However, a time of reckoning is approaching, evident in the kingdom's declining wealth and the chronic problems of the Saudi economy. Events since the 11 September suicide attacks and subsequent speculation about the activities of the radical Saudi dissident, Osama bin Laden, have refocused attention on politics and dissent in the kingdom. The substance of the discussion here, however, is the longer-term economic threat to the regime and the way in which the society is being affected by wayward and drifting domestic policies.

Consideration is then given to the increasing impact of globalisation as an engine of Saudi economic and socioeconomic restructuring and the approaching demise of the Saudi distributive–welfare state. Economic internationalisation—the most tangible form of 'globalisation'—is affecting Saudi Arabia as much as any other of the world's states. The Al Saud, too, are pressing for their country to be admitted to the WTO. The IMF does have policies which are relevant to Saudi Arabia's economic and socioeconomic future. The postmodern international world is thus impressing itself on a regime and a society which is in many ways still struggling to come to terms with modernity whilst desperately clinging to traditional family, tribal and religious values. In this new era, threats to Al Saud sovereignty are as evident in the slogans of the international economic fundamentalist as they are in those of the religious fundamentalist. The Al Saud are looking hard at their economy and at socioeconomic policy, and the motivations, difficulties and potential consequences of their decisions in these fields are considered here. Wealth squandered and wealth in decline is a prominent subtheme in the context of evidence that the ability of oil to provide a safety net for the regime is limited.

The nature of the Saudi political economy, particularly in the context of reform, globalisation and the winding down of the Saudi distributive–welfare state is the next theme dealt with. Fleshing out the political and societal aspects of Saudi economic functioning is important because the status quo is entrenched and too many vested interests stand to lose too much from substantial change. Yet substantial change is precisely what is being asked of the Al Saud in order to provide jobs for young Saudis, to oversee economic opening up and entry to the WTO, and to revive and diversify the country's stagnant oil-dependent economy, to mention just a few economic goals that have to date appeared to be all but beyond the regime's ability to achieve. Privilege based on kinship, regional ties and other forms of personalised relations are an all-pervasive feature of the Saudi economy. The term '*asabiyya* capitalism' has been developed here to help explain and understand the Saudi economic system, what it means politically, and the problems it presents for the regime as the state's income from oil increasingly falls short of what is required to provide for the future of the country in the way it has since the oil boom of 1973–4.

The dramatic effects that the 1973–4 oil boom had on the kingdom's political economy and social structure are discussed in Chapter 3, which looks at the political agenda of boom-time development and the rise of a Najdi-dominated rentier–distributive state and *asabiyya* capitalism, and with them the issues of rapid modernisation, urbanisation, education development, changing class structures, and informal and exclusive business practices—and their social consequences.

Chapter 4 examines the Saudi economy's continuing petroleum dependence, and thus also its vulnerability and the inevitability of the reform of the distributive–welfare state in the context of economic internationalisation.

The fifth and final theme, treated in Chapter 5, is that of the 'survivability' of the Al Saud ruling dynasty, the continuity of the Saudi political system, and regime resistance to political change in an era of reform. The resilience of Al Saud power—already traditional in a society which holds tradition sacrosanct—is explored. The surge in domestic dissent since the 1990 Gulf Crisis and the fragmented nature of the political opposition are dealt with as part of an examination of the state's security mechanisms, as well as its more subtle methods of social and political control, to determine how it is that the Al Saud have so far weathered all storms and look likely to keep doing so. A domestic focus is emphasised in this chapter, and indeed throughout the book, but the importance of certain elements of the kingdom's foreign policy and of international relations are also considered. Thus, the 1990–1 Gulf Crisis and War are acknowledged as the catalyst for the recent intensification of opposition to Saudi rule, and the influence of the Saudi–US relationship on the kingdom's internal politics and the continuing effects of 11 September 2001 are discussed in terms of their relevance to the regime's stability. So, too, is the phenomenon of Osama bin Laden and the Saudi nationals who participated in the convoluted wars fought in Afghanistan since the 1979 Soviet invasion.

Globalisation is revisited in Chapter 5, this time in the context of the information and communications revolutions, the Internet, cultural influence and censorship. Its still speculative cultural effects are looked at briefly, simply because they cannot be ignored. Saudi citizens themselves—even the young, modern and Western-educated—are certainly not ignoring them.[4] Young, well-educated, modern and at ease with the West they may be, but they are still very proud of their Arabian roots, their history and their traditions. Thus, while making no pretence to a comprehensive analysis of the brave new worlds of globalisation, postmodernity or cyber-politics, this book nevertheless does not shy away from these issues where they are relevant to socioeconomic and sociopolitical realities in the kingdom. An important sub-theme of this chapter is therefore dissident use of the Internet and the regime's response, particularly regarding the London-based groups: the Saudi opposition discovered e-mail and the World Wide Web in the early years of general public access, 1994–6, and were, in fact, at the cutting edge of new mediums of resistance. Also dealt with in Chapter 5 are issues relating to political developments in the kingdom and Al Saud resistance to political reform, coupled with the potentially crippling issue of succession to the throne, discussed there in detail.

Chapter 6 brings together the themes and conclusions that have gone before. Its main message is that the road of reform will lead to the restructuring of the Saudi oil state, with profound implications for Saudi citizens.

The Saudi 'rentier' state: a transformation fuelled by oil. Since no understanding of the current era of reform in Saudi Arabia can be reached without a realisation of what the 1973–4 oil boom meant for the kingdom, some key reference points need to be given.

---

[4] Whilst I was in the kingdom, a number of them expressed to me personally their concern on precisely such issues.

Oil was discovered in Saudi Arabia's Eastern Province in 1935 and production began in 1938. Until the oil boom of the 1970s, the Saudi state supported itself—in addition to relatively modest revenues from oil exports and from the *hajj*—by extracting taxes, duties and fees from the population and the economy.[5] With the boom, the Saudi state quickly metamorphosed into a 'rentier state' which prospered almost exclusively from the 'rents' received from the extraction and export of petroleum reserves. Large deposits of a limited and valuable resource such as oil have been likened to natural real-estate assets. Thus, revenues derived from the extraction and export of such a resource, a narrowly defined process which requires relatively little domestic development and production and which involves only a small minority of a state's population, has been described as the reaping of 'unearned income' (see Beblawi, 1987: 384) and the process has given rise to terms like 'oil rents'. Such income is derived from outside the domestic economy and is paid, principally, directly to the government which makes that government financially independent of its population, hence the use of terms such as 'rentier economies' and 'rentier states'. A rentier state then becomes the source of wealth domestically as one of its primary functions becomes that of distributor. The state becomes the patron of both the economy and of society. Within a short period, the role of granter-of-largesse and engine of the national economy is institutionalised. In this way, a rentier state also becomes a distributive, or 'allocation', state (see Luciani, 1987).

The basis of Saudi Arabia's 'rentier' status is, of course, oil. Applying to the kingdom the words of one scholar of the process of transformation that rentier status entails, it became 'petrolised' (see Karl, 1997: 80–81).[6] As a concept, the 'petrolisation' of Saudi Arabia

---

[5] The early Saudi state was a rudimentary one and still undergoing basic development at the time of the oil boom (see Chaudhry, 1997: 43–136).

[6] The cross-cultural, global applicability of the rentier–distributive model is made powerfully clear by comparing Terry Lynn Karl's study of the Venezuelan political economy with the Saudi case. For example:

> By setting into motion the long-term structural transformation of the economy and society that I have called 'petrolization', [the exploitation of petroleum] weakened non-oil interests and fostered the emergence of new social classes and groups whose fortunes were linked to the distribution of oil rents through state spending…

captures in a nutshell the environment which fostered the rise of a Najdi-based *asabiyya* capitalism, the Al Saud's legitimacy of largesse and, most importantly, the highly imbalanced structure of the Saudi rentier–distributive state which is now under threat and in decline.[7] But it is not the purpose of this book to reinvent the wheel as far as the formation and development of rentier states is concerned— even in the specifically Saudi case, although it must occupy an important place in this study.[8]

Modernisation, development and asabiyya capitalism.   During the period of 'petrolisation', haphazard modernisation and development of the country proceeded at an accelerating pace. Such rapid change

---

...incentives for other productive activities barely developed. (Karl, 1997: 80, 81)

Almost to the letter, the same words can be found in Kiren Aziz Chaudhry's important work on the Saudi political economy—for example: '...the market-driven sectoral development programs and the indirect distributive mechanisms set in place during the boom...resulted in the creation of entirely new social classes in Saudi Arabia.' (Chaudhry, 1997: 190)

See also Amuzegar's introduction to his comparative study of the OPEC countries for a summary of 'a heterogeneous group with shared objectives' (Amuzegar, 1999: 1–9). Detail on how the OPEC countries dealt with the sudden 'windfall' of oil rents is provided pp. 48–115, notably that, '[i]n all member countries, the public sector...engaged in direct production and distribution, albeit in each country with different rapidity, scope and depth' (p. 112).

[7] See the Glossary for a definition of the 'Najd' region of Saudi Arabia.

[8] For a concise discussion of the concept of the rentier state in the Saudi context, see Palmer, Alghofaily and Alnimir (1984); and in the broader context of the Arab world, see Beblawi (1987). Hazem Beblawi's insightful article appeared first in H. Beblawi and G. Luciani (eds), *The Rentier State*, vol. 2 of *Nation, State and Integration in the Arab World* (London: Croom Helm, 1987), and later in G. Luciani (ed.), *The Arab State* (London: Routledge, 1990). Chaudhry's book represents the definitive work on the development of the Saudi political economy (and, to a lesser extent, that of Yemen); for the phase of the kingdom's rentier–distributive metamorphosis, see Chaudhry, 1997: 139–92. Interesting comparative material is provided by Terry Lynn Karl, whose book on Venezuela parallels Chaudhry's book on Saudi Arabia. Although the latter is not one of her case studies, see Karl (1997) for a detailed study of the very mixed—even false—blessings that have come with 'petrostate' status; in this respect, see also Amuzegar (1999) for a detailed study of all the OPEC countries, including Saudi Arabia. See also Gause (1994: 42–58, 204n. 1) for an overview of the rentier status of the oil-rich Gulf Arab monarchies.

precipitated social and sociopolitical tensions marked, for example, by the seizure of the Great Mosque of Mecca in 1979, not during a time of economic adversity, but rather one of unprecedented wealth. This incident highlighted other, less desirable aspects of rentier status which had become entrenched in the Saudi political economy and which occurred in the context of the informal and opaque political–economic system based on kinship, *wasta* and other forms of personal relations which I have called '*asabiyya* capitalism'. *Asabiyya* capitalism boomed along with the state's income from petroleum exports and the many ambitious development programmes that followed; it is still fostering élite, bureaucratic/business patronage networks and is linked to the Al Saud's need for political support, particularly from the Najdi heartland of the kingdom.

Asabiyya capitalism promotes an environment in which acts that are regarded as overtly 'corrupt' in the West, flourish.[9] They include, for example, 'commission farming' and 'commission harvesting', terms used here to describe the business practice of agency, ubiquitous in the kingdom, whereby Saudi nationals who are part of the privileged *asabiyya* patronage networks act as agents, brokers and middlemen between foreign business or industry and the Saudi state in the negotiation and award of contracts. The agents charge commissions, sometimes substantial, as a percentage of the total contract value in return for their services; engaging the right agent or paying the right 'commission' can be the difference between a successful bid for a government contract and an unsuccessful one. The practice adds significantly to the cost of contracts for the Saudi state. Commission farming has been particularly prevalent in construction and infrastructure projects and in national armaments purchases.[10]

While issues of 'corruption' must be treated sensitively, evidence suggests that the Saudi population generally is becoming less tolerant of informal and exclusive business practices which are costing the state dearly. The Great Mosque incident indicated that regime

---

[9] Where appropriate, the term 'acts of corruption' has been employed in this work to shift the emphasis from the persons involved, who are acting in the societal context of Arabian *asabiyya* capitalism, to the act itself, thus implying that while the *act* may be regarded as 'corrupt', the people involved should not necessarily be regarded to be so.

[10] Agency also refers to the franchising of foreign business operations in the kingdom.

and élite excesses did not go unnoticed even during the initial years of the oil boom, the era of plenty. It also demonstrated that minority elements of the Saudi population were prepared to press home their dissatisfaction by drastic action. Accusations of regime favouritism and 'corruption' did not end with the execution of the Mecca rebels; similar and even more extensive and detailed criticisms have been prominent in post-Gulf War calls for political reform. In the era of globalisation, economic restructuring and financial restraint, these criticisms are likely to gain a stronger voice and, together with the external voices of the likes of the IMF and WTO, to contribute to mounting pressure on the regime for reform of the *asabiyya* system.

Structural dysfunctionality, globalisation and the momentum of reform. This book argues that the kingdom has already entered a period of wide-ranging change, the impetus for which is provided by the dysfunctional nature of the Saudi rentier–distributive state and by globalisation. It presents evidence to show that the Saudi 'petrostate' has been effectively dysfunctional for longer than it has been functional: the years 1983–6 saw the turning point in the kingdom's future as a state that could sustain rentier status. But despite the imbalanced nature of the Saudi economy, there is no doubt the Al Saud do wish to embrace globalisation, at least in its most tangible form of economic internationalisation. Saudi Arabia is, for example, eager to join the WTO; this is not surprising since, despite being among the first countries to apply for membership of the body, it is now one of the world's four largest economies still not a member. However, integration into a world economy is currently being pursued in tandem with minimal basic reforms to the kingdom's flawed economic and socioeconomic structures, and, even more emphatically, the Al Saud are resisting the political–economic and sociopolitical reforms now being suggested by the IMF as important adjuncts to a modern, sound national economic structure and administration. For Saudi Arabia, these non-economic reforms would mean a fundamental reformation of *asabiyya* capitalism. Meanwhile, the two principal 'architects of the new global economy'—the IMF and WTO—are pressuring the kingdom's rulers toward the formal demise of the Saudi rentier–distributive state. It is argued here that a clash of some kind is looming between the Saudi regime and these supranational financial–economic organisations.

Although the regime's goal is minimal disruption to business as usual, it is being argued that some renegotiation of the kingdom's élite networks will occur as part and parcel of reforms that are on the horizon. One outcome of the opening up of the Saudi economy to global influences is a narrowing of the élite base, with the possibility of a more extensive shake-up further down the road of reform. Even so, Crown Prince Abdullah, the effective head of state, is speaking the language of international finance and economics, and there is no doubt in which direction he will lead the kingdom. But reform under Abdullah, and probably under his successor too, will proceed very slowly and the evidence suggests it will remain incomplete. These will be points of conflict with the IMF and WTO in a post-Asian crisis world.

The present era of change essentially represents a reverse transformation, back to the economic and socioeconomic structures of a normative, extractive state. It can be conceptualised as the economic and socioeconomic upheaval of the oil boom running hesitantly and leadenly in reverse. Although dramatic political–economic and socioeconomic change is not new for Saudi Arabia, this re-transformation of the oil boom metamorphosis may ultimately represent an even greater upheaval than the first.

Saudi sociopolitics in the era of reform.   The analysis of the Saudi economy and socioeconomics leads on to an examination of its sociopolitics, i.e. national political opposition to the Al Saud and their regime and the regime's responses to sociopolitical challenges. As compared with Juhaiman al-Utaibi's Great Mosque rebellion of 1979, today's advocates of violence are choosing targets more disturbingly in tune with the broader society and now associated with the Al Saud and their alliance with the United States. But the Mecca rebellion was an early example of how violence could suddenly shatter the calm veneer of modern-day Saudi sociopolitics, just as the 1995 Riyadh and 1996 and 2001 Khobar bombings revealed glimpses of ongoing turbulence below the surface of order.[11]

---

[11] The 2001 Khobar bombing referred to is that of 6 October that year, which killed an American in addition to the Palestinian carrier of the device, after the 11 September suicide attacks on the United States. Controversy was launched by

Many of the complaints raised by Juhaiman in 1979 resurfaced in post-Gulf War dissent, indicating the persistence of some long-standing popular grievances against the regime. Religious ideology and imagery are invoked both by the regime and the diffuse political opposition in claims to legitimacy. Thus, the 'Custodian of the Two Holy Mosques', establishment *ulama*, radical young ulama, inspired young Saudis who fought in the *jihad* in Afghanistan, and ordinary, traditionally pious Saudis and their more secular, pragmatic counterparts are all players in the ongoing, mainly underground, sociopolitical drama being acted out in the kingdom.

While the Al Saud are finally and reluctantly showing signs that they are prepared, if necessary, to initiate serious socioeconomic reforms, it seems they are not prepared to make more than superficial concessions to popular opinion. Those caught between the old rentier–distributive economy and the new, regime-supported globalising economy, are the majority of the Saudi population. The regime is discovering that prosperity in the era of economic internationalisation involves more than the pure economics of GDP and budget statistics; the serious economic policy changes with which the kingdom is now confronted will have a significant impact on Saudi society. Population and employment statistics, for example, are not

the *Guardian* on 30 January 2002 over the involvement of mostly British nationals in a series of bombings which rocked the kingdom in 2000 and 2001. Three bombings—two in Riyadh and one in Khobar—occurred in November and December 2000. The first of these, in Riyadh on 17 November, killed a British national and wounded his wife; the third, in Khobar on 15 December, cost another Briton his sight and his right hand. Another three related bombings occurred in early 2001, in January and March in Riyadh, and on 2 May in Khobar, where a US citizen lost an arm and an eye from a parcel bomb (see the *Guardian*, 2002 for a summary of these events). Fourteen Westerners, mainly Britons, were arrested and Saudi authorities subsequently attributed the blasts to criminal activity concerned with the illegal alcohol trade. Four British men, a Canadian and a Belgian confessed to a range of offences, from involvement in illicit alcohol activity to the bombings, on Saudi television. The *Guardian* has presented evidence to back its allegations that the Saudi Interior Ministry concocted the story of a bootleg liquor feud and extracted confessions in order to conceal a serious internal security problem, probably involving supporters of Osama bin Laden (Kelso and Pallister, 2002; Kelso *et al.*, 2002; Pallister, Kelso and Whitaker, 2002; Norton-Taylor and Pallister, 2002). (Issues of subversion and coercion and repression by the regime are dealt with in Chapter 5.)

abstract concepts at ground level, they are socioeconomic realities for the educated young Saudis who cannot find work and who may not see their way clear to following the traditional social path of establishing their own (large) family in their own home. Socioeconomic issues such as unemployment and falling standards of living will form the principal link between economic reform and future sociopolitical unrest. Managing the retreat of the rentier–distributive state will be fraught with potentially destabilising political risks that will test the regime's mechanisms of survival.

The Al Saud are not dealing with the root problems of sociopolitical turbulence, but rather resisting the reforms ultimately required for a smooth transition to a truly modern—or even postmodern—and stable, state. The regime is not proceeding with economic and political liberalisation but dealing with structural problems piecemeal, through gradual, astute, but minor and incomplete compromises and concessions, underpinned by state censorship, systemic repression, active and brutal suppression when necessary, and absolute political authoritarianism. Ultimately the present sociopolitical status quo—namely destabilising moments within overall stability—is likely to remain unchanged for as long as the current conditions prevail.

Method of approach adopted for this book

This book aims to bridge studies which emphasise the sociopolitics of Saudi Arabia and those which focus on the kingdom's political economy. Society, as is implied by the composite terms 'sociopolitics' and 'socioeconomics', is the dynamic link between political and economic structures; this is the basic, underlying premise of the present work and the reason why the background to the historical and religious uniqueness of Saudi Arabia given below is so important. Even ground-breaking studies which do not treat the kingdom as an organic whole transgress the balance between elements which comprise the whole.[12]

---

[12] The recent work of two noted scholars of the kingdom, Kiren Aziz Chaudhry (1997) and Mamoun Fandy (1999), are therefore discussed in relation to arguments presented in this book in 'Sources and further reading'. Briefly, both Chaudhry and Fandy in their own ways recognise the dynamism of Saudi

The way in which religion, tradition, society, economy, politics and the state in Saudi Arabia build upon, interact and influence each other in the current era of reform is integral to the present narrative.[13] Unless the results of study are checked against the ground-level social reality, there is a risk that the analysis will drift wide of accurate conclusions. This book is, therefore, also an example of 'keep[ing] one's analytical feet planted firmly in the past and present' (Sick and Potter, 1997: 5)—the favoured approach of those with long experience of Gulf affairs.

In support of such an approach, it is worth observing that Western scholars have not developed frameworks within which the Arab and broader Islamic worlds can be adequately conceptualised, a view especially applicable in the case of Saudi Arabia and a reality that political scientists, sociologists and economists alike disregard at their peril. Thus, it is worth noting the comments of Fandy (1999: 14–18) on a series of theoretical trends which have failed to illuminate Middle Eastern political studies; he writes, specifically, (p. 14), 'I am always struck by what little relevance Western theory has to the world of the Arabs.' Hans-Heino Kopietz, formerly of the International Institute of Strategic Studies (IISS), believes '…it is nigh impossible to theorise…about [Saudi Arabia] at this time. Western social science still has a lot to learn about how non-western societies work' (Kopietz, H.H. 1999, pers. comm., 8 Dec.).[14] And

---

society; Chaudhry concentrates on its role in the political economy of the kingdom but does not convincingly analyse sociopolitics as such. Fandy, on the other hand, very appropriately emphasises the society aspect of Saudi sociopolitics, but disregards the economic factor.

[13] The particular nature of Saudi Arabia can be illustrated by the dilemma I faced in organising the 'background' chapter of this book. The original idea was to deal neatly with the 'ideological and religious foundations' of the modern state in one section, and with the state's 'political–historical background' in the following. However, a struggle ensued over the juxtaposition and intersection of historical chronology and the 'timeless' nature of religious ideology, and with the intertwining of sociopolitics, the influence of *muwahhidi* Islam and Al Saud religiopolitical legitimacy. In addition, tradition and the tenets of Islam weave an intricate web with other factors, such as tribalism and the historical circumstances surrounding the proclamation of the modern kingdom in 1932, out of which was formed the substance of the Saudi political economy and sociopolitics that developed through to and beyond the oil boom of 1973–4.

[14] Kopietz was Senior Defence Economist and Middle East Analyst at the IISS, 1980–90.

Alexander Bligh (1984: 2) discusses the 'major difficulty' of the kingdom's failure to 'fit into any political model familiar to a twentieth-century scholar brought up on Western precepts and ideologies'.

By and large, Western social scientists do not deal with the organic interactions between Saudi society, *muwahhidi* Islam, Arabian *asabiyya*, tribalism and extended family networks, and the importance of traditions, and between all of these and an authoritarian, religio-political ruling family. The acknowledgement of such connections was important in the development of the concept of *asabiyya* capitalism which is, in fact, a prime example—or even the very product—of the organic interaction of society with the political and economic structures of the developing oil-boom Saudi state.[15] The '*mudir* syndrome' is another such example; the term is used here to encapsulate the widely lamented Saudi work ethic predominant in the petrolised kingdom. Based on the Arabic word for 'director' (*mudir*), the coinage stands for the hierarchical attitude to employment rooted in concepts of honour and shame which has ramifications in the kingdom's policies on education, employment and the expatriate labour force, for example. It may also be seen as a vestige of a more traditional, 'closed' society.

However, Saudi Arabia is no longer quite the closed country it used to be. Although still reclusive, the kingdom is beginning to open up economically. Domestic economic, socioeconomic and political–economic structures are being challenged in the era of globalisation. But, it must be stressed that it is the Al Saud who have chosen to integrate their national economy into the globalising world economy. Such a move, regime spokesmen claim, is essential to the development of the Saudi export industry and for future economic prosperity generally. To achieve this goal, the Saudis have to conform, to some extent at least, to the economic 'architecture' being laid out by the IMF and WTO. This has been the willing

---

[15] This is not to suggest that Saudi Arabia has a monopoly on this type of societal manifestation. Paul D. Hutchcroft (1998), for example, writes of 'booty capitalism' and the creation of commercial élites which are tied to the state in the context of the Philippines, Indonesia, Thailand and Zaire (see especially his ch. 3, 'Patrimonial states and rent capitalism: The Philippines in comparative perspective', pp. 45–64).

decision of Saudi rulers, and it is the reality now being presented to the Saudi population. To speculate what the Saudis could or should have done and be doing financially and economically—perhaps drawing on their own cultural heritage to a significantly greater degree, for example—is not relevant to this work.[16] Economic analysis is therefore here conducted within the Western paradigm, although the socioeconomic inquiry is rooted much more in the Saudi reality.[17]

Without a proper grasp of the background, today's events and issues cannot be fully appreciated. These include the nature of Al Saud rule, the impact of the oil boom and the rentier transformation, the looming end of the rentier–distributive state, and the significance of social concern over the presence of Western forces in the kingdom and the cultural aspects of globalisation more generally. Historical context has been included in awareness of recent criticisms of other presentations of early Saudi history which do not fully acknowledge the heterogeneous nature of Arabia and the Al Saud's tenuous authority over territory.[18] Every endeavour has been

---

[16] This is a question that Clement Henry (1999c), for example, approaches in his article on the Islamic finance–globalisation dialectic. See also Abdullah Saeed (1993, 1995, 1996, 1998) for an elucidation of the Islamic system of finance as a basis of comparison with the Saudi system. See especially Saeed (1996: 12) and Henry (1999c: 31) on the not particularly Islamic Saudi financial industry. The Saudis have also adopted the Gregorian calendar for their fiscal year. Considering also that the regime likes to emphasise great development strides which have taken the kingdom into the twenty-first century 'ahead of time', the occasional acknowledgement of 'the new (Western) millennium' as a reference point for the modern era is not inappropriate.

[17] The postmodern world may be making inroads into Saudi society (see especially Fandy, 1999: 3–18), but this is occurring in conjunction with a continuing attachment to traditions. The social setting of contemporary Saudi Arabia is important for this book; a detailed exposition of Saudi traditions in modern life would make a fascinating study, but is not warranted here. However, signs of the development of youth subcultures are noted in Chapter 5, indicating a social future that will be as intriguing as it will be problematic for the kingdom's authorities.

[18] Chaudhry (1997: 46–7) is particularly sharp, but she does not provide evidence to sustain her attack. She states that '[a]t the turn of the twentieth century even the possibility of a single, lasting military–administrative authority in the Nejd was remote.' Indeed it was remote, but the detailed study of the period which led to the establishment of such an (Al Saud) authority does not necessarily imply it

made to highlight the Al Saud's usually loose tenure over conquered or co-opted tribes and their lands, and the constructed nature of the modern kingdom which was superimposed on its subject peoples and is still not as 'united' as its rulers claim.[19]

---

was inevitable. Chaudhry also over minimalises the importance of the *muwahhidi*-derived religiopolitical legitimacy of the Al Saud, something she neglects even when her study turns more overtly to sociopolitics (see Chaudhry, 1997: 293–9, 304–19).

[19] This book draws on the work of many scholars for the context it provides but, as this aspect is necessarily circumspect, Fandy's context-setting chapter, in particular, should be studied for a fuller understanding of the unique sociocultural background to contemporary Saudi Arabian affairs (see Fandy, 1999: esp. 21–50).

2

THE FOUNDING OF MODERN SAUDI ARABIA

STATE AND SOCIETY

By the mid-eighteenth century the central power of the Ottoman Empire, based in Istanbul, had for long been on the wane. Ottoman control over Arabia was mainly symbolic and was expressed with pomp and fanfare once a year at the time of the annual *hajj*, when a procession of pilgrims and officials and their military escort would wind its way down to Mecca from the imperial heartland, distributing largesse to significant tribes of the Hijaz and to the inhabitants of the holy cities of Mecca and Madina.

Other than a governor stationed in the Red Sea port of Jedda, the Ottoman sultan had no official representative answerable directly to Istanbul. Instead, in line with the mechanism employed in other far-flung, difficult to manage provinces, local families of note were recognised as the holders of local power, and their authority was not challenged as long as they funnelled revenue to Istanbul and did not disrupt imperial trade and military activity. In the Hijaz, the head of a noble family claiming descent from the Prophet Muhammad—a *sharif*—was charged with rulership on behalf of the sultan. The nearest other Ottoman presence was in the southern Iraqi port city of Basra, and across the Red Sea in the powerful province of Egypt.

Although the Hijaz was not a rich province and its ability to supply revenue for the imperial coffers was limited, the territory was still important: in a way which foreshadowed the prestige of the modern rulers of the Hijaz, '[p]ossession of the holy cities gave the Ottomans a kind of legitimacy and a claim on the attention of the world of Islam which no other Muslim state possessed' (Hourani,

1991: 226). As for the other regions of Arabia, Ottoman power was either unknown or completely ineffective. Increasing British maritime power challenged the Ottomans in the east of the peninsula and, in the lead-up to the First World War, a local power grew in the central, Najd, region of Arabia to challenge Ottoman authority in the Hijaz. It should not be surprising that, in the cradle of Islam, this new power should appeal to an Islamic ideology for its motivation and legitimacy. A combination of religious and temporal prowess gave rise to the Saudi dynasty in the 1770s. Its fortunes would vary over time and include two major incarnations—'realms' which would lay the foundations for ongoing Saudi claims to much of Arabia and ultimately lead to the establishment of the modern state of Saudi Arabia during the course of the first third of the twentieth century.

Saudi Arabia: ideological and political foundations

The original Saudi–Wahhabi 'religiopolitical' relationship.   Many contemporary, committed men of religious learning came to see the Arabia of the eighteenth century as one which existed in a state of *jahiliyya* akin to that which Muhammad knew before the revelation of the Quran.[1] Muhammad bin Abd al-Wahhab (1703–92) was one such *alim* and, possessed by the desire to witness a return to 'true' Islam, established through his determined preaching and strict piousness, a reputation as a reformer. Ibn Abd al-Wahhab belonged to the Hanbali *madhhab,* but had studied under scholars belonging to the other Sunni schools. His resoluteness, the strictness of his religious exegesis and his demanding philosophy appear to be the products of his own personality and life rather than being attributable solely to the Hanbali school (see Hopwood, 1982). One of his major sources of inspiration besides Quran and *hadith*, however, was the work of the Hanbali scholar, Ibn Taimiyya (1263–1328), whose teachings are generally regarded as strict, conservative and based on

---

[1] The nineteenth-century chronicler of the *muwahhidun*, Uthman bin Abdullah bin Bishr (d. 1873), provides an insight into the kinds of practices and beliefs which created the aura of *jahiliyya* (see Winder, 1965: 12–13. Winder cites Ibn Bishr frequently throughout his detailed study of nineteenth-century central Arabia). On *jahiliyya*, see also Christine Moss Helms (1981: 83–4; 121n. 3).

uncompromisingly literal interpretations of Quran, *hadith* and *sharia* (see Hourani, 1991: 179–81).[2]

The basic tenet of Ibn Abd al-Wahhab's message was the eternal unity of Allah; his 'basic text' (Hopwood, 1982: 29) was entitled *Kitab al-Tauhid*, 'The Book of Unity'.[3] His philosophy developed into a fierce and unyielding monotheism which included the indivisibility of religion and state. A religious-revival movement grew out of Ibn Abd al-Wahhab's activity *c.* 1740–1, and his followers came to be known as *al-muwahhidun*;[4] Wahhab himself became known—certainly by the followers of his teachings—as a *mujaddid*. The Arabian *muwahhidun* movement was a response to purely local conditions—the perception of *jahiliyya*—and pre-dated European colonialism in the Middle East.

After a short period of reforming activity under the protection of a local Najdi ruler, political opposition forced Ibn Abd al-Wahhab to move on; in 1744 he chose as his base the town of al-Diriyya in central Najd, just north of where Riyadh is today, and soon entered into a formal pact with its amir, Muhammad bin Saud (d. 1765). The formula was relatively simple: Wahhab promised the blessings of Allah, a just and noble cause and, through them, conquests with religious legitimacy, while Saud 'swore allegiance to the reformer in the cause of Islam and declared his readiness to undertake the jihad' (Rentz, 1972: 56). This alliance—upon which the first Saudi dominion, *c.* 1744–1818, was founded—was consolidated by the marriage of Muhammad bin Saud's eldest son, Abd al-Aziz, to a daughter of Abd al-Wahhab (see Troeller, 1976: 13). It was this original 'religio-political movement' (Esposito, 1991: 102)—'the effective union of

---

[2] See also notes 8 and 9 below.

[3] The Islamic philosophy of *tauhid* has its most direct expression in *sura* 112 of the Quran, *surat al-Ikhlas* ('The Declaration of [Allah's] Perfection', or 'Purity [of Faith]': see Asad (1984: 985) and Ali (1938: 2028)). This *sura* is also known by the name *al-Tauhid*. Asad (1984: 985) reports that according to 'a great number of authentic Traditions, the Prophet was wont to describe this *surah* as "equivalent to one-third of the whole Qur'an".' In his explanatory notes, Asad (1984: 985n. 1) writes of the term *al-samad*—which appears only in this *sura* and is uniquely applied to Allah—as comprising: 'the concepts of Primary Cause and eternal, independent Being, combined with the idea that everything existing or conceivable goes back to Him as its source and is, therefore, dependent on Him for its beginning as well as for its continued existence.'

[4] A less utilised name for the movement was *ahl al-tauhid*, 'People of Unity'.

political/military organisation and religious ideology' (Helms, 1981: 77)—which first gave the House of Saud its special religious status.[5] It led to *muwahhidi* acceptance of the Al Saud as 'legitimate and hereditary Islamic [rulers]' with their head bearing the title of *imam*, and it 'fundamentally distinguish[ed]' the rule of the Al Saud 'from other amirates and shaikhdoms of Central Arabia' and, indeed, from Saudi rule prior to the establishment of the alliance (Helms, 1981: 77, 81, 103–5). This status was to be inherited by subsequent generations of Saudis according to the Arabian customs of *nasab* and *sunna* and has thus been a foundation stone of Saudi political legitimacy since Ibn Saud began conquering central Arabia in the first decade of the twentieth century.[6]

Due to the successes of Wahhab's philosophy, the *muwahhidi* movement and the Saudi–Wahhabi religiopolitical alliance, the Arabian peninsula—excluding Yemen and Oman—is the only region in the Muslim world where the Hanbali *madhhab* is dominant.[7] The Hanbali school is generally regarded as the strictest of the four recognised Sunni branches of Quranic interpretation and observance.[8] On the other hand, James Piscatori (1983: 62–3) believes

---

[5] Esposito uses the term 'religiopolitical' specifically in relation to the Saud–Wahhab alliance; Hrair Dekmejian (1985: 7) employs 'religiopolitical fundamentalism' in a general sense. This rightly suggests that the Saudis were—and are—not unique in combining Muslim belief and political action. Hopwood (1982: 24–5) notes a similar, historical precedent in the Maghrebi *muwahhidi* movement founded by Ibn Tumart (*c.* 1078–1130) which, when allied with 'a more practical leader' (Abd al-Mu'min), founded the Almohad dynasty in Morocco and Spain. See also Lapidus (1990: 28–33).

[6] The term *sunna* is generically associated with the ancestral fame of nobility and virtuous deeds—temporal and/or religious—necessary for any family, clan or tribe to acquire in order to be honoured and attain continuing prestige (see Jafri, 1989: 4–6). The acquisition of such prestige, by benevolent means or through force (see Donner, 1981: 30–40), was a prerequisite to the attainment of power (see also the Glossary). *Sunna, nasab* and *hasab* (personal deeds of the individual) and the resultant accrual of personal, family and tribal honour, form the bases of the hierarchical structure of Arabian society.

[7] Hanbali law is the 'official school' of Saudi Arabia and Qatar (Ziadeh, 1995). A high proportion of Kuwaitis are also followers of the Hanbali *madhhab.*

[8] Ahmad bin Hanbal (d. 855), the founder of the *madhhab* which came to bear his name, was a leading figure in resistance to the attempts by the Abbasid caliph, Ma'mun (r. 813–33), to impose a single interpretation of Islam rooted in the ideas of particular rationalist theologians. Ibn Hanbal, who was persecuted for this

'conventional Western wisdom' has mistakenly labelled Hanbalis as the most 'unbending' among the Sunni *madhhabs*, and that the school possesses 'built-in flexibility' because, while strict where Quran and *hadith* are clear on a particular subject, it allows 'manoeuvrability' in interpretation and application where they are not.[9] 'Wahhabism' is a particular interpretation of the Hanbali school's teachings; despite any reputation the *madhhab* as a whole may have for the exercise of *ijtihad*, in its strictest form it is particularly austere, especially among those followers of the creed who identify themselves as *muwahhidun/salafiyya*.[10]

The first Saudi realm,[11] *c. 1744–1819.*[12]   Muhammad bin Saud, with the religious sanction of Ibn Abd al-Wahhab, began the small-scale expeditions which heralded the formation of the first Saudi realm. Muhammad bin Saud died in 1765, but within five years of his death '[a] new wave of religious enthusiasm [had] swept through [Najd], consciously modell[ed] …on the original rise of Islam

---

resistance, instead believed that the Quran and the *sunna* provided guidance enough; however, these two perennial sources of guidance were to be interpreted literally, with no concessions to any metaphorical ideals. Ibn Taimiyya and, in turn, Ibn Abd al-Wahhab, followed in this tradition (see Ziadeh, 1995; Hourani, 1991: 64–5, 179–81, 257–8).

[9] See also Hourani (1991: 180) on the Hanbali tradition, its 'strict' and 'literal' Quranic interpretation, and its recognition of *ijtihad*; Helms (1981: 80–3 and notes) traces a concise history of the stringent nature of Ibn Hanbal's thought, through to that of Ibn Taimiyya, to cast light on the orientation of the *muwahhidun*.

[10] For illumination on the *salafiyya*, see Shahin (1995): Ibn Hanbal is the 'articulator of classic salafiyah', Ibn Taimiyya 'contributed greatly to the evolution of the Salafiyah', and Ibn Abd al-Wahhab is presented as an example of the 'premodern Salafiyah'.

[11] I have adopted the term 'realm', notably employed by Nadav Safran (1985), since the other term most often applied to the early Saudi-conquered territories— 'state'—is a misnomer, in contrast to the modern kingdom founded in 1932. Furthermore, the dating of these early Saudi entities is an imprecise science, and has been given variously, for example, as 1747–1818 and 1818–92 (Omer, 1978: 275–81), and 1745–1811 and 1843–65/90/1902 (Fandy, 1999: 30, 41–3). Many historical accounts, such as those presented by Omer and Fandy, are confused; the definitive account is that given by Winder (1965).

[12] See the abbreviated genealogy of the Al Saud (Diagram 2.1), compiled to aid understanding of the historical events outlined in the following sections.

Diagram 2.1
SELECT GENEALOGY OF THE AL SAUD★

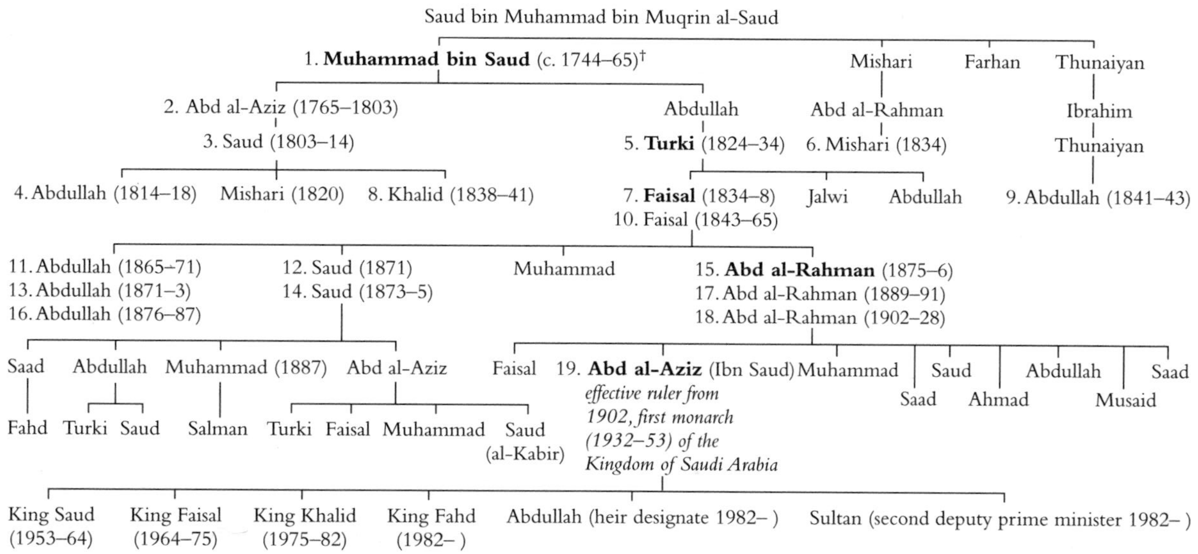

Saud bin Muhammad bin Muqrin al-Saud

1. **Muhammad bin Saud** (c. 1744–65)†

Mishari   Farhan   Thunaiyan

Abdullah   Abd al-Rahman   Ibrahim

2. Abd al-Aziz (1765–1803)   5. **Turki** (1824–34)   6. Mishari (1834)   Thunaiyan

3. Saud (1803–14)   7. **Faisal** (1834–8)   Jalwi   Abdullah   9. Abdullah (1841–43)

10. Faisal (1843–65)

4. Abdullah (1814–18)   Mishari (1820)   8. Khalid (1838–41)   15. **Abd al-Rahman** (1875–6)
17. Abd al-Rahman (1889–91)
18. Abd al-Rahman (1902–28)

Muhammad

11. Abdullah (1865–71)   12. Saud (1871)
13. Abdullah (1871–3)   14. Saud (1873–5)
16. Abdullah (1876–87)

Faisal   19. **Abd al-Aziz** (Ibn Saud) Muhammad   Saud   Abdullah   Saad

Saud   Saad   Ahmad   Musaid
(al-Kabir)

Abdullah   Muhammad (1887)   Abd al-Aziz   *effective ruler from*   Sultan (second deputy prime minister 1982–)
1902, first monarch
(1932–53) of the
Kingdom of Saudi Arabia

Saad   Abdullah   Muhammad (1887)   Abd al-Aziz

Fahd   Turki   Saud   Salman   Turki   Faisal   Muhammad   Abdullah (heir designate 1982–)

King Saud   King Faisal   King Khalid   King Fahd
(1953–64)   (1964–75)   (1975–82)   (1982–)

★ This significantly abbreviated genealogy is intended as an aid to the history presented in chapter 2. Numbers indicate the order of major Al Saud imams/rulers featured in chapter 2, from the beginning of the first Saudi–Wahhabi realm, c. 1744; their period of rule is in parentheses. Some other minor rulers also have their (brief) period of rule displayed. This genealogy ends with Sultan bin Abd al-Aziz, who is most likely to succeed to the throne after the current Crown Prince, Abdullah. Rulers in the line to Ibn Saud are printed in bold type.

† Muhammad bin Saud was the founder of the ruling dynasty, the original Ibn Saud.

Sources: Winder (1965); Lacey (1981); Bligh (1984).

eleven hundred years earlier', with 'the greater part of [Najd's] inhabitants' professing allegiance to the new *muwahhidi* creed (Glubb, 1960).[13] The late amir of Diriyya was succeeded by his son, Abd al-Aziz, who greatly extended the realm to control, albeit relatively loosely, an area exceeding that of the modern Saudi state. Riyadh was conquered in 1773; during the 1780s and '90s, territory along the eastern coast of Arabia, including al-Hasa (now the Eastern Province of Saudi Arabia) and what are today the states of Bahrain, Qatar and the United Arab Emirates (UAE), was subjected to *muwahhidi* control; parts of the Yemen along the Red Sea coast were added to the Saudi dominion; in 1802 the capture of Ta'if in the Hijaz was marked by a massacre of its inhabitants; and in 1803, Mecca came under Saudi suzerainty. Raiding was pushed ever further afield, most notably to the north, into Iraq and Syria (Safran, 1985: 9–12).

Abd al-Aziz's son, Saud, was the talented military commander responsible for most *muwahhidi* conquests; in 1803 when his father was assassinated at prayer, Saud became the ruler of the nascent mini-empire launched by his grandfather half a century earlier.[14]

---

[13] It is for this reason that the Saudis and their followers were almost universally referred to in Western sources as 'Wahhabis'. 'Wahhabi', however, implies the *muwahhidun* were and are followers of Shaikh Ibn Abd al-Wahhab rather than of Islam, and is therefore generally regarded by *muwahhidun* as a derogatory label in much the same way as Muslims resent the technically inaccurate, orientalist term of 'Mohammedan' to label the followers of Islam according to the Christ–Christian model. When asked if there were any official Saudi attitude on 'Wahhabi', the then Saudi ambassador to Australia, A. Rahman N. Alohaly (1995, pers. comm., 13 July), said the term was not acceptable to Saudi Arabians, and that it was used by 'those who are enemies of the kingdom'; he also, quite accurately, denied that *muwahhidun* constituted a sect (see also Ibn Saud's words on the subject, in al-Farsy, 1990: 20–1). For another explanation of the terms 'Wahhabism' and 'Wahhabi', their negative connotations, why their use persists, and alternative terms of reference, see Winder (1965: 1n. 1). The ubiquity of the term, however, has led even Saudi scholars to employ it (see, for example, Omer, 1978: 275; al-Farsy, 1990: 20). See also the brief definition in the Glossary.

[14] John S. Habib is one scholar who regards this dominion as having been an empire; he refers to 'the First Wahhabi Empire' (see Habib, 1978: 4). Troeller (1976: 14, 159) also refers to 'the Wahhabi Empire'. Mohammad Zayyan Omer (1978: 274–80), writing as associate professor of history at King Abd al-Aziz University (Jedda), employs 'state', 'realm' and 'empire'. Safran (1985: 28–72) writes of the third realm 'empire' created by Ibn Saud from 1902. Joseph A. Kechichian (1986: 56) refers to the first Saudi realm as 'the United States of Arabia'.

The religious mentor of this emerging realm, Muhammad bin Abd al-Wahhab, had been dead 11 years, but his legacy—and his sons and students—continued to inject his religious movement with vigour. Saud soon 'institutionalised' Wahhab's doctrine, and imposed a strict order on the tribes he controlled (see Safran, 1985: 12). From 1808 to 1812, Saud's tribal forces raided deeper into Iraq and Syria, as far as the vicinities of Baghdad, Damascus and Aleppo; although terror-stricken at the news of the approach of the *muwahhidun*, these major centres were never seriously threatened due to the 'primitive military system' employed by the marauders, which was oriented to raiding rather than to lengthy, organised campaigns and the garrisoning of conquered territory (see Glubb, 1960: 46–7).[15] The strategy was the traditional Arabian one of marauding, and winning or forcing the allegiance of tribes in order to gain access to their lands and their human and material resources; through these means influence and power were spread and a 'realm', or a 'dominion'—but not a 'state' or a coherently contiguous and administered body of territory—was forged.[16]

---

[15] Sir John Bagot Glubb, who as an officer in the British army participated in his country's imperial campaigns in the Arabian peninsula and Iraq in the 1920s and became familiar with the *muwahhidun* and their history, points to the use by the *muwahhidun* of intimidating tactics to keep subject a conquered population: 'Their policy of wholesale massacre…induced such terror that conquered populations hesitated to revolt, even if left without a garrison…' (Glubb, 1960: 47). He also summarises the feeling that at this time was beginning to be generated against the *muwahhidun*:

> …the savagery of their massacres of other Muslims, their greed for loot and their iconoclastic destruction of tombs and holy places, caused them to be regarded with hatred and repulsion by other professors of the Islamic faith. To the horror of the Muslim world, they even ventured…to desecrate in Medina the very tomb of the Prophet himself. (Glubb, 1960: 47; see also Troeller, 1976: 14)

This indication of the history of anti-*muwahhidun* sentiment in the Islamic world is relevant to the contemporary politics of the modern kingdom of Saudi Arabia.

[16] Such a dominion was fluid, and tended to ebb and flow according to the strength of successive rulers, according to 'unwritten desert law' (Troeller, 1976: 171). This 'law' has been interpreted by a British officer familiar with Arabian traditions before the imposition of nation-states after World War I:

> All Arab shaikhs base the territorial extent of their power upon their ability to enforce some order over the adjacent tribes, their power to enforce the

Despite the highly provocative nature of deep raiding to the north, it was *muwahhidi* control over the Hijaz, their imposition of austere religious mores in this holiest and most international of Muslim territories, and their interference in the annual *hajj* in general which roused the determination of the Ottoman sultan to put an end to the ascendance of the Saudi dominion. Originally commissioned by Sultan Selim III to subdue the rising force in Arabia, the Ottoman pasha of Egypt, Muhammad Ali, in 1811 sent an expedition to the Hijaz. Gradually the Egyptians gained the upper hand by capturing Madina in 1812, followed by Mecca and Ta'if in 1813. Then, in 1814, Saud, at the age of sixty-eight, died of a fever, to be succeeded by his son Abdullah. The succession was not smooth; another son of Muhammad bin Saud—the temporal keystone of the original Saud–Wahhab religiopolitical alliance—challenged Abdullah bin Saud. This son, Abdullah bin Muhammad, based his claim to the leadership precisely on the fact that he was the son of the founder of the Saudi–Wahhabi dominion. The challenge failed but the internal equilibrium of the Saudis was upset, creating conditions that encouraged defections to the Egyptians.

In 1818, a fresh Egyptian force razed Diriyya; Abdullah bin Saud and around 400 members of the Saud and Wahhab families were deported to Egypt.[17] Abdullah was eventually sent on to Istanbul, where he was executed. Due to the almost impossible logistics of maintaining control over eastern and central Arabia, the Egyptians soon withdrew to the Hijaz; thus, by late 1819 most of the Saudi–Wahhabi dominion had returned to unbridled tribal rivalry and feuding. The way was also paved for the emergence of a second Saudi realm only a few years later.

The second Saudi realm, c. 1824–91.   Soon after the Egyptian forces retired, content with authority over the commercially and religiously

---

payment of 'zikat' [taxes] by Beduin [*sic*], and their capacity to prevent and to avenge outrages and raids within the territorial limits claimed. (Shakespear, n.d.)

See Kostiner (1993: 181–2) for the way in which tribal allegiances were manipulated in territorial negotiations with the British as late as 1936.

[17] Diriyya has never been rebuilt. Atrocities committed by the *muwahhidun* were at this time matched by those committed by the victorious Ottoman–Egyptian forces under Ibrahim Pasha, son of Muhammad Ali (see, for example, Winder, 1965: 16–21; 55–6).

important province of al-Hijaz, Turki bin Abdullah bin Muhammad bin Saud—son of the challenger of Abdullah bin Saud in 1814—established a new Saudi centre in Riyadh in 1824.[18] The 'undiminished prestige of the Saud family—the font of pure Wahhabism' was a major contributing factor to the relatively rapid consolidation of Turki's position (Winder, 1965: 54). He quickly moved to extend his dominion—and the creed of the *muwahhidun*—following a pattern of expansion similar to the model that led to the founding of the first Saudi realm: small-scale campaigns with the eventual consolidation of influence and power in adjacent territories. In this instance, Turki wished to avoid antagonising the pasha of Egypt, so he expanded to the east; al-Hasa fell to him in 1830, and the Persian Gulf coast in its entirety recognised Saudi authority within another three years.[19] In an early display of Saudi acumen in foreign policy, Turki also sought to avoid a clash with the growing British presence in the Gulf. This approach was reciprocated by the British who, for their part, were content enough to live on friendly terms with the Saudis since they saw Turki's (re-)establishment of Saudi power as a stabilising factor on the peninsula (see Winder, 1965: 81–3).

Serious family dissent, which was to characterise the second realm, commenced soon after Turki began to consolidate new territory. In 1831 a cousin, Mishari bin Abd al-Rahman bin Mishari bin Saud, gained some tribal support and revolted. The revolt failed and Mishari was detained; however, in 1834 he managed to have Turki assassinated as he emerged from Friday prayers. Descendants of Ibn Abd al-Wahhab, known as sons of '*the* shaikh', by now possessed the adopted family name of 'Shaikh' and became known collectively as the Al Shaikh. Members of this revered lineage—who were by this

---

[18] For an account of the rise of Turki in 1823 to his takeover of Riyadh in 1824, see Winder (1965: 60–4). In his brief background to the Saudi succession in the twentieth century, Bligh (1984: 10–11; see also p. 106) presents a slightly different interpretation of events from the fall of Diriyya to the founding of the second realm. Winder's account is by far the better documented.

[19] Winder (1965: 65–81) carries a relatively full account of Turki's consolidation of power in Najd and his subsequent easterly expansion. It should be noted that Bahrain avoided 'Saudi control…in any permanent way' (Winder, 1965: 79). On Turki's devotion to educating his new subjects in *muwahhidi* religious practice, see Winder (1965: 86–7).

time regarded as the *muwahhidi* ulama *par excellence*—recognised Mishari as imam after securing their own safety. The importance of religious recognition from the senior ulama in the cause of political legitimacy is highlighted by Winder (1965: 96). However, Mishari's moment of glory was, literally, to be short-lived; Turki's eldest son, Faisal, hastily returned from a campaign against Bahrain, defeated Mishari and ordered him to be executed.[20] Following the hierarchy of importance in the *muwahhidi* order, Faisal, in presenting himself as imam, gave priority to establishing his legitimacy with the religious authorities of the Saudi realm before doing likewise with amirs and other, more secular political figures (Winder, 1965: 99). The Saudi grip on al-Hasa, Bahrain and Qatar was considerably loosened as a result of the disruption caused by this family feuding.

Then, in 1836, the now rebellious Pasha of Egypt, Muhammad Ali, as part of his war against the Ottomans, again sent a force to the Hijaz to move against Faisal in his home territory of Najd; the aim was to create a Cairo-centred empire at the expense of Istanbul. The Egyptians brought with them Khalid bin Saud, the brother of Abdullah bin Saud, whom they had defeated in 1818; Khalid was one of the many Saudis captured at the fall of Diriyya, and his fate in the Egyptians' plans was to be their proxy in Najd in the place of his cousin Faisal. Faisal distributed largesse to his subjects to quiet dissent in the face of the approach of the invading Egyptians in 1837 (Winder, 1965: 109)—an example of the virtual purchase of loyalty and political stability through largesse which is still a feature of modern Saudi domestic policy. Faisal was, however, defeated in 1838 and imprisoned in Cairo, and the Egyptians went on to conquer most of Arabia.[21] However, in the interests of the cohesion of

[20] See Winder (1965: 93–9) for the events surrounding Mishari's revolt, the murder of Turki and Faisal's triumph; see also Safran (1985: 14–15). Bligh (1984: 11, see also 106) does not mention Mishari bin Abd al-Rahman.

[21] For a detailed account of this latter Egyptian invasion, the installation and rule of Khalid, the fortunes of Faisal, the de facto 'partition' of Najd between Khalid and Faisal and, finally, Faisal's defeat and exile, see Winder (1965: 107–20). Winder's note on 'the lack of anything like modern nationalism in nineteenth-century Arabia, although it is true that Arabians had a sense of their Arabness' (Winder, 1965: 111–12), is also relevant for an understanding of some of the difficulties faced by Ibn Saud and his sons in the forging of a state in the twentieth century—the ultimate attainment of which may still be questioned, despite the building of the modern structures of state in contemporary Saudi Arabia.

the Ottoman empire, Muhammad Ali was forced by the European powers to relinquish his infant empire, and in 1841 most of his forces retreated from Arabia.

Khalid remained in Riyadh but was soon deposed by another relative, Abdullah bin Thunaiyan, who was, in the pragmatic fashion that had become characteristic of the senior *muwahhidi* ulama, pronounced imam. The saga continued when Faisal bin Turki returned to Najd after escaping from Egypt; Faisal opposed Ibn Thunaiyan who was in turn deposed in 1843, incarcerated and then killed by his captors in a family vendetta.[22] Faisal's return inaugurated a Saudi renaissance. In the words of Safran (1985: 16):

> Faisal's second reign (1843–1865) was the golden age of the second Saudi realm. Territorially, the realm was much smaller than the first and had little of its dynamism; but it had far greater acceptance externally and internally, representing as it did a transition from 'revolutionary Wahhabism' to 'Wahhabism in one country'.

It was during this period that the *muwahhidi* interpretation of Islam entrenched itself in Arabia; not surprisingly, it was centred in Najd and was 'more or less loosely followed elsewhere, the differences provid[ing] little or no ground for conflict' (Safran, 1985: 17). A relatively high degree of political stability fostered this consolidation of *muwahhidi* ideology; it was also an interesting period for the juggling of domestic and foreign policies on the part of the Saudi imam of central and central-eastern Arabia.

Faisal and the Ottomans exchanged recognition: Faisal paid an annual tribute to Istanbul and received in return the title 'ruler of all the Arabs'—in effect, a loose reference to the Arabs of the Arabian peninsula. Faisal, however, had to work hard—and, often, literally fight—to maintain his rulership in the face of constant tribal insubordination and open rebellion: the political stability referred to above was indeed only relative to the turmoil that had reigned since the fall of the first Saudi realm (see Winder, 1965: 149–78). The central authority in Riyadh was not wealthy; it depended on tribal

---

[22] For the detail of events from the Egyptian withdrawal, Khalid's rule and deposition by Ibn Thunaiyan, the latter's rule and his overthrow by Faisal, see Winder (1965: 131–48). Safran (1985: 16) prefers the version of Ibn Thunaiyan's death that has him poisoned at the hands of Faisal while in irons.

militias for its expeditions, and 'the entire realm was essentially a precarious confederation of tribes held together by the energy, will, and wisdom of the chief' (Safran, 1985: 17). Faisal resorted to force when it was necessary to maintain his dominance, but was usually prepared to be reconciled with rebels after disciplinary action had been taken. The tradition of allegiance to the ruler in the name of unity and Islam, espoused by the Saudis today, is illustrated in the attitude revealed by Faisal in a letter addressed to the rebels of Qasim in 1849:

Religion is of no avail unless it is expressed in a community and there can be no community without obedience. You refused our order and ceased obeying us. You know that war is a fire in which men are the fuel, and the killing of a single Muslim is costly to me; therefore, be not a cause for the shedding of your blood, but enter into that which you and your fathers entered before. (Faisal bin Turki, quoted by Ibn Bishr, cited in Winder, 1965: 160)

However, behind the religious message lay the nature of tribal politics, which demanded a policy of generosity and reconciliation, because '[f]rom the point of view of the would-be founder or ruler of a realm, it was necessary to treat some defeated opponents harshly to impress or deter others, but to treat most of them generously because enemies could easily become allies' (Safran, 1985: 26). Only through the consolidation of allies could the would-be ruler lay claim to the land, military manpower and other resources of the tribes. This dualistic policy of punishment and reconciliation remains a feature of Saudi coercion in the modern era.

Faisal followed a cautious foreign policy similar to his father's. Not wishing to disturb the Ottoman province of the Hijaz, he concentrated his aspirations in the east, where he likewise preferred to avoid conflict with British interests in the Gulf. With designs on Qatar and especially on the powerful and independent maritime shaikhdom of Bahrain, however, Faisal's ambitions conflicted with British interests. Faisal's rivalry with the Hijaz, epitomised in the 1846 invasion of the Najd by the *sharif*, Muhammad bin Aun, did not prevent him from claiming sovereignty over the Gulf principalities on the basis of the Ottoman sultan's cursory recognition of him as 'ruler of all the Arabs' (see Winder, 1965: 184). A series of wars ensued between the Saudi dominion and Bahrain; these finally came to an end in 1861 when Bahrain, which had enjoyed acts of British protection at crucial stages in the conflict with Faisal, was made a signatory to the 1853, British-brokered Perpetual Treaty of Truce and officially afforded British protection. Faisal was in no position to oppose British power in the region and modified his goals accordingly. Various Gulf coast statelets, however, including Bahrain after 1861, at some stage paid tribute to Riyadh—a gesture which underlines more the Saudi failure to bring these entities under direct control than any sign of Saudi dominance.[23]

The traditional Arabian style of *asabiyya* government exhibited during this golden era of the second Saudi realm was to be echoed by the next great Saudi ruler, Ibn Saud, the founder of the modern Saudi state:

Like the early Muslim state, Wahhabi Arabia in the nineteenth century represented a combination of traditional Arab patriarchal rule and a deeply felt religious ideal. The imam was commander-in-chief and chief justice as well as chief executive of the realm. All important matters domestic or foreign, political, fiscal and military were referred directly to the imam...

There was...some devolution of power from the imam to lower officials, the 'royal court' was small and informal. Its most important members were close relatives of the imam, whose loyalty transcended any local interests. In addition, the family of Sheikh Muhammad ibn 'Abd al-Wahhab also played a major role...

The device of using members of the imam's immediate family, especially brothers and sons, served two purposes. Firstly it helped to centralise the government in loyal hands, and secondly it helped to satisfy the conflicting aspirations of family members. (Winder, 1965: 203)

It was just such 'conflicting aspirations of family members' that led to the destruction of the second Saudi realm. Upon Faisal's death in 1865, his eldest son, Abdullah, became imam. But peace was not to reign: Abdullah's rule (1865–87) was to be interrupted by two complex periods of family rivalry which would virtually destroy the realm.

---

[23] Faisal's fortunes in international relations are covered in some detail by Winder (1965: 179–203, 217–22). For a brief account of Anglo–Saudi relations since the signing of the Maritime Truce in the Gulf in 1835, with a focus on Faisal's ambitions along the Gulf coast, see Troeller (1976: 15–18).

Firstly, Faisal's second son, Saud, coveted the leadership and soon entered into rebellion. A number of battles took place between the rivals and their respective tribal allies and, early in 1871, Saud took Riyadh and became imam (see Winder, 1965: 229–51; Safran, 1985: 17). In May of the same year, Ottoman forces from Iraq invaded the Eastern Province, proclaimed the deposition of 'all Sauds', and appointed an Ottoman governor to rule Najd from the security of the east (Winder, 1965: 252–5; see also Safran, 1985: 17–18). But family intrigue did not stop at this: the uncle of Abdullah and Saud, Abdullah bin Turki—that is, the brother of the former imam, Faisal bin Turki—mounted a successful coup against Saud. Abdullah bin Faisal joined his uncle in Riyadh, as imam once again (1871–3).

The second period of rivalry began immediately, with further battles between the imam and Saud bin Faisal, while the Turks attempted to dispose of them all (Winder, 1965: 255–7). Saud eventually prevailed over his brother in 1873 and became imam for a second time himself, but died in 1875 with the Saudi realm all but in total ruin. Infighting continued, however, as the youngest son of Faisal, Abd al-Rahman, took over the imamship from his brother Saud and resumed the war against his eldest brother, Abdullah. After further clashes, the sons of Saud entered the ongoing débacle in 1876 when they rose against their father's fraternal supporter, Abd al-Rahman. This development prompted Abd al-Rahman and Abdullah to be reconciled, and the rebellious nephews fled Riyadh to establish their own fiefdom in their father's power base south of Riyadh. Abdullah bin Faisal became imam for the third time—the eighth shuffle of the imamship in the 11 years since Imam Faisal died (see Winder, 1965: 262–3; Safran, 1985: 18[24]).

At this point, the ruler of the northern Najdi fiefdom of Jabal Shammar, Muhammad bin Rashid, asserted himself against Saudi rule—a significant move since Rashidi rulers had until then scrupulously maintained loyalty to the power in Riyadh. The 1880s saw Ibn Rashid gradually erode what little power the Saudis retained until, in 1887, prompted by another capture of Riyadh by the rebel

---

[24] Safran follows the wording of Winder very closely on occasions, yet also makes some errors of fact; Safran's wording in other places may also give an inaccurate impression of some events to those readers who do not refer to Winder's full and detailed history of this period of Saudi rule.

sons of Saud bin Faisal, he marched on the city, forced the expulsion of the young usurpers, and formally annexed the Saudi capital to his Shammari dominion (Winder, 1965: 263–72; Safran, 1985: 19). Abd al-Rahman bin Faisal made a number of attempts to regain the semblance of some territorial control, most notably in the great tribal revolt against Ibn Rashid in 1890–1; the challenge failed and Abd al-Rahman fled with his family to Kuwait where they remained in exile (Winder, 1965: 274–8).

Thus did the second Saudi realm come decisively to its conclusion in 1891—a realm that, even more than the first, had been marked by intrigue, internal dissent, and by acts of fraternal and tribal fickleness and civil war. This particular aspect of their history is not lost on the Saudi family today; nor is it lost on observers of the kingdom, who see in it a precedent for potentially fatal internal disruption. It is noteworthy that this predicament was, and is not unique to the Saudis. The Bahrainis also suffered from 'dynastic quarrels [which] resulted in a civil war' in 1842 (Winder 1965: 140); and even as late as 1995, the pattern was repeated in Qatar when, in June of that year, Shaikh Hamad bin Khalifa al-Thani deposed his father as amir in a bloodless palace coup.[25] The history of Saudi dominance of most of Arabia also provides an insight into the relations of the modern kingdom with its smaller Gulf Arab neighbours: in the period looked at thus far, successive Saudi rulers sought to expand their dominion at the expense of the independent Gulf shaikhdoms. Saudi Arabia today exercises great influence over

[25] The Qatari coup could, according to the Palestinian pan-Arab daily, *Al-Quds al-Arabi* (quoted in *Mideast Mirror*, 1995, vol. 9, no. 123), 'encourage other younger scions of the Gulf's ruling families to try to do likewise in their own countries'. Reporting on *Al-Quds*' commentary as well as quoting it directly, the *Mideast Mirror* states:

…there are fierce disputes within the ruling families of most of the other Gulf states that could result in similar outcomes.

…political change in the Gulf has tended to be…prompted by action from within ruling families…

The likelihood now is that 'the train of change in the Gulf sheikhdoms will not stop in Doha.' There are many problems and rivalries at the top of the political echelon in most Gulf states, and these are likely to heat up…portending 'peaceful transformations or bloody ones if they cannot be resolved by consensus'.

its neighbours, both through the Gulf Cooperation Council (GCC) and informally.[26]

Throughout the first two realms, *muwahhidi* doctrine prevailed in Najd as the common denominator of faith, yet it proved no match for political manoeuvring, tribal interests and rival ambitions; the message of Ibn Abd al-Wahhab may have inspired a religiopolitical expansion, but it was not sufficient to sustain the two Saudi political entities. The role of the ulama, as Safran (1985: 23) highlights, was to remain neutral and 'to sanction the authority of whoever prevailed'.[27] In modern Saudi Arabia, *muwahhidi* ideology is still of great importance for the prestige and legitimacy of the Saudi regime, and it is still the dominating factor which colours everyday life in Saudi Arabia. Despite the rhetoric to the contrary, political interests would appear to enjoy primacy over religious imperatives. A valid alternative interpretation is that Arabian cultural patterns and Islam—specifically *muwahhidi* Islam—have assimilated to the extent that, in Saudi politics, the two are virtually indistinguishable. In this case, those involved with the political imperatives of the state find appeal to religious legitimacy a convincing strategy, while those more concerned with a religious orientation to every aspect of life find recourse to political action in the name of Islam a natural and sincere option to achieve their goals. Thus, the historical evolution

---

[26] The *Mideast Mirror* (1995), again utilising *Al-Quds al-Arabi* in comment on the June 1995 Qatari palace coup, refers to the vital role of Saudi Arabia in the eventual outcome of the incident:

> In Qatar's case, it is regional heavyweight Saudi Arabia's attitude that will determine how things develop...
>
> The chances are that Riyadh, however displeased as it may be with Hamad's policies, will opt to stay out of the row within the al-Thani family. It learned from its recent experience in sponsoring the abortive secessionist rebellion in Yemen that interference in neighbors' internal affairs can prove very costly.

The comment, besides illustrating the regional power of Saudi Arabia, also provides an insight into the way Saudi Arabia's regional relationships are perceived in the Arab world. Another indication of the influence of Saudi Arabia on its small neighbours is illustrated in the results of a cultural inquiry made to the embassy of the United Arab Emirates in Canberra: in the process of ascertaining the extent of the Hanbali *madhhab* in the region, in this case in the Emirates, I was told to 'call the Saudi Embassy' (UAE Embassy, 1997, pers. comm., 11 Dec.). See the Glossary for basic information on the GCC.

[27] See note 51 and associated main text, below.

of *muwahhidi* Islam and Saudi sociopolitics are important when it comes to analysing the policies of the Saudi regime and the response/counter-response of regime and opposition.

The formation of the modern Saudi state

Ibn Saud on the march. The story of the foundation of the modern state of Saudi Arabia begins in Kuwait, where Abd al-Rahman bin Faisal and his family were exiled. It was his eldest surviving son, Abd al-Aziz (1881–1953), who was to assume the role of effective head of this branch of the family and who would lead the Al Saud back to power in Najd. According to Winder (1965: 278), Abd al-Aziz was, within 10 years of his exile, 'planning the bold raid which initiated his campaign to regain his patrimony'.

The 'bold raid' has long since passed into the realm of legend. It followed several years of unsuccessful manoeuvring on the part of Abd al-Rahman and Abd al-Aziz, allied with the amir of Kuwait, Mubarak bin Sabah. In January 1902, Abd al-Aziz made his way to Riyadh with a small contingent of followers, posted two separate groups at various points near the city and entered Riyadh secretly at night through ruined walls.[28] At dawn on the following morning, the infiltrators ambushed and killed the Rashidi governor of Riyadh and took the garrison of the citadel by surprise. The Riyadhis assisted Abd al-Aziz to secure the city and to rebuild its defences. The other exiled Saudis then joined the triumphant son in Riyadh, and Abd al-Aziz and his father agreed a division of responsibility: the father re-assumed the traditional title of Imam and managed administrative affairs while the son assumed the role of political and military leader (Bligh, 1984; 12–16; Safran, 1985: 30). The recapture of Riyadh was the first step in the conquest of territory that would eventually lead to the proclamation of the modern kingdom-state in 1932. It is, however, the event which the Al Saud have chosen to represent the foundation of the contemporary state and which was celebrated in January 1999 as the kingdom's centenary (by the

---

[28] See Glubb (1960: 55) and Safran (1985: 30); both accept the rendition of this event which puts the original group at 60 men, with the final infiltration group numbering 10. Bligh (1984: 13) presents the oft-cited figure of 40 for the number of Abd al-Aziz's party (however, 40 is an auspicious number in Semitic mythology).

Islamic calendar). Abd al-Aziz was extolled during the centenary celebrations as a man of military and leadership prowess, and equally as a man of religious piety—the consummate Saudi leader.

Ibn Saud (as Abd al-Aziz is popularly known[29]) then proceeded to gather support from the surrounding districts and, later in 1902, held his own against Rashidi attempts to relieve him of his newly acquired gains. Saudi expansion continued and, although modest at this stage, by June 1904 included the important Qasim district on the southern border of the Rashidi heartland. Ibn Rashid[30] enlisted Ottoman support and in July 1904 an inconclusive battle was fought between superior Rashidi and Turkish forces on the one hand, and the lesser forces of Ibn Saud and his Qasimi allies on the other. Ibn Saud nominally submitted himself to Turkish overlordship and was stripped of Qasim, which was to act as a neutral buffer zone between the Al Rashid and the Al Saud (see Glubb, 1960: 56; Safran, 1985: 30–2). Nadav Safran (1985: 32) provides an insight into the political outcome of these events, which he interprets as:

…a tribute to Ibn Saud's superior statecraft just as the battle itself was a tribute to his courage. The Turks had come into the battle with their vital interest in securing the Damascus–Madina railway wedded to the cause of ibn Rashid, who sought the destruction of Saudi power. By denying to the enemy coalition victory in the battlefield through his effective resistance, and then satisfying the particular interest of the Turks through nominal and temporary concessions, Ibn Saud broke up the coalition, placed himself with the Turks on an equal footing with ibn Rashid, and secured from both recognition of his power in the domains other than the Qasim that he had acquired so far.

This provides an early glimpse of Ibn Saud's diplomatic acumen confirmed in following years, as he and Ibn Rashid continued to pursue action against each other. In April 1906, Ibn Rashid was killed in this ongoing low-level war; in November 1906 the Turks abandoned Najd and, shortly after, Qasim was absorbed by Ibn Saud

---

[29] See Lacey (1981: 59–60, 60 note) on *Ibn Saud* as an honorary reference to the Muhammad bin Saud who founded the dynasty c. 1744.

[30] The founder of the rival Rashidi dominion, Muhammad bin Rashid, had died in 1897; the Ibn Rashid who at this stage opposed Ibn Saud was his nephew, Abd al-Aziz bin Mitab bin Rashid, a leader known for his chivalry but not for the political skills of his predecessor.

(Safran, 1985: 32–3; Glubb, 1960: 56–7).[31] Early in 1910, however, Ibn Saud suffered a temporary setback when, in alliance with Amir Mubarak of Kuwait and various tribes, he lost a battle against powerful tribal allies of the Rashids (Safran, 1985: 33). At this time, family dissent once again threatened the nascent Saudi realm in the form of up to eight of Ibn Saud's cousins, grandsons of his uncle, Saud bin Faisal.[32] The cousins, nicknamed *araif* (stolen camels recovered from an enemy in a counter-raid) after their retrieval from Rashidi captivity by Ibn Saud in 1904, used the opportunity of Ibn Saud's absence and defeat in an attempt to usurp his position. In league with the rebellious Ajman tribe, they established a base south of Riyadh. Ibn Saud defeated them in 1912. Some of the pretenders, reconciled, returned to Riyadh, while one fled to Hasa and the remainder to the Hijaz to join the Sharif of Mecca, the Hashimite Hussein who, since his appointment to the sharifate in 1908, had been asserting himself ever more vigorously beyond the borders of the Hijaz. In 1911, Hussein captured Ibn Saud's favourite (full) brother, Saad, and compelled Ibn Saud to sign an agreement which renewed his Ottoman allegiance and obliged him to pay tribute to Istanbul for Qasim through himself. But upon the return of his brother, Ibn Saud rejected his new pledges, citing a forced agreement that released him from his commitments (Troeller, 1976: 38–9; Lacey, 1981: 95–8, 100–1; Bligh, 1984: 17–18; Safran, 1985: 33–4).

---

[31] The turmoil which beset the Rashidi capital of Ha'il at this point epitomised the pattern of clan rivalry and family feuding in the interests of political ambition in Arabia. Glubb (1960: 57) has outlined the Rashidi dilemma:

> The great Muhammad Ibn Rasheed had raised his family to the highest pinnacle of greatness, but he had seized power by murdering nearly all his male relatives. It was a precedent which was to prove fatal to the dynasty. Mitab Ibn Rasheed [Abd al-Aziz's son and successor] had scarcely ruled for a year when he was assassinated by his cousin Sultan, who himself was murdered by his brother Saud Ibn Hamood. Nine months later, he also was assassinated...

This 'tragic tradition of internecine murder' (Glubb, 1960: 59) was eventually to give Ibn Saud his opportunity to destroy the Rashidi dynasty. See also Lacey (1981: 162–3).

[32] Lacey (1981: 533), Safran (1985: 33) and Bligh (1984: 114) number the rebellious cousins at eight, six and five, respectively; Lacey and Bligh also present differing genealogies of the cousins. Lacey's account of this episode (and his genealogy) appears to be the more accurate.

Far from entertaining any allegiance to the Turks, Ibn Saud moved against them in the east in May 1913. Frustrated since 1903 in his attempts to gain British co-operation, he acted alone. He was successful after a relatively short and bloodless campaign (Troeller, 1976: 21–5, 43–4; Safran, 1985: 35). However, in an act of *Realpolitik*, Ibn Saud pledged his allegiance to Istanbul anew; he cited mismanagement of Hasa on the part of the Turkish officials there, and claimed that he was, in any case, returning the province 'to the traditional state of affairs' (Troeller, 1976: 44).[33] As Gary Troeller (1976: 39) states, '[a]lthough he was anti-Turkish ibn Saud, like his forebears, was not adverse to pledging his allegiance to the Porte when it served his purpose' and, in this case, the purpose 'was probably [an endeavour] to prevent the Turks from taking any more punitive measures against him' (Troeller, 1976: 44). The end result was that in May 1914, Ibn Saud signed a treaty which confirmed him as a servant of the Turks in the role of governor of Najd and Hasa; this status, however, springing as it did from an act of 'political survival', was nominal only—in effect, Ibn Saud remained autonomous (Troeller, 1976: 55, 60–1).

Thus, by astute political manoeuvring, personal courage and the judicious use of military force, Ibn Saud had, on the eve of World War I, re-established Saudi dominance of central Najd–Qasim and Hasa. By gambling on the Turkish inability to retake Hasa and force his hand in the east, Ibn Saud had succeeded in making his realm a Gulf power of increasing strategic and political value. The stage was set for further Saudi expansion and the final destruction of Ottoman and Rashidi power in Arabia, against the backdrop of British regional hegemony.

The British, the First World War and post-Ottoman Arabia. During the nineteenth century, British relations with the Saudis were relatively insignificant. This situation gradually changed during the first quarter of the twentieth century. From 1903 Ibn Saud had been trying unsuccessfully to gain British support for his ambitions in the east against the Turks. The British imperative, as an extension of European policy, was to maintain good relations with the Ottoman

---

[33] The 'traditional state of affairs' was reference to previous Saudi dominance of Hasa.

Empire, so Ibn Saud's overtures were repeatedly turned down (Troeller, 1976: 34–6, 40, 46, 75; Kedourie, 1987: 29). But his desire—indeed, his need—for closer and more formal relations with the British did not diminish; in fact, he could not afford to offend the British since they were the pre-eminent Gulf power and were all that stood between the new Saudi dominion and the possibility of a Turkish invasion from the east (see Troeller, 1976: 50). This historical strategic vulnerability was brought home to the Saudi regime more recently with the 1979 Iranian Revolution and the 1990 Iraqi invasion of Kuwait; now, of course, the dominant Gulf power and the kingdom's protector is the United States.

Significantly, however, in 1914 the British India Office had come to see Ibn Saud as 'the strongest power in Arabia' (Holderness, 1914: IO memo). A June 1914 report by the British political agent in Kuwait, Captain W.H.I. Shakespear—a man on the ground in Arabia and personally acquainted with Ibn Saud—reinforced the change of mood in British policy on Arabia. He emphasised a general and growing Arab dissatisfaction with Turkish rule and the increasingly critical weakness of that rule (see Troeller, 1976: 64–5). The change of British attitude was transformed into a change of policy on the outbreak of war between Britain and Turkey on 5 November 1914.

Ibn Saud's ambitions were, however, dealt a blow when the British courted the former's enemy, Sharif Hussein of the Hijaz, prompted when the Ottoman sultan and caliph declared a *jihad* against Britain and her allies on 14 November 1914. The religious importance of the Sharif of Mecca invested the issue with great significance; if Hussein sided with the British, the Ottoman proclamation of *jihad* would be greatly diluted and, moreover, his support would help secure vital British bases and lines of communication in Egypt, the Suez Canal–Red Sea and Aden. If, on the other hand, Hussein declared for the Turks, he would also join alliance with the existing Turkish ally in northern Najd, the Al Rashid, thus making real a great threat to British interests in Arabia and the Gulf (Troeller, 1976: 76–7; Glubb, 1959: 58–9). The British position *vis-à-vis* Sharif Hussein and Ibn Saud is summed up by Troeller (1976: 81–2):

Using the same scale of religious, political strategic and military importance, it is readily apparent that ibn Sa'ud ran Sharif Husain a very bad second at the outset of the war—and for some time to come.

From the religious viewpoint, ibn Sa'ud stood at the head of a movement which was looked upon with a mixture of fear and disdain by many Moslems. His importance in this field was, in comparison with Husain, manifestly negligible. Politically, the Wahhabi leader had no influence outside the confines of central and eastern Arabia. He could not put himself at the head of an Arab movement which could to some extent coordinate comparatively sophisticated nationalist movements with tribal discontent.

The passage above sums up Ibn Saud's inferior military and strategic position as compared to Hussein's, the prestige value of being the custodian of the two holy cities of Mecca and Madina, and the prevailing perception of the *muwahhidun*. However, in keeping with his reputation for astute statesmanship, Ibn Saud continued to focus on the bigger and longer-term picture by pursuing his long-standing desire for formal relations with Britain. Although putting most of their weight behind Sharif Hussein, the British also deemed it to be to their advantage to entertain Hussein's Najdi enemy. Treaty negotiations occupied the whole of 1915; on 26 December 1915, the Anglo–Saudi Treaty was signed.[34]

Although no British–Sharifian alliance was formally cemented by a treaty—and although Hussein almost certainly knew of British and French machinations on the future of the Ottoman Arab provinces—on 5 June 1916, Hussein proclaimed the Arab Revolt against the Ottoman Caliphate and, in December of the same year, declared himself 'King of the Arab countries'. While Hussein was soon recognised by Britain and France as 'King of the Hijaz', Ibn Saud denounced this act as one of temporal pretentiousness on the part of a Hashimite supposedly descended from the Prophet. Although Ibn Saud refused to recognise Hussein's claim to kingship anywhere in the Arab world, he did fulfil minimal obligations to his British allies by announcing in November 1916 his support for the Sharifian-led Arab Revolt. In fact, this was almost the whole extent of Ibn Saud's capabilities at the time, since he was hard-pressed to maintain

---

[34] For a discussion of British considerations and an account of Ibn Saud's great haggling prowess in the treaty's negotiations, see Troeller (1976: 85–9). The treaty represented 'a turning point in Anglo–Sa'udi relations' and, as a result, '[r]eluctantly but inexorably Britain was drawn into the vortex of inner Arabian politics' (ibid., 90–1).

his own position in the face of serious rebellions by tribes supposedly under his control: helping the British by marching on the Turks' Rashidi ally was out of the question. Furthermore, in November 1916, Ibn Saud became 'Sir' Abd al-Aziz when he had bestowed upon him the award of Knight Commander of the Most Eminent Order of the Indian Empire (Troeller, 1976: 91–100; Lacey, 1981: 118–27).

British policy toward Ibn Saud vacillated and, during the period from late 1917 to early 1918, the British decided to be content with a minimal role for their Najdi ally; for his part, Ibn Saud could not make any major move without British approval and material support (see Troeller, 1976: 105–17). The result was that '[t]hroughout the war ibn Sa'ud's role was but a sideshow in comparison with that of his rival in the Hedjaz' (Troeller, 1976: 75). What did flourish during the war, however, was Saudi–Sharifian suspicion and hostility. This enmity was only to intensify in the following years when there was no common Turkish foe to distract the two rulers from rival ambitions. The first major clashes between the two occurred in May 1918, before the end of the war. Hussein suffered potentially serious setbacks, and the British, embarrassed by the fighting between their two Arabian allies, nevertheless continued their favour of the sharif. They made kings of his two sons, Abdullah and Faisal, in Transjordan and Iraq respectively, and formalised the boundaries of these new nation-states after the defeat of the Ottomans in the war. Though often angered at British attitudes, Ibn Saud maintained a consistently pro-British policy; he recognised that with the demise of the Ottoman Empire, the strategy that would best serve his interests was to entertain and do business with the new regional power (see Troeller, 1976: 130–50; Kostiner, 1993: 16–18, 35–42).

During the summer of 1920, British-brokered negotiations led to the signing of an armistice between Hussein and Ibn Saud (Troeller, 1976: 151–2). It was at this time and during these clashes that the new *muwahhidi* tribal–military force of the Ikhwan, moulded and wielded by Ibn Saud, entered into the equation, a force that elicited fear on the part of Hussein and wariness on the part of the British.[35] The Ikhwan provided Ibn Saud with a potent and, literally,

[35] The role of the Ikhwan in modern Saudi history is important and is the subject of some scrutiny below.

death-defying—or more accurately, death-welcoming—military force which also helped to re-confirm the original Saudi–Wahhabi religiopolitical alliance. After the negotiation of an uneasy truce with King Hussein of the Hijaz, Ibn Saud moved from strength to strength. In spite of, or because of, his feeling of vulnerability at the establishment of Sharifian kingdoms in the Hijaz and in Transjordan and Iraq, he 'endeavoured relentlessly to extend his frontiers to the limits of the early nineteenth century Wahhabi Empire' (Troeller, 1976: 159). Asir fell to him in 1920 and, in 1921, he dealt the final blow to the Shammari domain of the Rashidis when he captured Ha'il—a coup which provided him with great additional leverage in his conflicts with the rulers of the Hijaz and Kuwait.[36] In 1922 Ibn Saud brought himself even closer to the Iraqi and Transjordanian borders when he annexed Jauf. However: '…the manner in which Ibn Sa'ud decided on his conquests and his actual campaigns reveals that he had no master plan for a systematic conquest and expansion… It was not until the summer of 1921 that [he] embarked on a full-scale policy of expansion aimed at defeating his rivals (Kostiner, 1993: 54).[37]

It was also during this period that the British found themselves in a position akin to a tribal ruler, through the necessity of buying influence and loyalty with subsidies. A complicated balancing act resulted as the new foreign power attempted to keep a peace between its many clients that would be favourable to British interests (see Kostiner, 1993: 55–62; Troeller, 1976: 159–67; Lacey, 1981: 148–9). Included in this policy was the bestowing of favours and, in 1921, Britain recognised Ibn Saud as 'Sultan of Najd and its Dependencies'. Disputes between Ibn Saud, King Faisal of Iraq and Ibn Sabah of Kuwait over territory and tribes forced the British to draw

---

[36] On the fall of the Rashidi domain, see Kostiner (1993: 18–35, 45–52) and Troeller (1976: 167–74). Kostiner, in particular, puts the conquest of Ha'il in a clear perspective with the other theatres of Ibn Saud's conflicts and strategies of expansion.

[37] Elaborating on the impressive but ad hoc nature of this phase of Saudi expansion, Kostiner (1993: 54) goes on to state that Ibn Saud:

…attacked various arenas where an existing tribal dispute between loyal tribal groups and hostile rulers became acute. He was driven to assume responsibility in battlefronts through proselytism and the protection given to a loyal tribe, after which strategic interests impelled him to take a more aggressive approach.

borders arbitrarily in late 1922 (Troeller, 1976: 170–82); soon after, similar disputes over the Najdi–Transjordanian–Iraqi and Najdi–Hijazi borders led to failed negotiations—in the case of the latter dispute, the stage was set for Ibn Saud's conquest of the Hijaz and the eventual proclamation of a Saudi kingdom (Troeller, 1976: 189–211).

Hijaz conquered, kingdom proclaimed. As the 1920s progressed, Hussein's rule had been steadily undermined by a combination of the growing power of Ibn Saud and his own lack of astuteness; finally, by 1924, the Hijazi regime was on the point of collapse and only needed the *coup de grâce* to be delivered. Ibn Saud could afford to choose his moment, and the progress of events would soon present him with one.[38]

On 3 March 1924 the Kemalists in the new Turkish republic abolished the Caliphate; on 5 March, King Hussein established his Hijazi dominion as the seat of a new caliphate with himself as caliph. This 'bid for supremacy' further antagonised Ibn Saud and, when British subsidies were withdrawn on 31 March, Sultan Sir Abd al-Aziz prepared to make his move against his Hashimite enemy; he had the motivation and the means, and his British allies had withdrawn their restraining power along with their money (see Kostiner, 1993: 65–6; Troeller, 1976: 209, 216).

In August 1924 Ibn Saud's Ikhwan forces first took Ta'if, where a massacre of the inhabitants occurred. At this stage, Hussein's erstwhile supporters, the British, displaying competence in the art of king-breaking as well as king-making, precipitated the end of his already 'ineffective' rule by 'depriving' him of their support (Hourani, 1991: 319; see also Sonn, 1990: 214). This came in the form of British neutrality in what they chose to regard as 'a religious issue'. Nor would they allow Hussein's sons to enter Transjordan and Iraq into the war on their father's behalf (Troeller, 1976: 218–19; Kostiner, 1993: 67). Hussein was forced to abdicate on 3 October in favour of his son Ali; on 18 October Mecca fell to the Ikhwan.[39] Recognising

---

[38] Ibn Saud's Ikhwan had already won a major battle against Sharifian forces at Turaba in May 1919; success on this battlefield was followed up by the Najdi *muwahhidun* with concerted *dawa* and raiding (Kostiner, 1993: 31, 63–5).

[39] Glubb's statement (1959: 211) that Britain 'washed her hands of King Hussein' is not exaggerated: after abdicating, Hussein went into exile, first in Aqaba, then

the value of holding the holy city, Ibn Saud guaranteed the safety of pilgrims and, indeed, the *hajj* that year was successful. The Najdi sultan also diplomatically made conciliatory overtures and displayed openness to suggestion on the future of Mecca to the Muslim world (see Troeller, 1976: 220–2). In fact, Kostiner (1993: 66) presents evidence that Ibn Saud was aware of the tactical value of co-operation with other Muslim elements further afield, particularly in India, and was deliberately seeking to legitimise Saudi actions in their eyes.

Ibn Saud completed the conquest of the Hijazi kingdom–caliphate in December 1925; in January 1926 he followed the example of his vanquished rival by declaring himself 'Sultan of Najd and King of the Hijaz and its Dependencies'. Significantly, and ironically, a kind of de facto religious legitimation of Ibn Saud's conquests of the holy cities soon followed via official recognition on the part of the major European colonial powers who ruled over Muslim peoples: Great Britain, France, the USSR and the Netherlands. On 27 January 1927 the Sultan of Najd adjusted his title to become *malik* of Najd.[40]

In light of Ibn Saud's *fait accompli* in the Hijaz, the British negotiated a new treaty—the Treaty of Jedda, signed 20 May 1927—to replace the now obsolete Anglo–Saudi Treaty of 1915. Joseph Kostiner (1993: 111) believes that one of Ibn Saud's primary motives was his desire to negate 'any remnants of the image of himself as a vassal'. With image and honour such important commodities in Arabian tribal culture and, especially in light of increasing Ikhwan discontent with the 'unholy' Saudi–British alliance, Ibn Saud's concerns were understandable. Christine Moss Helms (1981: 78) believes his relations with the British were 'forced' almost from the outset, but this does not necessarily conflict with the view that it was Ibn Saud's far-sighted and astute statesmanship which guided his choice to throw in his lot with the British—an assessment of the situation that would not have been understood by the tribes of Arabia. It could be argued, as Helms (1981: 116–19) does, that his

---

in Cypress, after the British effectively barred him from Transjordan and Iraq (Troeller, 1976: 220; see also Kostiner, 1993: 69).

[40] Kostiner (1993: 104) discusses the motives and reasoning behind Ibn Saud's adoption of royal titles. See also note 49 and associated text below.

hand in alliance-making was forced by the reality of British power, and that he, unlike many of his contemporaries—Sharif Hussein being the most prominent example—succeeded by working intelligently with this reality rather than attempting to oppose it or to set too ambitious an agenda.

On the domestic front in the immediate aftermath of his conquest of the Hijaz, Ibn Saud set about building the administrative and other institutions of state. The development of this infrastructure involved much 'interplay... [with] traditional strategies of local politics' (Kostiner, 1993: 100); and, as will be seen, much strife sprang from the conflicting imperatives of a modern state on the one hand, and those of a traditional tribal sociopolitical system on the other. The tensions between the two were exacerbated by the *muwahhidi* world-view, which 'has clearly influenced all aspects of social, economic and political life' in central Arabia (Helms, 1981: 78). Indeed, this tension still exists, as demonstrated in the post-Gulf War Islamist dissent of the 1990s.

During this early phase of transforming a Saudi realm into a Saudi state, a number of precedents were set for what has become the Saudi way of ruling and dealing with political problems. For example, during less than successful attempts to integrate the Hijaz into the emerging state, many disputes between the relatively sophisticated Hijazis on the one hand, and the Najdi *muwahhidun* on the other, required arbitration. According to Kostiner, Ibn Saud '...apparently defused each outburst and partially satisfied all parties concerned, without ever devising a significant, lasting solution to their differences. The only measure that he pursued consistently was governmental consolidation, carried out by tightening his control over the realm' (Kostiner, 1993: 107).

Once having established his rule in the Hijaz, Ibn Saud initiated manoeuvres 'to avoid submitting to any further constitutional limitations on his powers' (Kostiner, 1993: 108). One outcome was that the elected council of Hijazi notables which Ibn Saud had initially fostered and which was capable of exerting decisive pressure on sociopolitical policy was, from August 1926, no longer elected but appointed; it 'was reduced to an advisory body at the disposal of Faysal [Ibn Saud's son and later king], who was vested with the real powers. The council retained only their right to ratify the budget and to represent public opinion' (ibid., 108). This move was to be paralleled nearly 70 years later with King Fahd's post-Gulf War inauguration of an appointed consultative council of notables. It was also in 1926 that the *muwahhidi* interpretation of Islam became 'the established state religion', with the result that 'Wahhabi belief strengthened Ibn Sa'ud's rule, leaving little temporal authority that limited the will of the king by law' (ibid., 106).

Many members of the Saudi family were appointed to leading positions in the newly created institutions of state; in general, a major goal of Ibn Saud was to centralise his authority. This policy alienated the Ikhwan and, together with their other complaints against their ruler—including Saudi relations with the British *kafirun* who were destroying their traditional lifestyle—led to a major revolt in 1927 which seriously threatened Ibn Saud's grip on power. The revolt was crushed, but in 1932 there was another rebellion, involving Hijazi malcontents and exiles and the Hashimites; it too was crushed, but the Saudis realised that further measures were required to integrate their territories more fully and to unite diverse subject populations. The result was the merging of the dual kingdoms of Najd and Hijaz. On 16 September 1932 the Kingdom of Saudi Arabia (*al-Mamlaka al-Arabiyya al-Saudiyya*) came into existence and Ibn Saud naturally became the first king of the modern monarchical state.[41]

The Al Saud–Najdi conquest of central and north Arabia, from the Red Sea to the Gulf, was complete and formally recognised, a result that was by no means inevitable; Ibn Saud's triumph on behalf of his branch of the family was 'the net result of generations of family rivalry' (Bligh, 1984: 11). In the current era of reform, the potential for debilitating family rivalry remains latent in the political structure of the kingdom.

The Ikhwan: a challenge to Saudi authority.   The relationship of Ibn Saud with the Ikhwan illustrates both the appeal and the tenuousness of Saudi religiopolitical legitimacy. The Ikhwan were Arabian

---

[41] Kostiner (1993: 163) writes that the 'establishment of a unified monarchical state served both to impress Saudi rivals outside the kingdom and to convince local tribes of Ibn Sa'ud's prowess', and that '[t]o foster feelings of regional loyalty to the government, Saudi leaders introduced the new [unified monarchical] institutions in accordance with common tribal practices.'

Bedouin tribes who had 'migrated' from a nomadic life and settled in the belief that settlement facilitated proper religious practice. Ibn Saud encouraged this '*hijra*'—with the approval of the ulama— because settled populations were easier to control. Inspired by a religious fervour which included a belief in martyrdom to earn a place in Paradise and by the belief that Ibn Saud was leading them into a new Islamic era akin to the days of the Prophet, these *muwahhidi* tribes became the core of Ibn Saud's army of conquest from 1918 (see Habib, 1978: 3–86; Kostiner, 1993: 35–42, 72–9; Helms, 1981: 84–8, 111, 127–50; Troeller, 1976: 128–30; Glubb, 1960: 57–8).[42]

After conquering the Hijaz, Ibn Saud sought to expand the territory under his control by sanctioning Ikhwan raids and *dawa* into what is now Kuwait, Jordan and Iraq; in fact, the Najdi amir was recorded as claiming hereditary family rights to a contiguous stretch of territory from Najd through western Iraq to northern Syria (see Helms, 1981: 110, 250–1; Abir, 1993: 4)—territory corresponding to that which became the sphere of influence of the first Saudi realm, however tenuously and fleetingly. Such claims did not have a religious basis but were promoted by encouraging Ikhwan religious zeal. Through further conquests or conversion to the *muwahhidi* creed, Ibn Saud hoped to bring more tribes—and thus their tribal lands—under his patronage. These ambitions ran counter to British colonial interests and Ibn Saud was eventually forced to be content with his north-central Arabian kingdom. His problem then, however, was the Ikhwan, because he 'could not accommodate both the Ikhwan and the British' (Helms, 1981: 253–4).

Ibn Saud's dealings with the British, his acceptance of the European fixed-borders concept of state, and the resultant suppression of raiding, looting, proselytising and '*jihad*' (against non-*muwahhidi* Muslim tribes) quickly became causes of Ikhwan complaints.[43]

---

[42] Although the Ibn Saud-sponsored *muwahhidi* revival began in earnest in 1912, the Ikhwan played their first major part in the shaping of modern Saudi Arabia in the 1919 Khurma and Turaba clashes against Hussein. Habib (1978: 87–102) deals specifically with the Ikhwan role in these Najdi–Hijazi engagements.

[43] Glubb (1959: 211) attempts to express what he thinks must have at this stage been going through the mind of many an Ikhwan warrior regarding their ruler:

Now [after 20 years of war and plundering] …[this] same Ibn Saud was telling them that they were not to raid Iraq or Trans-Jordan because they were at

In fact, Ikhwan discontent dated from the time Ibn Saud began consolidating his rule over the Hijaz and centralising his power: they and their traditional lifestyle were being marginalised in the process of building a modern state—a result not undesired by Ibn Saud, who 'seemed...determined to weaken the Ikhwan' (see Kostiner, 1993: 100–117).[44] The strategy of deliberately encouraging a fervent, militant religious movement inevitably carried a risk of tenuous control. The view that Ibn Saud fostered the Ikhwan and used them politically, while lacking any personal ideological commitment to them or firm control over them is strongly argued by Glubb (1960: 57–8), Kostiner (1990: 231; 1993: 39) and Troeller (1976: 38, 114, 129–30, 210). Considering this volatile state of affairs, it was only a matter of time before the two clashed; in November and December 1927 a major Ikhwan tribe challenged Ibn Saud's authority by raiding into Iraq—the motive apparently being to protest at Ibn Saud's 'selling out' to the British, and to force him 'to return to tribal modes and values' (Kostiner, 1993: 121).[45]

The rebellion gained momentum and eventually led to the Battle of Sibila in March 1929; Ibn Saud was victorious, but it was only with British co-operation and assistance that the Ikhwan were finally destroyed in January 1930. The transition from 'revolutionary Wahhabism' to 'Wahhabism in one country' which began during the second realm, was now complete (see Safran, 1985: 56).[46] Before the final defeat of the Ikhwan, however, Ibn Saud employed a tactic that was to become a hallmark of Saudi religiopolitical

---

peace. Had their leader become a renegade from the true faith? Had he been seduced by the pleasures of this world or by the lure of heathen gold?

Habib (1978: 138–9) narrates an encounter between an Ikhwan messenger and Ibn Saud in which the former reputedly refused to acknowledge the latter as a true Muslim.

[44] Troeller (1976: 210) reveals that Ikhwan discontent pre-dated the conquest of the Hijaz, and that even as early as 1920, 'many of ibn Sa'ud's followers were incensed at their leader's deference to the British...'

[45] For an account of the background and lead-up to the Ikhwan rebellion, see Kostiner (1993: 72–117).

[46] For a full account of the Ikhwan rebellion, including the British role, see Habib (1978: 136–55), Helms (1981: 250–74) and Kostiner (1993: 117–40). More concise accounts are contained in Safran (1985: 49–54) and in Abir (1988: 4–6; 1993: 4–5).

strategy: he turned the tables on his opposition by presenting himself as the better Muslim, publicly accusing his opponents of sectarianism, fanaticism and of living 'against the instruction of the Shari'a' (Ibn Saud, 1929a). The cloak of piety is one the Al Saud have always worn; their right to wear it is something they have had to defend continually and pointedly against challenges both domestic and international since their conquest of the Hijaz. They are still defending it today as, in the era of globalisation, the Saudi dynasty faces new challenges to its religiopolitical legitimacy.

Reflections on paradoxes. The process of Ibn Saud's rise to dominance relied on a number of apparent paradoxes and contradictions which the subjects of the king, as well as others in the world Muslim *umma*, were asked to digest. In many cases they failed to do so, with the result that some of these deep-rooted paradoxes and contradictions are now haunting the Saudi regime. For example, despite the fact that he perhaps had little choice in the matter, Ibn Saud had no compunction about dealing with the British, even though the Muslim world had criticised the Hashimite–British alliance. Ibn Saud's 'primary goal was to secure the rights of his family to rule in Central Arabia', and the British were seen as 'a convenient vehicle' to secure those rights (Helms, 1981: 118–19).[47]

Likewise, despite Muslim disapproval of Hussein's self-proclaimed kingship, Ibn Saud, in turn, took the 'remarkable' step of proclaiming himself a king—the first ever in central Arabia (Helms, 1981: 110). This move away from Muslim leadership titles such as caliph and imam was due, according to Helms (1981: 109–10), to 'outcries from Islamic communities throughout the world' over the Saudi conquest of the Hijaz. Kostiner (1993: 103) refers to 'growing international Muslim pressure' to curb the Ikhwan's 'drive for [the] purification' of the Hijaz after its conquest which led to extraordinary political manoeuvring by Ibn Saud in an attempt to placate the divergent religious sensibilities of volatile domestic and important foreign Muslim populations. The *muwahhidun* lent to Arabian politics and life, then as they do today, a uniquely conservative ideological

---

[47] The tribal roots of Arabian society also played a major part in producing 'often contradictory and asymmetrical' processes as the new Saudi state developed, giving rise to what Kostiner (1990: 229) calls 'a convoluted process of state formation'. The role of tribalism in Saudi sociopolitics is discussed below.

environment not necessarily enjoying favour in the wider *umma*; in fact, the *muwahhidun*, the Ikhwan in particular, have a reputation for a religious élitism which has even extended to a view of themselves as the only true Muslims (Helms, 1981: 92, 98, 131). Glubb (1959: 211) wrote, 'to the Ikhwan all the world but themselves were heathen'.

This attitude often expressed itself in contemptuous and self-righteous behaviour during raiding and in battle, notoriously so during the 1924–5 Hijaz campaign at Ta'if: '...extreme religious fervour turned comparatively unsanguine traditional encounters into massacres. In many instances, the Ikhwan killed all males, regardless of age' (Troeller, 1976: 210).[48] The Hijazis, who were not *muwahhidun*, did not initially welcome their conquest, although many Hijazi tribes were susceptible to the *dawa* of their Najdi conquerors (see Kostiner, 1993: 62–70). Thus, in the interests of wider Muslim acceptance, Ibn Saud abandoned his *muwahhidi* religiopolitical title of imam in favour of sultan and *malik*.[49]

This move toward a more official secularisation of Saudi rule, at least in name, presented problems of its own, and Ibn Saud found it

[48] Of the Ikhwan and their tradition of massacre, Helms (1981: 144) writes: 'In battle, they frequently killed everyone [that is, mainly non-*muwahhidi* Muslims], including women and children, believing that they alone were the representatives of a pure Islam'. Aburish (1995: 20–1) paints a similar picture, describing the Ikhwan as 'Bedouin hordes' (see also Glubb, 1959: 210). Such portrayals provide an insight into Ibn Saud's use of force in the conquest of his kingdom (see also Aburish, 1995: 13, 23–4, 27), although many accounts, probably accurately, state that Ibn Saud was never in full control of the Ikhwan, and that he was often 'deeply saddened' at news of Ikhwan excesses (see Habib, 1978: 113–14, on the 1924 Ta'if massacre). Glubb (1960: 44–5, 47) briefly narrates comparable behaviour on the part of the Ikhwan's forebears during the first Saudi realm with the massacres at Karbala and Ta'if, and writes that '[w]holesale massacre had become the corner-stone of their policy', and that, '[t]he Wahhabis murdered in cold blood every male human being, even small children, but women were rarely, if ever, molested.' Regarding the killing of women, if the reports are accurate, it appears as if Ikhwan conduct deteriorated—or their 'cleansing' became more thorough—in the twentieth century (see, for example, Troeller, 1976: 209–10). These excesses on the part of the Ikhwan are in conflict with the presentation of Islam as the *din* (religion/way of life) of peace and mercy, and thus can be criticised by Muslims on religious grounds.

[49] Ibn Saud's father, Imam Abd al-Rahman, died in 1928. See note 40 and associated text above.

necessary to build further on his specifically *muwahhidi*-style legiti-macy domestically; it was, after all, the *muwahhidi* religious estab-lishment which had, for nearly two centuries, bestowed a special religious weight to Saudi dynastic rule.[50] In essence, any ruler of the heartland of the Islamic world, if not overtly religious in his own right, had at least to be seen to be enjoying strong religious creden-tials and the support of the ulama. The process of gaining and maintaining this religious backing, however, becomes more prob-lematic in a modern state with expanding institutional structures and government, and even more acute for a royal family growing in numbers. Thus, the Saudis became the 'protectors of the two holy places' (Mecca and Madina), and looked to Muslim tradition for the religious sanction of their rule among their subjects and among Muslims internationally.

According to what may be described as orthodox Sunni Muslim tradition, unjust and even degenerate rule is better than the anarchy of no rule or the turmoil of revolt, as long as the ruler does not deny Islam.[51] This tradition has proved to be the basis for a greater abso-lutism whereby the seizure of power is purported to be sanctioned by Allah and disobedience is almost equivalent to heresy. In this respect, the following extracts from a speech made by Ibn Saud to tribal chiefs in 1929 are illuminating:

You people of Nejd…you all know that we are your masters and descend-ants of your masters and that, by the will of God and the word 'unity' and the sword we are your Kings.

…God has always been with me and has always revealed to me those who wish to harm their religion, king, and country (Ibn Saud, 1929b).

---

[50] *Muwahhidi* criteria for political legitimacy were: preserving the unity of the *umma*, avoiding *bida* (innovation), combating *fitna* (dissension/civil strife) and *shirk* (polytheism/idolatry), obeying *sharia* and, in general, promoting the *salafi* way of life through *dawa* and *jihad* (see Helms, 1981: 81, 84, 97, 103, 104, 106, 108).

[51] This tradition is traceable to at least the eleventh and twelfth centuries and to the Muslim philosopher, al-Ghazali (d. 1111). See Hourani (1991: 144–5, 162) for a concise explanation of this line of thinking. Surprisingly, it still persists in the modern Islamist opposition—a spokesman for the once prominent Saudi oppo-sition organisation, the Committee for the Defence of Legitimate Rights (CDLR) was, during its heyday, quoted as saying: 'Rulers should be acceptable to the people. The monarchy is acceptable as an alternative to chaos. We can live with the king so long as he gives us basic rights' (reported in Richards, 1994).

Ibn Saud justified, i.e. legitimised, his own rule on the basis of central Arabian tradition and a new form of European-style kingship and, at the same time, on religious tradition and the blessing of Allah, all equated with the formation of a Western-style state under (British) imperial tutelage. In this way, the Saudi dynastic regime 'became God's representative on earth' (Helms, 1981: 99)—a rather convoluted legitimating ideology containing within it the paradox of 'a secular government the authority of which was based on a divine right to rule' (Helms, 1981: 251).

As observed above, a major challenge to the Saudis' divine right to rule was mounted by the Ikhwan at a critical time of state consolidation. Half a century later the Al Saud would discover, to their dismay, that the legacy of the Ikhwan did not die in 1930, and since the 1991 Gulf War, the parallels between contemporary United States hegemony and that of Britain in the pre-Second World War period have not been lost on the opponents of the Saudi regime, nor on the regime itself, which is acutely aware of the sensibilities of its population. The dilemma posed by the pursuit of national interest and foreign policy as the regime sees fit—including major alliances with Western powers such as the United States—in the face of less than favourable public opinion, gives rise to many convoluted policies. The paradoxical Saudi religiopolitical ideology of legitimacy has clearly not been trouble-free and as the twenty-first century unfolds, it may prove to be one that is increasingly difficult to sustain.

Sociopolitics and the religious nexus

The centralisation of power and the building of a functional bureaucracy and the infrastructure of state begun in 1925, has continued. This process has had a substantial boost since the 1950s as the financial windfall from the commercial exploitation of oil gathered momentum. But many hundreds of years of traditional tribal culture cannot be radically transformed in a few decades. Although the destruction of the political power of tribal and nomadic culture has actively and largely successfully been pursued in the process of state development, tribalism is still an important factor in Saudi sociopolitics. The fact that the modern state of Saudi Arabia also occupies the heartland of Islam adds another, deeply religious dimension to sociopolitics in the kingdom. The Al Saud still appeal to the religiopolitical legitimacy of their forebears and, in the manner first realised by Ibn Saud after his conquest of the Hijaz, possession of the holy cities of Mecca and Madina are used to bolster this legitimacy at home and throughout the Muslim world.

These factors often combine in unpredictable ways and interact with other elements of Saudi Arabia's socioeconomic and sociopolitical structures, the most significant of which are the wealth and the royal–bureaucratic–business élite networks created by the oil and development booms which transformed the kingdom's political economy; world economic trends, especially the ongoing process of global economic integration; local demographics and class structures; and relations with Western states, particularly with the United States. Despite popular Saudi claims that the kingdom's phenomenal development programme had catapulted the country into the twenty-first century by the early 1990s, it is still doubtful whether the institutions of state are themselves developed or sophisticated enough to formulate and administer strategies and mechanisms with which to manage economic and socioeconomic reform effectively. This contrasts with what appears to be a greater ability on the part of the regime to circumvent domestic sociopolitical unrest and to deal with it once it has occurred.

While the development of the physical infrastructure of the country has been impressive—at least at first glance—these achievements may prove to be superficial given the antagonistic forces at work below the surface of this society where the world of Saudi sociopolitics is largely located. It is the interaction between this world, domestic socioeconomics and the ability of the Saudi state to manage reform and challenges to its traditional authority that will determine the future of the kingdom. For this reason, an acquaintance with the most important basic elements of Saudi sociopolitics—religion, tribalism, and family solidarity and factionalism—is necessary.

Quran, sunna and ulama. Epitomising the Al Saud appeal to Muslim faith, as well as weak institutionalisation, are the upholding of the Quran and the *sunna* of the Prophet as the state's constitution and the implementation of a strict Hanbali interpretation of *sharia* law. These hallmarks of the state have been recently re-affirmed officially (Basic Law of Government, 1992: Articles 1, 7, 8),[52] diplomatically (Alohaly, A.R.N., 1995, pers. comm., 13 July), and by King Fahd himself (Saudi Press Agency, 1997c).[53] The vital link between the theocratic nature of Saudi Arabia and its rulers—i.e. between Quran, *sunna* and *sharia*, and the Al Saud—is the religious establishment, the ulama. Although the original Saud–Wahhab religiopolitical relationship has undergone stresses and modifications since its founding—especially in the twentieth century, with the balance of power shifting in favour of the Saudi side of the equation—this religiopolitical link is still strong. It is now a traditional, firmly entrenched relationship, whereby the Saudis foster, recognise and sanction conservative ulama in return for official religious approval, and it continues to be the basis of the critical nexus between the Saudi royal family and Islam. Nevertheless, the Al Shaikh have been playing a diminishing role, to the advancement of 'commoner' ulama who are of less 'noble' heritage (see Bligh, 1985: 48).[54]

---

[52] The 'Basic Law of Government' is a royal decree of King Fahd which was presented to the nation (through the powerless Council of Ministers) in a constitution-like form. Article 1 reads as follows: 'The Kingdom of Saudi Arabia is a sovereign Arab Islamic State. Religion: Islam. Constitution: The Holy Quran and the Prophet's Sunnah (traditions)' (Basic Law of Government, 1992: Article 1. See also Mutabbakani, 1993: 20 and *Saudi Arabia Index*, 2000a for prose versions of this first article). (The royal decrees of 1992 and other issues of Saudi political development are treated in Chapter 5.)

[53] Whilst chairing the meeting of the Council of Ministers at Salam Palace in Jedda on 4 August 1997, King Fahd, as reported by the Saudi Press Agency (1997c), said that 'ever since its unification [Saudi Arabia] has based and is still basing all its political, economic and social orientations on the principles of the true Islamic faith and the teachings of its tolerant creed', and 'stressed that the country was committed to this sound Islamic path and would not deviate from it, considering the gracious Koran and the tradition of the chosen prophet [*sic*] ...as its constitution, by which to realize justice and spread virtue.'

[54] One of the major themes treated by Alexander Bligh (1985) in his article on the Saudi religious élite is the decline in the prominence and influence of the Al Shaikh in Saudi religiopolitical affairs. As Fandy (1999: 36, 254n. 22) points out, the Al Saud–Al Shaikh relationship is not a black-and-white matter of secular/political–religious alliance: '...both families are religious, although the religious credentials of the Sheikh family are stronger, and both of them are prominent tribal families, although the Sauds have long been more powerful...both families are part of the tribal and religious "asabiyya of Saudi Arabia".'

As a reference point, it is relevant to note what has become the established role of the ulama in Muslim society, namely that of mediators of religious authority and legitimacy for essentially secular political regimes seeking to present an image of Islamism. This has been assessed and summed up by Mamoun Fandy (1999: 25) as follows:

> With the exception of the da'wa (missionary) state in Medina under the leadership of the Prophet, Islam historically has been secondary to the 'a'ila [family]; its main function has been to support the cultural hegemony of the ruling tribe/dynasty. This interaction between state and Islam brought about certain adjustments to Islam rather than the other way around; the state was not adjusted to become Islamic; rather, Islam was adjusted to support the state. In this arrangement, the state has used the 'ulama to justify the policy choices of the ruling elite. The function of the 'ulama is thus to establish the hegemony of the ruling amir and his family. The 'ulama solidify the hegemony of the amir and his family because the interpretation of the Shari'a principles has traditionally been their exclusive domain.[55]

The establishment ulama in Saudi Arabia are no exception: they are widely perceived to be very close to the regime, although the latter is also to some extent limited by prevailing Islamic mores (see Fandy, 1999: 37). Proximity to the regime is not the case for a significant segment of younger ulama, however, who perhaps could be accused of being too close to 'the caprice of popular feeling' (see Hourani, 1991: 69). They include figures who were at the forefront of dissent in the kingdom in the 1990s when one could properly speak of a rift between the ruling family and the conservative ulama on the one hand, and more radical younger ulama and sections of the general population on the other. Although currently resubmerged beneath the surface of Saudi society, this rift has become significant in the struggle for religious legitimacy between the Saudi regime and the Islamist opposition. For detailed discussion of this

---

[55] See also Fandy (1999: 36–8); Gause (1994: 13, 15–17). Albert Hourani (1991: 69) provides a more benign, idealistic interpretation of the role of the ulama in Muslim states. See also Hourani (1991: 141–6) for further elaboration on the relationship between political rulers and the ulama, as well as a concise presentation of the early Muslim attitudes in the sphere of power and authority.

topic, see Chapter 5. Here it is enough to point to the critical nexus which exists between the Al Saud and Islam, between regime and ulama, which has been described as a 'two-edged sword' (Salameh, 1980: 7; Esposito, 1991: 111; see also Gause, 1994: 31–2).

On the subject of the establishment ulama's subservience to the regime, scholars are unanimous in their assessment: 'Two centuries after Ibn Abd al-Wahhab', writes Hrair Dekmejian, (1985: 147), 'his descendants of the Al Shaykh family have become the monarchy's official apologists.' Piscatori (1983: 60–1) believes the ulama are straight forwardly 'agents of the state' because they have become 'bureaucratised', and therefore 'depend on the government for their salaries and positions'. Mordechai Abir (1993: 181) agrees, claiming that the Saudi ulama 'almost automatically' legitimise 'every act' of the royal house and, in return, benefit from royal largesse. The role of the religious establishment in the kingdom is also transparent to non-Saudi foreign service personnel, one of whom perceives them as '…trained and docile religious scholars' (Australian diplomat 1, 1995, pers. comm., 17 Aug.). Describing another variant of the ulama–state relationship in a discussion of the Saudi 'religio-political orientation', Joseph Kechichian (1986: 53) writes that, by working together, political and religious authorities both 'derive a dose of legitimacy', while Tamara Sonn (1990: 214) goes further: 'The Hanbali "*ulama*" of the state are on Sa'udi salary…they are drawn from elite families themselves; their fortunes are closely allied with those of the Sa'udis. They therefore routinely support those measures that protect the security of the state.'

Although a 'process of sanctioning the deeds of the house of Saud has been going on since the eighteenth century' (Bligh, 1985: 37),[56] in the twentieth century this process also included the institutional

---

[56] Derek Hopwood (1982: 26) concludes that religious legalists traditionally 'were dependent for their position on the amir' in central Arabia before and during the period of Ibn Abd al-Wahhab's ascent. A wider historical perspective reveals that the existence of religious élites in the employ of Muslim rulers is not without well-established precedent, '[f]rom perhaps the thirteenth century' (Hourani, 1991: 160); nor is the contemporary Saudi–ulama relationship unique in the modern Arab world—for example, Iraqi ulama were seen to be subservient to Saddam Hussein in declaring a *jihad* against the forces opposing Iraq after the 1990 invasion of Kuwait, a declaration diametrically opposed to that of the Saudi ulama, who supported the Saudi position against Iraq.

co-optation of the ulama so that they have become the virtual appendage of a modern regime. This co-optation was advanced significantly after the death in 1969 of the Grand Mufti of Saudi Arabia, a member of the Al Shaikh religious dynasty. Instead of replacing him, the third monarch of modern Saudi Arabia, Faisal bin Abd al-Aziz (r. 1964–75), enacted two changes which together more or less abolished what little independence and real political influence the ulama had retained to that date. The first was made in September 1970 when, nearly eight years after originally promising to do so, King Faisal created a ministry of justice with a religious shaikh as the inaugural minister of that portfolio. Since the new minister—and now all religious courts throughout the country—answered to the prime minister, the independence in, and sole responsibility for interpretation of the *sharia* hitherto exercised by the Grand Mufti were subsumed under the state (see Bligh, 1985: 43, 48). Secondly, in 1971 King Faisal created a 17-member 'Council of Senior Ulama' which had none of the independence and personal authority once wielded by the Grand Mufti.[57] In the words of Alexander Bligh, '[f]or the first time a permanent forum was brought into being to serve the King in his future need for religious authorization and approval', and, '...the council marked the end of the Al al-Shaykh era in Saudi history' (Bligh, 1985: 39).

Implicit here is one area where institutionalisation has been very successfully implemented by the state. Yet there is no legitimate institutional channel for the open expression of differing opinions within the ulama, let alone channels for the assessment and potential implementation of fundamentally alternative views. Religious figures who hold alternative views on important issues, which may have political connotations and may be regarded by the regime as radical, are caught between their chosen strategies of personal appeal to the authorities and unauthorised preaching on the one hand, and regime attempts to co-opt them, threats and the risk of imprisonment on the other. Thus, outside a defined and relatively small, rigid

[57] During the era of post-Gulf War dissent in the kingdom and, more specifically, immediately following the formation of the CDLR political reform organisation in May 1993, the fifth Saudi monarch, Fahd bin Abd al-Aziz, reinstated the position of Grand Mufti. The elderly Shaikh Abd al-Aziz bin Baz, then head of the Council of Senior Ulama, was appointed Grand Mufti, a position he held until his death in 1999. The position carries the rank of minister.

and brittle area of institutionalisation, there exists an unofficial space of religious activity potentially threatening to established state interests.

The importance of the politico-religious nexus to the power structure created by the Saudis becomes clear when set in the context of the constitution issue as follows: (*a*) There is no legally binding written constitution; (*b*) the Quran and *sunna*, despite centuries of entrenched tradition, are to some extent still subject to interpretation, especially in periods of rapid technological and social development when Quranic principles have to be applied in new situations and circumstances—which means Saudi Arabia's 'constitution' is fluid; and (*c*) the agents of Quranic and Prophetic exegesis, the ulama, are effectively controlled by the Saudi regime—which means the regime in reality also controls the interpretation and application of the kingdom's unwritten 'constitution' on a day-to-day basis. This measure of control, coupled with control of the generally respected religious establishment, and the institutionalisation of rule by royal decree with no popular representation, makes clear the absolute nature of the power of the Saudi monarchy.

The kingdom's religious significance sets the Saudi regime apart from others in the Muslim world which also have a subservient ulama, and both regime and ulama bear a unique burden in the Islamic world at large for this reason. Kechichian (1986: 63) points out the benefits that accrue to the Saudis from the religiopolitical relationship, on an international as well as a domestic level: 'In Saudi Arabia, it is the government (politics), as the guarantor of the safety of Muslims and of the Holy cities, which undoubtedly derives a dose of legitimacy, within both the Kingdom and the Muslim world, from this source of influence (religion).' The Saudi monarch is routinely referred to in the kingdom and in its public relations material internationally as 'the Servant' or 'the Custodian' of 'the Two Holy Places' or 'the Two Holy Mosques'[58], a title which plays overtly on the dynasty's religious legitimacy and is aimed particularly at the Muslim population across the world; indeed, Piscatori (1983: 61) has referred to this special status as the Saudis' 'primary claim to govern'. As an extension of this role, the Saudi regime has been careful to promote itself as a benefactor of Muslim communities

---

[58] There is even a 'Custodian of the Two Holy Mosques Cup' football competition in Saudi Arabia, which has enjoyed the personal patronage of Saudi kings.

globally, typically by sponsoring the building of mosques. Awareness of the necessity of this image was recently reconfirmed by King Fahd when he was reported to have 'devoted part of the session [of the Council of Ministers, Jedda, 4 August 1997] to talking about the continuing interest and attention of the Kingdom of Saudi Arabia in the houses of God...both inside and outside the kingdom, on account of its strong faith in its role in the life of Muslims...' (Saudi Press Agency, 1997c). Many millions of riyals are expended every year by the king, both personally and on behalf of the Saudi regime, in this exercise in global Muslim patronage which, besides mosques, includes the financing of Islamic centres—large complexes which may incorporate, for example, one or more mosques, a school and a cultural activities facility—and the distribution of Qurans.[59]

Saudi religiopolitical legitimacy is also fostered in the Islamic world through an active foreign aid programme that promotes Saudi Arabia and its ruling family as patrons of Muslim causes worldwide. During the Soviet occupation of Afghanistan, for example, Saudi Arabia encouraged the *jihad* view of the conflict in the Arab world and backed up this campaign with substantial funding of the

---

[59] Saudi largesse in these and other projects is a well-known reality in Muslim communities in Muslim and non-Muslim countries alike and is widely and keenly coveted. The following recent examples are typical: personal contributions from King Fahd built the Muslim World League's headquarters in Madina at a cost of US$26.67 million; other contributions have financed 'the distribution of millions of copies of the Holy Qur'an and its translations printed at the King Fahd Printing Complex in Madinah' (see M2 Presswire, 1997); a large donation from King Fahd is contributing to the renovation of the revered Al-Azhar mosque in Cairo (Abdullah, 1997); in Gibraltar, the opening on 8 August 1997 of the King Fahd Mosque—built with a donation from the monarch—was attended by a number of high-profile Saudi dignitaries and was televised live to the Middle East by the media enterprise started by a brother-in-law of King Fahd, the Middle East Broadcasting Centre (*Saudi Gazette*, 1997c; IPR, 1997b); in Malaga, Spain, on 11 August 1997, one of King Fahd's favourite sons, Prince Abd al-Aziz, laid the foundation stone for the King Fahd Islamic Centre—a five-storey building which will be funded by the king and which will include a 16-classroom school, two mosques and a cultural centre (IPR, 1997c); another 'King Fahd Mosque' was inaugurated near Paris in September 1997—an event attended by the Imam of the Great Mosque in Mecca as part of an extensive international programme which saw him visit many Islamic centres and organisations in the United States (IPR, 1997e).

Pakistan-based Sunni *mujahidin* groups. Arabs throughout the Arab world were also unofficially encouraged to fulfil a religious obligation by joining the *jihad*. A significant aid role has also been played in Bosnia–Hercegovina.[60] Other theatres of unrest, such as Azerbaijan, have also provided a stage for Saudi Arabia to play out its image of Muslim patriarch whilst pursuing its national interests—in the Azerbaijani case, by again opposing those of Iran.[61] Domestically, and internationally in the Muslim world, such involvement is used to great public relations effect.[62]

On the other hand, this prestigious position carries with it an equally high responsibility in the eyes of the world *umma*, and to some extent it legitimises a general Muslim interest in Saudi affairs. This can sometimes extend to criticism of, and hostility toward the royal family, particularly on issues concerning Mecca, Madina and the *hajj*. For example, the 1979 siege of the Great Mosque of Mecca was not only a disaster in its own right but very damaging to the religious prestige of the Al Saud, as were the *hajj* stampedes of 1990, 1994 and 1998, and the Mina fire of April 1997.[63]

The 1979 Mecca siege also proved damaging for the ulama; facing 'a dilemma' and displaying indecision, 'the Mecca incident marked a new low point for the Saudi ulama and provided irrefutable proof of their political weakness' (Bligh, 1985: 48). A point that

[60] The Saudi roles in Afghanistan and Bosnia–Hercegovina provide fascinating examples of radically different and apparently contradictory foreign policies. They are also good examples of how foreign and domestic policies intersect and how both can change according to the imperatives of national interest. The influence of Arab veterans of the Afghan war in the domestic politics of a number of Arab countries, including Saudi Arabia, were already a significant factor in contemporary Arab affairs before 11 September 2001.

[61] One of the major Saudi goals in Afghanistan was to counter Iranian influence.

[62] After supplying 478 kilograms of medicine and medical appliances 'for the Muslims of Azerbaijan' in August 1997, the Saudi Ministry of Health issued a public statement declaring that 'the supplies were dispatched as per the directives of [the] Custodian of the Two Holy Mosques King Fahd to alleviate the suffering of Azeris following Armenian aggression on their country.' The Saudi Arabian Health Minister, Dr Osama Shubukshi, said that '[t]his assistance comes in line with King Fahd's support to Muslims all over the world' (Saudi Press Agency, 1997b).

[63] These and other *hajj* incidents, and their effect on the image of the Al Saud are discussed in Chapter 3.

can be drawn from Kechichian's analysis of the siege is that even before the Saudi ulama supported the regime in the incident, their subservience to Saudi interests was already recognised and opposed by the rebels: 'What the Mecca rebels rejected were the levels of corruption within the Royal Family and the inevitable acquiescence of the ulama to such behavior. Clearly, what is implied in the accusations made by the attackers is that the ulama have reconciled themselves to exercising their religious authority in tandem if not in the shadow of the political authorities' (Kechichian, 1986: 62).

Events since the 1990 Gulf Crisis have demonstrated that significant sections of the Saudi Arabian population share the basic grievances of the 1979 rebels, although the expression of this feeling now takes various forms—mostly peaceful, but also including violence, albeit of a more sophisticated kind if the 1995 Riyadh and 1996 Khobar bombings are any measure.[64]

The role of the establishment ulama in supporting the regime during incidents such as the 1979 siege and the 1990–1 Gulf Crisis–War, increasingly binds the Saudi regime and the establishment ulama to each other, despite the latter's inferior partner status in the relationship. The cynical political reality of this symbiotic, mutually reinforcing relationship is becoming increasingly difficult to conceal from aware, educated Muslims, many of whom openly characterise it as one of 'false impression[s]' and 'facade[s]' (see Bligh, 1985: 43, 45). Consequently, both the Al Saud and the establishment ulama are subject to attack on religious grounds from dissenters domestically and internationally (a topic of more detailed discussion in Chapter 5).

Tribalism, asabiyya and the contemporary Saudi state. While the overt and official emphasis is on Islam as the ruling ideology of the kingdom, there is another underlying dimension to the formation of the modern Saudi state, namely tribalism. The success of Abd al-Aziz's state-building exercise owed as much to tribal imperatives as to appeals to the religious sentiments of (mainly *salafi*) Arabians. In the absence of any Arabian concept of a state with fixed borders, it was Ibn Saud's use of Islam and tribalism—often in tandem, sometimes

---

[64] These incidents are covered in more detail in Chapter 5; the 1979 siege of the Great Mosque is analysed further in the next chapter in relation to the kingdom's oil boom period.

in apparently contradictory ways, but usually cleverly—that enabled him to forge his kingdom in the mould of a modern state. Saudi Arabia, a new nation-state in the European sense, is still a very traditional, if increasingly complex society, and this is naturally reflected in Saudi sociopolitics and socioeconomics today. This is again an example of the Saudi Arabian paradox: a 'post-traditional' absolute monarchy has developed the trappings of modern state institutions, but traditional hierarchical, tribal–kinship values largely determine all its procedures, decision-making and general conduct (see, for example, Hudson, 1977: 17, 165–82; Palmer, Alghofaily and Alnimir, 1984; al-Hegelan and Palmer, 1985; Palmer *et al.*, 1989; Kostiner, 1990).[65]

Closely linked with tribalism in the Arab context is the key concept of *asabiyya*, developed by the fourteenth-century Maghrebi Arab scholar, Ibn Khaldun (1332–1406) as part of his theory of the cyclic rise and fall of dynasties. Derived from the verbal root *'asaba* (to tie, bind, wrap...), *asabiyya* is defined as 'zealous partisanship...party spirit, team spirit, esprit de corps...tribal solidarity, racialism, clannishness, tribalism...' (Wehr, 1976: 615). As 'a product of...kinship linkages and blood ties...[*asabiyya*] is usually translated [by scholars of the Middle East] as "group feeling"' (Lindholm, 1996: 52–3; see also Ibn Khaldun, *The Maqaddimah*, 1967 edn, vol. 1: 361–5). The term has also been variously summed up as: '...a corporate spirit oriented towards obtaining and keeping power' (Hourani, 1991: 2); a 'natural sentiment...tribal bonding or the sentiment of group solidarity that results from kinship, blood ties, and common descent' (Lapidus, 1990: 28); a 'cultural energy...the will to power...[a constituent of] the formula for cultural hegemony' (Springborg, 1992: 272). Although first coined around 600 years ago, the concept and ideals of *asabiyya* are still current: '...the idea of tribal asabiyya...is the reasoning that has been locally in use for millennia, and continues as the organizing principle most referred to by the people [of the Middle East] themselves' (Lindholm, 1996: 61). Moreover, '...asabiyya is central in the "cultural imaginary" of the Middle Eastern world...the strength

---

[65] The '*mudir* syndrome' (the term, based on the Arabic word for 'director', is my own), which presents the kingdom with work ethic and employment problems, is an example of this legacy. These issues and the problems arising from them are discussed more fully in Chapters 3 and 4.

of a solidary kinship ideology, metaphorically expressed through asabiyya, is the factor that permits the expansion of tribal groups into positions of power...' (Lindholm, 1996: 54–5).[66]

What is striking in the study of the history of early Saudi politics is the crucial role tribal imperatives have played in the outcome of important events. 'Fickleness' was the term employed earlier in this chapter to describe actions such as the switching of allegiances in mid-battle, wholesale desertion immediately before battle, or the betrayal of an allied garrison by opening gates for assailants.[67] But what may often seem unpredictable about the tribal role in Arabian politics ceases to be so when the complex sociopolitical and physical environments in which the system operated are considered. Safran (1985: 25–6) refers to 'an ethos of opportunism', but goes on to elaborate on the tribal imperative as follows:

Neither settled nor bedouin tribes had a lasting interest in an overarching state unless their particular tribe controlled it, since the state merely exacted taxes and tribute and was in no position to offer desirable services. A chief who would attempt such an enterprise was therefore to be [initially] resisted, joined if he appeared to be succeeding, shaken off if he appeared to be faltering, and deserted in favor of his enemy if the latter seemed stronger.

---

[66] For an indication of the broad meanings the concept of *asabiyya* has taken on in the discussion of the modern Arab state, see Michael Hudson (1977: 35–7), Basam Tibi (1990: 128–30), Hourani (1990: 307–8) and Fandy (1999: 6–9, 91).

[67] A classic example of this kind of behaviour occurred during the fratricidal war between Abdullah bin Faisal and Saud bin Faisal in 1873. Saud, with Bedouin allies from the Ujman, al-Murra, Dawasir, Qahtan and Mutair tribes, led an expedition against the Utaiba tribe, which was allied to Abdullah. The battle which resulted demonstrated 'Bedouin self-seeking at its worst. In its early stages, when the 'Utaibah were being hard pressed by Mutair attacks, the Qahtan (secretly in league with Abdullah?) suddenly turned on Saud's personal cavalry and captured most of his horses; then they wheeled again against Mutair. As the battle degenerated into near chaos, the Qahtan withdrew with their booty' (Winder, 1965: 261). See also Lacey (1981: 98) on the 'wayward bedouin politics' which resulted in the capture of Ibn Saud's brother, Saad, by the *Sharif* of Mecca in 1911. Lacey (1981: 115) also cites Captain William Shakespear, shortly before his death as part of the Saudi camp fighting the Rashidis at the battle of Jarrab in 1915: '...[Bedouin] are quite capable of being firm friends up to the battle and then suddenly changing their minds and going over to the other side in the middle of it.'

Within what Lindholm (1996: 62) calls the 'vague cultural unity...
[the] entwining net of kin...' created by the *asabiyya* ideal, Hasan
al-Naqeeb (1990: 3–4) sees tribalism as part of a coherent sociopolitical system in the Arabian peninsula, in which 'the tribes and
tribal alliances are...units governed by political tribalism in a general perspective...' (see also Helms, 1981: 21–3). In such an environment, it should come as no surprise that religious credentials and
the force of arms are not the only legitimating criteria exploited by
the Saudis: political acumen in a traditional, tribal context also
played a significant role in securing for the Al Saud their dominance
in a new state. Commenting on the concept of *asabiyya*, Hudson
(1977: 36) draws attention to 'the importance that [Ibn Khaldun]
placed on group feeling as an element of political culture apparently
outranking in significance even such other bases as royal authority
and religious merit. [Ibn Khaldun's] emphasis on group feeling
provides an important clue to one of the main roots of political
legitimacy in the Arab world.' Ibn Saud thus could not ignore the
imperatives of the Arabian tribal milieu in consolidating his rule;
beneath the rhetoric of religiosity, he worked with Arabia's tribal
sociopolitical system to underwrite the legitimacy of his family's
hereditary claim to the territories that made up the new Saudi
kingdom.

It is also worth noting that, from the very beginning of the Saud–
Wahhab alliance in 1744, the Saudis began bolstering their religiopolitical legitimacy by intermarrying with the Wahhab family. These
matrimonial arrangements 'proved to be particularly advantageous
for the Al Saud' (Helms, 1981: 103), and were unsurprising in the
context of the power relations of the traditional culture of the
region. When Ibn Saud set about reconquering territory for a Saudi
realm, 'tribal power and the tribal value system were unprecedent-
edly salient in the Saudi state' as it emerged (Kostiner, 1990: 229).

James Piscatori (1983: 68) points out that, '[b]y using force and
manipulating an Islamic ideology', the Saudis created a state and
promoted 'a general loyalty towards themselves as a kind of super-
tribe'; Holden and Johns (1981: 530) also refer to the Al Saud as a
'super-tribe'. Further indicating the way in which tribalism and
Islamic ideology interacted in Ibn Saud's strategies, Ghassane
Salameh (1980: 5) has written: 'The tribe has consistently provided
the basis for social and political organization in the Arabian

Peninsula. Any attempt to increase power beyond the tribe has invariably been based on religion' (see also Salamé, 1989: 70–1).[68] In this context, the words of Helms (1981: 113) are pertinent: 'Principally through the Wahhabi movement, Abd al-Aziz and previous Saudi rulers had been able to transcend tribal and urban loyalties while still using their social structure as a basis for political manipulation.' Thus, 'the [modern] Saudi state that emerged was a renewed version of a traditional chieftaincy... [which] is evident from the tentative and fragile co-operation among its tribal groups and the personalized, noninstitutionalized rule that Ibn Sa'ud exercised' (Kostiner, 1990: 228). However, there is a case for going even further and arguing that while *salafi* Islam may have provided the Saudis with a homogenising ideological appeal, it was tribalism that not only provided the Al Saud with 'a basis for political manipulation' but also dictated practical strategy at a grass-roots level and cemented the Saudi grip on power.

The reality of Arabian tribal culture made it prudent for Ibn Saud to cater to tribal sensibilities in the traditional manner, in keeping with the Al Saud 'super-tribe' analogy,[69] the key elements of which lay in tribal intermarriage and the patronage of a tribally-based National Guard (see below)—both dating from the Ibn Saud era—and in the domination of the developing state structures by the Saudis and their related aristocratic families. On the first of these strategies, Salameh noted: 'It is remarkable in a tribal society that one tribe could gain the degree of hegemony attained by the Saudis. This can be attributed not only to the crucial Wahhabi connection, but also to the family practice of arranging strategic marriages with other powerful tribes' (Salameh, 1980: 5; see also Kostiner, 1990: 230; Abir, 1988: 4; Abir, 1993: 3–4).

Speculation on the number of Ibn Saud's wives has not settled on a definitive figure, but 22 is often quoted—although reference to

[68] Salameh and Salamé are the same author; Salamé (1989) is a revised version of Salameh (1980).

[69] Tribal culture was so strong that even the Ikhwan—'brothers' in a zealous form of Islam and theoretically equal regardless of tribe, and supposedly contemptuous of any social organisation other than an 'Islamic' one—settled overwhelmingly in *hijar* which were not only founded on traditional tribal lands, but dominated along tribal lines. The Ikhwan also frequently fought under tribal banners (see Helms, 1981: 130–42 and accompanying notes, 144; Kostiner, 1990: 231).

'hundreds' of wives is also not uncommon. A former Saudi Ambassador to Australia, A. Rahman N. Alohaly (1995, pers. comm., 13 July), is confident that Abd al-Aziz, in accordance with orthodox Quranic teaching, was never married to more than four wives at any one time, although he allowed that the king also had numerous concubines (see also Bligh, 1984: 39–40; Aburish, 1995: 31; Abir, 1988: 4).[70] Aburish reveals that these unions yielded 42 sons and an 'unknown number of daughters'; he also states that '[Ibn Saud] married into over 30 tribes and used these links to get closer to them and gain their support' (Aburish, 1995: 31).[71] This practice may be interpreted as a way of offering potentially hostile families a stake in the state as part of the ruling élite; wives were also taken from among defeated tribes and families for the same reason (see Abir, 1988: 6–7; 14n. 3; Lacey, 1981: 163). Winder (1965: 156) specifically mentions 'the marriage bond' between the Saudis and the powerful Rashids of Jabal Shammar during the golden era of the second Saudi realm. Strategic tribal intermarrying by key members of the Al Saud has continued since the time of Ibn Saud.

A bastion of tribalism is still to be found in the National Guard, which had its origins in the 'White Army'—formed around 1930 and composed of Bedouin, many of whom were the remnants of the Ikhwan. This military force became a haven for certain tribes, and 'strict attention was paid to tribal composition in the various regions [of the kingdom]' (Helms, 1981: 272). Chiefs' sons entered service as officers, 'others as...soldiers', and 'recruits [became] economically dependent upon the state...thus facilitating [the state's] control over them' (Salameh, 1980: 8).

The legacy of these strategies is manifested in, among other aspects of contemporary Saudi Arabia, the 'relatively rigid social structure' which, according to Abir (1993: 3), is at least partly due to the population's tribal origins; and, as late as 'the middle of the twentieth century...[the] tribe and clan were still the most important socio-political substructures in Arabia' (Abir, 1993: xvi), by which time tribal–kinship relations had already played their part in determining the élites of the country. Kostiner (1990: 237) has

---

[70] Varying definitions of 'marriage' should be allowed for.
[71] See also the detailed list of Ibn Saud's sons, numbered at 43, in Lacey (1981: 526–9), and a similar list of sons, numbered at 45, in Holden and Johns (1981: 552–5).

more to say about the position of tribalism during the period of Saudi state formation:

> In contrast to the limits of tribal power, tribal values prevailed in Ibn Sa'ud's polity; they suited the patrimonial regime, which left the old social structure intact. A dualism thus prevailed in Saudi state building. But whereas in the 1920s centralization and tribalism were alternative contending value systems, the next three and a half decades were dominated by centralizing and development policies that still encapsulated a simmering tribal infrastructure.
> ...In governmental decision making, informal tribal practices loomed behind the bureaucratic procedures and institutions.

As state development accelerated under King Faisal, 'major socio-cultural change' was not sought, and during the reigns of Khalid (r. 1975–82) and Fahd (r. 1982–), tribal heritage and values have even been re-emphasised as positive personal and societal credentials (Kostiner, 1990: 241, 247). Kostiner (ibid., 245) also writes of extensive 'patron–client networks' which 'created a large clientele dependent on the royal family'; and Fandy (1999: 242–3) points to Al Saud penetration of the country's civil society, to the extent that 'Saudi Arabia has become, literally and figuratively, synonymous with its royal family'. These attributes of Saudi society are the central factor in the informal politico–socioeconomic system of '*asabiyya* capitalism' introduced in the following chapter.

All the interpretations of (Saudi) Arabian sociopolitics discussed above present tribalism as the bedrock of power and point toward a tangible and ongoing role for tribal–kinship relations in contemporary, day-to-day sociopolitics. However, it would be a mistake to believe that tribalism in Saudi Arabia is still as dominant or monolithic an institution now as it was in even the recent past. In fact, even during the early period of state consolidation—and while he was manipulating tribalism—Ibn Saud was also forced to 'undermine' tribal loyalties to create political stability (see, for example, Helms, 1981: 111, 131; 149n. 29; 146).[72] Most recent thinking on

---

[72] See also the discussion above in the section on the Ikhwan, specifically, Ibn Saud's weakening and final destruction of the tribally-based Ikhwan in the interests of developing a European-type state entity. For an account of the Saudis' use of 'sedentarisation as a means of detribalisation', see Fabietti (1982).

this topic tends to the view that, although the overt political role of tribalism has been greatly diminished, its social legacy lives on. Thus Piscatori (1998, pers. comm., 15 May), for example, doubted the strength, and therefore the relevance of tribalism in modern Saudi politics. However Fandy (1999: 23)—while expressing 'extreme caution' regarding use of the term 'tribe'—implies that tribalism is still a major factor in Saudi sociopolitics and one that even rivals Islam (see Fandy, 1999: 48, 194, 232, 245–6). Madawi al-Rasheed believes the issue of the contemporary sociopolitical role of tribalism requires further exploration to ascertain, for example, 'how far tribal affiliations cut across political affiliations'; although identity in the kingdom today is rapidly and dramatically diversifying as a result of modernity, tribalism 'for identity and [purely] socially is…[still] important' (al-Rasheed, M., 1998, pers. comm., 22 May).[73]

In fact, the diverse population of Saudi Arabia, historically distinguished by regional and religious cultures within Islam as well as tribe, has become relatively more integrated since state-building, modernisation and development were consolidated during King Faisal's reign. The principal result of this process—even as the traditional, formal structures of tribalism have decayed—has been the intermingling of tribal culture with the institutions and bureaucratic procedures of the state; thus the 'imprint' of tribal values 'is evident throughout the Saudi kingdom—on its territorial setting, political regime, social structure, and collective identity' (Kostiner, 1990: 248). The legacy of this culture lingers on in contemporary Saudi psychology: hence the importance of the nature of *asabiyya* and the central role of tribalism in Saudi history in understanding the social, political and economic relations in modern Saudi Arabia (see, for example, Fandy, 1999: 34–5, 91).

Thus, without straying too far into the field of anthropology, 'neo-tribal' might perhaps be an appropriate term to define Saudi Arabia today, since tribalism continues to permeate the society even

---

[73] It is interesting to note that when engaged on the subject of tribalism, some younger Saudi Arabians claimed the tribe is no longer such an important issue, except in the case of those who do not have 'good roots'. This attitude contrasts with a surprisingly strong general attachment to 'traditions' (Saudi nationals 1998, confidential and informal sources, Riyadh, Jan.–Mar.).

as the young state continues to consolidate and modernise. Fandy (1999: 31), for example, testifies to the persistence of a tribal psychology into the modern (and postmodern) era. Indeed, in questioning the stereotyping of modern Saudi society as 'traditional', Fandy opposes labelling in terms of absolutes and instead advocates a narrowing of the concept of tribalism to one of 'familialism' (Fandy, 1999: 10, 23–5). He presents this as a more accurate representation of the society and a better aid to understanding the contemporary kingdom. In expanding on the nature of Al Saud power and legitimacy, for example, he writes: 'The hegemony of the royal family and its world outlook in Saudi society is not made of islam [*sic*] alone, but islam mixed with 'asabiyya (solidarity or group feeling) and the dominant ethos of familialism ('a'iliyya) within the larger context of qaraba (closeness both in space and social relations) society' (Fandy, 1999: 23).[74] In this way, Islam in Saudi Arabia merges with the extended family and with wider personal social relations within the overall, historical–cultural context of *asabiyya* to form the fabric of day-to-day life and interaction at every level and in every facet of society, including politics, the bureaucracy and business. This is a vitally important observation in the study of Saudi Arabia in the era of reform the country has now entered, as will be demonstrated in the following two chapters.

The royal family and the throne.   By the mid-1970s, estimates of the number of Saudi princes ranged as high as 20,000 (see Henderson, 1994: 6–7), and thus there was clearly plenty of scope for the exercise of royal privilege and the practice of *asabiyya*.[75] Despite the

---

[74] *Qaraba*, from the verbal root *qaruba* (to be near, to come near, approach...), is also defined as 'relation, relationship, kinship' (Wehr, 1976: 754). (Fandy employs a lower-case 'i' and the plural 'islams' to denote the many different official and unofficial interpretations, levels of understanding, and social practices of Islam in different Muslim cultures.)

[75] Anthony Cordesman (1997: 201n. 30) quotes a range of 2,000 to 7,000 princes, with the 'higher figure represent[ing] many sons with little or no influence who are descended from collateral branches of the family. The 2,000 figure is a rough estimate of the number who have any real influence.' Alexander Bligh (1984: 3–4) as long ago as 1984, however, also quoted the figure of 2,000 to 7,000. Both David Long (1996: 64) and Saad al-Fagih (1998, pers. comm., 16 Sept) have cited 10,000 princes as an estimate for the mid-1990s. Simons (1998: 23) refers to '20,000 princes and princesses'; *Saudi Arabia Index* (2000b) cites 6,000

recent checks in the overt tribal nature of Saudi society, the dominance of state institutions by the Saudi royal family is intrinsically
based on family and clan loyalties: four generations of males of the
royal lineage occupy strategic positions throughout the military and
government bureaucracy—an 'amplified nepotism' according to
Salameh (1980: 8; see also Salamé, 1989: 74, 79). Kostiner (1990:
239) writes that 'regional administration [has been] monopolized
by branches of the Saudi family and its hand-picked aides.' This follows the historical and cultural patterns of Arabian *asabiyya* as originally outlined by Ibn Khaldun (and of Fandy's *qaraba* society):

> ...a ruler can achieve power only with the help of his own people. They
> are his group and his helpers in his enterprise... It is they with whom he
> fills the administrative offices, whom he appoints as wazirs [ministers of
> state] and tax-collectors. They help him to achieve superiority. They share
> in all his other important affairs. (Ibn Khaldun, *The Maqaddimah*, 1967 edn,
> vol. 1: 372)

Family networks have thus permeated state structures, which serve
as 'a meeting ground for the different branches of the royal family'
(Salameh, 1980: 8). However, Saudi rule is currently dominated
by one branch of the family, the Sudairis, itself dominated by the
'Sudairi seven', i.e., the seven full brothers who are sons of Ibn Saud
and one of his three Sudairi wives, Hassa bint Ahmad al-Sudairi.[76]
Fahd bin Abd al-Aziz, the present king, is one of the seven. Prince
Sultan bin Abd al-Aziz, Second Deputy Prime Minister, Minister of
Defence and Aviation, Inspector General, and probably the next
heir designate after Crown Prince Abdullah succeeds King Fahd, is
another.[77] Prince Na'if, the Interior Minister, is yet another, as is the
powerful governor of Riyadh province, Prince Salman. Na'if and
Salman are senior candidates for the throne after Sultan.

---

princes. Moreover, this princely population is growing at a rapid rate—by 40–5
males per month according to one estimate (see Woollacott, 1996). The number of princes is another area of haziness surrounding the kingdom, but the figure is certainly many thousands, and growing.

[76] The Al Saud are from the Anaza tribe; the Sudairis are a 'powerful Bedouin
dynasty from northern Najd [who have] intermarried with all the branches of
the Sauds' (Abir, 1993: 9).

[77] Prince Sultan's eldest son, His Royal Highness General Khalid bin Sultan bin
Abd al-Aziz, was Commander of Joint Forces during the 1991 Gulf War.

This branch of the family, 'having very early chosen the state apparatus as the means to augment its power, [has] exercised an almost hegemonic influence' over the processes of government (Salameh, 1980: 8). Sudairi moves to increase their influence in key areas of the state in fact began c. 1962 (Abir, 1993: 104); by early 1966, Sudairi leadership of the royal family was acknowledged in British diplomatic despatches (Man, 1966a[78]). The consolidation of power within the House of Saud on the part of the Sudairi seven during the reign of King Khalid and immediately after the succession of Fahd is described by Aburish (1995: 52) in a way which concisely illustrates the nature of factional politics and the jostling for positions of power, influence and prestige within the extended royal family:

The Sudeiri seven, with Fahd in the lead, became the power behind the throne and proceeded to take steps to eliminate or restrict the power of other groups within the family. In the process they undermined the seniority system...and the family council, the two authorities in the succession process. The sons of their [half-]brother, the late King Saud, were denied jobs in the Government and obstacles were placed in their way to prevent them attaining any positions of importance. The sons of King Faisal were allowed to occupy official positions...but the Sudairis saw to it that they were denied any real power... Of course, the sons of Fahd, Sultan and the rest of the Sudeiris became merchants, ambassadors, governors and generals. In total, the Sudairis and their sons held 63 key government positions. (*See* also Man, 1966a)

Abir (1993: 106), in explaining opposition within the royal family to the Sudairi clan, describes the Sudairis' 'endeavours to monopolise power' as indicative of 'dynastical tendencies'. In this respect, Sudairi power moves represent an attempt to establish a dynasty within a dynasty (see Abir, 1993: 69, 98, 103–7), which has obviously important implications for succession to the throne. However, unlike during the earlier Saudi realms, in the modern era the extended royal family has maintained its basic cohesiveness. It has sought to exploit the nation's oil wealth and modernise, whilst at the same time attempting to maintain a traditional, authoritarian,

[78] Morgan Man was British ambassador to Saudi Arabia from October 1964 to July 1968.

patron–client family dynasty, with few concessions to further political development. From this state of affairs an institutionalised procedure of succession has failed to evolve; the question of succession continues to present hazards for the Saudi dynasty—a subject of closer scrutiny in Chapter 5.

Conclusion

One of the lessons that Saudi history has to teach is that nothing can be taken for granted: the dynasty has historically been an unstable one, and the modern period has yet to prove conclusively that in its current incarnation Saudi domination of Arabia will survive indefinitely. The royal family's original religiopolitical alliance with the Al Shaikh has evolved into a series of well rehearsed religious public relations exercises supported by a transparently subservient, if traditionally conservative, ulama. This alliance, and the religious legitimacy of the Al Saud, were not sufficient in the past to guarantee Saudi longevity; indeed, the principal factor in the dynasty's success appears to have been the personal strength and charisma of individual leaders. While this factor was crucial in the past—in the premodern, entirely tribal environment that existed before the First World War—it is less relevant today, in an age where absolute monarchies that still very much display the legacy of a tribal history and clan factionalism are quite an anachronism. However, a royal family in the era of the postmodern global village is not necessarily headed for extinction.

To date, pessimistic views of Saudi 'survivability' have consistently been proved wrong. There is nothing on the immediate horizon which would suggest the days of the Al Saud are numbered, but the horizon is also certainly not clear. Significantly, it was the chief economist of a leading Saudi bank who, in commenting on the economic outlook for the Saudi budget in 1998, observed that there were '…grey clouds on the horizon' (Taecker, K., 1998, pers. comm., 9 Mar.), and these are bringing uncustomary clouds into the lives of the Saudi population. The socioeconomics of the kingdom is the field in which the future of its political structure, if not the regime's stability, will probably be decided.

New economic shocks are now jolting the regime and threatening to impact on the socioeconomic status quo centred on the

Najdi *asabiyya* bureaucratic–business élite networks created in the aftermath of the oil boom of 1973–4, when the still-infant state suddenly metamorphosed into a rentier–distributive oil kingdom. The dilemmas of modernisation and development in general have evolved into dilemmas of economic and socioeconomic management, and these now present the Al Saud with a new kind of challenge for which the regime is armed with little experience. These problems are accentuated by the inefficiency of the Saudi bureaucracy, and by the wastage and dubious and exclusive business practices which all burgeoned in the oil boom era. The longer that unpalatable reforms are delayed, the greater the negative impact they will have on the sociopolitics of the kingdom. It is to these issues that the next two chapters turn in analysing how the domestic political economy and socioeconomics are being shaped by global forces over which the Al Saud exercise limited control.

3

THE OIL BOOM AND MODERNISATION

THE RISE OF *ASABIYYA* CAPITALISM
AND SOCIAL STRESS

The personality of Ibn Saud, the religiopolitical legitimacy of *muwa-hhidi* Islam, and manipulation of the sociopolitics of tribalism, may have been sufficient to sustain the founder of the modern Saudi state, but they have not been the only handles on power. Since the discovery of large reserves of oil in the late 1930s—and especially since the oil boom of the early 1970s—wealth distribution policies, and the development and modernisation of the Saudi state and economy have increasingly been incorporated into the royal family's strategy for a popular patriarchy and political security. Delivering to its citizenry the benefits accruing from oil revenues and economic development, and being seen to be doing it Islamically and in accordance with cultural mores, are fundamental pillars of the Saudi right to rule. Although the Al Saud have been successful in maintaining a generally stable government and their own legitimacy in the eyes of the majority of the Saudi population, all has not gone smoothly. Development and the socioeconomic policies of the last quarter-century may yet reveal serious flaws as the regime struggles to adapt the kingdom to a future in which global economic integration is an important objective.

A number of significant reorientations in the social bases of the Saudi political economy have occurred since the formative period of the modern kingdom, 1925–32; these have entailed the destruction and creation of entire social classes in a society that was once popularly acclaimed as classless. But no change was as significant as that precipitated in 1973–4 by the oil boom. Thereafter, development programmes multiplied and accelerated, especially under the aegis of Crown Prince (now King) Fahd after the assassination of King Faisal in 1975. These programmes and the money which made them possible changed the social as well as the physical face of the kingdom: the influx of massive wealth from oil 'rents' reincarnated Saudi Arabia as a distributive state almost overnight.

A by-product of the development and modernisation of the Saudi state and economy has thus been the unleashing of forces for social change. Hitherto, social change for the benefit of a relatively narrow segment of Saudi society has been one of the unofficial, self-serving goals of those charged with implementing and managing the development process. Unsurprisingly, the profoundly conservative, traditional and religious elements in Saudi society—which today still give it its essential character—have been sources of tension with the forces of change throughout the development process. Development and modernisation, then, like religion, have in some ways become a two-edged sword for the regime. With the advent of the rentier state, the rapid transformation of a traditional, tribal society has caused serious social strains which have occasionally erupted in an Islamically-expressed, radical conservatism, one that is socially and religiously conservative, but politically radical and militant in practice. The Saudi royal family staked its original claim to power on Islam, and rests its continuing claims to power on hereditary authority, Islam and development. Reconciling these factors and staying in control in a stable sociopolitical order have been the overriding concerns, even the 'obsession' (Nehme, 1994: 632), of the Saudi regime.

One way that the Al Saud have been able to manage sociopolitical pressures has been by the manipulation of state revenues. This has been a key domestic policy in order to buy a great degree of popular legitimacy in the role of traditional patriarchs. As generous patrons, buoyed by a firm grip on the state's purse strings, the Al Saud have been able to lavish an enormous range of gifts and subsidies upon their clients, the Saudi people. The legitimacy of largesse has been a strategy to ensure political stability which is in harmony with the social heritage of Arabia: leaders are expected to fulfil certain responsibilities and obligations toward their tribe in return for allegiance. As noted in the preceding chapter, the Al Saud have assumed the aura of a 'super-tribe', with the Saudi population effectively in the role of the tribe writ large; regime and people are entwined in an unwritten but understood patron–client relationship often referred to as 'the Saudi social contract'.

The strategy of patronage, as a conduit for oil wealth, has also been a vehicle for the pursuit of personal goals and enrichment on the part of individual royals and other senior figures of the regime, at the expense of broader state interests. Indeed, as noted already, the ascent of the Saudi rentier–distributive state gave rise to an enlarged *asabiyya*-based political economy with the wholesale creation of new, predominantly Najdi, bureaucratic–business élites and networks based on family and other personal contacts, and *wasta*. Favouritism, mismanagement and widespread wastage, and the institutionalisation of exclusive business practices were hallmarks of this era. These have fed back into the real discontent that existed below the usually quiet surface of Saudi society and damaged Al Saud religiopolitical legitimacy both at home and abroad. This chapter looks at, among other related topics, the path that boom-time development and modernisation has taken in Saudi Arabia, the formation of the Saudi rentier–distributive state and the rise of *asabiyya* capitalism, the Al Saud strategy of public largesse, and what they all mean in the Saudi context.

Boom-time development and the transformation of a state: the legitimacy of largesse, asabiyya capitalism and social change

Development in the Saudi Arabian context. A specific developmental dilemma has emerged for the Saudi regime because of the political significance attached to state largesse bestowed upon Saudi society. Scholars of Saudi socioeconomics and others involved with the kingdom on a professional basis are unanimous in observing that 'obvious political gesture[s]' (Mohamedi, 1993: 15) permeate economic planning on the macro level, and lurk behind almost every economic decision on the micro level (see also Nehme, 1994: 638–9). Bill and Springborg (1994: 430) write of 'the subordination of rational economics to political calculations' on the part of the regime, and even some senior economists who have worked in Saudi Arabia tacitly acknowledge the political nature of certain subsidies (see SAMBA, 1998b: 6–7). Grand-scale largesse is a relatively recent phenomenon, associated with the kingdom's petroleum-industry fortunes, although its roots lie deep in the traditional patriarchal *asabiyya* sociopolitical customs of Arabia.

Driving the Al Saud's strategy of public subsidies has been the country's oil wealth which, following the knock-on effects of the 1973 oil embargo, saw average Saudi crude prices sky-rocketing from around US$2.70 per barrel in 1973 to around US$9.80 per barrel in 1974. The value of Saudi oil exports jumped from almost US$5,850 million in 1973 to more than US$32,500 million in 1974. Saudi export earnings from oil averaged around US$44,160 million per annum in the twenty-four years from the 1974 oil boom to 1997, with oil export revenues reaching a peak of nearly US$111,000 million in 1981—a year in which a high international price for oil coincided with high Saudi production (see Table 3.1). Although the value of non-oil exports and services have followed a pattern of more or less steady annual increases—reflecting progress (albeit slow) in economic diversification—the vast bulk of Saudi export earnings in the modern era has always been, and still is, derived from the petroleum sector.[1]

---

[1] It is appropriate at this point to draw the reader's attention to some specific difficulties involved in dealing with Saudi statistics. In this study, for example, it is interesting to compare the statistics of the Saudi Arabian Monetary Agency (SAMA)—the government central bank—with figures provided by the World Bank, for the total value of Saudi export earnings (Table 3.1 col. 6). A cursory look at the World Bank's figure for the total value of Saudi exports of goods and services for 1976 (US$37,388 million), 1980 (US$106,765 million), 1986 (US$22,790 million) and 1996 (US$60,221 million) reveals differences ranging from only US$62 million (1986) to a substantial US$3,116 million (1996) (see World Bank, 1998; 1999: 219 and cf. Table 3.1). For a third set of comparable statistics, see also CDLR (1995a: 35, t. 3); the CDLR-commissioned researchers' sources include the IMF, the OPEC Statistical Bulletin and the Centre for Global Energy Studies (CGES). It is relevant to take note of the caution offered by the CDLR-commissioned authors:

> While all of the sources we have accessed quote impeccable authorities such as the IMF, OECD, World Bank, IEA etc., these, in turn, depend solely on the Saudi authorities themselves for specific, detailed and accurate financial data and here we find a hole… Any statement from whatever source that purports to give an accurate assessment of the current financial situation in Saudi Arabia must, in our view, be unsoundly based. (CDLR: 1995a: 31–2. See also Chapter 4, notes 3, 10, 14)

Table 3.1.

GUIDE TO SAUDI ARABIAN OIL EXPORT AND INCOME FIGURES, 1969–2000

	Oil exports (million barrels p.a.)	Arabian Light Crude oil price: annual averages (US$/barrel)[1] (cf. WTI prices)	Total value of oil exports (US$m.)	Total value of other exports (US$m.)	Total export earnings incl. receipts for services (US$m.)
1969	1,020.05		1,839	22	1,997
1970	1,174.17	1.30	2,155	26	2,323
1971	1,528.19	1.65	2,583	7	2,742
1972	1,992.53	1.90	3,892	15	4,125
1973	2,560.34	2.70	5,849	27	6,233
1974	2,891.68	9.76	32,587	80	33,314
1975	2,409.39	10.72	27,174	119	28,136
1976	2,939.64	(12.23) 11.51	35,510	121	36,707
1977	3,142.05	(14.22) 12.40	40,228	122	41,758
1978	2,812.70	(14.55) 12.70	36,847	144	38,615
1979	3,218.47	(25.08) 17.26	57,861	150	60,051
1980	3,375.69	(37.96) 28.67	100,563	156	103,685
1981	3,291.54	(36.08) 34.23	110,956	873	116,304
1982	2,058.40	(33.65) 31.74	72,935	956	78,456
1983	1,431.08	(30.30) 28.77	44,626	1,032	49,808
1984	1,167.89	(29.39) 28.06	36,161	1,263	41,536
1985	780.72	(27.99) 27.54	25,844	1,546	30,950
1986	1,190.02	(15.04) 13.73	18,000	2,123	22,728
1987	973.12	(19.19) 17.23	20,366	2,771	25,651
1988	1,245.49	(15.97) 13.40	20,144	4,171	26,607
1989	1,217.50	(19.68) 16.21	24,023	4,274	30,808
1990	1,642.42	(24.52) 20.82	39,960	4,287	47,278
1991	2,382.11	(21.54) 17.43	43,462	4,090	50,461
1992	2,408.98	(20.57) 17.94	46,396	3,760	53,623
1993	2,296.92	(18.45) 15.68	38,505	3,774	45,562
1994	2,275.27	(17.21) 15.39	38,024	4,476	45,847
1995	2,296.13	(18.42) 16.73	43,416	6,494	53,390
1996	2,236.01	(22.16) 19.85	54,109	6,456	63,337
1997	2,257.33	(20.61) 18.76	53,183	7,389	64,829
1998	2,332.48	(14.39) 12.26	32,472	6,253	43,455
1999	2,087.68	(19.31) 17.43	44,745	5,810	55,928
2000	2,282.38	(30.37) 26.77	70,637	6,615	82,031

Source: Saudi Arabian Monetary Agency (SAMA, 1998: 15, 298–301, 314; SAMA, 2001); BP Amoco (1999b); BP (2001).
[1] Average annual prices of the benchmark crude, West Texas Intermediate (WTI), are provided (in parentheses) for comparison.

The Saudi regime, like those of the other Gulf Arab rentier states, is not dependent on tax revenue and is therefore financially independent of its population. Helen Lackner (1978: 213) outlined, early in the kingdom's emergence as a rentier state, how Saudi Arabia departed from the developmental norm and how the process has been harnessed politically, economically and socially: 'Oil revenues have allowed the regime to assert its control over the country as they have enabled it to consolidate its political hegemony by paying subsidies to the tribes and by buying off any potential opposition. For the same reason the regime is in control of economic development and, less directly, of social transformation.'[2]

It was the oil boom of the 1970s that spawned the entire contemporary Saudi bureaucracy and the state institutions whose primary function it was to distribute oil 'rents' through society. Massive petroleum revenues have enabled the state to bestow the new fruits of those export earnings upon its population in the form of modern infrastructural development and subsidies which include, for example, free education and health care with ultra-modern facilities; token charges for utility services (including water, electricity and gas) and petrol; subsidised staple foods such as bread, rice and sugar; the importation of foreign labour for much of the country's heavy manual and menial work; and no income tax (see Beblawi, 1987; Amuzegar, 1999: 98; Royal Embassy of Saudi Arabia (London), 1997; Chaudhry, 1997: 150–5; Curtiss, 1995: 48; Bill and Springborg, 1994: 429–30, 431; Nehme, 1994; Wilson and Graham, 1994: 54, 176, 178–9). The use of the term 'Saudi welfare state' is not uncommon (see, for

---

As a measure of the research conducted for the CDLR report, the pessimistic estimates of Saudi budget deficits for the years 1990–3 were actually dwarfed by more substantive figures presented by the Saudi American Bank: from a total deficit of US$54,380 million (CDLR, 1995a: 32–3) to approximately US$78,000 million (see SAMBA, 1997: 2). Continuing Saudi economic dependence on the petroleum sector, the dubious nature of Saudi statistics, and Saudi financial problems are topics of more detailed analysis in the following chapter.

[2] The precedent of tribal subsidies established in the early history of the modern Saudi state (1926–47), 'which effectively absorbed a large part of state revenue', is described by Tim Niblock (1982: 90–1, 105n. 85). Niblock (ibid., 77) regards 1947 as the year in which 'oil revenues began significantly to transform the economy'. Abdelrahman al-Hegelan and Monte Palmer (1985: 49) suggest that Saudi Arabia may be 'the prototype' of a rentier state.

example, Amuzegar, 1999: 96–9; Cordesman, 1997: 74; Wilson and Graham, 1994: 54), and has even been employed and emphasised by the Saudis themselves (Royal Embassy of Saudi Arabia, London, 1997). Social security in the kingdom is an 'endeavor…which the state diligently maintains… The Social Security budget has been subject to constant upward reviews, rising in 1993 from [US$400 million] to [US$720 million]. Payments are made through 76 offices serving all regions of the Kingdom' (Ministry of Information, n.d.: 10; also Ministry of Information, 1997: 69, 107–10[3]). These are figures of which the government is proud. State expenditure on social welfare becomes even more significant in light of the relatively small Saudi population, 12.3 million nationals according to the 1992 census.[4] Moreover, spending on social welfare accounts for only a fraction of budgetary resources allocated to 'human resource development' and to 'health and social development' (see SAMA, 1998: 306–7).

The distributive–welfare state is an important element in what has been termed 'the Saudi social contract'; this incorporates the Al Saud strategy of the 'legitimacy of largesse', which has consistently allowed the regime to 'buy off any potential hostility long before it has time to develop into anything like a serious threat' (Lackner, 1978: 216; see also, for example, Amuzegar, 1999: 99; Cordesman, 1997: 47, 73–6; Wilson and Graham, 1994: 81, 178, 185; Beblawi, 1987). The strategy of largesse, however, has developed into a pillar of the regime's legitimacy and now colours every aspect of the kingdom's political economy, socioeconomics and sociopolitics. According to one source, the Al Saud rely on two types of legitimacy: ideological, largely through a co-opted ulama; and 'functional', through the use of subsidies (Piscatori, J., 1998, pers. comm., 15 May).[5] However, social welfare is also an Islamic ideal which is

---

[3] These and countless similar publications are printed and distributed in their hundreds of thousands by the Ministry of Information. They are usually variations on the constantly recurring themes of the enormous achievements which have been made in all fields of economic, developmental, social and religious endeavour since Ibn Saud's foundation of the modern kingdom.

[4] The controversy over Saudi population statistics is treated in the following chapter.

[5] Piscatori's basic outline of Al Saud political legitimacy is the standard one. The 'legitimacy of largesse' is my term—it corresponds to Piscatori's 'functional legitimacy'. Saudi 'ideological legitimacy' was presented in some detail in the previous chapter.

now broadly sanctioned in contemporary Islamic interpretation within the concept of *zakat*, thus further illustrating the difficulty, if not futility, of any attempt to separate clearly religious/ideological issues from secular/state issues and, indeed, from everyday life in Saudi Arabia.

Kiren Aziz Chaudhry distinguishes between a 'welfare state' which is re-distributive, and a 'rentier state' which is distributive. According to her model, the application of the term 'welfare state' to Saudi Arabia is technically incorrect.[6] True to its 'rentier' status, the Saudi regime is, rather, a distributor of wealth gained directly from overseas as oil 'rents' rather than a redistributor of wealth gained from the population through taxation: it is a state of patron largesse. The development of institutions in such a distributive state 'diverge[s] from classical patterns of state-building as [its] bureaucracies emerge in response to the need to allocate rather than to appropriate revenue' (Chaudhry, 1997: 26; see also Beblawi, 1987).

From the Saudi regime's viewpoint, '[w]hat has been achieved in the Kingdom [in the 25 years from 1970 to 1995] is a unique blend of material and social development' (Royal Embassy of Saudi Arabia, London, 1997: 2). How far the Al Saud have been in control of the overall processes of development and modernisation and their social consequences, however, is debatable. Before oil revenues became significant in 1947, according to Tim Niblock (1982: 94–5), economic development was subordinated to 'security-related projects' in the interests of consolidating both a unified modern nation-state, and Al Saud power in that state (see also al-Awaji, 1989: 50). During the 1950s, when oil revenues climbed from more than US$56 million in 1950 to be sustained above US$290 million from 1955 (SAMA, 1998: 11), development planning and spending were not 'coherent' or 'consistent'; rather, '[d]ecisions on disbursement… [were] taken in a random and uncontrolled fashion, with no clearly established objectives…', a situation which reflected a still young and very loose state structure (Niblock, 1982: 95–6).[7]

---

[6] Chaudhry writes with the benefit of more than a decade to research her topic. Reference to 'the Saudi welfare state' is, however, ubiquitous. The term 'distributive–welfare state' is used in this book to describe the increasingly complex political–socioeconomic nature of the modern Saudi state.

[7] Indeed, the process of state formation—in contrast to the mythology favoured by Saudi officialdom of the 'unification' of the (non-existent) state of Saudi

During the oil boom of the 1970s and 1980s, the decision-making process entered a new phase of disarray. The only firm decision, spurred by the influx of oil rents, appears to have been to transform the function of the state to wholly one of distribution. This entailed the abolition not only of taxes but of the taxing institutions of the state, with the result that 'the new distributive organs of the Saudi bureaucracy became the exclusive motor of the economy in the 1970s' (Chaudhry, 1997: 141). In the rush to develop the state as distributor of largesse and to achieve unbridled growth in the various sectors of the national economy under their charge, the new bureaucracies and individual bureaucrats were effectively given a free hand to manage resources as they saw fit, often in accordance with personal whim. With 'no vision of the…future', growth for its own sake was the principal goal of government policy (see Chaudhry, 1997: 155, 142, 143, 172). The results of this oil-rent driven, growth-induced bureaucratic labyrinth were: 'unguided' planning, despite the adoption of five-year development plans; a lack of bureaucratic co-ordination; and even competition between government agencies (Osama, 1987: 33; Chaudhry, 1997: 139–92; al-Awaji, 1989: 55–6). Thus, as economic restructuring reached 'cataclysmic' proportions (el-Mallakh, 1982: 13), unhealthy patterns began to emerge and to characterise the 'new' Saudi oil state—it was an environment which, as will be seen shortly, opened the way to a wholesale resurgence of patronage, favouritism and nepotism as the Saudi political economy and socioeconomic system were literally re-formed.

However, the destruction of the tax state, argues Chaudhry, also effectively blinded the new distributive state, since the social and economic contacts and overall socioeconomic structures required

---

Arabia—had barely been completed by the 1950s. According to Chaudhry (1997: 48–50), it was not until the end of the 1940s that the early Saudi state was able to complete the process of establishing 'a national market with a uniform legal system and a single measure of exchange' while in the process creating a centralised bureaucratic administration. Even so, the key to this painstaking success was the conquest of the Hijaz which made available to Ibn Saud the human and material resources of this comparatively rich western region of Arabia. Since 'a stable constituency for the state did not even exist until the 1940s', a milestone was thus reached in 1950 when 'twenty years of expansion and centralization culminated [with] Ibn Saud issu[ing] the first comprehensive unified income tax legislation' (see Chaudhry, 1997: 69, 76).

to extract taxes and regulate the economy atrophied as they lost their relevance.[8] Their decay soon resulted in the loss of the state's ability to gather socioeconomic data and ultimately meant that it 'no longer knew much about the society it ruled' (Chaudhry, 1997: 167). This situation resulted in severe distortions in the distributive and developmental processes.[9] This analysis is supported by the Saudi academic Abdul Rahman Osama; writing on the inadequacies of the development strategies adopted in the Gulf Arab states during the boom period, he notes that '[t]he lack of basic information creates difficulties in decision-making in the formulation and implementation process, and the gap is filled with subjective judgements and guesswork...' (see Osama, 1987: 31–3). He goes further, however, claiming that the results of such 'haphazard guesswork... [do] not constitute development' at all (ibid., 1987: 33; for a discussion of OPEC countries in a comparative context, see Amuzegar, 1999: 48–50, 213–16).

In rejecting a purely economic definition of development, Osama reinforces the general Saudi emphasis on the social aspects of developmental processes (Osama, 1987: 5–6). He writes that '...the real criterion of development is efficiency, the control and direction of resources according to plans and programmes with clear objectives, and the ability to direct human capabilities towards the achievement of these objectives'; indeed, he proposes a more complete definition of development, as '...an intricate, integrated, interactive process occurring within a matrix of complex and constantly interacting relations among the political, economic, social, administrative and educational constituents of society' (ibid., 6, 8). As will be demonstrated below, Saudi state efficiency is extremely low, the direction and quality of education questionable, recent economic performance

[8] Explaining this predicament in a straightforward cause–effect manner, Chaudhry (1997: 164–5) writes:

The direct taxes that the government had so painstakingly put in place in the four decades prior to the boom were not just economic tools or the source of government funding; they were also an important source of information without which distributive policies themselves could not be effectively (let alone equitably) carried out.

[9] See Chaudhry (1997: 139–92) for her full account of the rise of the Saudi distributive state in the 1970s and all its consequences.

has been very poor, social attitudes are still contributing to high unemployment due to disdain for jobs in a whole range of economic sectors, and political development has been virtually non-existent. Indeed, Osama argues, the flaws of 'fallacious' development, which 'has the appearance of development but lacks the substance [of a] continually productive base' will inevitably lead to 'disastrous consequences' unless policies are reviewed and action implemented (Osama, 1987: 17, 19, 176).

Helen Lackner (1978) pre-empted Osama in her study of how rentier status was distorting the developmental process in Saudi Arabia:

One reason why Saudi Arabia's situation is unique is that the country's wealth has not come as a result of the development of the country's internal productive forces, but from the sale abroad of a raw material whose exploitation requires few workers, only about 20,000. Although oil is a Saudi Arabian resource, its exploitation is effected through external agents. The income generated from oil is paid directly to the regime from abroad, it forms a direct support for the political *status-quo*. Oil income has not been *the product* of internal economic development, on the contrary it is *its cause*. This reversal of standard principles of development has deep consequences for Saudi Arabia socially, politically and economically. (Lackner, 1978: 213, author's emphasis. See also Beblawi, 1987.)[10]

Thus, official Saudi claims of success in 'material and social development' should be questioned—especially in light of the fact that some sectors of Saudi society have not fared well in various developmental/distributive processes.[11] Distortions and less than complete success in these processes have led one generally optimistic analyst to conclude that the kingdom in the 1980s was '…a "quasi-developed" as opposed to a "developing" country' (Huyette, 1985: 135). The 1990s saw no significant change in circumstances requiring a reappraisal of the 'quasi-developed' label, in spite of repeated claims that Saudi Arabia 'has reached the twenty-first century ahead of time'

---

[10] See also Wilson and Graham (1994: 171); and Birks and Sinclair (1982), who write of a 'dualistic pattern of development' which left most Saudi nationals outside the 'modern sector'.

[11] Issues of poverty in Saudi society are discussed in more detail in the following chapter.

(Alohaly, A.R.N., 1995, pers. comm., 13 July).[12] Hence the pertinence of an inquiry which focuses more closely on the links between Al Saud power and socioeconomic development and change.

State largesse in Saudi Arabia is operated by the ruling and bureaucratic–business élites of a traditional–authoritarian–distributive political system which has gradually and far from flawlessly institutionalised control over the economy.[13] The revolutionary

---

[12] Claims that are true only 'in a very superficial way', according to an Australian diplomat with extensive service in Saudi Arabia (Australian diplomat 1, 1995, pers. comm., 14 July). This assessment of Saudi Arabia's development progress remains current despite recent postmodern portrayals of the kingdom (see, for example, Fandy, 1999: 10–12). The view that Saudi Arabia 'is a very complex mix of the "traditional", the various forms of modernities, and the postmodern' (ibid., 10) is actually an updating of the familiar discussion of the Saudi modernisation dilemma. (Some of the social issues resulting from the impact on the kingdom of aspects of 'postmodernity' are treated in Chapter 5.)

[13] James A. Bill and Robert Springborg (1994: 24, 24n. 26) have adapted a pre-existing taxonomy of political systems according to (political) developmental strategies and present four categories: democratic–populist, traditional–authoritarian, traditional–distributive, and authoritarian–distributive. Saudi Arabia, as an example of the second category in this modified taxonomy, exhibits the following characteristics:

> Security for the ruling house is the overwhelming obsession of the political strategists who direct these governments. Political participation is severely restricted, and all important decision making is monopolized by the central figures in the ruling establishment. Although these governments distribute in varying degrees the goods and services that they control, this is not a high priority on their political agendas. (Bill and Springborg, 1994: 25)

The criteria Bill and Springborg use for listing Saudi Arabia with Jordan, Morocco and Oman in the traditional–authoritarian category, rather than with Bahrain, Kuwait, Qatar and the UAE in the traditional–distributive category, lie mainly in statistics used to measure the degree of modernisation achieved by Middle Eastern countries (see Bill and Springborg, 1994: 17, t. 1.1). Saudi Arabia's relatively poor record when compared with its smaller Gulf neighbours is taken as evidence of the regime's lesser commitment to the distributive function of the state.

Chaudhry (1997: 139–92) unequivocally categorises Saudi Arabia as a distributive state. The history of the modern Saudi state leaves in no doubt the seriousness with which the Al Saud have taken their role as patrons and distributors of largesse. However, material results should not be confused with actual practice and intent. Thus, I have favoured the combined term of 'traditional–authoritarian–distributive' which I think better describes the cultural, political and economic nexus embodied in the rule of the Saudi dynasty.

decision to abandon taxation in favour of the distribution of oil wealth—which has had many, profound and uncalculated economic and social consequences—was ultimately 'made out of expediency' (Chaudhry: 1997: 146). In other words, the strategy of largesse clearly serves, first and foremost, a political agenda. It was not a policy without precedent: 'political exigencies' played a role in the winding back of various taxes during the 1950s and 1960s (Chaudhry, 1997: 77), and the regime's constant concern with domestic security can only be appreciated if the relationships between political power, economic control, development, and the Saudi bases of legitimacy are understood.

Fareed Mohamedi drew attention in 1993 to the link between economic and political dilemma: 'With domestic and foreign politics hindering [economic] policy changes that could increase revenues and/or decrease spending, how will the government control the budget deficits which have averaged close to 13 per cent during the last four years?' He went on to write that, even according to optimistic calculations, the Saudis will be facing 'deficits of 8–10 per cent of GDP in the next several years' (Mohamedi, 1993: 16).[14] Saudi budgetary performances since this forecast have proved Mohamedi's view conservative. But even worse from the Saudi perspective is the fact that after budget deficits were clawed back to something resembling a respectable level in the years 1995 to 1997, the collapse of oil prices during 1998 again faced the state with the prospect of severe financial difficulties. The dramatic recovery of oil prices in 1999–2000 dispelled any sense of another imminent crisis, but have done

[14] Mohamedi is chief economist and a former head of country risk and oil market analysis at the Washington, DC-based Petroleum Finance Company. Previously, he was vice-president and a senior analyst in the sovereign risk unit at Moody's Investors Service, and was the principal analyst for rating several Gulf countries, including Saudi Arabia. Gross Domestic Product (GDP) can be calculated in various ways but is, ultimately, the total value of final goods and services produced in a country. 'Final' means GDP does not include intermediate goods and services which are used to produce other good and services. Thus, GDP is equal to: sales to households for final consumption (excluding imports since they are produced abroad) + expenditure by firms on plant and equipment (investment expenditure) + government expenditure (on goods and services, not social expenditures such as health and welfare) + expenditure by foreigners on the country's exports.

nothing to alter the kingdom's dependence on oil or the potentially crippling liabilities associated with such dependence.[15]

Of urgent concern to the regime, therefore, is that dramatic falls in oil revenues and newly expanding budget deficits at any time in the future will significantly slow the development process, especially its industrialisation and economic diversification objectives. At least equally important is the fact that renewed budgetary problems will interfere with the regime's distributive capacity and its image as patron in a socioeconomic environment which already displays gross inefficiencies, imbalances and inequalities. In turn, the consequences of fiscal restraint also have potentially serious political ramifications. These concerns are known to have been shared by, among others, the Bank of England, the US Federal Reserve, the IMF, and at least one US government credit agency in the wake of the 1991 Gulf War (see Mohamedi, 1993; Wilson and Graham, 1994: 195–6; CDLR, 1995a: 47–8n. 2), when strong rumours of a Saudi financial crisis coincided with an evident rise of internal dissent in the kingdom. More importantly, renewed budgetary difficulties only increased pressure on the Saudi regime from the international financial industry to tackle much more vigorously the task of economic restructuring and relinquish altogether the role of distributive patron. In the meantime, the oil boom economy has transformed Saudi Arabian society; but the new social structure has barely had time to establish itself and already further changes are on the horizon.

The Najdiisation of the state. Essential to the formation of the modern state of Saudi Arabia was the creation of a unified national market, a goal only achieved by the end of the 1940s[16] and which necessitated the 'systematic destruction of internal barriers to exchange and of the social groups that profited from them…' (Chaudhry, 1997: 50, 134). The first socioeconomic group to be destroyed was the Najdi tribal confederations, along with their nomadic livelihood—the final battle between the representatives of this group and the emerging Saudi state was, literally, fought at Sibila in 1929, and by the time the kingdom was declared in 1932 the subjugation of this group and its (political-)economy was complete. By 1950 the

---

[15] Fiscal questions are dealt with in more detail in the following chapter.
[16] See note 7 above.

guilds and the smaller merchants of the Hijaz, who had provided
the emergent Saudi state with an economic stepping-stone in the
formation of a national economy, had likewise been destroyed in
favour of the large commercial houses of the Hijazi merchant élite
of Jedda (see Chaudhry, 1997: 47–100, 131–6). These early socioeconomic transformations of the modern Saudi state are important
illustrations of the fact that dramatic and rapid change in Saudi
socioeconomics is not unprecedented, and that state and market
formation is an exercise that is socially both destructive and cre-
ative, as, too, is economic restructuring.

Chaudhry's research is valuable for shedding light on these processes. See, for example, the following concise summary of the four
decades of Saudi socioeconomic changes which preceded the present structure of the Saudi state, society and economy:

[T]he process by which the institutions that governed the national market
were forged was brutal. Between 1925 and 1973 the Saudi state underwent
several transmutations in which forces antithetical to the formation of a
national market and a centralized administration were (in most cases quite
literally) eliminated. The protagonists in these conflicts changed over time,
but each successive consolidation signalled a narrowing of the social basis
of the state. In sequence, the material foundations, institutional constructs,
and ideational systems of the autonomous nomadic tribes, the Al Saud's
tribal armies, the guilds, and the smaller merchants were destroyed. In each
case, they were destroyed after having been directly instrumental in the
creation of the new national order and having come into conflict with the
next rung of social groupings whose co-optation was necessary for the
centralization and expansion of national institutions. (Chaudhry, 1997: 99)

Chaudhry concludes: 'By the 1960s the aspiring commercial-
industrial elites of the Hijaz had formed the social basis of the newly
created national market; previously independent business communities were utterly transformed into a dependent corporate group
with strong institutional ties to the economic ministries' (ibid.,
1997: 99). But, by the time the Hijazi merchant élites had established themselves as the kingdom's pre-eminent socioeconomic
group, their position was already being undermined. The stage had
been set for the definitive ascent of an entirely new socioeconomic
formation: the Najdis. The rise of this group from the Al Saud's
own heartland is a classic case of *asabiyya* in action, and testifies to

the centrality of *asabiyya* ideals in the Arabian historico-cultural milieu.[17] The inexorable progress of the Najdiisation of the Saudi state, of course, began with the forging of the kingdom.

When Ibn Saud completed the conquest of territory which became the basis of the modern Saudi kingdom, members of his family and other select Najdis became the 'new Saudi ruling class—the aristocracy' of the new state (see Abir, 1993: 3–9).[18] However, this naturally privileged position of power did not imply economic and commercial expertise and, indeed, the ruling élite was obliged to rely on the more cosmopolitan, sophisticated and technically experienced Hijazis to establish a national economy and bureaucracy; indeed, the Hijazi administrative system was 'adopted as the basis for the central management' of the new state (al-Awaji, 1989: 50, 52), and the Hijaz itself served as the early state's administrative–bureaucratic 'nerve centre' (Kostiner, 1990: 238; 1993: 174). This broad reliance on the Hijaz was epitomised by the fact that the Saudi national capital was only officially transferred from Jedda to Riyadh in 1961. Even until the mid-1970s, some national agencies could not afford the move to Riyadh, because of a more complete reliance on Hijazi expertise.[19]

As ministries and other bureaucratic headquarters were relocated to the principal Najdi city and traditional seat of Saudi power, Hijazi staff were dismissed and replaced by Najdis. This facilitated Najdi domination of the bureaucratic middle ranks, and by 1969 they occupied 61% of senior bureaucratic positions—a process which continued over the course of the 1970s (see Chaudhry, 1997: 94, 170, 170n. 86). By 1973 Najdis commanded the collective Saudi

[17] See Chapter 2, 'Tribalism, asabiyya and the contemporary Saudi state'.
[18] The earlier phases in the development of this 'aristocracy' could also be described as the consolidation and entrenchment of 'a cooperating coalition based on personal, ad hoc arrangements among [tribal] leaders and between them and the ruler [in this case, Ibn Saud]' (see Kostiner, 1990: 226). Elements of this form of rule were still in operation from the 1925 milestone conquest of the Hijaz until the final subjugation of the Ikhwan in 1930. See also Kostiner (1990: 243) for a brief summary of the constituencies of emerging class structures.
[19] See Chaudhry (1997: 170n. 86). The important agency cited as an example of the later move was SAMA. Riyadh's future as 'a modern capital' was marked out for it in 1954 by King Saud, and by 1956 construction of new ministry buildings was under way (Holden and Johns, 1981: 179).

bureaucracy and were in a position to favour kin and the new 'clusters of clients' during the boom era (Chaudhry, 1997: 170–1).[20] The direct hand of the ruling class was also active during this period of bureaucratic reformation, with the highest government officials being chosen by the king himself or by senior princes. Selection was based on loyalty, family affiliation and social status (see Islami and Kavoussi, 1984: 17–18)—practices consistent with those of the early, much more strongly tribally oriented days of the kingdom under Ibn Saud (Kostiner, 1990: 236).

As noted in the preceding chapter, although tribalism as a political force had been significantly diminished during the period of state formation, the legacy of tribal culture and identity lingered on in Saudi society and permeated the institutions and bureaucratic procedures of the state. Mamoun Fandy, whose analysis of contemporary Saudi sociopolitics stresses more particular and focused manifestations of Arabian *asabiyya*—i.e. *qaraba*[21] and 'familialism'—similarly concludes that '…the ethos of familialism saturates the whole political system' (Fandy, 1999: 24). Kinship relations operating within the *asabiyya* ideal have naturally continued: the structures of state institutions presented no obstacle to Najdi *asabiyya* networks. It was only a matter of time before the Najdi ruling élite consolidated their power throughout the state and the economy.

Blood ties are not the only basis of *asabiyya* relationships, however: 'affiliation' also enters into the equation in group solidarity (Hudson, 1977: 36). Ibn Khaldun originally posited that: 'Client relationships and contacts with…allies have the same effect as (common descent)… Whenever such a client relationship exists between a tribe and its clients before the tribe has obtained royal authority, the roots of the relationship are more firmly intertwined…' (Ibn Khaldun, *The Maqaddimah*, 1967 edn, vol. 1: 374–5). The crucial point here is alliance and clientism *before* the acquisition of absolute political power. 'Only in the rarest cases is a distinction made between (common) descent and the client relationship. The position (of clients) is the same as that of close or blood relatives. However, if [the rulers] choose followers after they have obtained royal

---

[20] Abir's much less detailed account dates definitive Najdi dominance of the bureaucracy as occurring during the 1980s (see Abir, 1993: 117–19).
[21] See Chapter 2, note 74 and associated main text.

authority, their royal rank causes them to make a distinction between master and client, and...between close relatives and clients or followers' (ibid., vol. 1: 375).

Thus, close clients and allies may, in effect, be accepted as honorary kin, and 'eventually conceptualized as...blood kin' (Lindholm, 1996: 53); and, '...familialism is an expansive system that benefits from those outside it who exhibit exceptional qualities that merit inclusion in the qaraba system' (Fandy, 1999: 31). In this way, a certain amount of flexibility and fluidity of inclusion and exclusion permeates 'group solidarity'. This flexibility not only helps to explain the progressive Najdi domination of Saudi state institutions through the favouring of kin and clients but also sheds light on the decline and rise, demise and establishment, of individuals, groups, social classes and patron–client networks as the Saudi state and political economy developed, modernised and changed, a story that continues today in the era of globalisation and Saudi economic restructuring.

The rise of Najdi asabiyya capitalism.   With a firm grip on political power and the state bureaucracy, the next step for those sharing in the Al Saud–Najdi *asabiyya* system was the exploitation of this advantageous position also to dominate the Saudi economy. The 1970s oil boom provided both the means and the extra incentive, if any were needed, to consolidate a Najdi-centred political economy, a process that took place rapidly and decisively with the birth of the new distributive state produced by the oil boom—a state that 'united Nejdi political and bureaucratic elites with a private sector of their own making, their own kin' (Chaudhry, 1997: 140).

Bureaucratic favouritism based mainly on kinship and the *wasta* mechanism fuelled the rise of the new business class, through practices common in such situations the world over. Thus the negotiating of all manner of bureaucratic procedures, such as obtaining various licences and permits and registering lucrative agencies, were smoothed for the favoured. Also a characteristic of this period of Saudi socioeconomic development was the trading of inside government information on development projects, tenders, and the like (Chaudhry, 1997: 162). Many observers of the kingdom have pointed out that this is not uncommon in societies where profits are to be made—Chaudhry (1997: 162) is one of these, but she also claims that Saudi Arabia is a special case because of 'the amounts of money involved and the proportion of economic activity covered [and] because the distribution system was deliberately constructed to facilitate the entry of nationals into intermediary positions between the government and foreign companies'.[22] This last development in particular is of great significance in the virtual institutionalisation of commission farming, a practice which became synonymous with doing business in Saudi Arabia, discussed below in the context of exclusive Saudi business practices.

Such formal and informal institutional arrangements furthered Najdi business ascendancy. An example of the former was placement of all the kingdom's chambers of commerce under the auspices of a Riyadh-based confederation in 1981, the Saudi Confederation of Chambers of Commerce, Industry and Agriculture, thus marking the formal end of the importance of the Jedda Chamber of Commerce. It also symbolised the end of dominance of the Hijazi merchant élite who, by this time, were unable to defend their position as the principal allies of the Najdi political–military aristocracy. Informal arrangements included the large-scale movement into private business of senior bureaucrats, who thus became links between business and government with intimate knowledge of and contacts in both sectors (see Chaudhry, 1997: 160, 163; see also Palmer *et al.*, 1989: 18–19; Islami and Kavoussi, 1984: 20). Another link in business–government relations was the deliberate business-family strategy of 'donat[ing] a member to government service' (Kay, 1982: 176). Consequently, although the government did not have an open policy of helping Najdis specifically to enter into business, it was well-connected Najdis who were best able to capitalise on the kingdom's booming oil economy and transformation into a distributive state. Fandy (1999: 30) explains how certain families prospered as a result of royal family largesse:

...the money coming from oil rent is distributed to enforce the earlier qaraba hierarchy...to consolidate an already existing hierarchy of qaraba

---

[22] The informal and exclusive, *asabiyya*-based political–business relations of Saudi Arabia and the practices they spawn, are not without parallel in highly diverse regions of the developing world. In Venezuela, for example, the advent of the oil state 'destroy[ed] weak but traditional elites [and] created a new dominant class with strong vested interests in the fate of the oil sector' (Karl, 1997). See also Chapter 1, note 15, for the coining of the term 'booty capitalism' (Hutchcroft, 1998) in relation to the Philippines, Indonesia, Thailand and Zaire.

relations... Thus families loyal and close to [the] Al Saud were given a bigger share [of boom-time wealth] than those whose loyalties were suspect. (See also Fandy, ibid., 38–9, 246–7; Beblawi, 1987: 388.)

At the same time, of course, modernisation and development, at least on a superficial level, were proceeding apace. As a result, after 'the massive programmes of industrial, agricultural and infrastructural development... [of] the late 1960s and the 1970s... economic developments are themselves now steadily transforming the social structure by expanding the size and significance of those social groupings on whom the operation of the economic infrastructure depends' (Niblock, 1982: 78). In other words, the proliferation of Najdis in the Saudi business and bureaucratic classes—through blood and regional allegiances—is an ongoing and self-perpetuating affair. Interlinking and interacting *qaraba* networks form a vast, personalised web throughout the Saudi socioeconomic structure from the highest levels of the élite down, to construct an all-encompassing politico–socioeconomic system.

Natural aids to Najdi economic ascent were not merely regional affiliations but also the socially fractured nature of the new state, which served to reinforce regional identity. Even after the (united) Kingdom of Saudi Arabia was proclaimed in 1932, it is wrong to refer without qualification to a 'Saudi society' in the historical context, as Kostiner (1990: 226; 1993: 183; cf. Salamé, 1989: 80) does, implying a greater level of homogeneity than actually existed. Differences between the *muwahhidun* and other Sunni *madhhabs*, as well as those of the Shiites, between Hijazis and Najdis and those from the south and the east, between the urban centres and rural districts, between nomads and farmers, and between the traditional and the 'modern', are factors that contributed to a society that even today is not as homogeneous as is generally believed.[23] The Hijazis and other significant non-Najdi elements of the Saudi state were, in the

[23] Even highly placed Saudis cautiously acknowledge the 'well-known fact that the Kingdom was composed of quite different areas as regards population conditions [and] local circumstances...' (al-Awaji, 1989: 50). Despite the use of the term 'Saudi society' to refer to an entity that existed in name only, Kostiner, in dealing comprehensively with the politics of Saudi state formation in the early- and mid-1930s, does make it clear that significant regional differences—and

first instance, conquered peoples and, as the new state consolidated itself, coerced and co-opted peoples.

One example of this heterogeneity is the deep religious divide between the roughly 90% of the population who are Sunni and the minority Shiite population, concentrated in the oil-rich Eastern Province (formerly al-Hasa); smaller Shiite communities live in Asir and the Hijaz. As with the Sunnis, who in Saudi Arabia are predominantly Hanbali but among whom may be found followers of the other *madhhabs*, so the Shiite population is also subdivided.[24] Of the Shiite population of Saudi Arabia, David E. Long (1991: 11) has written: 'the Shias have never been fully integrated into the political, economic or social life of the country.' In fact, there has been a long history of Saudi and *muwahhidi* prejudice against, and persecution of the Shiites, and the Shiite population has, in turn, been a significant source of political and civil disturbance (see below, Chapter 5). Madawi al-Rasheed (1998: 125–6) has discussed the discourse of the Saudi Shiite political opposition in which the concept of *asabiyya* is employed to explain the establishment of the Saudi state and the nature of Najdi 'cultural, political and religious domination' of that state. The economic dimension of Al Saud–Najdi *asabiyya* flowed naturally from the establishment of this domination, an interpretation of the Saudi political economy reinforced by Patricia Springborg's definition of *asabiyya* as 'the will to power… [a constituent of] the formula for cultural hegemony' (Springborg, 1992: 272).

---

reluctance to accept Saudi rule on the part of recalcitrant Najdi tribes even after the defeat of the Ikhwan—were a major hurdle in Ibn Saud's attempts to forge a modern state (see Kostiner, 1990: 238; 1993: 163, 173–7, 184). A less than homogeneous society still confronts the Saudi state. While it continues to hinder the growth of a sense of national unity, it is utilised by the regime to promote the fragmentation of an already divided political opposition (issues treated in Chapter 5).

[24] The exact size of the Shiite population is unknown, but has been variously estimated at 7–20% of the total Saudi population. The US State Department (2000: section 2.c) has put the Shiite population at 'roughly 500,000 of nearly 14 million citizens'. Most predominant are the followers of the twelfth imam (Eastern Province), with Ismailis (seventh imam: Asir and Hijaz) and Zaidis (fifth imam: Asir) also represented.

Asabiyya capitalism institutionalised.[25] What occurred during the restructuring of the Saudi political economy during the boom period was, at root, a demonstration of the state's role in the socioeconomic sphere and revealed the links between Al Saud power and socioeconomic development and change:

> ...class stratification in distributive states is likely to be an exclusive function of state spending patterns; in this extreme form of corporatism, the state not only reorganizes or promotes, encourages or disbands, existing occupational groups but actually *creates* entire sectors... oil revenues...empower the state to create new social groups from whole cloth. (Chaudhry, 1997: 26, author's emphasis.)

The 'extreme corporatism' of the Saudi state clearly has the power to include and exclude individuals, families, clans and 'entire sectors' of society, in a way that has become a fact of life in Saudi Arabia but is nevertheless in accordance with a flexible system of *asabiyya* capitalism. This power is just one aspect of the patron–client relationship of the regime and the citizenry. The use of largesse within a patrimonial, kinship-oriented society is, of course, by no means a novel concept in Arabia. However, these characteristics took on increasingly grander proportions in the Saudi sociopolitical–economic system during the oil boom era as the national economy integrated, developed and became wealthier, resulting in the entrenchment of the *modus operandi* variously characterised as favouritism, cronyism, nepotism and corruption.

---

[25] Some sensitive issues are broached in this discussion, and it is appropriate to draw attention at this point to the fact that exclusive, patron–client business practices and informal political–business relations are by no means a purely Saudi phenomenon. Nor by treating issues which may be classified as an analysis of 'corruption' in Saudi Arabia is it meant to imply that corruption is not a serious problem elsewhere, including in 'democratic' and 'developed' Western states and institutions (see, for example, Transparency International, 2002). The difference is that socially-sanctioned favouritism and exclusive business practices have found institutionalised form in the kingdom. For a pessimistic overview of 'corruption' in the Arab world in general, see Jabbra (1989: 4–5). For an extensive treatise that focuses on the economic cost of corruption globally and which argues that reform of the state is a necessary element in the complex remedy for corruption, see Tanzi (1998).

Although accounts of 'corrupt' political–business practices abound, many of these are rhetorical in nature. Chaudhry, however, documents well a number of early cases of favouritism; but these, she argues, were isolated, and tend to highlight the measures put in place, especially from the early 1930s to the late 1950s, to prevent corruption and profiteering by members of the royal family and the bureaucracy. Corruption, she maintains, 'was severely punished in all recorded instances', and even princes were targeted—by Prince (later King) Faisal—in a royal ordinance of 1934–5.[26] Faisal also enacted a law in 1956 which prohibited, with severe penalties, private business engagements on the part of public servants and princes. These early attempts by the infant government to regulate potentially corrupt practices were motivated by the pragmatism of income maximisation; the emerging, pre-boom state could ill afford to lose too much of its national revenue to corruption, a situation that changed with the oil boom (see Chaudhry, 1997: 61n. 32, 62, 62n. 41, 87–8, 88n. 106, 93n. 120, 94n. 125).

Despite the discouragement of outright corruption motivated by fiscal austerity in the pre-boom period, corruption was apparently regarded as a separate phenomenon from officially sanctioned favouritism. Of this latter practice during the formative years of state institutions there is firm evidence. An illustration of the practice of royal favouritism in the period of relatively low tolerance of corruption, and a harbinger of what would become the norm during the 1970s, was the 'large favour' bestowed on the Riyad Bank in 1967 by granting it the management of government accounts. The bank, a concern mainly run by four prominent Najdis with tribal pedigrees, won at the expense of the National Commercial Bank (NCB) which was owned by Jeddans of Yemeni extraction, despite its being the lesser institution of the two (Chaudhry, 1997: 94n. 125).

The line between favouritism and blatant acts of corruption during the pre-boom period may have been a fine one, but it also appears to have been clear. After the boom, however, it became distinctly blurred. This shift was symbolised by the official repeal in 1976 of the 1956 law which criminalised partnerships between state officials and private business (see Chaudhry, 1997: 88, 88n. 106,

---

[26] Critics might say that 'all recorded instances' are key words in this argument.

162, 162n. 65). Najdi *asabiyya* capitalism was already well entrenched by the mid-1970s, but from 1976 conditions were ripe for its unchecked spread, and indeed for its informal institutionalisation. Quoting the results of a survey conducted on the eve of the boom era, Chaudhry (1997: 171) records the attitudes of senior Saudi—that is, principally Najdi—bureaucrats as follows, and comes to inevitable conclusions:

...72 per cent of the respondents said that they thought favoring a relative or a clansman was a 'social duty', and 26 per cent openly admitted seeing employment in the civil service as an opportunity to combine public and private interests. After 1975, when the prohibition on civil servants' participation in private business was lifted, bureaucrats openly engaged in partnerships with the private sector. State contracts, subsidies, and development programs quickly created a business class that mirrored the social background of the upper cadres of the bureaucracy. Merchants, entrepreneurs, and businessmen who maintained strong personal, economic, family, or tribal ties with state functionaries prospered.

Furthermore, a later study of the Riyadh-based Saudi bureaucracy, published in 1985, confirmed the 'centrality' of favouritism to the operations of the bureaucracy: a widespread general practice not confined to the upper echelons of society, favoritism had indeed become the norm. Despite acknowledging the fact that not all civil servants were in a position to indulge in favouritism, the study found that 23% of the senior bureaucrats surveyed thought that 'virtually all of their subordinates were in the business of granting special favors', and a further 30% indicated that 'a majority of their subordinates granted preferential treatment to friends and relatives' (al-Hegelan and Palmer, 1985: 64). Not just civil servants were prone to indulging in favouritism; the granting of *wasta* was expected from the Saudi public (al-Hegelan and Palmer, 1985: 63). According to Abdelrahman al-Hegelan and Monte Palmer (1985: 65), the practice is 'socially acceptable if not desirable'. They claim that respondents to their survey 'indicated that the process of favoritism was present in the fabric of Saudi society'. Shirley Kay (1982: 181) also confirms these views: '...traditional values have come through into the modern state in Saudi Arabia: a man's first loyalty is to his family, then his tribe, then his country. Nepotism is a virtue and it would shame a man to refuse to help or give a job to a close relative'. Osama (1987: 59) argues that '[a]dministration is a cultural and social product which reflects the values of society as a whole'—a fact which he claims helps explain the 'weak performance of government agencies [in the oil producing countries of the Arabian peninsula] in spite of their adoption of models of administration copied from those in advanced countries.'

Ultimately, the results of such all-pervasive favouritism had a debilitating effect on the efficiency of the bureaucracy, creating client–bureaucracy friction, the reluctance to delegate authority on the part of supervisors and to accept authority on the part of employees, as well as the institution of practices such as the requirement for multiple signatures and an over-centralised control in general (al-Hegelan and Palmer, 1985: 55–65). A more recent indication of the problems of Saudi bureaucratic efficiency was seen in early 2000 when Crown Prince Abdullah personally ordered measures be taken to improve the performance of government agencies (*Saudi Gazette*, 2000). Osama (1987: 21) mentions tribalism when addressing the issue: 'long-held tribal traditions [constrain]' the functionality of the state through 'the problems of wasting time, disdaining manual work, favouritism and partiality, and the distribution of wealth and other rewards according to ascribed social status rather than achievement.'

These broadly defined social attitudes also feature among the explanations offered for a general lack of innovation and efficiency in the Saudi bureaucracy, which in turn impacts negatively on national economic development (Palmer *et al.*, 1989: 12–13, 20ff.; al-Hegelan and Palmer, 1985; Osama, 1987: 21). Significantly, the empirical research conducted by Palmer *et al.* reveals that senior Saudi bureaucrats themselves regard cultural disposition as relevant to low bureaucratic innovation: 86.2% of the respondents in their survey thought that various explanations for low innovation listed in the category 'culture' were either 'very important' or 'important' (Palmer *et al.*, 1989: 23, t. 3). Respondents who rated cultural factors as the most important explanation for low bureaucratic performance made up 13.9% (Palmer *et al.*, 1989: 23, t. 4).[27] The contentious role

---

[27] One of the authors of this article, Abdelrahman al-Hegelan, was a senior Saudi bureaucrat in the Ministry of Finance when it was published.

of 'culture' in Saudi socioeconomic functioning is treated further below.

From a position of political and bureaucratic strength within the Saudi state, the step to the institution of *asabiyya* capitalism on the part of the Najdi-dominated élites was a short one. Informal business–political relations and exclusive business practices flourished. With the influx of massive oil revenues the political and bureaucratic–business élites of Saudi Arabia grew very wealthy, and by means which many, including Saudi citizens, would not always regard as legitimate. Abir implies that the very creation of an entire, Najdi-dominated state–business élite provided a basis for the ubiquity of unethical practices, albeit along the lines of the traditional allegiances of family, clan and region. He provides a concise overview of the process of wealth accumulation on the part of those who shared in the system of Najdi *asabiyya* capitalism:

Widespread corruption in the Saudi government was nourished by the numerous multi-billion defence, infrastructure and other development contracts. The kingdom's spending spree and commission system at every level of economic activity enriched many Saudis, particularly senior members of the Saudi ruling class and their 'constituencies' as well as Saudis related to the technocratic upper-crust…members of the royal family… amassed [fortunes] through parasitical involvement (fictitious partnerships) in the country's trade and other economic activities… [and] bribes offered by foreign contractors [were] freely accepted by their associates and members of the royal family. The patronage and commission systems were in fact major means by which the regime channelled wealth to the ruling class and the new elites and through them to all levels of the middle class. (Abir, 1993: 73; see also Beblawi, 1987: 386–8)

Greater social context is provided by Fandy (1999: 30): '…what can be conceived of as "corruption" and nepotism in a discourse where meritocracy and legalism are the dominant criteria can be construed as another form of wealth distribution in a qaraba-centred discourse…'. However, he immediately qualifies this statement: 'This is not to condone corruption; rather, I merely seek to explain how money and power are allocated within the Saudi system.' The 'system' to which Fandy refers is that of *asabiyya* capitalism, the organic roots of which are further emphasised: 'Ending this system of the allocation of values on the basis of qaraba means ending political and economic participation, as most Saudis know it' (Fandy, 1999: 31).

Within the élite, members of the wider royal family—the core of the Najdi aristocratic class—found a new source of sociopolitical power as beneficiaries of, and through ongoing participation in the Saudi economy that was generated by the oil boom:

…economic strength and political power within the royal family have become increasingly closely interlinked, a modern counterpart to the political strength and tribal allegiances of the past, with princes wielding influence by manipulation of their economic interests in the form of financial capital and employment, rather than by control over numbers of fighting men. (Birks and Sinclair, 1982: 206)

Palmer, Alghofaily and Alnimir (1984: 19) write that '[p]olitical leaders have become the preeminent economic decision makers in the rentier state. It is their values, far more than the marketplace, that dictate economic policy.' And Jahangir Amuzegar (1999: 96–7) states that '…the al-Saud ruling family had a monopoly on high public offices and exerted unparalleled influence over all major economic decisions through business partnerships and blood relations with the local business community.' Unsurprisingly, therefore, favouritism and informal and exclusive business–political relations, provide another link between the economic and the political spheres of Al Saud rule, and for the purposes of this study, more specifically between Saudi economic management/mismanagement on the one hand, and political liability on the other. Several serious instances of political protest have already occurred in the kingdom in which complaints against royal and regime corruption have figured.

An example of the links between bureaucratic inefficiency, favouritism, acts of corruption and socioeconomic manipulation can be seen in the way the Saudi Real Estate Development Fund (REDF) managed its affairs from the mid-1970s to the mid-1980s. The REDF was supposed to provide access to oil-boom wealth to a broad base of Saudi citizenry through interest-free loans to facilitate the purchase of private housing. Chaudhry's research here, as in most other aspects of her history of the Saudi political economy, is meticulous. She is in no doubt that the REDF's priority was the distribution of funds, in accordance with the task assigned to it by the emerging distributive state. This took precedence over the planning of how such distribution was to be accomplished; thus approximately US$12,000 million was 'injected...into the construction sector without ever codifying its lending priorities and procedures'. The results included: 'massive misallocation to wealthy applicants who... were using loans to finance commercial building projects'; '[m]ultiple loans to families for the same project'; the preparation of annual reports 'based on information that was fragmentary and at least partially fabricated'; and the 'disappearance' of 'large tranches of cash', including 'an unexplained discrepancy' of approximately US$2,274 million for the period 1975–84 which was revealed by careful analysis of the REDF's own, dubious, reports. Strong criticisms of this state lending institution made by the World Bank in 1978 included the observation that 'political considerations' would prevent a much needed, thorough reorganisation of the REDF. The report was ignored, unbridled abuses continued, and the results were 'catastrophic' for the Saudi real estate sector (see Chaudhry, 1997: 237–8).

A similar example is that of the Saudi Industrial Development Fund (SIDF) which was charged with the distribution of interest-free loans to promote the development of the industrial sector. Although beginning well, with contracted management from Chase Manhattan of New York, the performance of the SDIF declined markedly in 1977 when Saudi management took over the reins. At this point, project assessment ceased and the SDIF began lending to 'inexperienced, aspiring industrialists with strong political and kinship connections to the political and bureaucratic leadership'. By 1986, it was estimated by the Riyadh Chamber of Commerce that more than 35% of SDIF-funded projects were in default (see Chaudhry, 1997: 238–41). Yet another example of unethical links between government and private business interests in the banking and finance industry is provided by the 1999 finding against Abd al-Ra'uf Khalil, a former Saudi government official, in the Bank of Credit and Commerce International (BCCI) scandal. Khalil was ordered to pay US$1,100 million to BCCI liquidators after a US judge found that he had received millions of dollars in return for posing as a nominee in BCCI's secret acquisition of the First

American Bank in 1982, and that he had also allowed his name to be used by BCCI to conceal enormous losses, and helped divert more than US$250 million from BCCI into a brokerage he partly owned. Another Saudi, Ghaith Pharaon, had already been found guilty of fraud in the case. BCCI collapsed in 1991, leaving 100,000 creditors owed more than US$10,000 million 'after a massive fraud' (Cave, 1999).

These three examples are not atypical cases. According to many sources with intimate personal experience of the mechanisms of the Saudi bureaucratic–business networks, favouritism and 'corruption' have been described as 'glaring' (Australian diplomat 1, 1995, pers. comm., 14 July[28]). In a report echoing the disappearance of the funds managed by the REDF, this diplomatic source also revealed that shortfalls of up to US$17,000 million were known to have occurred between calculated oil revenues and what should have reached the central coffers during the oil boom (see also Sick, 1997: 21). The same source also quoted the opinion of a US oil and gas economist that 'what we [in Western business] would call corruption is endemic' (Australian diplomat 1 1995, pers. comm., 14 July). A well-placed private industry source was of the view that 'corruption is legal' in Saudi Arabia (Business consultant, 1996, pers. comm., 1 May; see also Byman and Green, 1999a: 19–22), while two former chairmen of the Arabian American Oil Company (Aramco), both of whom had lived in the kingdom 'for decades', are on record as saying that 'corruption has been accepted and unquestioned' (Taubman, 1980).

These sources thus support Chaudhry's findings on the, albeit loose, institutionalisation of what in Western establishments would be regarded as overt corruption, as do claims that '[c]orruption is built into Saudi Arabia's five-year economic plans', whereby 'huge [and] unnecessary construction projects' are incorporated into development strategies in order to 'generate corrupt payments' in the form of commissions on contracts (see Taubman, 1980). It is interesting to note at this point that a number of IMF papers dedicated to issues of global corruption have identified 'highly discretionary' state capital projects as a major conduit for the misuse of state funds for personal gain (*IMF Survey*, 1997d: 375; see also *IMF*

[28] This diplomat served in Saudi Arabia for four years in the 1990s.

Survey, 1997a; *IMF Survey*, 1998; Tanzi, 1998: 568, 576). The IMF has found that enlarging the size and complexity of projects or the construction of 'cathedrals in the desert' in the interests of commission farming on the part of those involved in planning and approval processes is not uncommon worldwide, 'especially when the controlling or auditing institutions are not well developed and institutional controls are weak'. Moreover, '[i]n the extreme case of a totally corrupt country, the productivity of the projects becomes almost irrelevant' (*IMF Survey*, 1997d: 375–6).

Accounts of the construction of expensive white elephants in Saudi Arabia are numerous—one such example being a state-of-the-art opera theatre built in Riyadh in the late 1970s to early 1980s which 'has never been used' even though it cost 'a fortune' to build (Senior Australian diplomat, 1999, pers. comm., Feb.–Mar.). Commission farming is the most likely explanation for this project although it is possible, but not probable, that second thoughts about the impact of opera on conservative *muwahhidi* sensibilities was behind the royal order banning its use. It is nevertheless true that the very idea of opera performances in the *muwahhidi* heartland where, even in the late 1990s, a cinema could not be found, remains absurd.[29] At the very least, this particular case represents the almost total lack of coherent planning—and accompanying waste—which has

---

[29] An Australian diplomat serving in Saudi Arabia who was personally taken to see the opera theatre believes that Crown Prince Abdullah was behind the order to ban the theatre's use in the interests of conservative religious political support (Senior Australian diplomat, 1999, pers. comm., Feb.–Mar.). Narrating a conversation with a 'wealthy merchant', Kay (1982: 175–6) cites the case of weekly flights abroad to seek the 'cultural activities' which were non-existent in Saudi Arabia; when asked why he himself made no effort 'to introduce theatre, cinema or concerts to Saudi Arabia', the 'immediate reply was that the people were not ready for it'. It is interesting to note, however, that a special 'opera' was commissioned for the 1999 centenary celebrations. Entitled *The Knights of Tawhid*, the dramatic performance extolled the feats and piety of Ibn Saud as it told the story of the conquest of Riyadh and the 'unification' of the kingdom according to Islamic principals. The 'libretto' was in classical Arabic poetic form and, complete with laser lighting, digital sound effects and a cast of hundreds, it was performed at the opening ceremony of the annual National Guard event, the Janadriyya cultural festival (pers. observ. 1999, Janadriyya, 23 Jan.). The opera was written by Badr bin Abd al-Muhsin bin Abd al-Aziz, a grandson of Ibn Saud and a prominent poet, and founder of the Saudi Arts Society.

characterised the Saudi development process since the oil boom. Hegelan and Palmer (1985: 49) not only write of 'inordinate waste' and 'mismanagement', but imply that the Saudi government was well aware of this state of affairs even by the mid-1980s (see also Palmer, Alghofaily and Alnimir, 1984: 20). Considered opinion on this subject appears to be almost unanimous across the decades: 'Easy money…reduced financial discipline within the bureaucracy, and allowed careless budgetary allocation, waste, unsavoury practices and widespread corruption' (Amuzegar, 1999: 217).

The incidence of favouritism, *wasta* and acts of corruption in the kingdom has frequently drawn the attention of observers of Saudi Arabia writing from a standpoint which is not always dispassionate and has occasionally received lavish and sometimes lurid publicity in the media. Geoff Simons (1998: 26–31) writes of the 'culture of corruption' and presents a general but highly coloured account of Al Saud transgressions and misuse of ill-gotten personal wealth. To infer that corruption in Saudi Arabia stems from the culture is contentious.[30] Whilst philosophising on whether greed, vanity and other forms of 'corruption' are part of human nature rather than a reflection of any particular culture is not a concern here, it is nevertheless relevant to note that the manifestation of favouritism in Saudi Arabia, which forms an important basis for many corrupt practices, does stem largely from traditional attitudes which promote kinship allegiances. This should not come as a surprise, since the kingdom is a developing nation and traditional attitudes still have great currency in Saudi society.

Thus, the indigenous social conditions underlying the formation of personalised business networks—here summed up as the *asabiyya* heritage—were a natural part of Saudi society before they, just as naturally, were extended to and became entrenched in the new state institutions (see, for example, Beblawi, 1987: 386–9). Moreover,

---

[30] While Simons links corruption and culture in a negative sense, Peter Iseman (quoted in Taubman, 1980) approaches the issue in a more conciliatory way, as does Kay (1982): 'That the morals are different from ours can lead foreigners to accuse [Saudis] of hypocrisy or immorality. A state handling billions of dollars with growing sophistication must, we feel, be corrupt if it does not run on our lines… Bribery is a widely accepted way of obtaining contracts and spreading wealth; it does not cause the same moral agonising that it does in the West' (Kay, 1982: 181). See *The Economist* (1999a) for an attack on this argument.

there is no question that the primacy of the family in life is possibly the most cherished of traditional Saudi values: in the unambiguous terms of Fandy (1999: 24), '…the discourse of 'a'iliyya [familialism] permeates the Saudi public discourse… suggesting a continuity in the patriarchal, familial organization of society.' Hegelan and Palmer (1985: 65) also reflect on 'the fact that Saudi society is very much a family oriented society in which few values other than religion take precedence over family loyalty' (see also Kay, 1982: 176, 181). This obviously has its positive aspects as well as negative manifestations.[31]

A specific form of dubious business practice which has received particular attention is commission harvesting by members of the royal house and other Saudi élites acting as agents and middlemen, especially in negotiating and awarding lucrative arms and construction contracts. Dilip Hiro (1993: 9), addressing the period of King Fahd's reign, writes of 'a scandalous rise in corruption', claiming that kickbacks as high as 30% of the value of construction and armaments contracts were not uncommon. One of the more notorious Saudi arms deals was, and still is, the 1986 Al-Yamamah contract and the associated later contracts with Britain. The commercial significance of the oil-for-arms Al-Yamamah deal—worth approximately US$28,173 million (Norton-Taylor and Pallister, 1999)—was later to spill over into Saudi sociopolitics and to play an important role in Saudi–British relations with respect to UK-based Saudi dissidents (see Chapter 5).[32] In other sectors, contractors paid up to

---

[31] See the preceding chapter, 'Tribalism, *asabiyya* and the contemporary Saudi state'. Saïd Aburish (1995: 69) refers to the '…obsolete family/tribal ways in which the House of Saud continues to govern…'. Aburish's entire book, as its title implies (*The Rise, Corruption and Coming Fall of the House of Saud*), revolves around Al Saud 'corruption', whether real or alleged. Both Aburish and Simons are, in fact, examples of the rhetorically assertive writing on Saudi Arabia referred to above.

[32] A good, remarkably dispassionate account of Al-Yamamah as a case example of how the unofficial Saudi commission system operates was provided by the Committee Against Corruption in Saudi Arabia (CACSA, 1999a; also 2002b) on a well-presented Internet site. CACSA, a US-based dissident organisation, ran their site for several years to mid-1999; from late 1999 to late 2002, however, the site appeared to be inaccessible. Dissident accusations over Al-Yamamah do not appear to be unfounded (see, for example, Kelsey and Koenig, 1994a; Norton-Taylor and Pallister, 1999). On the international arms trade and commissions globally, IMF staffer, Vito Tanzi (1998: 563), reported that '[s]ome experts have

40% of the value of the contract to Saudi 'commission entrepreneurs' (Chaudhry, 1997: 154. See also Islami and Kavoussi, 1984: 79–81; Abir, 1993: 117–18.)

In 1977 a 'Tender Law' was passed, which represented an attempt on the part of Prince Fahd, then the Crown Prince under King Khalid, to (*a*) limit commissions to 5%, and (*b*) limit agent representation to no more than ten foreign companies. Both measures can be interpreted as an attempt to minimise the destabilising effects of prevailing, excessive commission practices by institutionalising the sharing of the commission pie more equally among the middle classes; however, these limits are believed to be regularly flouted (see Abir, 1993: 73; Chaudhry, 1997: 154, 161; Taubman, 1980; *Wall Street Journal*, 1981). An earlier attempt—at least on face value—to short-circuit the commission system with regard to arms-related purchases was made when the Saudi Council of Ministers, under the direction of the Minister of Defence and Aviation, Prince Sultan, declared unlawful the payment of commissions to agents and brokers for arms and defence equipment (Resolution no. 1275, 15 Sept. 1975. See Lerrick and Mian, 1982: 102–3). However, within three months of this resolution, Crown Prince Fahd stated publicly that there was 'no objection' to Saudi agents being appointed on behalf of arms manufacturers 'in the fields of maintenance, services, and construction' (Fahd bin Abd al-Aziz, interview in *Al-Anwar*, 28 Nov., 1975, cited in Lerrick and Mian, 1982: 103, 103n. 30). In general, 'certain ambiguities do exist with respect to the scope of the prohibitions' (Lerrick and Mian, 1982: 104).[33]

The ultimate victim of excessive commission practices is, as one Saudi protest organisation points out, the general Saudi population (CACSA, 1999a); and the CDLR refers to 'the business culture of commissions' which they claim adds up to 25% to the country's import bills (CDLR, 1995a: 45). The drain on national wealth can be appreciated when the mechanism of commission harvesting is outlined. Put simply, a contract may be awarded to a company

---

estimated that as much as 15 percent of the total money spent for weapons acquisition may be "commissions" that fill somebody's pockets.'

[33] On the official Saudi system of agency, see Lerrick and Mian (1982: 94–139) and, for a more concise outline, Presley (1984: 143–4).

which has made the best personal contacts and which co-operates by inflating its quotation to incorporate the cost of 'commissions'; these can sometimes run to many millions of dollars and represent a system of 'thinly veiled bribes' which lends legitimacy to the counter-claim that the foreign companies involved are equal partners in the process (see Eigen, 1998; Taubman, 1980; CDLR, 1995a: 43; see also *The Economist*, 1999a). The *Wall Street Journal* (1981), for example, highlights the role of American companies' complicity in commission payments, and quotes a Saudi's response to accusations of 'corruption': 'If there's a corruption problem in Saudi Arabia, it's because [Western traders] taught us how' (see also Kelsey and Koenig, 1994b, 1994a).[34] However, as demonstrated here and in other studies of the kingdom, purely indigenous forms of corrupt behaviour and extreme socioeconomic biases born of favouritism and the *wasta* mechanism flourished in the boom period, including—besides commission farming—profiteering by way of land speculation, inequitable land distribution, dubiously administered loan and subsidy schemes, and fiascos in the agricultural sector (see Taubman, 1980; Chaudhry, 1997: 172–85).[35] The trading of inside government information obviously facilitates these practices among the broader élite.

The burden on national resources is accentuated even further when the cost of projects that are actually unnecessary—such as unusable opera theatres—are also taken into account. In these cases, it is not only the extra cost to the state's treasury of commission payments that depletes the coffers, but the entire cost of the project. Even where contract bids have not been excessively inflated to pay for sometimes extremely high commission rates, the most competitive bid for a contract may not be successful because the right contacts and agents were engaged by a competitor, a state of affairs that

[34] Despite the alleged association with arms commissions of some significant Western names, such as that of Mark Thatcher (see Kelsey and Koenig, 1994a), it should be noted that governments and private companies involved in dubious commission practices are not only Western ones. For example, Ignatius (1981b) provides details of an oil-buying scandal involving commissions which precipitated 'a brief coup against the Thai government', and Taubman (1980) specifically refers to corruption concerning the South Korean Hyundai construction company.

[35] These issues are taken up again in more detail in the following chapter.

has been officially recognised by the (powerless) Saudi Council of Ministers in a 1975 communiqué:

[t]he Government has noticed recently that the costs of execution of its projects has been increasing continuously and exceeding all reasonable limits... A number of brokers have given some companies the impression that they can obtain work for them in the Kingdom, using the broker's personal influence, in spite of the high prices quoted by these companies. (Quoted in Lerrick and Mian, 1982: 103–4.)[36]

Saudi political opposition movements in exile, which are quite open in their accusations, routinely charge the royal family and other regime authorities of corruption and of squandering the wealth of the nation. The objections of opposition factions, especially the overtly Islamic opposition, target not only the regime's privileged access to national wealth, but also the way wealth is used by the ruling class as a whole and by prominent individuals in particular. (These issues are dealt with further in Chapters 4 and 5.)

Further socioeconomic change: urbanisation and new class structures. The Najdiisation of the state and the development of a Najdi *asabiyya* political economy were not the only results of the oil-boom transformation of the Saudi state. In fact, if there is one single physical development above others that has contributed to the changing face of Saudi society, it is the phenomenally rapid and profound urbanisation of the population in the latter half of the twentieth century. Indirectly fostered by the regime's early agenda of sedentarising tribes to aid the state-building process, urbanisation was also encouraged by the processes involved in the construction of a national economy, especially the hectic development and modernisation which followed the oil boom and which virtually dictated greater migration to, and centralisation around the rapidly expanding major

---

[36] Some reasonably well documented cases of the commission mechanism are available. Besides the sources cited previously on the Saudi–British Al-Yamamah arms contracts see, for example, the *New York Times* (1980) and Ignatius (1981a, 1981b) for relatively detailed accounts of commission payments and other dubious practices involving strategic business liaisons between foreign companies and governments on the one hand, and (often senior) Saudi princes on the other. The cases cited involve the telecommunications and oil industries.

cities (see al-Awaji, 1989: 56, 58; Kay, 1982: 172–5). The tremendous rate of urbanisation can be measured by the fact that in 1960 only 30% of the Saudi population lived in cities (Islami and Kavoussi, 1984: 45); by 1980, 66% was urbanised, and by 1997 this figure had climbed to 84%, which is also significantly higher than world averages (World Bank, 1999: 193). At the same time, the nomadic population has dropped from being the majority of the kingdom's population earlier last century, to between 5% and 25% of the population by 1993 (see Kostiner, 1990: 243; Abir, 1993: xvi; also Kay, 1982: 172–4, 183nn. 7, 9; Birks and Sinclair, 1982: 200).

Along with education, urbanisation has been a major contributing factor to changing class structures in the kingdom, particularly through the development of an urban lower class and the establishment of a middle class (Islami and Kavoussi, 1984: 44–56; Abir, 1993: 72–3). These aspects of modernity represent the beginnings of a significant social transformation in a relatively short period of time, especially considering the much-vaunted 'classless' nature of traditional society in Arabia out of which the new classes are forming.[37] Western concepts of 'class' have only become relevant to a study of Saudi Arabia since the extensive implementation of oil-boom development and modernisation programmes, and new class structures do not yet have deep roots in the society. On the other hand, Saudi society is still very hierarchical and is traditionally based on tribal, family and personal honour: '…"modernizing"—that is,

---

[37] See Abir (1993: 3) for a brief treatment of the 'classless' nature of the regions of Arabia that were to become 'Saudi' Arabia, and contrast this with Kay's account of the impact of the oil boom in the 1970s: 'class divisions and social snobbery are becoming more apparent as wealth is shown in possessions' (Kay, 1982: 175). A distinguished British diplomat who served in Saudi Arabia commented that conspicuous consumption in the kingdom was typical of 'the temptation of the newly rich', which he found 'deplorable' but understandable (Former British ambassador to Saudi Arabia, 1998, pers. comm., 26 May). However, Fandy (1999: 246–7) points out that those who benefited most from Al Saud boom-time largesse were 'those who were already prominent before the oil boom. The newly rich families are thus not exactly "nouveau riche", the money has gone to the oldest and most reputable families and tribes.' By Fandy's account, 'newly rich' equates with the acquisition of great wealth by already prestigious families. Thus, 'conspicuous consumption' in the early years of boom-time wealth was most likely a reflection of a sense of established social superiority. (See Chapter 2, note 6, for a concise account of the bases of Saudi social hierarchy.)

"Westernizing"—wealth, has not led to the Westernization of social structures and values' (Fandy: 1999: 246–7).[38]

The recent formation of a middle class is, however, an important development. This fledgling class has recently been described as 'growing', and forms one of the principal bases of the expanding Saudi financial sector (SAMBA, 1998g: 12). The role it has had in the development of national life—other than in the economic sphere—has been limited, except for the significant part that the Najdi entrepreneurial class has played in consolidating a Najdi-dominated *asabiyya* capitalism in the wake of the oil boom. William Rugh (1973: 17), in an analysis which remains valid today, wrote: 'Saudis with a secular education have broken less new ground in the social sphere than they have in the economic. Traditional factors such as kinship and religion still are very important in Saudi social behavior...'.[39] Rugh's major criterion for inclusion in 'the New Middle Class' is a 'secular education', but he also points to the existence of 'a distinct non-secular group in the middle class' (Rugh, 1973: 7ff., 11). This should hardly surprise; more surprising would be if, even after a quarter-century of rapid development, anything more than a very small percentage of the new middle class were absolutely secular. Spokesmen for two major Saudi political opposition groups, who are themselves from the new Saudi middle classes and are unapologetically Islamist, claim that the social orientation of the middle classes remains distinctly Islamic (al-Masari, M., 1995, pers. comm., 3 July; al-Fagih, S., 1998, pers. comm., 20 May; see also Rugh, 1973: 19).

Abir (1993: 186) admits that the 'liberal' middle class is a 'minority', whilst at the same time placing much importance on its role in Saudi sociopolitics. Abir (1988: 8; 1993: 3, 29, 70–1) gives only a passing glance at the ascent of Najdis; compared with Chaudhry's, his treatment of the 'new middle class elites' and of 'the technocratic

---

[38] This social hierarchy is still important today with regard to labour, workforce and employment issues (see Chapter 4).

[39] This point emphasises the fact that state development in Saudi Arabia has outstripped societal adjustment to the pace of modernisation. It is also important in analysing the development and nature of political opposition to the regime and the roots this opposition has in Saudi traditions and socioeconomics. See, for example, Article 2 of the mission statement of the liberal, US-based CACSA, quoted in Chapter 5, for deference to Saudi traditions and Islam.

upper-crust' is superficial, his definition of these new classes hazy, and the importance he attaches to them in Saudi sociopolitics is, with hindsight, over-emphasised. However, like Rugh, Abir's explanation for the rise of this class appears to depend largely on modern education, as opposed to Chaudhry's more detailed and convincing emphasis on the dynamics of the rapidly transforming Saudi political economy that came with the birth of the distributive state (see Abir, 1988: 34–59; 1993: 15–23). The importance of education in contemporary Saudi socioeconomics, however, should not be underestimated, and indeed it is an important key to the success of future economic restructuring and the sociopolitical stability of the kingdom—a fact of which the regime is well aware.

The sociopolitics of education in the Saudi oil state. Saudi Arabia's wealth in oil resources has provided the means for broader economic and national infrastructure development. This has, in turn, necessitated, and fuelled a natural desire for improvements in education. The development of the nation's human resources has been undertaken with enthusiasm by successive Saudi administrations, and '[t]he record since the early 1970s has been rather impressive' (Islami and Kavoussi, 1984: 46; see also Mutabbakani, 1993: 41–6). In a list of 'astonishing achievements', Saleh Mutabbakani reveals that during the 1950s, only three secondary schools existed in the country and that the entire student population was less than 54,000, whereas from 1970 to 1992 total student enrolments at all levels of education rose from 547,000 to 2.9 million. The breakdown of the figures for this period shows an increase from 397,000 to 1.9 million children receiving primary education, from 77,000 to 550,000 students receiving intermediate and secondary education, and 'an amazing thirty-eight times surge' in higher education from 7,000 students in 1970 to 268,000 in 1992 (Mutabbakani, 1993: 41–2).

In spite of these impressive statistics, however, there is still much room for development. The Fifth Development Plan, for the years 1990 to 1995, projected figures by level of education for Saudi nationals who were expected to enter the Saudi labour force during this period, and they are revealing (Ministry of Planning, ?1989: 127, t. 6.5). While 12% of new entrants were expected to go into the labour force with university training, 25.8% would do so with secondary schooling, 10.5% would have completed intermediate school, 22.1% would look for work with only elementary school behind them, and 15.7% would do so with not even elementary schooling (see Table 3.2, which also gives estimates of total numbers of expected labour force entrants, with figures for males and females. Diagram 3.1 illustrates the Saudi education system). Without indicating how accurate these estimates proved to be (no analysis of previous performance is offered in the five-year plans), the Sixth Development Plan for the 1995–2000 period set forth improved projections, reflecting the expectation that better-educated Saudis across the board would flow into the labour market (see Table 3.3). Even so, '[e]stimates indicate that 27.9 percent of new labor market entrants during the Sixth Plan period will be dropouts from elementary level and adult vocational training programs' (Ministry of Planning, ?1994: 171).

Reservations as to the quality of Saudi education are commonplace and sometimes severe: Osama (1987: 127–52), for example, delivers a stinging condemnation of Arab, Gulf and, especially, Saudi education systems and their sociopolitical underpinnings. Abir (1988: 39–40, 45, 48) likewise draws attention to the poor quality of Saudi education.[40] The persistence of high illiteracy rates continues to present basic obstacles both the state and individual Saudis have to overcome before meaningful nation-wide development can be claimed to be firmly on track. While world illiteracy averages have been listed at 38% and 21% for females and males respectively, 50% of adult Saudi females were judged to be illiterate in 1995, compared with (a still high) 29% of the adult male population (World Bank, 1999: 193; see also Hardy, 1992: 30, 30n. 86). Despite these and other doubts over the structure and quality of the Saudi education system, the role of this accelerating educational process in creating a new class of Saudi citizen should be acknowledged. Indeed, while Abir (1988: 34–59; 1993: 15–23) places much emphasis on the

---

[40] See also Lacey (1981: 176) for aspects of Saudi tradition which highlight differences between the Saudi and Western approaches to education. In fact, the Saudi Ministry of Planning has outlined 'a number of key issues [in the education sector] for which remedial measures are needed' (see Ministry of Planning, ?1994: 268, 270, 273–6, 283). The performance of a majority of Saudi academics during the Centennial Conference in Riyadh, 24–8 January 1999 was mediocre at best, and was notable for a general lack of adherence to accepted academic practices (pers. observ. 1999, Riyadh, 25–8 Jan.).

Diagram 3.1

FLOW CHART OF EDUCATION AND TRAINING

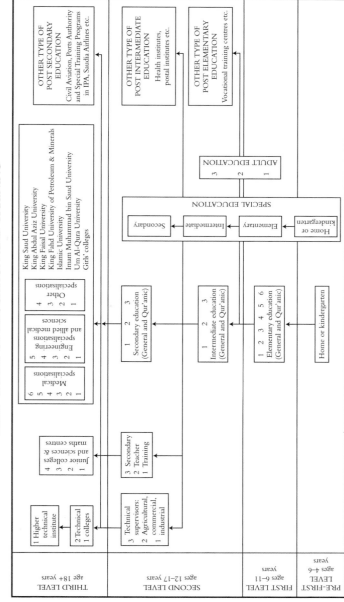

Table 3.2

NEW ENTRANTS TO THE LABOUR FORCE BY LEVEL OF EDUCATION

(estimates, 1990–95)

Highest level of education completed	Male	Female	Total	%
		New entrants to the labour force		
University (total)	38,300	30,300	68,600	12.0
Engineering	4,700	0	4,700	0.8
Natural sciences	4,100	4,700	8,800	1.5
Medical sciences & health	2,300	1,000	3,300	0.6
Statistics, mathematics and computer sciences	3,000	2,100	5,100	0.9
Economics & Business	3,700	1,600	5,300	0.9
Social sciences	8,600	10,400	19,000	3.3
Teacher education	5,400	5,200	10,600	1.9
Religious studies	6,500	5,300	11,800	2.1
Junior colleges: technical (total)	7,400	0	7,400	1.3
Industrial	5,700	0	5,700	1.0
Commercial	1,700	0	1,700	0.3
Secondary school★ (total)	139,500	9,000	148,500	25.8
General education	103,100	7,500	110,600	19.2
Technical & Vocational	36,400	1,500	37,900	6.6
Intermediate school★ (total)	56,700	3,800	60,500	10.5
Elementary school★ (total)	114,800	12,200	127,000	22.1
Less than elementary (total)	85,500	4,900	90,400	15.7
Pre-service adult vocational training (total)	72,400	0	72,400	12.6
Total	514,600	60,200	574,800	100.0

Source: Kingdom of Saudi Arabia Fifth Development Plan (Ministry of Planning, ?1989: 127)

★ Includes students who withdrew without completing the next level of education or training program.

Table 3.3
NEW ENTRANTS TO THE LABOUR FORCE BY LEVEL OF EDUCATION
(estimates, 1995–2000)

Highest level of education completed	New entrants to the labour force			
	Male	*Female*	*Total*	*%*
University★ (total)	73,800	40,900	114,700	17.4
Engineering	10,100	0	10,100	1.5
Natural sciences	10,000	5,500	15,500	2.4
Medical sciences and health	5,500	2,600	8,100	1.2
Commerce, mathematics and computer sciences	12,700	4,100	16,800	2.6
Agriculture, zoology and nutrition sciences	2,600	700	3,300	0.5
Social sciences and Islamic studies	24,900	23,500	48,400	7.3
Teacher training	8,000	4,500	12,500	1.9
Technical Colleges (total)	12,800	0	12,800	1.9
Secondary School★ (total)	209,600	11,500	221,100	33.5
General education	172,000	8,900	180,900	27.4
Technical and vocational	37,600	2,600	40,200	6.1
Intermediate school★ (total)	119,800	7,800	127,600	19.3
Elementary school★ (total)	66,200	13,800	80,000	12.1
Less than elementary (total)	62,400	4,700	67,100	10.2
Pre-service adult vocational training (total)	36,600	0	36,600	5.6
Total	581,200	78,700	659,900	100.0

Source: Kingdom of Saudi Arabia Sixth Development Plan (Ministry of Planning, ?1994: 179).
★ Includes students who withdrew without completing the next level of education or training program.

correlation between 'modern education and the rise of new elites', the effects of educational development were predicted in the early 1980s:

> As a result of the growth of higher education, a new professional middle class is emerging in Saudi Arabia, which is likely to become quite powerful both in its numerical strength, and its control over the economy. This class is likely to demand participation in economic and political decision making. However...this class is still very small and is not likely to become an important social force until the 1990s. (Islami and Kavoussi, 1984: 48; see also Rugh, 1973: 20)

More importantly, Abir (1988: 40–1) adds to Chaudhry's account of the rise of the Najdi bureaucratic élite by drawing attention to unequal opportunities in the developing Saudi education system of the 1960s and 1970s.[41] This was a system of subsidies of limited or unequal availability and uneven quality which favoured the middle, upper and ruling classes and the urban population in general. Najdis and Hijazis were thus the main beneficiaries. But the role of education in the 'new' Saudi distributive state was also a conservative one: the *muwahhidi* religious establishment of the state, which had traditionally been a powerful influence in Saudi education but which had lost ground under King Faisal, began regaining that ground from 1978 under the influence of Crown Prince Fahd (see Abir, 1988: 20–48). Abir (ibid., 41) maintains that Fahd 'was well aware of the ulama's contribution through indoctrination to the regime's stability and also needed their support in the power struggle within the ruling class.'

A relatively higher political profile during the 1990 Gulf Crisis reminded the regime that an educated middle class might entertain aspirations to greater political participation. In the aftermath of the 1991 Gulf War renewed pressure began to be applied to this new middle class in an attempt to neutralise it, in effect, a stopgap measure taken in light of the less than complete success of the education system to produce citizens who would not think and act in political terms. The 'younger Saudi generation'—i.e. the beneficiaries of Saudi educational development over the last 30 years—'it is hoped,

---

[41] Rugh (1973: 12–13, 17) also points out the usefulness of 'the old asset of family background' when coupled with the value of a modern education.

will use their acquired education for the good of their society and country' (Mutabbakani, 1993: 43). How 'the good of their society and country' is interpreted by this up-and-coming generation, however, may differ from the version preferred by the established political élite.[42] Al Saud expectations as regards education and the sociopolitical role of the newly educated were enshrined in the 1992 Basic Law of Government (Chapter 3, 'The constituents of Saudi society', Article 13): 'Education aims at the inculcation of the Islamic creed in the young generation and the development of their knowledge and skills so that they may become useful members of society who love their homeland and take pride in its history.' This statement is immediately preceded by: 'The State shall foster national unity and preclude all that may lead to disunity, mischief and division' (Basic Law of Government, 1992: Article 12).

Of course, the homeland that young, educated Saudis are asked to love is the Arabian kingdom of the Al Saud, and the history in which they are expected to take pride is the history forged by the Al Saud's struggle to create their kingdom[43]—a kingdom in which young Saudi citizens must recognise their place as subjects and clients of their royal patrons. An example of one of the goals of the Saudi education system was seen at the January 1999 Riyadh Centennial Conference, which was an exercise in regime endorsement seeking academic respectability (pers. observ. 1999, Riyadh, 24–28 Jan.). The censorship of papers well in advance of the conference not only raised serious questions as to the sincerity of Saudi efforts to introduce a rigorous, inquiring and independent academic tradition in the kingdom, but suggested that education, like economic policy, is subordinated to political imperatives.[44]

---

[42] The role of this new class in albeit muted calls for reform at the time of the 1990–1 Gulf Crisis, is explored in more detail in Chapter 5.

[43] The links between Saudi education and the Al Saud interpretation of history were amply demonstrated in the centenary celebrations of 1999, which marked 100 years by the Islamic lunar calendar of Ibn Saud's recapture of Riyadh in 1902, an event whose celebration as the founding of the state of Saudi Arabia may well be questioned. Rather, it marked the re-establishment of Saudi rule over the district around Riyadh, and the beginning of the conquest of territory that would lead to the proclamation of the modern kingdom in 1932 (see Chapter 2).

[44] My own paper on Saudi aid to Bosnia was censored, albeit insignificantly. However, the experience left me in no doubt that any paper which took criticism

Therefore, it should come as no surprise that the emphasis in modern, non-religious Saudi education is on basic, technical and scientific knowledge, where the achievements of both the state and of students are also politically safe. A good example of the incursion of political imperatives into education policy was provided during the reign of King Saud when, in 1955, studies abroad were curtailed and students were recalled, and when '[p]olitical science and other "dangerous" fields of study were banned' (Bligh, 1984: 80–1). However, no form of modern education can be completely safe for the ruling élite. Scientific and technical education are very relevant to the kingdom's economic development, but have in the past also been areas of under-achievement—and in any case, two leading Saudi dissidents are men of science: Saad al-Fagih, a surgeon, and Muhammad al-Masari, a physicist. As will be discussed in the following chapter, a significant component of the next phase of Saudi socioeconomic change is renewed emphasis on the restructuring of the education system to serve the goal of Saudiising the workforce and relieving the problem of youth unemployment.

---

beyond the accepted Saudi norm of offering advice on how to do a good thing better, would not have been accepted for inclusion in the conference. I was originally asked to submit my paper more than 12 months in advance of the conference (al-Rubiyya, M.A. 1997, pers. comm., 8 Nov. [17/7/1418H]). Conference topics and themes were also defined in advance—prospective participants could choose from among 18 subjects concerning Saudi Arabia (al-Dawood, N., 1997, pers. comm., 29 July [1/4/1418H]): 'The foundation of the Saudi state'; 'The late King Abdul Aziz'; 'The unification and construction of Saudi Arabia during the reign of King Abdul Aziz'; 'The continuation of the construction of Saudi Arabia after the late King Abdul Aziz' (that is, the 'life, personality and method of government and administration' of one of the three subsequent kings, Saud, Faisal or Khalid); 'Saudi Arabia under the Custodian of the Two Holy Mosques: King Fahd'—that is, either (*a*) 'life, personality and method of government and administration', or (*b*) 'major achievements in his reign'; 'Development of the Saudi systems of government'; 'The development of the governmental institutions'; 'Education'; 'Scientific research and its institutions'; 'Social development'; 'Intellectual and cultural activities'; 'The economy and the infrastructure'; 'Health care services'; 'Security and defense'; 'The private sector and its role in development'; 'The religious status of the Kingdom'; 'The Kingdom's achievements in the service of Islam and the Muslims'; 'Saudi international relations'.

Early warning signs

The cumulative stresses associated with rapid modernisation and development mounted as the 1970s progressed. The Al Saud–Najdi domination of the kingdom's politics and economy, the virtual institutionalisation of a Najdi *asabiyya* capitalism, and bureaucratic inefficiency and wastage, have led both to the employment of state resources in the legitimacy of largesse and to the significant squandering of those resources. These developments occurred in conjunction with the transformation of the society by rapid urbanisation, an unprecedented expansion of education and the formation of new social classes, momentous changes which did not come without some sociopolitical cost to the Saudi regime.

The potential exists for state wastage, favouritism and exclusive business–political relations to precipitate political disquiet, especially when these issues are combined with religiously fuelled dissatisfaction over the Islamic credentials of the regime and of individual royals. Opposition elements are well aware of the relation between the Al Saud's political and religious legitimacy, which is constantly emphasised and reinforced by the Al Saud themselves. Vigilance is required on the part of the regime to maintain the credibility of these links, domestically and internationally, because the nexus between the political and the religious is a vital one for Saudi claims to the right to rule. Any points of weakness caused by inappropriate personal behaviour or the inadequate fulfilment of their religious responsibilities as the custodians of the Islamic heartland, present the opposition with potentially powerful ammunition in their campaigns against Al Saud rule.

An example of Al Saud vulnerability to attack on their conduct of religious affairs came in 1994 when the CDLR produced a 16-page report on the regime's management of the the annual *hajj*, compiled in the aftermath of the stampede which claimed, officially, 270 lives (CDLR, 1994a).[45] From the outset, the report refers to Saudi 'mismanagement, lack of professionalism, favouritism and indifference', and then presses claims of 'patronage', 'individualistic interests', 'red tape', 'commissions', 'bribes' and 'blackmail' (see CDLR, 1994a: 2, 8–9, 12).[46] Irrespective of the CDLR's own uncertain religiopolitical

---

[45] The CDLR (1994a: 2) claim that more than 2,000 pilgrims died.

[46] Blackmail allegedly results after 'many *mutawwifin* [*hajj* brokers] fail to accommodate their pilgrims': in Mecca, after having already paid for their *hajj* packages,

orientation, the report was a blow directed at the heart of the Al Saud's religiopolitical legitimacy, although its effect was not quite as profound as the dissidents had hoped. Saad al-Fagih, the founder of the CDLR offshoot organisation, the Movement for Islamic Reform in Arabia (MIRA), who prepared the report for the CDLR, has stated with hindsight that, '[t]he report was embarrassing to the regime at its time but the regime was more concerned with the "annual" disasters than with the report. There [have] been some improvements in Hajj preparations but there [has been] no strategic change in administration' (al-Fagih, S., 1999, pers. comm., 25 May).

Criticism of *hajj* management spilled into the mainstream Western media after the Mina fire of April 1997 which officially killed 343 pilgrims.[47] The following quote from the *Daily Telegraph*'s diplomatic editor, Christopher Lockwood (*Electronic Telegraph*, 1997), is

---

the pilgrims are then asked for more money to rectify the situation (CDLR, 1994a: 12). In the meantime, pilgrims are forced to sleep 'in the main roads, on the bridges or inside the tunnels', a 'phenomenon' that is becoming increasingly more prevalent (CDLR, 1994a: 9, 12). The political opposition blames the Saudi government for this situation, since they claim that favouritism within the *mutawwifin* allows unethical practices to occur, and that unethical practices in the overall management of the holy precinct degrades the entire pilgrimage experience both physically and religiously. Evidence of unethical practices on the part of *hajj* agents was provided in March 2000 when Saudi authorities cancelled the licences of seven agents for 'major violations against the rights of pilgrims' and suspended the licences of another 25. Of a total of 415 agents, complaints against 60 were reported (al-Tuwaim and al-Amri, 2000).

[47] Unofficial and dissident sources maintain the death toll, mostly among South Asian pilgrims, was between 2,000 (Syed, 1997a) and at least 4,000 (Muhammad, 1997; CDLR, 1997). The latter claim from the leader of the London-based Islamist movement, Al-Muhajiroun, purports to be supported by the Saudi Health Ministry—no doubt the 'insider sources' associated with the CDLR (see CDLR, 1997), given the links that developed between Al-Muhajiroun and the CDLR in 1996–7. In light of wind speeds of 36–40 km. per hour (*Al-Qimam*, 1997b) and temperatures of around 42 degrees Centigrade (Amayreh, 1997), the fact that approximately 70,000 tents were destroyed in the fire (Amayreh, 1997; CDLR, 1997; Lockwood, 1997; Syed, 1997a) suggests a figure of only 343 dead would be a mercifully low toll. Official Saudi sources, without actually giving a number for the tents destroyed, proudly claimed that 63,635 replacement tents were quickly erected for the affected pilgrims (*Al-Qimam*, 1997a).

an example of the kind of reporting that will not help Al Saud religiopolitical public relations:

> Among the titles of King Fahd, Saudi Arabia's absolute ruler, none is more important than that of Custodian of the Two Holy Mosques. It is at once his greatest claim to legitimacy and, potentially, his greatest liability. With grim regularity, people have died by the hundred during the hajj.
>
> The deaths of so many people this year, and the injuries sustained by up to 2,000 more, come as a severe embarrassment to the government.[48]

Perhaps even more damaging was the suggestion by a Jedda-based Indian diplomat that most of the victims could have been saved if Saudi authorities had taken timely and appropriate action (Amayreh, 1997). In a corroborating article citing 'US and Saudi intelligence sources', the claim has been made that the pilgrims were actually locked into the huge tent compound by a fence erected and guarded by Saudi security personnel and were unable to escape (Syed, 1997b). Quoting 'a prominent Arab observer'—a 'more moderate' source— Lockwood (1997) reveals that the prevailing feeling about *hajj* management is not optimistic:

> This fire is not the first and it will not be the last… The problem is not so much the money—[the Saudis] have spent plenty of money. The problem is that the regime will not trust people from outside to run things in Mecca. All the people involved are Saudi security people and they are simply not up to it.
>
> … This reflects on their claim to be suitable as custodians. ('Arab observer', quoted in Lockwood, 1997)[49]

---

[48] It should be emphasised, however, that organising an event of such massive proportions as the annual *hajj*, and managing it through to completion without incident is no small task. Any government in Saudi Arabia—indeed, any government anywhere in the world which had to cater for an event of similar magnitude—would be hard-pressed to manage the *hajj* without incident year in, year out. In fact, events of much lesser magnitude and significance in the Western world, football games in particular, have likewise claimed a disproportionately high number of lives 'with grim regularity' (for details of many sports disasters, see Nando.net, 1995).

[49] The other sources quoted by Lockwood were the Al-Muhajiroun leader, Omar Bakri Muhammad, and the CDLR's Muhammad al-Masari.

The CDLR issued a communiqué on the tragedy and, in characteristically rhetorical style, commented on the issue of the undoubtedly vast amounts of money spent on *hajj* sites.[50] Most of this money, according to the CDLR (1997), went to 'commissions…palaces, royal hospitality and secret services', the 'meagre remainder' being 'mis-managed' and spent 'without vision'. Syed (1997b) has quoted 'a Saudi intelligence source' as saying the *hajj* priorities of Saudi officials are catering for 'VIPs and political security'.[51]

Independent reports on earlier tragedies establish a history of questionable management of the most important international Muslim event. For example, during the 1990 *hajj* stampede in which 1,426 pilgrims were officially confirmed as having been killed, researchers who compiled a country study of Saudi Arabia for the US Library of Congress concluded that the new pedestrian tunnel where pilgrims died was 'overcrowded and inadequately ventilated' (Library of Congress, 1992).

However, not all has been catastrophe and condemnation, and the following account describes some of the more positive aspects of the Saudi conduct of the *hajj*, despite the 1997 catastrophe:

…the tragic Mina blaze aside, the Hajj season went generally smoothly, with the Saudi authorities offering nearly excellent services to the pilgrims. State-of-the-art services and accommodations ranged from air-conditioned marble pavement to computerized billboards featuring prayer times and were everywhere at and around the two spacious Grand Mosques in Mecca and Medina. Cold water was available round-the-clock through

[50] For an indication of the sums expended on expanding and upgrading facilities in and around Mecca, see Ministry of Information (1998: 59–65; 1993a: 35–109). Saudi sources present a figure of more than US$636.26 million which has been spent over 'the last few years' prior to 1998, and a figure of more than US$1,546 million for work completed in the 1980s (Ministry of Information, 1998: 59–65). Without specifying a time frame, the CDLR (1997) quote Saudi claims of 'US$19 billion [spent] on expanding and upgrading Hajj facilities to ensure the comfort and safety of the pilgrims'.

[51] See also CDLR (1994a: 9, 11–12). See al-Awaji (1989: 50) for an account of the historical preoccupation with 'security affairs' on the part of the Saudi authorities. For an example of the public relations weight given to the king and crown prince in 'receiving congratulations from prominent [international] Islamic personalities' at the *eid* for the 1992 *hajj* season, see Ministry of Information (1993a: 5, 7).

ubiquitous fountains at the two sanctuaries. Furthermore, there was no shortage of food throughout the pilgrimage term... (Amayreh, 1997)[52]

Indicative of the importance given to their role as hosts of the holy places is the 1993 Ministry of Information publication, *At the Service of Allah's Guests*. The 176-page booklet is both a *hajj* guide for pilgrims and a government public relations effort reinforcing Saudi religiopolitical legitimacy. Chapter 5, 'Services of the Custodian of the Two Holy Mosques' Government [*sic*]', in particular, highlights the latter purpose. A short appendix addressing safety issues (Ministry of Information, 1993a: 173–4) reads: 'Most of the tragic individual incidents during the Hajj seasons are due to negligence, misuse of tools and failure to benefit from planned arrangements.'[53] It is interesting to note that of 14 points addressed in this appendix, six concern fire safety. After a fatal stampede in 1998, a Saudi journalist was quoted as saying that 'pilgrims frequently overlooked or ignored safety instructions' (*Electronic Telegraph*, 1998), which bolsters the regime's claim that accidents are due to pilgrims' transgressions of safety regulations, despite the meticulous care of the authorities. Nevertheless, after the loss of another 118 lives in the 1998 stampede, the regime was no doubt relieved, and not entirely for altruistic reasons, that there were no major incidents during the 1999 and 2000 *hajj* seasons.

Islam, traditional values and development. The propaganda battle over the competence of *hajj* management is just one of the fronts on which the Al Saud are striving to maintain their status as legitimate

---

[52] See also *Al-Qimam* (1997a, 1997b) for the official Saudi account of events concerning the Mina fire tragedy and a general portrayal of commendable *hajj* management.

[53] On every point the regime makes, however, there is a counter-claim by the opposition: Masari (quoted in Lockwood, 1997) implies that the incidence of disasters is linked to the authorities' treating pilgrims 'like cattle', which directly challenges official claims that pilgrims are treated with consideration and respect, and that disasters are effectively the fault of the pilgrims themselves—or are the result of 'fate and divine will' (CDLR, 1994a: 14; see also CDLR, 1997). The privileged treatment of VIPs, and the 'patronizing [of] pilgrims'—as in the *At the Service of Allah's Guests* booklet—are also condemned as un-Islamic, and the suggestion is made that disasters occur even more frequently than is known but are covered up (CDLR, 1994a: 14).

religiopolitical rulers of the bulk of the Arabian peninsula. The noted Saudi poet and long-serving former ambassador to the United Kingdom, Ghazi al-Gosaibi, as long ago as 1977 when he was Minister for Industry and Electricity, publicly lamented 'the emergence of a consumer society whose material requirements are endless'. He went on to state that '[s]piritual restraint...becomes imperative...[W]e should go back to the purity of our faith and abide by its principles' (Gosaibi, quoted in Islami and Kavoussi, 1984: 56[54]). These are interesting comments from a man noted as a 'Western-educated [technocrat]...the doyen of the Saudi intelligentsia' and as an opponent of the contemporary religious opposition to the Saudi regime (Abir, 1993: 71, 80, 118, 180). It once again demonstrates the role Islam plays in the lives of the majority of Saudi citizens and the central place it has in society through the melding of religious and traditional values.

Even in the realm of state administration, bureaucrats responsible for the vast development projects of the last quarter century have acted as agents of conservatism and have provided yet another link in the chain that binds Saudi society, politics, religion and tradition. For Palmer *et al.* (1989: 26), this is not difficult to explain: besides a relatively low exposure to Western influences compared with other regions of the Middle East, Saudi Arabia is, '[p]olitically...the protector of Islam. Traditional values must be preserved. To do otherwise would be heresy. Senior Saudi administrators clearly see their role as one of preserving traditional values.' The result of this socio-religious orientation is that '[c]hange is not perceived as an unmitigated good. Social continuity rivals the desire for modernity and change' (Palmer *et al.*, 1989: 21).

Yet, despite the conservative environment, socioeconomic change during the boom period has been rapid and sweeping, and Western influence has been making inroads into Saudi society. However, these changes have not occurred without some difficulty and even occasional tragedy on the road of development and modernisation. The introduction of television during the 1960s is a good, if notorious, example. In 1965 Prince Khalid bin Musaid bin Abd al-Aziz—

---

[54] The technically correct transliteration of Gosaibi's name, as employed by Islami and Kavoussi, is *Qusaibi*. Gosaibi is the name by which he is widely known in the West. He served as ambassador to the UK from 1992 to 2002.

a grandson of Ibn Saud and nephew of the reigning king, Faisal—led a 'puritanical protest' against King Faisal's modernisation programme, with the new television transmitter on the edge of Riyadh as the main target. The prince was killed and, a decade later, his brother, Faisal bin Musaid, assassinated King Faisal; this second son of Prince Musaid was then of course executed (see Dekmejian, 1985: 140, 1994: 628; Bligh, 1985: 41–2; Piscatori, 1983: 66; Lacey, 1981: 369–71).

This violent 'neo-Ikhwan' opposition to television echoed similar, earlier misgivings over radio in the 1920s and 1930s when, believing virtually all innovations to be evil, the ulama opposed its introduction.[55] For a further illustration of the hyper-conservative nature of the most extreme followers of *muwahhidi* Islam during this period, see Helms (1981: 252–3): 'Even the bicycle was viewed as the "vehicle of the Devil"'—*bida* and dangerous.

Although the dominant *muwahhidi* milieu of the kingdom did not augur well for a smooth development process from the very first, juxtaposing traditionalism and modernism before the influx of significant oil revenues from 1947, according to Niblock, is 'inappropriate':

> While the commercial sector constituted the principal instrument through which Saudi Arabia was increasingly drawn into the economy of the capitalist world and the principal channel through which outside ideas penetrated the country (until the oil sector assumed these roles), the commercial sector was itself dependent on and given encouragement by the 'traditional' framework which surrounded it. (Niblock, 1982: 95)

Conflict between the cautious new order being implemented by the Al Saud on the one hand, and the representatives of the traditional status quo—most notably the Ikhwan and the ulama—on the other, was clearly discernible before 1947. However, the extreme stresses of modernisation are only a very recent phenomenon and are directly linked to the development of the country's oil resources. Since the oil boom especially, scholars have emphasised the 'contradictions

---

[55] The legendary persuasive powers of Ibn Saud on this issue came to the fore: he had recitations of the Quran transmitted to prove the virtuous potential of such technology (see, for example, Bligh, 1985: 40; Holden and Johns, 1981: 103; Lacey, 1981: 369).

emanating from the clash between modernity and tradition' (Kechichian, 1986: 66) and, indeed, Al Saud rulers, Faisal in particular, appear to have been very aware that development policies would antagonise the population. Accordingly, they have employed the strategies of religious justification and, occasionally, of moderating adjustments to development programmes accompanied by a toning down of the pro-development rhetoric. On the eve of his formal ascent to the throne, Crown Prince Abdullah is now doing exactly the same, thereby maintaining the conservative face of rule in addition to signalling that the kingdom has entered another new era, that of economic restructuring and globalisation, topics dealt with in the following chapter.

King Faisal, who in fact initiated 'a semi-revolutionary program of modernization' (Kechichian, 1986: 60), provides a good historical example of the strategy of religious justification for change. He openly linked Islam and development—or 'progress'—endorsing the latter in language designed to sway the conservative adherents of the former:

Our religion… requires us to progress and advance and to bear the burden of the highest tradition and best manners. What is called progressiveness in the world today, and what reformers are calling for, be it social, human or economic progress is all embodied in the Islamic religion and laws.

We are going ahead with extensive planning, guided by our Islamic laws and belief, for the progress of the nation… We have chosen an economic system based on free enterprise because it is our conviction that it fits perfectly with our Islamic laws and suits our country… (Bin Abd al-Aziz al-Saud, (King) Faisal, n.d.)

It should be emphasised that 'semi-revolutionary' in the ultra-conservative environment of Saudi Arabia of the late 1950s to the early 1970s does not have the same connotation as it has in the developed world. 'Semi-revolutionary' modernisation projects in the Najd, for example, include the opening of classrooms for women which in 1963 necessitated the use of the National Guard to control demonstrations in Buraida against such an innovation (see Lacey, 1981: 363–4; Parssinen, 1980: 159). It is the relative nature of 'semi-revolutionary' in the Saudi context that leads others to describe Faisal as a 'gradualist' in his general approach to modernisation and, specifically in relation to reform for women, his programmes 'can hardly be termed revolutionary [yet] the departures from the established cultural norm were nevertheless radical within the context of dominant customary attitudes' (Parssinen, 1980: 153–4).

Faisal, therefore, may not have sought 'major sociocultural change' (Kostiner, 1990: 241), but change inevitably accompanied the development process, despite its relatively measured pace at this stage.[56] The major social and cultural—and political—forces needing balancing were recognised by observers in the 1970s: '[t]he pace of rapid development, once embarked on, cannot be readily checked. How to carry it through without sacrificing the essential values of their own society is seen as one of their major problems by those who rule Saudi Arabia' (Kay, 1982: 182). Michel Nehme (1994: 641) has raised the dilemma that still troubles Saudi rulers today, in the era of globalisation, as it did in the oil boom era of the 1970s and 1980s:

...the societal and cultural values of Saudi society before the implementation of the development plans, were basically those of a tribal community with a static traditional mode of production. That raises the following question: how is the Saudi ruling class going to maintain all their previous values in a society that is changing so rapidly on the road to modernization?

Nehme (1994: 632) has also outlined the strategy of successive Saudi monarchs in the oil era: 'Realizing that the society was divided between two major elements, the conservatives and the modernizers,

---

[56] Lacey (1981: 363–8) presents a delightfully personal and accessible narrative of King Faisal's struggle to reform female education—that is, to introduce it—in the face of *muwahhidi* conservatism. In the process, Lacey (1981: 368) reveals the king's own attitude to the broad issue of conflict between tradition and modernisation: 'Faisal denied the then modish assumption that if you want to modernize a country you must forcibly destroy its past', and thought that, instead, '[t]radition...should be made the ally of development, not its victim.' And quoting Faisal: 'We want to go forward on solid ground...not find ourselves in a quicksand.' My own experience with Saudi citizens leads me to conclude that Faisal's words still speak for the majority of the population, a conclusion supported by recent statements from Crown Prince Abdullah which echo Faisal's. There is, however, a question mark hanging over the youth of the kingdom and how committed they might be to traditional values in the era of globalisation—an issue treated in Chapter 5.

the Saudi government decided to please both by giving the latter what they wanted, modernization, in the name of what the former valued most, Islam.' Such a reconciliation was, and is, no easy task, since change 'was considered as a threat to the community' (Nehme, 1994: 632). The result has not necessarily been a good one for the royal family: it has produced a state that is 'an anachronism in political terms in the Twentieth Century...a breeder of rampant materialism while it bears the cloak of asceticism' (Lackner, 1978: 216). The path that has led to this sociopolitical condition has been replete with contradictions, paradoxes and extremes, and has at times been difficult to sustain.

The struggle the regime has undergone to maintain its poise and a working relationship between its religiopolitical legitimacy, societal traditions and a profound national development programme, has occasionally been revealed in outbreaks of hostility against the kingdom's rulers. These outbreaks, some of which have been of the most extraordinary kind and have shaken the regime to its foundations, did not materialise out of nowhere; on the contrary, they further demonstrate that beneath the usually calm surface of Saudi society there is a very real stratum of considerable discontent. Recent evidence of this state of affairs includes the major bombings in 1995 in Riyadh and 1996 in Khobar—and probably a series of smaller-scale bombings in 2001–2. But these more contemporary examples of turbulence were not without an even more dramatic precedent, namely the 1979 siege of the Great Mosque in Mecca.

The 1979 siege of the Great Mosque of Mecca.[57]   Political ineptness, waste, extravagance and other excesses characterised the reign of King Saud bin Abd al-Aziz, who followed his father to the throne in 1953. Within Saudi Arabia, it was a period of struggling consolidation and change for the still–infant state; throughout the Arab world, nationalist pride was riding the crest of Nasserism. These factors combined to create an unsettled sociopolitical environment which has been described by more than one scholar as 'simmering

---

[57] The reader will not need reminding that religious extremism and tragedy also occur in the Western world; for example, the siege of the Branch Davidian compound at Waco, Texas, from 29 February to 19 April 1993 which left 86 cult members and four US law enforcement personnel dead.

unrest' discernible 'just below the surface' (see, for example, Holden and Johns, 1981: 183; Lackner, 1978: 97). Exasperation at the growing incompetence and decay of morality in the court resulted in a power struggle within the royal family and, finally, in the deposing of Saud, who was replaced by Faisal in 1964.[58] Faisal's reputed wisdom and competence, and his personal integrity and piety settled the situation at court and within the kingdom, and his programme of incremental but steady national development was implemented. This, of course, led to the clashes with ultra-conservative traditional and religious values outlined above.

For King Faisal personally, the final clash with the opponents of his projects and style of rule came on 25 March 1975 with his assassination. His gradual but firm approach to modernisation died with him. The regime's development programme was then accelerated in the late 1970s under the aegis of King Khalid or, more precisely, Crown Prince Fahd, who virtually ruled by proxy. Even so, already '[b]y the end of 1975, Saudi social structure was remarkably changed' (Nehme, 1994: 636): it was a society beginning to reflect 'the unprecedented strains of rapid development' (Piscatori, 1983: 64). Focusing on the unique religious orientation of the kingdom, John Esposito (1991: 112) emphasises that, '[f]or many, rapid modernization undermined Saudi Arabia's Islamic way of life'. Others used even more dramatic terms: 'dislocations caused by change', a 'sense of societal disintegration', '[i]deological disorientation', the rending of the 'socioideological fabric of the kingdom' (Kostiner, 1990: 243–4, 247), and 'the ideological and social cleavages in a society increasingly suffering from the culture shock of haphazard and rapid modernization' (Dekmejian, 1985: 137) are typical of the expressions used to describe the effects of rapid modernisation in the late 1970s.

A dissenting view of the Saudi developmental process is offered by Riad Ajami (1987: 130): 'Political stability in Saudi Arabia has been unusually high for a country undergoing rapid industrialization

---

[58] For a good account of this period, sociopolitical unrest and court intrigues, see Abir (1993: 27–50), Bligh (1984: 43–83), Lackner (1978: 59–64, 89–100), Holden and Johns (1981: 176–201). A concise account is presented by Henderson (1994: 8–12). Lacey (1981: 299–357) covers the era of Saud in his characteristically personal but sensitive style.

and modernization.' However, Ajami immediately adds the following qualification: 'Yet, stability is easily maintained during a period of unprecedented budgetary surplus.' Regardless of the overall pattern of political stability and state largesse in the era of plenty, the strains of development were about to show in the violence that erupted six years into the oil boom period.

On 20 November 1979, heavily armed opponents of the Saudi regime seized control of the Great Mosque of Mecca as 50,000-odd people were celebrating the Islamic new year, the turn of the century 1399–1400 in the Muslim calendar, at the conclusion of the *hajj*.[59] The insurgents demanded that the ulama withdraw their support from the Saudi royal family in what Nazih Ayubi (1982–83: 274) has described as 'social criticism of, and political protest against, what they regarded as the false and opportunistic utilization of Islam to hide corruption, decadence, and oppression, as well as subservience to the "foreigner".' In pamphlets and 'letters' produced in the years of activity before open insurgency, the elderly Shaikh Abd al-Aziz bin Baz, then head of the Council of Senior Ulama and a former teacher of the rebel leader, Juhaiman al-Utaibi, was singled out for criticism. The establishment ulama as a collective were also attacked for accepting payments from the regime and for using Islam to support the 'treacherous' rule of the Al Saud. Even the legitimacy of Ibn Saud himself and the foundations of the modern state he had forged were attacked (Kechichian, 1986: 58–65, 1990: 12–15; Buchan, 1981: 515, 518).

During the siege itself, five demands—a 'summary' of al-Utaibi's 'political message' (Kechichian, 1990: 12)—were broadcast over the mosque's public address system:[60]

1. The adoption of socio-cultural values which are based on just Islamic values rather than corrupt Western emulations, and the breaking of diplomatic relations with Western states which are exploitative in nature.

---

[59] The rebels numbered 'about two hundred' according to Piscatori (1983: 66), 'three to five hundred' according to Ayubi (1982–83: 274).

[60] From *Intifadat al-Haram 1400H–1979* (The Sacred Uprising), (London, 1981), reproduced in Kechichian (1990: 12). The bracketed comment in point 3 is Kechichian's.

2. The overthrow of the 'treacherous' Al Saud monarchy and the establishment of a just Islamic government, as well as full accountability of the Al Saud's wealth, stolen from the Saudi people.
3. The declaration that King Khalid and his co-rulers [read the ulama and the ruling family] who governed with divine guidance, are unjust and sinful because they encouraged foreign exploitation of the country.
4. The end of petroleum exports to the United States because of its rejection of Islam and of Muslims; the national wealth should not be squandered and petroleum exports should be limited only to meet the country's economic needs.
5. The expulsion of all foreign civilian and military experts who are dominating the Arabian Peninsula.

After a bloody siege of nearly two weeks, Saudi security forces recaptured the mosque.[61] Juhaiman and 62 other surviving insurgents—41 Saudis and 22 Arabs of other nationalities—were subsequently publicly beheaded in eight different cities throughout the kingdom. It goes without saying that the incident was a damaging embarrassment and public relations disaster for the Al Saud. Writing of these consequences, Joseph Kechichian (1986: 58) states that the siege 'was not just an incident…but a blow to the prestige of the House of Sa'ud'. David Holden and Richard Johns (1981: 530) write that 'damage to the credibility of the super-tribe [Al Saud] in terms of its competence to provide stability was difficult to calculate, but it was not negligible.' A 'senior American intelligence official' (quoted in Taubman, 1980) maintains that the siege 'jolted' the royal family and led to a 'crackdown on corruption'.

The rebellion highlighted concern over modernisation, Western influences and issues relating to the decay of socioreligious values. How deep these feelings ran in Saudi society was difficult to determine, just as it is today. What is certain, however, is that these feelings do exist and that, from time to time, they come to the surface in unpredictable and often startling eruptions such as the 1996 Khobar bombing. In this respect, it is instructive to read that there

---

[61] For evidence suggesting Saudi forces had the vital assistance of élite French units, see Kechichian (1986: 69n. 21) and Paul (1980: 3–4 and notes).

was, and still is, 'widespread feeling that the attackers of the Great Mosque erred in their choice of target but that they expressed valid objection to the decline of public morality' (Piscatori, 1983: 70); this opinion is, for example, held by Saad al-Fagih, a leading dissident of the post-Gulf War Saudi political opposition (see Fandy, 1999: 154).

Dekmejian writes that while the neo-Ikhwan movement that culminated in the seizure of the Great Mosque drew support from both urban and tribal groups, 'many Saudis considered seizure of the Sanctuary as a doctrinally illegitimate act and a tactically foolhardy move.' Factors thought to have contributed to the rebels' 'alienat[ion from] the broad spectrum of mainstream Saudi Islamists' include an element of 'tribal puritanism', and 'the Ikhwan's messianic ideology' (see Dekmejian, 1994: 628). At this point, the tribal factor in the siege should be highlighted: the rebels' leader, as his name indicates, was a member of the Utaiba tribe—one of the powerful Ikhwan tribes which revolted in 1927 and were crushed by Ibn Saud.[62] Ikhwan messianism was evident in the fact that Juhaiman's rebellion presented a companion, Muhammad bin Abdullah al-Qahtani, as the Mahdi—the eschatological doctrine of the Mahdi is marginal to mainstream Sunni Islam.[63]

More to the point today, however, is Dekmejian's belief that the Great Mosque incident 'represented the "tip of the iceberg" with respect to the widespread revivalism that emerged in the 1970s in Saudi society' (Dekmejian, 1994: 628). The siege was also the harbinger of troubles in the Eastern Province. Beginning with violent riots just after the seizure of the Great Mosque, the kingdom's Shiite minority began nearly ten years of dissent. *Muwahhidi* persecution of the kingdom's Shiites—tacitly admitted for the first time during

---

[62] It should also be noted that King Faisal's assassin was born to Prince Musaid of a Rashidi mother (Shammar tribe); Prince Musaid himself belonged to the Sudairi branch of the family, having been born to Ibn Saud from Jauhara bint Saad al-Sudairi. Thus, a thread of tribal antagonism and family factionalism can be seen weaving its way through major acts of defiance directed against the regime well into the modern era. Tribal loyalties undoubtedly remained important in the early period of the kingdom.

[63] This doctrine entered Shiite Islam through contacts with Christian messianic concepts and then, along with related or derived sufi mystical thought, influenced popular Sunni belief.

the November 1979 riots by Deputy Interior Minister, Prince Ahmad bin Abd al-Aziz (Buchan, 1981: 525)—and the inspiration of the Iranian Revolution, precipitated these events in the east. Kechichian (1990: 5n. 22), however, speculates that the Shiite riots and Juhaiman's revolt may not have been 'a pure coincidence'. Moreover, Kechichian (1986: 69n. 21) presents the astonishing, but 'unverified' suggestion that the Great Mosque siege was much more serious than has been revealed and represented a potentially kingdom-wide rebellion, while Abir (1988: 163n. 41) cites King Khalid and Crown Prince Fahd as admitting that, had the rebels chosen different and more politically oriented targets rather than the Great Mosque, the consequences for the regime 'might have been far more serious' (cf. al-Fagih, cited in Fandy, 1999: 154).

The observation that the chaos manifested at the end of the 1970s may have been only 'the tip of the iceberg' echoes Dekmejian's earlier, prophetic view that the '[m]ore complex...problem of...the growing Islamist opposition' will present greater difficulties for the Al Saud far into the future (Dekmejian, 1985: 146). Firm evidence of the validity of this conclusion is contained in the post-Gulf War demands of would-be reformers; for example, the 1991 'Letter of Demands' delivered to King Fahd and the 1992 'Memorandum of Advice' presented to Shaikh bin Baz bear more than a passing resemblance to the 'five main points' of Juhaiman's revolt listed above. Fagih and another prominent post-Gulf War Saudi dissident, the now notorious Osama bin Laden, for example, continue to cite 'un-Islamic' behaviour, the 'squandering' of state resources, 'corruption', and the lack of strategic national planning as major causes of grievance against the regime (see Fandy, 1999: 154–5, 186–7; al-Fagih, S. 1998, pers. comm., 20 May and 28 May).[64]

Like the devastating Khobar bombing of 1996, the insurrection at the Great Mosque may have proved less disturbing to the Al Saud if real evidence of external interference had been proved. However, despite some variations on Hanbali doctrinal norms, Juhaiman and his insurgents were born of the legacy of *muwahhidi* Islam and

---

[64] Masari and the now limping CDLR, of course, also continue to share these views (al-Masari, M., 1998, pers. comm., 20 May and 26 May). Unlike Fagih/MIRA and Bin Laden, however, Masari/CDLR have been marginalised in oppositional discourse (issues treated in more depth in Chapter 5).

the Ikhwan—ironically and not atypically in Saudi sociopolitics, from the same sources of legitimacy upon which the Al Saud base their right to rule. Whilst sharing the same *muwahhidi* heritage, the November 1995 Riyadh and June 1996 Khobar bombers were more the products of an internationalist Islamic commitment and outrage born and nurtured in the wars in Afghanistan and the Gulf. An indication of the greater political acumen of the contemporary militant opposition was displayed in their choice of targets, a US-operated Saudi National Guard administration centre in Riyadh and a US Air Force barracks in Khobar. Both were symbols and physical manifestations of what is being seen by an increasing number of Saudi citizens as an American occupation of their country. Anti-US feeling has palpably grown in the kingdom in the aftermath of the 1991 Gulf War, and the new Saudi militant opposition—if it can be referred to as a whole—has tapped into this feeling and is tacitly appealing to it for at least moral support. How effective and persistent this radical Saudi opposition will prove to be, however, is another question. As displays of radical opposition, history may record the various bombings in Riyadh and Khobar of 1995–2002 to be little more than a flash in the pan: deadly monuments to a defined post-Gulf War phase of Saudi sociopolitics. On the other hand, as US hegemony in the region increases with the global 'war against terrorism' in the aftermath of the airliner hijacking and suicide attacks against US cities on 11 September 2001, radical opposition may well intensify. In the meantime, the Al Saud will not be comforted by the knowledge that the new radical Islamist opposition is more sophisticated than their neo-Ikhwan forebears.[65]

[65] See Chapter 5. As with *hajj* disasters and the Mecca siege, the Riyadh and Khobar bombings also have much in common with similar acts in the Western world; for example, the Oklahoma City bombing of 19 April 1995. This single incident, in which an American Gulf War veteran utilised a truck bomb in a way similar to the one that the Khobar bombers would use later, was far more devastating than the Riyadh and Khobar bombings combined. The Oklahoma City bombing—executed on the anniversary of the FBI's assault at Waco (see note 57 above)—as an expression of radical opposition to a national government on the part of loosely affiliated (fundamentalist Christian) religious and right-wing organisations and individuals, has direct and startling comparative value with Saudi Arabia.

Conclusion

Since the proclamation of the modern kingdom of Saudi Arabia in 1932, the country which dominates the Arabian peninsula physically, economically, religiously and politically has been subject to enormous changes and stresses. As Chaudhry has documented, the social bases of the Saudi political economy have undergone several transformations in a cycle of destruction and creation on the way to establishing a unified national economy. The Najdiisation of the bureaucracy was all but a *fait accompli* on the eve of the oil boom of 1973–4, a situation which facilitated Najdi economic dominance when the distribution of oil wealth became the priority of the state. This was the era of plenty, which began when state revenues more than trebled in less than a year. Saudi Arabia became a rentier and a distributive state, and politically the kingdom moved from a traditional–authoritarian to a traditional–authoritarian–distributive political system. Oil rents and their distribution fuelled increasingly rapid modernisation and development. Elaborate subsidies and social services fuelled 'the Saudi social contract' and 'the Saudi welfare state'. These formed the substance of the legitimacy of largesse which became an entrenched strategy, the goal of which was to placate a population faced with revolutionary socioeconomic changes and with no stake in government.

Just how much control the Saudi regime has had over distributive and developmental processes is questionable. The formulation of five-year development plans, themselves of a dubious nature, have only yielded dubious and unsteady results in, for example, education and urbanisation in the kingdom—both now becoming areas of socioeconomic liability for the regime as pressure for economic restructuring mounts. However, despite the largely unplanned, ad hoc nature of development, the resulting reconfiguration of Saudi society and of economic power could not have displeased the ruling dynasty; the rise to socioeconomic prominence of Najdis and their allied clients during the 1970s and 1980s only reinforced the dominance over the kingdom of those from whom the Al Saud have traditionally drawn their most significant domestic political support. From the effective Najdiisation of the state, the establishment of a new Najdi bureaucratic–business élite through blood and regional favouritism—summed up in the concepts of *asabiyya* and *wasta*—was only a relatively short and natural step.

Although the ideals of Arabian *asabiyya* had always been a part of the Saudi political economy, it assumed larger-than-life proportions in the larger-than-life capitalism unleashed in the kingdom with the oil boom. Oil boom capitalism accelerated and consolidated an increasingly Najdi-run state *asabiyya*, building on the Najdiisation of the state from the early 1960s as the national economy became more firmly established. In this context, *asabiyya* capitalism, as has been said, can be conceptualised as the Arabian version of Asia's so-called 'crony capitalism', thought to have been a significant contributing factor in the economic crisis which crippled many East and South-East Asian countries for around two years from mid-1997. Such parallels may prove a source of at least some discomfort to the Al Saud at some stage in the future; as will be argued in the following chapter, a significant confrontation is looming between Saudi Arabia's *asabiyya* capitalism and the forces of global economic integration.

In the wash of oil wealth and the flurry of development activity, the way was open for mismanagement and waste, and for favouritism, nepotism and the institutionalisation of informal and exclusive business practices on the part of the new Najdi bureaucratic–business élite and those with the right connections. In financial terms, these practices have cost, and are still costing the Saudi state very dearly; they have contributed greatly to the broader picture of poor economic performance, as will be seen in the following chapter. These less edifying aspects of Saudi *asabiyya* capitalism have obscured and complicated the processes of government, and a lack of transparency and ultimately of accountable governance has undermined confidence in the regime; this is reflected in the literature of the political opposition which represents the perspective of a worrying proportion of the Saudi population from the Al Saud point of view.

In the drive to become 'an advanced and self-sufficient Kingdom' (Mutabbakani, 1993: 42), there were always going to be contradictions and conflict between the goals of forging a technically sophisticated economy and society on the one hand, whilst maintaining sociopolitical calm and passivity on the other. On the path to achieving these goals, there have been numerous conflicts with traditional values and religious conservatives. In general, however, 'the government was able to defeat the arguments of the hardline traditionalists' (Mutabbakani, 1993: 42).[66] But 'defeating arguments' has been among the lesser of the regime's problems in reconciling development and modernisation with conservative *muwahhidi* and traditional mores—the struggle for the future of Saudi society has occasionally erupted into physical clashes which have unsettled the Al Saud, the 1979 Great Mosque siege being a prime early example. Later, the 1995 and 1996 bombings in Riyadh and Khobar marked the beginning of a new era of political violence. The Khobar bombing of October 2001, which killed an American, and followed on a series of six bomb attacks between November 2000 and May 2001, added to tension and uncertainty in the kingdom after the 11 September attacks against the United States. The depth and extent of sentiment which could potentially be turned against the regime was reaffirmed in the emotional period following the United States' launching of its military action against Osama bin Laden and the Taliban regime in Afghanistan. The recent acts of hostility represent progress from traditional socioreligious rebellion against the Al Saud to a contemporary form of radical protest popularly defined as 'political Islam', issues dealt with in detail in Chapter 5.

Questions relating specifically to regime 'corruption' have been openly raised in major acts of opposition as well as in the propaganda war levelled against the Al Saud since the siege of the Great Mosque. From unethical business–political relations and personal excesses to the way that the regime manages religious affairs, such as the *hajj*, the Al Saud have had to endure many barbs from their opponents at home and abroad. In the case of Saudi Arabia, such issues can easily be given a religious significance, with potentially serious consequences for the Islamic legitimacy of the Al Saud; to date, Saudi rule has been able to withstand such assaults.

With the dawning of the era of economic globalisation, however, the Saudi economy and, by extension, the broader Saudi socioeconomic system, stand to suffer from many practices spawned by the boom period. The bureaucratic–business élites and the patronage networks of Saudi *asabiyya* capitalism are about to be buffeted by

[66] Mutabbakani was referring to the issue of female education.

yet another phase of socioeconomic change early in the new millennium. How they will respond remains to be seen: the majority of the current élite may not be inclined to stand idly by while their position is eroded. One likely outcome of economic restructuring and globalisation is a narrowing of the base of *asabiyya* capitalism—that is, a growing divide between socioeconomic classes and between the 'haves and have-nots', as is already being witnessed in developed countries. As government spending and 'the Saudi welfare state' are reined in and the upper echelons of the élite buy into the privatisation process, a new Saudi super-élite in direct partnership with investing foreign companies will come into being. Again, these issues are treated in detail in the following chapter.

Since oil wealth and distribution policies have been linked to the political imperatives of the security and stability of the Al Saud regime, any obstacle to their ability to continue purchasing a basic level of sociopolitical stability is going to be of concern to the regime. The acute financial difficulties that came with the 1998–9 collapse of oil prices magnified these concerns, facing the regime with the prospect of socioeconomic adjustments which in themselves—even with generous funding—could result in further unsettling sociopolitical consequences for Al Saud rule. The dramatic recovery in oil prices as a result of OPEC production cuts in April 1999 does not alter the longer-term scenario for the kingdom. The breaking of a 17-year run of budget deficits with a surplus in 2000 is likely to represent only a temporary surfacing out of the red: Saudi Arabia's revenue base is as chronically unstable as oil prices are volatile. The observation that political stability 'is easily maintained during a period of unprecedented budgetary surplus' only emphasises the significance of the end of the era of Saudi budgetary surplus—indeed, the looming end of the Saudi distributive–welfare state.

4

THE RESTRUCTURING OF
AN OIL STATE

THE CHALLENGES OF ECONOMIC REFORM
AND SOCIOECONOMIC CHANGE IN THE ERA
OF GLOBALISATION

Bar the occasional spike in the price of oil, Saudi boom times are over. Crown Prince Abdullah, the effective ruler of the kingdom since King Fahd's 1995 illness, has publicly admitted as much. The oil boom, which really began in earnest in 1974 and continued through the 1980s in spite of the first signs that it could not and would not last forever, amounted to a revolution for the Saudi economy and society. The effects of the end of the boom, although they will be drawn out over a longer time frame, stand to be as significant as those of the boom itself. In Saudi Arabia, the end of the era of plenty has as much political as economic significance: appeasing the population and potential political opposition with an elaborate system of direct and indirect subsidies became increasingly problematic as the 1990s progressed. Put simply, budgetary difficulties have greatly interfered with the regime's ability to sustain its strategy of patronage and largesse.

The legitimacy of largesse as a strategy is now nearing the end of its life as development and modernisation processes continue, and as the time has come for Saudi Arabia to develop and integrate its own human resources into the economy more fully. Economic problems have contributed, and are still contributing, to pressures on the regime to reduce subsidies and the reliance on imported labour. Yet Saudi development planners face a quandary in that the economic

141

remedies envisioned for the near future will only exacerbate the socioeconomic imbalances that have so far remained obscured and manageable. For example, great wealth was created as a result of the development of the country's oil resources, yet pockets of poverty remained—and now evidence suggests that the stratification of society is intensifying and that an unequal distribution of wealth is becoming even more pronounced. These realities have combined with other economic and socioeconomic factors, such as over-reliance on the petroleum sector, often substantial budget deficits since 1983, increasing state debt, high levels of imported labour, and high unemployment rates amongst Saudi nationals, creating challenges for the Saudi regime which may turn into sociopolitical pressures more serious than those witnessed to date.

The forces of international economic rationalism, whose ostensible goal is the integration of national economies into the modern, transnational economy, are now dictating even more forcefully that structural changes in the Saudi economy must be implemented. Governments worldwide, including that of the Al Saud, are under pressure to decrease their direct involvement in economic management. This adds an extra political, or ideological, dimension to the pressures on the regime to reform its political economy and its socioeconomic policies. Specific pressure to implement these changes has periodically been sharpened by a series of financial crises: the Saudi economy can no longer afford the luxuries associated with the years of the oil boom. Pressure for the winding-down of the Saudi distributive state and the fundamental socioeconomic adjustments which must necessarily accompany such an economic restructuring is building momentum. Even if only partially implemented, these adjustments to the way Saudis have known life over the last quarter-century will be dramatic, and have the potential to be destabilising sociopolitically if they meet with resistance. Implementing economic reforms, managing the associated socioeconomic adjustments and dealing with any sociopolitical fallout are the tasks currently facing the Saudi regime.

This chapter focuses on the economic difficulties of the Al Saud and the way that predominantly low and unstable oil prices, the heavy financial burdens of the 1991 Gulf War, and the extravagances of *asabiyya* capitalism have contributed to them. Evidence is presented here which suggests that the significant rises in oil prices from late-March 1999 represent little more than temporary relief for the kingdom's chronic long-term economic and socioeconomic difficulties and may, in fact, reintroduce a degree of complacency among those involved in strategic decision-making.

Oil prices, Saudi budgetary planning and the momentum of economic reform

An economy dependent on oil. The Saudi economy is not as healthy today as it once was—or rather, the dependencies and flaws in post-boom Saudi developmental processes are revealing themselves in their full severity. The heady days of the 1970s and early 1980s oil boom are well and truly over, but despite attempts at economic diversification, the kingdom's economy is still dependent on oil. As a clearly observable consequence, Saudi revenues are prone to extreme fluctuations, with fiscal planning remaining vulnerable to forces largely outside the control of the government. After the immediate post-Gulf War financial shock, improvement in the country's economic fortunes was largely due to strong oil prices in 1996 and 1997; then financial crisis loomed once more in 1998 with the virtual collapse of oil prices, and again, the recovery of financial poise in 1999–2001 was due to strong oil prices.

These pendulum swings in fiscal fortunes are not conducive to sound national management in any sphere of the economy or society. Such extreme fluctuations are precisely what many influential economists and organisations, including global powers such as the IMF, would like to see reduced through the acceleration of long-delayed strategic economic reforms. Although 'now…the oil sector contributes only about one-third to total GDP' (SAMBA, 1998d: 4), the importance of oil to the Saudi economy is understated by the GDP figures: it still accounts for approximately 90% of export earnings and 75% of budget revenues (CIA, 1999).[1] An insight into the mysteries of the Saudi economy and an indication of the persistent,

---

[1] The CIA's 1999 assessment of the Saudi economy estimated that the petroleum sector contributed 40% to the kingdom's total Gross Domestic Product (CIA, 1999).

if not entirely transparent, importance of the petroleum sector, are given by the following accounts:

> Saudi Arabia's economy remains driven by oil and oil revenues. Sales of crude oil comprise approximately 35 percent of the Kingdom's GDP, and oil indirectly accounts for far more through oil industry contracts [which stimulate other economic sectors]… Although other sectors of the economy contribute hefty amounts to the Kingdom's overall GDP, their real levels are difficult to discern, especially given the government's recycling of petrodollars through industrial and agricultural subsidies. (Wilson and Graham, 1994: 171)

> …more than two decades after Saudi Arabia committed itself to a strategy of diversifying away from dependence on oil, the energy market continues to determine the health of its economy. Despite expensive efforts to promote industrial development with cheap energy, low-cost finance, protectionism and central planning, the kingdom today remains … essentially an oil-based economy. (O'Sullivan, 1996)

Saudi Arabia is not alone—it shares this dilemma with the other Gulf Arab oil producers, and, although the oil industry as a whole 'has always suffered from poor information', it has become clear to analysts that major oil exporters 'have become progressively more dependent on oil revenues in absolute terms' (Stevens, 1996: 399, 392).[2] An important point, however, is that while a great deal of lip-service has been paid to it, adequate levels of economic diversification

---

[2] Kuwait, where petroleum accounts for nearly half of GDP, is the most oil-dependent of all the GCC states: 90% of Kuwait's export revenues and 75% of the government's income are from oil. For Oman, petroleum accounts for around 40% of GDP, and for 75% of export earnings and government revenues. The figures for Qatar are 30% of GDP and around 70% of export earnings and 66% of government revenues. The UAE's overall dependence on oil, natural gas and petrochemicals amounts to about the same as Saudi Arabia's dependence on the oil sector. Bahrain, the only GCC state without large oil reserves, augments its production with the refining of imported crude; even so, petroleum production and processing account for about 30% of GDP, and for around 60% of export receipts and 60% of government revenues (see CIA, 1999). Paul Stevens (1996: 392) cites oil as accounting for 75% of merchandise exports for OPEC countries, with these governments' revenues being 'equally dominated by oil'. Oil dependence is, in fact, more likely to be understated than overstated. On the prospects for the oil industry's becoming more transparent in the future, Stevens (1996: 399) is pessimistic.

have still not been reached. As the Saudi five-year development plans come and go, not only has much of the non-oil sector of the Saudi economy remained largely dependent on state oil rents, but many attempts ostensibly designed to diversify have only increased the reliance on oil (see Osama, 1987: 35; Kanovsky, 1994: 40, 46, 76). Referring to the Saudi economic performance of 2000—the year which saw a budget surplus for the first time in eighteen years—a report by a major Saudi bank described a 'high dependence on oil' as one of three major 'imbalances' in the Saudi fisc that needs to be eliminated (SAMBA, 2001: 8). In 2001, as the kingdom moved into its seventh five-year plan period, not much has changed, although tentative restructuring efforts were stepped up in 2000 and 2001.

Thus, the price of oil remains of crucial importance to Saudi economic planning and, by extension, to the development of social projects, such as health services, and of projects in the socioeconomic sphere, such as the implementation of new, industrially-oriented emphases in the education and training of young Saudi nationals. In other words, the structure of the Saudi rentier–distributive state is still firmly in place. This basic liability, recently brought home to the Al Saud yet again with the oil price crash of 1998–9, has provided the regime with renewed incentive to diversify the economy, especially by encouraging manufacturing and non-oil exports, and by embarking on an extensive programme of economic restructuring according to formulae recommended by the advocates of economic globalisation. The privatisation of state-owned enterprises and the fostering of the private sector in general as government economic intervention retreats, the opening of the economy and financial system to foreign investment, reining in *asabiyya* capitalism and introducing greater transparency are among the reforms being pressed upon the Saudi regime and which challenge the 'new' Saudi state created by the oil boom.

Wake-up calls: From the 1980s to 2001 and beyond. Much is made of the 1986 collapse of oil prices but, in fact, the edge had already been taken off the oil boom with the recession which began to bite in 1982–3, caused by Saudi Arabia's unsuccessful attempt to halt the softening of world oil prices by progressively cutting its export volumes from 3,375.69 million barrels per annum in 1980 to a mere 780.72 million barrels per annum in 1985 (see Table 3.1 p. 80). This cut in oil exports to the world—paralleled, of course, by cuts in production (see SAMA, 1998: 313)—was in line with the kingdom's role as OPEC's 'swing producer', whereby Saudi oil output was increased or decreased to match supply and demand in an attempt to regulate world oil prices. As a consequence, Saudi oil revenues declined dramatically (see Table 3.1).

The kingdom's sacrifice was in vain; other OPEC countries discounted their oil prices to maintain sale volumes and, in July 1985, Saudi Arabia renounced the role of swing producer and increased its oil production in a measure designed to rescue its rapidly deteriorating economic position. The combination of price discounting and ignored production quotas led to the collapse of oil prices in 1986, when they fell to an average of US$13–14 per barrel—and reached lows of US$8–10 per barrel in mid-1986— from an average price of more than US$27 per barrel in 1985 (see Table 3.1; Kanovsky, 1994: 26–7). Despite implementing a slowdown in spending and drawing heavily on foreign reserves, the government saw its budget deficit soaring from 6.4% of GDP in 1983 to 25.3% of GDP in 1987 (see SAMA, 1998: 125, 306; Kanovsky, 1994: 19–21, 73–4; Wilson and Graham, 1994: 181–2). The disruption was so great that a budget was not presented by the Saudi government in 1986; Chaudhry (1997: 269n. 1, 273) refers to 'the lost year' and 'the disarray of the Saudi fisc'. The oil price crash of 1986 caused official government revenues from oil to more than halve, from around US$42,575 million in 1985 to around US$20,027 million in 1987 (see SAMA, 1998: 306).[3]

---

[3] The value of oil revenues for 1985 and 1987 quoted above are taken from SAMA's presentation of figures from the Ministry of Finance and National Economy. These figures are at odds with those drawn from previous SAMA annual reports, which are presented elsewhere in SAMA's 34th annual report (cf. SAMA, 1998: 11): for the overlapping years of 1981–8, the figures do not agree. Both these listings are, in turn, at odds with figures provided in the national balance of payments summary on pages 300–1 (see SAMA, 1998: 11, 300–1, 306–7). Even if statistics could be taken at face value, working with Saudi figures and finances presents many problems, including uneven correlations between the Gregorian and Hijria calendars, changes in the dates of the regular Saudi fiscal year, the failure to issue a budget for 1406–7H (1986), the 'amalgamation' of the 1410–11H (1990) budget with the budget of 1411–12H (1991) (see SAMA, 1998: 306–7), and the 'revision' of the methods used to classify foreign assets which had the effect of almost doubling the kingdom's liquid foreign exchange reserves from 1996 (see IMF,

As a result, the Saudi economy has been struggling since the mid-1980s.[4]

High budget deficits continued throughout the remainder of the 1980s and into the 1990s (see Table 4.1) and, as highlighted by Fareed Mohamedi (1993: 16), deficits of at least 8% of GDP were forecast into the mid-1990s. Besides a lower oil price, the direct and indirect expenses of two Gulf wars—both financially costly to Saudi Arabia—and of military and security expenditures in general, took their toll of the Saudi economy. Considering a bill of between US$50,000 million and US$70,000 million for the 1991 Gulf War, arms purchases since the war of around US$50,000 million, and up to US$30,000 million lost in aid to Iraq during the first Iran–Iraq Gulf war (1980–8), the Saudi economic position in the decade 1985–95 can be characterised as not in good health (see, for example, Kanovsky, 1994: 57–71; Krimly, 1999: 257–8; Kechichian, 1999: 242, 249; Cordesman, 1997: 58; Allen, 1996; al-Rasheed, 1996a: 18; Curtiss, 1995: 51; Wilson and Graham, 1994: 189; Hardy, 1992: 31).

It is no secret that world financial institutions, at least during the dark economic days of the early 1990s, have been concerned and 'raised questions about how deep the Saudi official (as opposed to royal) pockets really are' (Mohamedi, 1993: 14); British banks avoided the Saudi line of credit and one US government credit agency almost downgraded the kingdom's credit rating in March 1993. The IMF also issued warnings and advice centred on simple logic: spending needed to be reduced or revenues needed to be increased (Wilson and Graham, 1994: 195–6; see also Mohamedi, 1993; CDLR, 1995a: 47–8n. 2; *The Middle East*, 1993b: 27). While constraining spending would not only mean scaling back national infrastructure development but also the reining in of subsidies and the welfare state, increasing revenues would mean increasing taxes

---

2000b: 666). Different listings which provide different figures for the same areas of economy only serve to confuse the picture of Saudi finances further. Chaudhry (1997: 273) states that from 1982, it was also 'impossible to compare [budget] allocations across sectors' because of 'repeated changes in the budget format' (see also notes 10 and 14 below).

[4] Saudi Arabia's dilemma then, as it is now and as it will be in the future, was not unshared; for example, in 1997, Stevens (1997: 135) referred in apocalyptic terms to 'the failing economies' of the GCC (see also Stevens, 1996: 401).

Table 4.1
SAUDI BUDGET STATISTICS, 1981–2002

	Budget deficit/surplus (US$m.)	Ratio of deficit/surplus to GDP (%)
1983	−6,878.7	6.4%
1984	−12,728.1	12.8%
1985	−13,921.9	16.1%
1986	−16,289.8	22.5%
1987	−18,615.5	25.3%
1988	−13,417.9	17.6%
1989	−9,319.1	11.2%
1990 & 1991★	−42,773.5	19.2%
1992	−17,933.2	14.6%
1993	−17,103.0	14.4%
1994	−9,288.3	7.7%
1995	−7,328.4	5.9%
1996	−5,081.9	3.7%
1997	−4,272.4	2.9%
1998	−12,817.1	9.6%
1999	−9,716.0	6.9%
2000	+6,072.0	3.5%
2001	−6,675.0	3.6%
2002[†]	−5,060.0	2.8%

Sources: Saudi Arabian Monetary Agency (SAMA, 1998: 125; 2001), Saudi American Bank (SAMBA, 2002a: 2) for 1983–2000; SAMBA (2002b: 2) for 2001–2..

★ The budgets for 1990 and 1991 were amalgamated.

[†] Statistics for 2002 are SAMBA mid-year forecasts. SAMBA (2002b: 2 note) advises that in June 2002 the Saudi Central Department of Statistics 'revised GDP data for 1996–2001'.

and fees and/or instituting new ones—in other words, the rentier–distributive basis of the Saudi oil state required basic reassessment.

In fact, such a reassessment was avoided even as gloomy budget forecasts were eclipsed by the actual deficit: in 1991 it was around 19% of GDP; in 1992 it was nearly 15% of GDP; by 1993 it was still more than 14% of GDP (see Table 4.1). Only in 1994 did the pessimistic forecast of a near-8% deficit show on the balance sheets, thus looking like a relatively positive achievement (see SAMBA, 1997: 2; SAMA, 1998: 125). Commentators describing the Saudi economic state of affairs at the time routinely employed phrases such as 'economically enfeebled' (*The Economist*, 1995: 21), '[t]he fragility of the economy' (Evans, 1996: 9), and 'Saudi Arabia is broke' (Rossiter, 1995).[5] Chaudhry (1997: 269), looking back over

---

[5] Dr Caleb Rossiter is director of the Washington-based advocacy group, the Project on Demilitarisation and Democracy. He was referring to the fact that Saudi

the era in question, wrote of '[t]he economic crisis of the 1980s and 1990s'.[6]

However, the fiscal situation continued to improve, with the years 1994 to 1997 seeing the deficit steadily reduced; in 1997 it was brought down to only 2.9% of GDP (SAMA, 1998: 125; SAMBA, 2001: 1; see Table 4.1).[7] It was, in fact, during 1995 that many commentators, sometimes in unjustifiably glowing terms, implied the kingdom's economic woes were behind it (see Curtiss, 1995; Cooper, 1995a), although others, looking at longer-term prospects, did not share this optimism (*Middle East Monitor*, 1995; Collett, 1995), while Paul Stevens (1996, 1997) predicts a gloomy future for all the

---

Arabia was forced to borrow from European banks in order to pay for arms purchases from the United States. Other 'petrolised' states shared in this financial predicament; Terry Lynn Karl, for example, has claimed that the Venezuelan government suffered from a 'spending addiction' (see Karl, 1997: 164–9), a charge that can be equally directed at the Saudi regime. For a striking Saudi–Venezuelan economic comparison, see Karl, ch. 8, 'From boom to bust: The crisis of Venezuelan democracy'. Democracy, of course, has never been at stake in Saudi Arabia, but the decline in the economic fortunes of major oil producing rentier states from the early 1980s was not an isolated experience.

[6] Other indicators support the view that Saudi finances were experiencing serious difficulties during this period. For example, 'Swiss banks, where Saudi princes and institutions still have huge sums on deposit, say they have difficulty in assessing Saudi Arabia's economic picture, but note that deposits have dwindled to a trickle in recent months' (Borowiec, 1995).

[7] Saudi Arabia's nominal GDP was also reported to have grown by a healthy 7.1% in 1997, with real GDP growth registering 1.9% (SAMBA, 2001: 1). Saudi economic and financial figures that are dealt with and presented by analysts are provided by the Saudi Ministry of Finance and National Economy, by SAMA and, occasionally, by the Ministry of Planning. In an earlier report on the Saudi economic performance of 1996, SAMBA (1997: 1) wrote that 'the very high overall nominal economic growth rate seen in 1996 of 8.6 percent is unlikely to be repeated… "real" GDP for 1996 grew by 2.3 percent'. SAMBA (2001: 1) lists a 1996 real GDP growth rate of 1.4%. By way of further illustrating the haziness and constant revisions surrounding analysis when dealing with Saudi statistics, it is worth noting that the US Central Intelligence Agency estimated 1996 Saudi real GDP growth at 6% (CIA, 1997). The World Bank has listed both a 2.4% GDP growth rate (World Bank, 1998) and a 1.4% GDP growth rate (World Bank, 2001b) for 1996. In any case, the 1996 real GDP growth rate was below the 3.3% average for the 10 years 1987–97, but 'a marked improvement' on the growth rates of –0.7% to 0.5% from 1993–5 (SAMBA, 1997; see also O'Sullivan, 1996). These 1993–5 figures reflect the economic impact of the 1991 Gulf War and the resulting financial difficulties.

countries of the GCC. Summing up the swings in international concern over this period, together with a hint that all is not necessarily well regarding future economic development, Edmund O'Sullivan wrote as follows in late 1996:

> It is four years since reports first emerged that Saudi Arabia, burdened by the costs of paying for the Kuwait crisis and high general spending commitments, was experiencing serious economic difficulties. For a period, it seemed that the country with the largest economy in the Arab world was teetering on the brink of financial collapse.
>
> It is too soon to believe that the kingdom has found a sustainable development path, but the worries have largely evaporated. (O'Sullivan, 1996)

Despite less than sound budgetary planning and the Saudi government's '[consistent failure] to meet its financial obligations' (ibid.), a former chief economist at the Saudi American Bank (SAMBA), Kevin Taecker (1998, pers. comm., 9 Mar.), regards the financial crisis scare of the early to mid-1990s as 'silliness' and 'uninformed', a view shared by the Director of the Oxford Institute for Energy Studies, Robert Mabro, who believes it 'was exaggerated from outside' (Mabro, R., 1998, pers. comm., 14 May).[8] It should be noted, though, that King Fahd is quoted as saying in a cabinet address in August 1995 that, 'We have succeeded in dealing with the (financial) crisis' (see Cooper, 1995a; Curtiss, 1995: 48; see also Cooper, 1995b: 34). In an attempt to allay fears, the king in effect acknowledged that there had at least been a disturbing perception of financial crisis which was widespread and serious enough to warrant it being put firmly to rest by no less a figure than the monarch himself.

The goal of the Saudi Sixth Five-Year Development Plan (1995–2000) was 'to eliminate the government deficit completely by the end of the year 2000' (SAMBA, 1997: 3); on current analysis, even with high oil prices leading to the first budget surplus in 18 years in 2000, consolidating and sustaining this goal—which has been

[8] Taecker, also a former US Treasury attaché to the US Embassy in Riyadh, is known to be sympathetic to and very optimistic about Saudi Arabia's economic challenges (Australian diplomat 3, 1998, pers. comm., 23 Feb.). SAMBA merged with the United Saudi Bank (USB) in 1999 to create the kingdom's second largest bank. Before the merger, *The Banker* (1999: 124) ranked SAMBA, a joint Saudi–Citibank venture, as sixth in the Arab world for 1998–9 and pronounced it one of the most profitable in the Middle East region.

carried over to the Seventh Five-Year Plan—will remain elusive.[9] The temporary relief of the years 2000–1, after more than two years of relatively high oil prices, promises to remain temporary. Undermining confidence in the ability of the Saudis to manage their economy efficiently, especially in the face of adversity, are practices such as those outlined by Chaudhry (1997: 167):

Government statistics were literally manufactured in the Ministries of Finance and Planning. All but the first of the various Five-Year Plans begin with fictitious parameters based on unsupported assumptions and proceed to build even more fantastic projections. In 1981 the budget format was 'reformed' to make already opaque figures even more impossible to interpret.[10]

Lower than expected oil prices, together with low demand from Asian countries due to the Asian financial crisis—then in full force— were already presenting the Saudi economy with 'two grey clouds on the horizon' by the beginning of 1998 (Taecker, K., 1998, pers. comm., 9 Mar.; see also SAMA, 1998: 159).[11] The average export

[9] Whether citing the aims of the five-year plans offers any comfort at all, though, should be considered in the light of the opinion of at least one professional previously directly involved with Saudi Arabia, that the plans 'are not worth the paper they're written on' and that they, 'at best...are an expression of hope' (Australian diplomat 1, 1995, pers. comm., 14 July).

[10] It is interesting to note that even the (1996) Annual Report of the Saudi Industrial Development Fund, a division of the Ministry of Finance and National Economy, points to the unavailability of 'full details of economic statistics', and resorts to the repetition of basic statistics, presumably to disguise a dearth of solid information, and to present a stridently optimistic and much less than full picture of the state of the kingdom's industry (see SIDF, 1996: 24–5). Moreover, 'insider' industry publications, such as the Dubai-based *Gulf Business* magazine, have lamented '[t]he traditionally sketchy flow of information [in this case, on Gulf oil companies' investments in foreign oil companies]', which 'does, of course, make it difficult to obtain a clear picture of the success or otherwise of Gulf involvement in [foreign-based] companies' (Hussain, 1998). Cordesman (1997: 197) emphasises that sources of data on Saudi Arabia '...are at least in partial conflict. There is no consensus over demographic data, budget data...'. See also note 3 above; note 14 below; Chapter 3, note 1; and the section on sources in 'Sources and further reading' below.

[11] According to BP Amoco (1999a), '[t]he key feature of the oil market in 1998 was the deep and prolonged fall in crude oil prices. Prices fell almost continuously

price for Saudi crudes in 1997 was around US$18.70 per barrel; by January 1998 this price had already been revised downward for the year to a projected US$14–15 per barrel (SAMBA, 1998a: 1). By mid-February 1998, world oil prices were reported to have 'fallen to their lowest levels since 1994'; the average price of Saudi crudes had dropped to lows of around US$11.50 per barrel before recovering somewhat to around US$12.50 per barrel—a level which was clearly '…too low…to meet planned 1998 objectives' (SAMBA, 1998b: 1; 1998c: 1). A rise in the budget deficit to US$5,000 million—about 3% of GDP—that had already been planned for 1998 had by March 1998 been revised upward to about US$8,000 million, corresponding to a rise to approximately 4.8% of GDP (see SAMBA, 1998a: 2; 1998b: 5–6; 1998c: 1). What appeared to be a reasonable worst-case prognosis during the first quarter of 1998 once again proved to be over-optimistic as world oil prices slumped deeply mid-year and virtually collapsed in December.[12] With the price of Arabian light crude dropping to below $10 per barrel from June to August, and to around $8 per barrel in December, the 1998 budget deficit eventually came in at more than US$12,800 million—9.6% of GDP (SAMBA, 2001: 1; see also Table 4.1).[13] This final deficit figure does not include approximately US$9,600 million in loans taken from the national oil company, Saudi Aramco,

---

throughout the year, yielding an annual average Brent [a benchmark North Sea crude blend] price of $13.11, 32% below 1997 and the lowest since 1976.' Overall energy consumption fell by 1.5% in 'recession-hit Asia'. Specifically, Asian oil consumption fell by 2.7%, while demand for oil in 'the four Asian crisis economies' fell by a massive 11.1%. Demand for oil in Japan—the world's second largest consumer—fell by 4.2%, a fact which 'reflect[ed] its persistent economic recession' (BP Amoco, 1999a). Oil production for 1998 rose by 1.4%, which 'significantly exceeded growth in demand'. While non-OPEC production 'was effectively flat', OPEC's production rose by 3.2%, mainly as a result of a more than 80% increase in Iraqi production, to 2.2 million barrels per day, under the terms of the UN 'oil for food' programme. Apart from Iraq, OPEC production decreased 0.1% (see BP Amoco, 1999a).

[12] The price per barrel of the two common benchmark crudes, West Texas Intermediate and UK Brent, in December 1998 dropped to US$11.31 and US$9.80 respectively (IMF, 1999a: 72).

[13] For analysis at the time, see EIU, 1999a; 1999f; SAMBA, 1999.

and from Abu Dhabi to prop up the budget during the year (see Allen, 1998).[14]

In February 1999 the gloomy trend was forecast to continue as oil prices remained severely depressed. Even though the 1999 Saudi budget deficit was expected to be reined in, a shrinking GDP—with real GDP estimated to have declined by a startling 10.8%—resulted in an initial budget deficit to GDP ratio prediction for 1999 of approximately 9.7%. Slowing GDP growth was also predicted for all Middle Eastern and North African economies in 1999, but the oil-dependent GCC economies were expected to fare worse—with negative real GDP growth rates—than Arab countries with more diversified economies (IPR, 1999a, 1999b). The trends underlying these pessimistic forecasts have tended to lend veracity to a confidential report compiled on Saudi Arabia by the IMF in late 1995 and subsequently leaked to a British financial industry publication. It revealed that IMF projections indicated the Saudi budget deficit would, in a reversal of the 1993–5 trend, soon rise once again to 10% of GDP (see *The Banker*, 1995). The financial difficulties created by low oil prices also put pressure on the Saudi currency, the riyal, which is pegged at 3.745 riyals to the US dollar. Over the course of late 1998 to early 1999, the Saudi Arabian Monetary Agency (SAMA, the kingdom's central bank), was forced to 'adjust' interest rates and to draw on reserves to defend the riyal against devaluation (EIU, 1999k; Allen, 1998), a predicament which 'highlight[ed] the continuing weakness of the Saudi economy, its dependence on oil income, and its lack of transparency' (EIU, 1999b). Recalling the unflattering impressions of the mid-1990s, one British newspaper reported at the time that '[t]he problems

---

[14] Wilson and Graham (1994: 191–2) are sceptical about the level of Saudi deficit spending:

> The real figure may be substantially higher since Saudi budget figures are notoriously inaccurate and often serve as rough guidelines for spending. There are also large discrepancies between projected and actual figures; the latter are usually released the following year and purport to show real revenues and expenditures. However, many expenditures such as defense spending and payments to the royal family occur off-budget.

The CDLR-commissioned researchers offer a comparable evaluation and conclude that this state of affairs 'makes a nonsense of all analysis of the present and future financial health of Saudi Arabia' (see CDLR, 1995a: 33).

caused by the low oil price have been sufficiently severe...that at least one leading US bank—Citibank—has placed [Saudi Arabia] on its "watch list" alongside countries such as Brazil' (Brummer, 1999).

A stay of this decline appears to have been engineered, however, by concerted action on the part of major world oil exporters early in 1999 to cut oil production. The strategy was to reduce a global over-supply of oil and thus to promote a recovery in oil prices. After two failed attempts to secure new, lower oil production quotas during 1998, in mid-March 1999 Saudi Arabia led the effort to ensure agreement among the world's most significant oil producers to reduce output.[15] Once again, Saudi Arabia made the greatest sacrifice, with a pledge to cut production by 585,000 barrels per day (bpd), to 7.438 million bpd.[16] A total of 2.1 million bpd—3% of the daily worldwide supply—was pledged to be cut from collective production for one year, from 1 April 1999 to the end of March 2000. The strategy proved to be effective almost immediately. The benchmark crude, West Texas Intermediate (WTI)—which was languishing at around US$12.40 per barrel in early March 1999—had risen to around US$18.40 per barrel by the end of April, and broke a 19-month high in July on its way to settling in the US$21-range during August. This progress caused alarm among global energy supply professionals and prompted speculation that OPEC had gone too far with its corrective measures (*The Australian*, 1999). Progress continued, however; by the end of September, WTI was fetching more than US$25 per barrel to represent an effective doubling of oil prices in six months, and in mid-March 2000 it breached

[15] The ten active OPEC members, Saudi Arabia, Iran, Kuwait, the UAE, Qatar, Libya, Venezuela, Algeria, Nigeria and Indonesia, were joined by non-OPEC oil producers, Norway, Mexico and Oman, in an accord agreed in the Hague on 12 March 1999. OPEC ratified the agreement at the cartel's ministerial meeting in Vienna on 23 March. Iraq, subject to UN sanctions and the restrictive 'oil for food' programme, has not been an active member of OPEC since its August 1990 invasion of Kuwait.

[16] OPEC's second-largest oil exporter, Iran, agreed to cut production by 264,000 bpd. Final quota cuts for the smaller producers were sketchy, and compliance rates—although high—were not 100% (88% in May 1999 and 91% in June among OPEC producers; see Shiels, 1999). For figures on oil production cuts to which the other, smaller, producers agreed in March 1999, see *USA Today* (1999) and Habiby (1999).

the US$34 mark—the highest seen since the Gulf War-inflated prices of 1991.

Despite the dramatic recovery in oil prices, any gains for Saudi Arabia were largely eaten up by the lower production quota and corresponding falls in oil export volumes. Non-oil activity had also slowed, and sustained higher oil prices were in any case only expected to deliver a medium-term boost to the economy (EIU, 1999h; 1999j). The beneficial effects of higher oil prices were predicted to filter through the Saudi economy only during the year 2000, which they in the end did to a greater extent than predicted. In the meantime, despite continuing very strong oil prices, zero growth in real GDP was forecast for 1999, accompanied by predictions of only moderate gains of up to a maximum of 2% growth by the year 2003 (EIU, 1999f; 1999h; 1999j). These estimates were revised upward in light of unexpectedly high oil prices from April 2000, after the March 2000 OPEC meeting which raised production quotas for member states.[17] In the final analysis—at least, as final as any analysis can be for Saudi Arabia—negative 0.8% real GDP growth was reported for 1999 (IMF, 2002). As expected, rising oil prices in 1999 were not reflected very noticeably in that year's budget, but they made 2000 a good year fiscally for the Saudi government: the 1999 deficit came in at more than US$9,716 million (approximately 6.9% of GDP), while the government broke its

---

[17] The important and closely monitored OPEC meeting in Vienna of 27 March 2000 marked the end of the 12-month period of price-supporting production cuts agreed in March 1999. A new agreement did not come easily, and was reached (minus Iran) in the early hours of 29 March. The new agreement restored production quotas to pre-March 1999 levels with an effective overall OPEC production increase of 1.716 million bpd (including Iran): Saudi Arabia's adjusted quota thus returned to 8.023 million bpd. A price target range was announced by the Saudi Oil Minister, Ali al-Nuaimi: US$20–$25/barrel for UK Brent (US$21.50–$26.50/barrel for WTI). An absolute general crude range of US$22–$28/barrel was further proposed by the Algerian Mining and Energy Minister, Chakib Khelil. In the month following the agreement, oil prices stabilised in the US$25–$27/barrel range (WTI) before surging once again through May, to reach more than US$37/barrel by mid-September 2000. For reporting and analysis of the March 2000 OPEC meeting see, for example: WTRG (2000); Platt's (2000); Reuters (2000); Macalister (2000); McKenna (2000). A follow-up OPEC meeting in late June 2000 failed to produce any action that resulted in lower crude oil prices.

17-year run of budget deficits in 2000 with a US$6,072 million surplus (SAMA, 2001). The 2000 surplus represented 'around 3.5 percent of GDP' according to the IMF (2001: 1; see also IMF, 2002, and Table 4.1). Despite this encouraging result, the actual 2000 surplus reported by SAMA at the end of 2001 was substantially down on earlier forecasts of a US$12,000 million surplus (see AFP, 2001b; SAMBA, 2001: 1, 2). This higher figure was itself a downgrading of an even earlier 2000 forecast of a US$14,000 million surplus, which reportedly reflected 'a higher level of Aramco expenditures or off-budget spending than…anticipated' (SAMBA, 2001: 6). Growth in real GDP for 2000 was reported at 4.9% by the IMF (2002).

Any perception that the oil price boom of 1999–2000 had solved Saudi Arabia's economic problems, however, was misfounded. The welcome combination of increased production (officially) from April 2000—to more than 8 million bpd—and very strong prices could by mid-2001 be seen to be coming to an end. Oil prices and Saudi GDP were, in fact, as early as April 2000 forecast to weaken and to 'rise gently', respectively (EIU, 2000a). The 11 September 2001 airliner suicide attacks against New York and Washington pushed the United States—the world's largest economy and energy consumer—toward official recession and further increased political instability in the Middle East. These events, with the world economy moving into recession, signalled lower oil prices to come. OPEC cut production three times in 2001, removing 3.5 million bpd from the global supply in a fruitless attempt to support its target price range of US$22–8 per barrel. The 2001 Saudi budget was predicated on a price for Saudi oil of US$22 per barrel at 8.7 million bpd—planning criteria which were already compromised very early in the year (SAMBA, 2001: 2, 4–5). In mid-November 2001, the price of the North Sea Brent benchmark crude fell below US$17 per barrel for the first time since June 1999. Saudi oil sells for about $2 less than Brent and, after the third OPEC output cut, Saudi Arabian oil production stood at 7.541 million bpd. As a result, one early 2001 forecast predicted a budget deficit of US$2,000 million, representing a deficit to GDP ratio of approximately 1.3% on GDP that was forecast to contract by 2% (see SAMBA, 2001: 1–2). Another, later, estimate from the Riyad Bank forecast the 2001 deficit to come in at US$3,200 million (see AFP, 2001b). A final revision of the 2001 deficit forecast—to US$6,675 million—was officially announced by the Saudi Ministry of Finance and National Economy in a statement issued on 8 December 2001. The slide back into the red was set to continue unabated into the following year as the Saudi cabinet also announced that the 2002 budget would carry a deficit of US$12,016 million (see, for example, Reuters, 2001h). In terms of the national account, the kingdom in 2002 was preparing—with a price of between US$15 and US$17 per barrel forecast for Saudi oil—to revisit the figures produced in 1998 when the price of oil collapsed.

Ultimately, the period of high oil prices 1999–2000 will prove to have been of only limited and temporary benefit to the kingdom, and in fact only reinforces the 'devastating volatility' (Amuzegar, 1999: 152) of its revenue flow. Moreover, the sobering news does not end with the falling oil prices of late-2001. OPEC's November 2001 deferment of a fourth production cut for that year heralds the dawning of an era in which the organisation cannot manage global oil supply and prices on its own. OPEC states agreed to cut another 1.5 million barrels from their daily production, but from January 2002, and only if non-OPEC producers—especially the major producers Russia, Norway and Mexico—collectively agreed to cut output by a further 500,000 bpd. The compliance of non-OPEC producers with OPEC strategies cannot be assumed to be a foregone conclusion; dissent on the part of just one major non-OPEC producer on one occasion will more than likely result in at least a short-term financial tragedy for all OPEC producers.[18] Russia, in particular, is reckoned to be set on the strategic economic path of high volumes of oil and gas exports based on a low price dependency, and will therefore be an unreliable player in OPEC-non-OPEC production/price co-ordination deals (see Zhdannikov and Lannin, 2001).[19] OPEC can only look forward to repeated struggles with non-OPEC producers if the difficulties involved in the first

---

[18] Regarding the OPEC dilemma of November–December 2001, the cartel's Venezuelan secretary-general, Ali Rodriguez, 'warned of an "unimaginable" collapse in oil prices [in 2002] if non-OPEC rival producers did not agree to cut output in tandem with the cartel' (AFP, 2001a).

[19] See also note 29 below.

attempt at securing such co-operation are any measure (see, for example, AFP, 2001d; Reuters, 2001g). Even after deals are sealed, all the countries concerned—both OPEC and non-OPEC produc-ers—need to honour their cutback commitments to ensure the effectiveness of the strategy of decreased production.

The Centre for Global Energy Studies believes that OPEC, by making production cuts conditional on non-OPEC cuts, 'has intro-duced a new degree of uncertainty into the market' (CGES, 2001). This comes on top of an oil market that has become increasingly uncertain and volatile since 1986 (Stevens, 1996: 400). A unified stance on the part of all the world's oil producers will, in fact, be-come more difficult to achieve as commercial reserves of oil are dis-covered in the economic zones of more and more countries of the world.[20] Saudi Arabia, as the OPEC cartel's most powerful member, will for the foreseeable future inevitably face difficult choices that centre on the equally damaging sacrifices of low prices in competi-tion with non-OPEC producers on the one hand, and loss of mar-ket share through decreased production in attempting to defend prices on the other. The economic and social costs to the kingdom of such sacrifices will only increase with time.

Paul Stevens foresaw these developments in his major critiques of 'the conventional view of ever growing dependence upon Gulf oil' and that the international oil market would amble along much as it had always done (Stevens, 1997: 135; 1996: 391). Stevens' argument is based on the following recent developments in the oil industry and specialist observations of the field: (*a*) revolutionary advances in oil exploration and development technologies have lowered the cost of oil production and increased recovery rates, thus making previously uneconomical (non-OPEC) fields worth developing; (*b*) oil companies are being offered increasingly attractive invest-ment terms by (non-OPEC) governments to explore for and develop new reserves; (*c*) the trend towards privatising or commercialising (non-OPEC and non-GCC) state-owned national oil companies is improving efficiency which translates into increased production capacity; (*d*) non-GCC OPEC producers, such as Venezuela, Nigeria

---

[20] To cite just one example for illustration, significant new reserves of oil are still being discovered in the Caribbean, in addition to fields that have already been a boon to the economy of Trinidad.

and Algeria, have been more successful in attracting foreign investment to their upstream production operations, which promises to
improve efficiency and production capacity significantly; (*e*) at some
stage, probably before the end of the first decade of the twenty-first
century, Iraqi oil will re-enter the market on a large scale; and
(*f*) the countries of the former Soviet Union, including Russia, are
likely to attract significant new foreign investment in oil exploration, development and redevelopment of existing fields as legal and
political operating contexts become settled and problems of export
routes are resolved (see Stevens, 1997: 138–9; 1996: 396–400).

The former Saudi oil minister and founder and chairman of the
Centre for Global Energy Studies, Ahmad Zaki Yamani, has publicly expressed an opinion on the future of the oil industry that is in
keeping with Stevens'. In June 2000 Yamani raised eyebrows when
he asserted that by 2005 oil prices would have suffered another
crash (see Brandreth, 2000). Yamani's well-founded prediction did
not stop at five years:

Thirty years from now there will be a huge amount of oil—and no buyers.
Thirty years from now, there is no problem with oil. Oil will be left in the
ground. The Stone Age came to an end not because we had lack of stones,
and the oil age will come to an end not because we have lack of oil … I am
a Saudi and I know we will have serious economic difficulties ahead of us.
(Yamani, quoted in Brandreth, 2000).

Yamani's reasoning is almost identical to Stevens': basically, '…on
the supply side it is easy to find oil and produce it' (Yamani, quoted
in Brandreth, 2000). As part of the overall bleak scenario for oil producers, Yamani also cited new automobile technologies which will
eventually revolutionise the demand for energy away from petroleum (see Brandreth, 2000; Fagan, 2000). Stevens, too, addresses the
issue of demand for oil; he argues that at the same time that non-
GCC oil supply is set to continue expanding, world demand for oil
'may also begin a long term fundamental decline' (see Stevens,
1997: 139–40). A former chief economist at the Shell oil company
has summed up a particular view of the oil industry which does not
augur well for the future prosperity of Saudi Arabia and other major
petroleum producers whose economies remain dependent on oil:
'People in the industry would not be surprised by a vision of the

future with relatively weak prices, but punctuated by occasional price shocks' (quoted in Fagan, 2000).

The veneer of improving fortunes during the mid-1999–mid-2001 period barely veiled the deep and serious structural flaws in the Saudi economy. Looking beyond short-term oil price fluctuations, Saudi Arabia's status as a distributive and welfare state, if not its technical status as a rentier state, is under threat.

The sustainability of the rentier–distributive state.   Saudi Arabia's fiscal patterns over the course of the 1980s and 1990s were not ones that would lead to the sustained elimination of deficits in the near future, and it was observed that the (temporary) recovery in oil prices from April 1999 'will not obviate the need for deeper economic restructuring' (EIU, 1999b). The economic problems are more complex than erratic oil prices and budget deficits. For example, 17 continuous years of deficit financing (1983–99 inclusive) have resulted in the 'rapid depletion' both of liquid reserves of foreign exchange and of total foreign assets (*MEED*, 1997a; Krimly, 1999: 261–2; Kanovsky, 1994: 19–21; Allen, 1996; Wilson and Graham, 1994: 192). Foreign exchange reserves were readily available to finance the government's deficit spending, while non-liquid foreign assets had to be liquidated to help make up the shortfalls. Immediately after the 1991 Gulf War, the kingdom's foreign assets were 'believed to be precariously low' (Pike, 1992: 10), and were all but officially admitted to be 'almost depleted' (Krimly, 1999: 262).

The post-Gulf War political environment in Saudi Arabia was more restless than it had been since the height of the Arab nationalism inspired by Egyptian President Gamal Abd al-Nasser in the 1950s and 1960s, and economic issues were an important element in the overall presentation of this recent surge in political discontent. A glimpse of the political fallout precipitated by the Saudi government's economic management as practised to date, and by the depletion of foreign assets in particular, is provided in the CDLR-commissioned 'Country Report'. In the notes to part two (which were written by the CDLR), reference is made to 'a top secret telegram' dated 6 August 1994, which was sent to the president of the Consultative Council by King Fahd, related to an also secret cabinet report on the state of the kingdom's finances. In this report, '…the regime admits for the first time that all reserves accumulated in the

1970's and early 80's had been completely exhausted by the end of [1988]' (CDLR, 1995a: 47n. 2).[21]

This dire situation, purportedly admitted only to itself by the regime, stood in contrast to the official figures for liquid reserves and foreign assets at the time. However, the official, publicly available figures for both classes of assets clearly show they had been steadily run down from 1983 (see Table 4.2[22]). Referring to data for total accumulated funds, the CDLR (1995a: 47n. 2) claimed that the official figures were 'completely unrealistic': 'Even if we interpret the regime's admission conservatively, assuming that gold and foreign currency reserves needed to back the Riyal of roughly 30$bn were untouched by the end of 1988, we must assume that the entries under "funds accumulated" [for 1988 listed as US$93.33 billion; see CDLR, 1995a: 35, t.3]…must be erroneous by at least 60$bn.'[23]

As a result of the seriousness of fiscal affairs in the early 1990s, the cabinet report apparently 'suggest[ed] vast increases in fees and taxes' (CDLR, 1995a: 47n. 2).[24] Various extractive measures were

---

[21] The CDLR obtained copies of these documents and published them as an appendix to their 'Country Report' (see CDLR, 1995a: 50–7). King Fahd's telegram is numbered 3141/S and dated 29/02/1415. The Ministry of Finance and National Economy report referred to in, and attached to the telegram, takes the form of a cabinet memorandum, numbered 9223; this includes another document, 'Proposals and suggestions to increase resources from some of the utilities and services', also published in the CDLR appendix. The CDLR, and now its offshoot, MIRA, have consistently proved accurate in commentary and forecasts on Saudi Arabian sociopolitical and economic developments, which reflects the positioning and reliability of their informants in the kingdom.

[22] Table 4.2 also provides comparative data on the UAE's liquid foreign reserves and Singapore's total foreign assets to help put the Saudi figures into some kind of perspective. The IMF lists the population for the three countries in 1992 as 16.96 million, 2.04 million and 3.26 million, respectively, and for 1993, as 17.35 million, 2.1 million and 3.36 million, respectively (IMF, 1999b: 654, 772, 670). Thus, on a per capita basis, even accepting the official figures at face value, Saudi Arabia's foreign liquid reserves and assets and, by implication, the management of them, compare poorly with its tiny neighbour and with Singapore, which is not only tiny but not endowed with any natural resources.

[23] Gause (1997: 68) quotes foreign currency reserves of US$20 billion held by SAMA to support the Saudi riyal.

[24] The cabinet committee which authored the 1994 economic report was headed by the then Minister of Finance and National Economy, Muhammad Abal-Khail,

indeed proposed by the government—and in some cases imposed, but then withdrawn in the face of social and business opposition—in an attempt to redress the poor state of the national fisc (Chaudhry, 1997: 274–5, 286). In the event, a revival of state rental income from oil spared the regime from having to press on with such relatively radical reforms at this time.

High oil prices and subsequent progress in reducing the budget deficit in 1996 and 1997 undoubtedly went some way toward halting the trend towards the evaporation of liquid reserves and foreign assets. What did have a very positive impact on the kingdom's reserve holdings, however, was a 'revision' by the Saudi fiscal authorities of the methods used to calculate the kingdom's holdings of foreign exchange. At an analysis-confounding stroke of a pen, Saudi foreign exchange holdings from 1996 were rejuvenated, on paper at least: independent confirmation of the status of these reserves is not available. In a note on Saudi Arabia in the 'International Liquidity' section of its *International Financial Statistics* publication, the IMF reports that '[b]eginning in January 1996, the [Saudi] authorities provided revised data on *Foreign Exchange*…after reviewing their methodology for classifying foreign assets' (see IMF, 2000b: 666). The new, 'revised' figures and the explanatory note were first published by the IMF in March 2000. On the other hand (using the figures presented by the IMF before the publication of 'revised data' from 1996), once liquid reserves had stabilised around the US$7,500 million mark in 1997–8—from a high of US$32,236 million in 1981—rising oil prices from late-March 1999 can be seen to have had little immediate impact on the kingdom's reserves (see Table 4.2, 'Saudi liquid foreign reserves minus gold').

Regardless of the true levels of Saudi assets and rising oil prices, as late as December 1999 the Economist Intelligence Unit (EIU, 1999m) expected the kingdom to be a regional economic laggard

---

who had occupied his post for 20 years. A 'widely respected figure', and one who has been 'credited with persuading the country of the need for austerity measures…', he was replaced in the 2 August 1995 cabinet 'shake-up'—a move which was reported as unexpected (See Cooper, 1995a). His departure was described as 'largely his own choice' (ibid.) and was probably in order to pursue his own business interests in the private sector (al-Fagih, S., 1999, pers. comm., 25 Aug.).

Table 4.2

SAUDI ARABIAN FOREIGN ASSETS, WITH COMPARATIVE FIGURES
FOR THE UNITED ARAB EMIRATES AND SINGAPORE (US$ MILLION)

Year	Saudi liquid foreign reserves minus gold[1]		UAE liquid foreign reserves minus gold	Total foreign assets (cf. Singapore)[2]	
1972		2,383	–	(1,755)	2,892.7
1973		3,747	91.7	(2,373)	4,590.1
1974		14,153	452.9	(2,669)	19,918.3
1975		23,193	987.9	(3,157)	38,941.3
1976		26,900	1,906.5	(3,344)	51,229.4
1977		29,903	800.3	(3,699)	59,082.0
1978		19,200	811.8	(5,046)	58,521.5
1979		19,273	1,432.3	(5,777)	61,729.3
1980		23,437	2,014.7	(6,425)	87,398.9
1981		32,236	3,202.2	(7,332)	130,041.9
1982		29,549	2,215.5	(8,373)	137,952.8
1983		27,287	2,072.4	(9,349)	126,774.3
1984		24,748	2,286.9	(10,664)	111,303.1
1985		25,004	3,204.3	(12,308)	88,216.7
1986		18,324	3,369.9	(12,932)	74,574.0
1987		22,684	4,725.3	(14,455)	68,502.0
1988		20,553	4,433.5	(16,536)	62,165.5
1989		16,748	4,456.6	(19,795)	60,518.0
1990		11,668	4,583.9	(26,770)	56,667.5
1991		11,673	5,365.4	(32,301)	55,794.3
1992		5,935	5,711.8	(40,385)	57,380.5
1993		7,428	6,103.7	(48,191)	51,556.7
1994		7,378	6,658.8	(55,759)	49,548.7
1995		8,622	7,470.9	(68,673)	46,472.6
1996[3]	14,321	(6,794)	8,055.5	(76,419)	52,355.1
1997	14,876	(7,353)	8,372.3	(80,561)	58,485.9
1998	14,220	(7,520)	9,077.1	(74,441)	46,889.1
1999				(75,786)	
1st quar.	17,060	(8,265)	8,989.9		42,114.8
2nd	14,021	(7,159)	9,212.0		
3rd	14,095	(7,921)	9,636.2		
4th	16,997	(not available)	10,675.1		
2000					
Jan.	16,236				
Feb.	16,188				
Mar.	16,488				
Apr.	16,128				
May	16,843				

Source: International Financial Statistics, IMF, Washington DC (various issues).

[1] Gold reserves do not exceed the non-gold reserves listed by the IMF. Saudi gold reserves 1992–99 were valued between US$214 million and US$239 million.

[2] Figures for Singapore (rounded) are listed in parentheses.

[1, 2] Data for Saudi Arabia corresponds to that presented by Cordesman (1997: 61).

[3] Saudi fiscal authorities provided the IMF with 'revised data' on liquid foreign exchange reserves 'after reviewing their methodology for classifying foreign assets' (IMF, 2000b: 666). The 'revised' figures are effective from January 1996, and are first listed by the IMF in March 2000. 'Pre-revision' figures are retained (in parentheses) for some continuity of analysis.

in 2000, and that the Saudi government would continue drawing on its foreign assets 'to meet spending commitments'. Foreign assets, by official accounts, still remain 'substantial', according to the EIU (ibid.). Foreign exchange holdings—which only record liquid reserves, such as treasury bills and bank deposits but do not reveal transfers of reserves to investments with higher earnings, such as bonds (see *MEED*, 1997a)—may not be quite as depleted as the most pessimistic assessments might indicate (nor perhaps as flush as the 'revised' figures might suggest), but the warning signs are unmistakable.[25]

While repeating the familiar lament that '[i]t is extremely difficult to find accurate and official figures on the liquid reserves of the Saudi government', F. Gregory Gause in 1997—that is, even before the oil price crash of 1998—wrote that 'it is clear...the [Saudi] government cannot finance continued deficits' from its reserves (Gause, 1997: 68, 81n. 10), a situation that, moreover, also faces Kuwait and, to a lesser extent, all the other GCC states (see ibid., 68–9). Although the EIU estimated the kingdom's total net official foreign assets at US$82,500 million as of 1998 (EIU, 1999f), foreign exchange reserves as of March 1999 were, in contrast, estimated at 'only around' US$7,500 million, 'representing import cover of only 2.1 months...', a level which is contributing to the vulnerability of the riyal (EIU, 1999b; cf. Table 4.2; see also Allen, 1998). EIU estimates of Saudi foreign exchange holdings for the first two quarters of 1999 were US$6,800 million and US$5,560 million respectively (EIU, 1999l).[26] Not only have the state's reserves dwindled, but private Saudi assets held abroad are reported to have fallen by approximately US$30,000 million since the beginning of 1996 (al-Dabbagh, 1999).

[25] The IMF's measurement of international liquidity as displayed in its country pages—the source used for Table 4.2—include, in the case of Saudi Arabia, the US dollar value of SAMA's holdings of IMF Special Drawing Rights (SDRs), reserve position in the IMF, and (principally) foreign exchange reserves: the sum of these is used by the IMF to calculate 'total reserves minus gold' (see, for example, IMF, 2000a: xv). The value of the kingdom's gold reserves are not significant (see Table 4.2, note 1). Worthy of mention is the IMF's resort to vaguer language when presenting Saudi statistics: 'approximately end of period', compared with a more definite 'end of period' for most other countries, including the UAE (the fiscal year for both Saudi Arabia and the UAE is the Gregorian calendar year).

[26] These EIU foreign exchange figures for 1999 equate to the IMF's listing of pre-revision figures for the same period; they make up the bulk of 'Saudi liquid foreign reserves minus gold', as listed in Table 4.2.

The rising price of oil in 1999, however, presented a ray of sunshine as far as the kingdom's assets were concerned, since the US$6,072 million budget surplus of 2000 is believed to have gone some way toward rebuilding foreign assets. The IMF (2001: 1) reported that SAMA's 'net foreign assets rose to cover about 10 months of prospective imports'; in addition, the Saudi government is reported to have used some of the surplus to accelerate the implementation of state investment projects (IMF, 2001: 1). The government also used surplus revenues to settle overdue payments to farmers and contractors (SAMBA, 2001: 6–7; IMF, 2001: 1). Nevertheless, many details of the 2000 surplus—why, for example, it wasn't more than it was, and exactly how it was used—typically remain a mystery (see SAMBA, 2001: 6–7). The year 2000 may have been a good one for the Saudi government, but the consequences of 17 years of deficit financing will present Riyadh with formidable challenges for many years to come.

One of the enduring negative legacies of the deficits is public debt. The same 1995 IMF report that predicted a return to double-digit budget deficit-to-GDP ratios also warned that the Saudi public debt would rise to 110% of GDP by the year 2000 if 'reforms' were not 'put in place' (see *The Banker*, 1995). One major Saudi bank has stated that '[t]he total debt of the central government is not reported...estimates based upon accumulated annual budget deficits and known borrowings by government companies suggest a figure...in the range of $125 billion at end-1997' (SAMBA, 1998e: 3). In fact, the growth of the kingdom's public debt, mostly incurred through domestic borrowing to finance budget deficits after the unsustainable drawing down of reserves, has in recent years been 'spectacular' (Krimly, 1999: 262). By late 1998, total public debt was estimated to be 'approaching 100% of GDP' (see SAMBA, 1998f: 8); the 1998 debt was eventually reported to have peaked at 104% of GDP (Hirst, 1999). EIU estimates in 1999, however, had the Saudi public sector debt rising from 87.4% of GDP in 1997 to 109.9% of GDP in 1998—in approximate dollar terms, a rise from around US$127,780 million to US$144,740 million (EIU, 1999f).[27]

---

[27] Saudi GDP declined in 1998 as a result of the crash in oil prices, from US$146,200 million in 1997 to an estimated US$131,700 million for 1998 (EIU, 1999f). The elusiveness of tangible Saudi economic statistics is once again illustrated by

By early 1999, domestic debt alone was threatening to exceed 100% of GDP (EIU, 1999a; 1999d). Official foreign debt—unpopular from the Saudi point of view and downplayed by the government—by the end of 1997 stood at an estimated US$6,000 million/4% of GDP (SAMBA, 1998e: 3; cf. Wilson and Graham, 1994: 194–5). The total external debt of both the public and private sectors for 1997 was estimated by the EIU at US$24,415 million/16.7% of GDP, and for 1998 at US$30,300 million/23% of GDP, and was forecast to rise in 1999 to US$32,730 million/24.5% of GDP (EIU, 1999f). The 1999 forecast was actually revised upward in April 2000—after a year of dramatically-rising oil prices—to US$34,024 million (EIU, 2000a).

Regarding the total Saudi public sector debt, however, the more 'significant factor' is that around US$6,000 million per year is already allocated to servicing the sum total of the government's existing liabilities: 'a substantial portion of budgetary resources... [which is] more than 12 percent of recent budgets' (SAMBA, 1998e: 4). Worse still, projected continuing budget deficits for the foreseeable future will demand '[a] steady increase in both domestic and external debt' in order to cover the deficits (EIU, 1999g). The EIU has also forecast that total external debt will rise, albeit modestly, to US$34,660 in 2001, which will 'reflect... rising short-term debt and borrowing by government agencies' (EIU, 2000a), and that total public debt will run at around 120% of a forecast average GDP of US$154,760 million for the years 2001–2003 (EIU, 1999f).[28]

---

comparing these EIU 1997 and 1998 GDP estimates with those of the World Bank for 1999 for which year, when the dramatic recovery in oil prices began in March, the kingdom's GDP was listed as only US$128,892 million (World Bank, 2001a: 297). SAMBA (2001: 1) lists Saudi nominal GDP as follows: 1997, US$143,550 million; 1998, US$127,700 million; 1999, US$139,000 million.

[28] On 'growing government indebtedness', which is described as 'alarming', see also Wilson and Graham (1994: 191–8). They write that the

[c]omposition of [domestic medium- and long-term debt] is intriguing because its exact size is unknown...SAMA has never clarified how many development bonds have been issued, or what percentage has been placed with banks or with government agencies. This information has even been refused to...domestic banks, which have been solicited and pressured to take the paper. Estimates vary wildly... (Wilson and Graham, 1994: 193).

A return to budgetary surplus in 2000 resulted in 'stabilised' government debt, but in no significant reduction in debt (SAMBA, 2001: 2). In February 2001, SAMBA (2001: 2) estimated the government's domestic debt at US$162,700 million/101% of GDP.[29] The IMF (2001: 1) put the government's domestic debt for 2000 at 95% of GDP. Other estimates at the end of 2001 put domestic debt at 107% of GDP (see Fahmy, 2001). SAMBA (2001: 8) has described 'the high level of debt' as one of the three principal 'imbalances…in Saudi government finances', and has predicted that, with a return to deficit in the 2001 fiscal year, there is 'not…much room for debt reduction'. The bank regards a 60% debt to GDP ratio to be 'prudent', but that this 'would take many years' of financial discipline and economic reforms (SAMBA, 2001: 9).

The economic circumstances outlined above emphasise the significance of the 1994 Saudi cabinet report suggestion that 'vast increases in fees and taxes' be implemented, and the fact that it echoed similar conclusions arrived at by the IMF and a host of economic and political analysts since the Gulf War. The report also emphasised that Saudi Arabia's financial managers and political leaders have for some time been well aware of problems in the kingdom's economic structure and of what measures may be required to rectify such an unsound structure. The net result of the regime's failure to act effectively is that the underlying patterns of Saudi economic management have still not been addressed. International pressure for the reform of the Saudi rentier–distributive state has been building up and will intensify.

The dilemma is this: continued absolute reliance on oil rents entails a vulnerability that cannot be lessened without significant changes to the whole economy and the way it is managed. Many of these necessary changes are unpalatable socioeconomically and, by extension, politically. Rolling back the distributive function of the

---

For yet another startling account of the burgeoning domestic and foreign debt of the Saudi government, see Kanovsky (1994: 74–5). It should be emphasised once again that although the accuracy of specific economic data for Saudi Arabia often cannot be ascertained, important basic trends can still be plotted.

[29] The foreign debt of the world's second-largest oil exporter, Russia, stood at around US$140,000 million in late 2001. This level of debt has been cited as spurring Russian desire to pump as much revenue-generating oil as possible (see Zhdannikov and Lannin, 2001).

state and the legitimacy of largesse are significant steps the Al Saud have, not surprisingly, been reluctant to take. Saudi budget, balance of payments and GDP figures for 2000 may have elicited sighs of relief from the regime, but 'macro-economic imbalances [and] structural rigidities in the budget' (IMF Staff Report, cited in *The Banker*, 1995) hang over the Saudi economy like an executioner's axe. Unless addressed, these economic weaknesses will only exacerbate further the vulnerability of the Saudi budget to oil price fluctuations, particularly as the predictions of the future of the oil industry by the likes of Stevens and Yamani come to pass.

The reforms the IMF has in mind—and the IMF is by no means alone in its prognosis and prescriptions—relate to the liberalisation of restrictions on foreign investment and the implementation of 'a well-defined privatisation programme' (IMF Staff Report, cited in *The Banker*, 1995). Saudi Aramco, SABIC (Saudi Basic Industries Corporation, the holding company for the kingdom's principal petrochemical concerns), and Saudia (the national airline, now Saudi Arabian Airlines) were specifically mentioned in this regard (ibid.; see also *MEED*, 1997b). Pressure on the Saudi regime to conform to the doctrines of economic globalisation—put forward as 'a fundamental source not only of economic growth but also of structural change' (*IMF Survey*, 1997b: 153)—has only increased since the time of the 1995 IMF report (see, for example, *MEED*, 1997b). SAMBA (2001: 9) has recommended that a strategic goal of the government should be to cap oil revenue needs at 50% of the budget—a goal that is as clearly revolutionary as it is long-term.

Reducing the reliance on foreign labour; eliminating subsidies for consumer utilities, for industry, and for thousands of minor royal family members; reforming the civil service; introducing a greater degree of transparency in economic and financial processes; and reforming the excesses of *asabiyya* capitalism are other serious structural reforms being urged upon the Saudi political economy. Together, they spell the end of the Saudi distributive state. In the wake of these reforms, and with further economic development and diversification—industrialisation in particular—the end of the Saudi rentier state will also be in sight. The unsustainability of the Saudi rentier–distributive political economy has been apparent for many years and the era of rentier opulence is drawing to a close.

Economic and financial globalisation: Another challenge to Al Saud sovereignty?

'Globalisation' and economic internationalisation. 'Globalisation' has been a source of increasing debate in recent years. The effect of this internationalising force has been to induce change in the nature of the economic, political, social and cultural dimensions of the world's geopolitical regions, nation-states and local communities. The multifaceted changes associated with these developments have generated intense interest among theorists contemplating and ana-lysing the complex and sometimes opposing forces at work in an increasingly integrated world.[30] The interaction between the vari-ous dimensions of globalisation is very relevant to any study of developing countries, including Saudi Arabia, for whose society and regime the principal elements associated with the spread of global-isation clearly have potentially serious implications. These elements include the revolutions in information and communications tech-nologies and, to a lesser extent, in transport—'the real driving force[s] behind globalisation' (Schulze and Ursprung, 1999: 302; see also Fuchs and Koch, 1996: 165–6).[31] They also include 'the *adop-tion of some form of market economy and democratic rule of law* in an increasing number of countries' (Schulze and Ursprung, 1999: 303, authors' emphasis).

Since this chapter is concerned with the economics of Saudi sociopolitics, the emphasis of the approach to globalisation here in the first instance is obviously on its economic dimension, which is the most solid empirically and most sound theoretically. Some economists maintain there is 'no generally accepted definition of internationalization or globalization...so there are no generally accepted propositions concerning its implications' (Kemp and Shimomura, 1999: 1). Others—based on extensive discussion and some qualifications—settle on 'global economic integration' as a

---

[30] See, for example, the wide-ranging contributions, from a variety of approaches, on all aspects of 'globalisation' in the volume edited by Eleonore Kofman and Gillian Youngs (1996), and the more novel treatise of Benjamin Barber (1996).

[31] The information and communications aspects of global integration, in particu-lar, are proving problematical for the Al Saud. For example, they are presenting serious implications for the regime's policies of public opinion manipulation and censorship (issues treated in the relevant sections of Chapter 5).

brief working definition (Schulze and Ursprung, 1999). With reference to economic globalisation, it is worth noting that:

...a sober interpretation of the available data points to the fact that the economic reality at the turn of our century does, in no way, resemble the notion of a single and uniform global economy... Even though the economies of advanced industrial countries are currently more integrated than they used to be—especially as far as capital markets are concerned—substantial home biases still exist and do not seem on the verge of disappearing. Moreover, a detailed analysis of the empirical facts clearly demonstrates that the extent to which individual countries and industries have been exposed to global market integration is not uniform. (Schulze and Ursprung, 1999: 345)

Thus, 'globalisation' in the economic sense may be described as the ongoing process of the opening up of economies—'economic internationalisation' being the favoured term in economist circles (Mitchell, D., 1999, pers. comm., 23 June; Schulze and Ursprung, 1999: 301). According to the generally accepted formula, economic opening up means unrestricted international trade and investment, encompassing the free flow of goods, services and financial capital. This, in general terms, is the formula being presented to Saudi Arabia and with which the regime is experimenting.

While the kingdom appears to be moving slowly but apparently surely in the economically 'global' direction, the dearth of sound information on Saudi political and economic processes makes an assessment of progress and predictions of any outcome beyond the immediate future difficult. The academic economists, Günther Schulze and Heinrich Ursprung (1999: 346), point out that 'it is impossible to unambiguously determine the influence of globalisation on the conduct of national fiscal policies without resorting to empirical investigations'. The results of any such study concerning Saudi Arabia, if one were ever to be conducted, would be at best dubious in the sociopolitical circumstances that have traditionally prevailed, and of course still currently prevail, in the kingdom.

That Saudi Arabia is attracted by the lure of the potential economic benefits of a more integrated global trading community has been proved by the kingdom's application in 1993 to join the General Agreement on Tariffs and Trade (GATT) and its stated desire to become a member of the World Trade Organisation (WTO) (see, for example, *Saudi Gazette*, 1997a).[32] In 1997 the Saudi Minister of Industry and Electricity, Hashim bin Abdullah bin Hashim Yamani, announced that his ministry was preparing a study on a new industrial policy 'to meet the new international climate and future challenges' (Yamani, 1997), a process which, in meeting WTO membership criteria, was expected to 'provide opportunities and challenges' for Saudi industry (see *Al-Hawadith*, 1997). Yamani has claimed that membership of the WTO will prove to be of 'immeasurable' benefit as 'a major step in opening up foreign markets to Saudi products and facilitating access to Saudi markets for foreign firms' (see IPR, 1997d). Although also intensifying competition in the domestic market, it would thus help to achieve the goal of increasing industrial exports, particularly in the petrochemical industries (see IPR, 1997d; *Al-Hawadith*, 1997).

Other sources have confirmed Saudi Arabia's industrial export drive, which is crucial for the future success of Saudi economic diversification. For example, Fahd Aslimy—the Assistant Secretary General for Export, Saudi Export Development Centre—has stated that Saudi industry is currently geared to replacing imports. To illustrate, he revealed that most of the 1997 industrial output, worth around 70 billion riyals (US$20.14 billion), went to the local market. However, he stressed that, in the longer term, Saudi industry has 'no choice' other than to look to export because of a 'shortage of local markets, which are limited, and excess capacity'. This export drive will be assisted by the fact that Saudi products are being made to international standards (Aslimy, F. 1998, pers. comm., 7 Mar.; see also Sharani, 1998). Clearly, WTO membership will aid this process.

Although seeking to join the WTO 'on the favourable terms granted to developing countries', senior Saudi industrial and commercial officials admit that WTO membership will require changes to the kingdom's economy, trade practices and regulations (Reuters, 1997a; *Saudi Gazette*, 1997a), a process by no means guaranteed to proceed smoothly. For example, after the third round of negotiations

[32] Saudi Arabia is the only GCC country not already a member of the WTO. The WTO was founded in 1995 as a result of the latest Uruguay Round (1986–94) of GATT; GATT itself was established in the aftermath of the Second World War to promote free global trade, but is now succeeded by the WTO.

on Saudi Arabia's application to join the WTO, in May 1997, trade diplomats said the kingdom 'must do more to present detailed offers on market access' (see Reuters, 1997a). Other predictions are proving prophetic: 'implementation of wide-ranging reforms is still expected to be a long process...as many of the reforms required for WTO membership, including measures such as easing restrictive practices in the banking sector, are likely to be strongly resisted by vested interests in the kingdom' (EIU, 1997; see also Henry, 1999a: 3–4; 1999c: 29–34).

Just before the November 2001 WTO meeting in Qatar, Saudi officials began playing down the kingdom's prospects of joining the organisation in 2002. A member of the Saudi team negotiating with the WTO over membership was quoted as saying he did not expect that his country would join the WTO before late 2003; the chief economist of Saudi Arabia's largest bank, the National Commercial Bank, also stated that Saudi WTO membership would 'probably take a long time' (Isa, 2001b). The Saudi position initially promoted at the time was that WTO membership would compromise a number of Islamic principles, which the kingdom simply was not prepared to do. The real problem, however, was that extensive economic and legal reforms required by the WTO before the kingdom could be admitted had not been implemented (see Isa, 2001b; Reuters, 2001a). A Saudi offer to carry out the reforms after admission was rejected by the WTO, and Saudi officials subsequently blamed the kingdom's delayed entry on 'unclear and inflexible WTO rules' (Reuters, 2001a; Isa, 2001b). By mid-2002 accession negotiations were described as 'stalled' (SAMBA, 2002b: 9; see also SAMBA, 2002a: 28).

Encouragement for Saudi Arabia to become more fully involved in the race toward economic internationalisation is coming from the United States (see Kalicki, 1999) and further impetus is also being provided by the other Gulf Arab states of the GCC which are similarly seeking the perceived benefits of more liberal international trade via WTO membership. According to the chairman of the Saudi Chambers of Commerce and Industry, by 1997 the GCC states had collectively drawn up 'a globalization program in...preparation to join [the WTO]' (see *The Riyadh Daily*, 1997b). The creation of 'a single Gulf market' is also on the GCC agenda (Avancena, 1997), a goal recently given fresh emphasis by Crown

Prince Abdullah (*The Emirates News*, 1998), and reinforced by strong advocacy on the part of the United States at the Gulf '99 Conference in Abu Dhabi (see Kalicki, 1999). Programmes and plans may be being designed, but the reality is that the effects of globalisation have been making incremental inroads into Saudi Arabia for some time. Salamé (1989: 78) maintains that the oil boom 'almost overnight, intimately linked [Saudi Arabia] with the international capitalist system'. In 1987 the Gregorian calendar year was adopted for the issuance of Saudi budgets, an act which 'reflect[ed] the degree to which state revenues were increasingly tied to international financial and commodity markets', and representative of the growing influence of 'the new internationalization' (Chaudhry, 1997: 269n. 1, 270). The IMF has confirmed the trend more generally by stating that the decade 1985–95 was 'a period when the global integration process was in full swing' (*IMF Survey*, 1997b: 154).[33]

The IMF has consistently been a powerful advocate of economic internationalisation, and the organisation is committed to ensuring the process continues to develop apace. IMF publications are a rich source of information on how this major international economic body perceives the course that globalisation should follow since it actively promotes the creation of 'the global economy' and the economic architecture needed to support it (*IMF Survey*, 1997b: 158).[34]

---

[33] 'Global integration' did not begin in 1985, nor did it end in 1995 (see Schulze and Ursprung, 1999: 305, 305n. 13, 307, 307n. 15, 308; *The Economist*, 1998f: 62; *IMF Survey*, 1997b: 153, 155). Moreover, the momentum of 'globalisation' is by no means trailing off; in 1999, foreign direct investment worldwide grew by 25% to US$827 billion, and cross-border merger and acquisition activity rose by more than 33% to US$720 billion (*The Economist*, 2000a; 2000b). By the end of the first half of 2000, 'despite a slowdown in the second quarter', cross-border merger and acquisition activity had risen by another 26%, involving transactions worth US$1.9 trillion (*The Economist*, 2000c).

[34] In presenting an alternative view to that of the IMF, Ignacio Ramonet, writing for *Le Monde Diplomatique*, names four organisations prominent in promoting globalisation:

Financial globalisation is a law unto itself and it has established a separate supranational state with its own administrative apparatus, its own spheres of influence, its own means of action. That is to say the [IMF], the World Bank, the Organization for Economic Cooperation and Development (OECD) and the [WTO]. These four powerful institutions are unanimous in singing the praises of 'market values', a view faithfully echoed by most of the major organs of the media. (Ramonet, 1997)

It is interesting to note that a report at the Fund's economic forum on 5 May 1997 at IMF headquarters in Washington was introduced as follows: 'Globalization…is a fundamental source not only of economic growth but also of structural change, presenting policy-makers with both new opportunities and challenges' (*IMF Survey*, 1997b: 153), and the very same catch-phrase—'opportunities and challenges'—was then echoed by Minister Yamani in August 1997, soon after the May WTO–Saudi negotiations on the kingdom's application to join the WTO. Other such in-vogue economic slo-gans in general circulation are now being heard from other Saudi ministers; for example, the Minister of Planning, Khalid bin Muhammad al-Gosaibi, whilst promoting privatisation and foreign investment at the Gulf 2000 Conference said that the kingdom 'must accelerate productivity growth and strengthen…international com-petitiveness' (al-Gosaibi, 2000). The entire thrust of the Gulf 2000 Conference itself, organised by the *Middle East Economic Digest* and held in Abu Dhabi on 28–9 March, is indicative of the economic trend washing over the Arab Gulf states as it is elsewhere: entitled 'Energy, infrastructure and finance in the Middle East', its empha-ses were 'the need for private sector investment in infrastructure projects and the opening up of regional economies to meet the challenge of globalisation' (*MEED*, 2000).

The global drive for 'transparency' and 'good governance'. Senior Saudi officials like Minister Yamani, for example, appear quite prepared to discuss the challenges facing the kingdom's industries, but the hur-dles are not just economic. The global challenges increasingly being referred to by, most notably, the IMF, the WTO, the World Bank and the Organisation for Economic Cooperation and Development (OECD), and also by a host of other organisations and individual economists and commentators, are basically political. Transparency, corruption, democratic governance and social development—world-wide—are all now receiving almost as much attention as purely economic issues. The point being made is that, in line with the imperatives of globalisation, the quite substantial economic reforms

---

Moreover, the IMF—the world's principal macroeconomic interventionist organisation—is not without strong criticism in mainstream economic circles (see Sachs, 1998; *The Economist*, 1999c).

required in many developing countries cannot be sustained without accompanying political and even social reforms. The drive to economic internationalisation and the promotion of economic consistency and stability, according to the architects of the global economy, also demands a measure of globalisation of democratic political principles to ensure minimum safeguards against the economically debilitating effects of a lack of transparency and of corruption (as defined by the Western-based supranational economic organisations).

The drive to greater global political–economic transparency is a concerted one, to which significant world economic personalities are adding their weight. The former, long-serving managing director of the IMF, Michel Camdessus, for example, has outlined 'seven building blocks…for a globalized world'; his 'fourth building block' is 'the "golden rule" of transparency, now truly seen as the key for modern management, economic success, and rational behavior of global markets' (Camdessus, 1998).[35] Transparency, according to Camdessus (1998), must go hand-in-hand with 'integration…into the mainstream of the globalizing world economy' on the part of developing countries, with 'an increasingly open and liberal system of capital flows', and with 'the definition of international standards and codes of good practices'.[36] Significantly, his strong advocacy of globalisation included concern for social issues and 'political accountability' (Camdessus, 1998). Camdessus's views are strongly supported by the organisation he headed (see, for example, Anjaria, 1999; Ouattara, 1999; *IMF Survey*, 1999). The post-Camdessus IMF is likely to be even more politically astute, more concerned with

[35] Camdessus resigned suddenly, if not entirely unexpectedly, from the IMF's top post in mid-November 1999, effective from February 2000. He remains the longest-serving managing director in the IMF's history, with 13 years in the position.

[36] The IMF is developing mechanisms to promote these goals, and is actively 'expanding its activities and its mandate' in fields it regards as important to international financial stability. Two established measures include the General Data Dissemination System (GDDS) and the Special Data Dissemination Standard (SDDA) which, among other objectives, are designed to promote transparency in the economic and financial data of all IMF member countries (see the IMF Internet site at: http://www.imf.org/external/standards/index.htm; and 'Standards and codes' at: http://www.imf.org/external/help/index.htm; and at: http://dsbb.imf.org/; also *IMF Survey*, 1997b: 156–8; Fischer, 1998: 23).

political issues and social policies in client countries, and tougher on corruption, than it became during the last few years under Camdessus's guidance (see Gray, 1999a, 1999b; Hartcher, 1999).

Vested interests in existing and opaque political–economic arrangements that are driven by patron–client relations and personalised networks have led some commentators to speculate that a 'stable world system [of 'global capitalism']' is not assured (Sachs, 1998: 20). There is growing consensus among economists that not only is transparency required for the successful implementation of appropriate structural reform of national economies but also, increasingly, that some form of democratic political system is a prerequisite of prosperous participation in the emerging international economy: 'One standard should apply for participation [in global economic planning]: democratic governance, since the only reliable way to build for the future is through participatory political processes' (Sachs, 1998: 19; cf. Schulze and Ursprung, 1999: 303). Camdessus's fifth 'building block' of a new global economy is 'good governance, which is equally essential for strong economies and properly functioning democracies… competing for excellence in governance is the modern face of statesmanlike responsibility' (Camdessus, 1998). Obviously, for many developing countries and would-be participants in a global economy, including Saudi Arabia, this implies unwelcome substantial reform of the existing political structures (see also *Middle East Monitor,* 1995).

The IMF, as a powerful participant in global economic planning, is continually reinforcing the links between transparency, 'good governance'—by proffered definition, of a democratic/participatory kind—and economic success. At a 1999 Berlin conference, IMF Deputy Managing Director, Alassane Ouattara, delivered a keynote address entitled, 'The political dimensions of economic reforms' (Ouattara 1999). He emphasised that '…development rests on three pillars: good economic policy; a conducive legal and political environment; and attention to equitable social development.' He did not, however, allow the case for transparency and the links between economic and political reform to rest at these few words, but continued more forcefully:

The 'new' economic policy debate revolves around issues like transparency, accountability, governance, consensus and participation. Five or six years ago, these concepts were not at the center of our reflections, but they have always applied. In fact, the countries that have developed successfully over sustained periods of time are those that have achieved transparency, accountability, governance, consensus and participation, or at the least, have prevented shortcomings in these areas from gaining the upper hand. What the Asian crisis has also shown is that if such shortcomings do gain the upper hand, economic decline can occur, even after long periods of success. (Ouattara, 1999)

The Asian financial crisis, which struck with full force in October 1997 and only eased during 1999, shook the global economy and provided a lesson to national rulers and economic planners everywhere in the developing world that no economy was immune from collapse, even apparently strong economies—a fact that the Saudi regime must find uncomfortable.[37] Although the attention of the IMF and World Bank had turned to issues of transparency and good governance before the Asian economic collapse, the crisis and the resultant notoriety of 'crony capitalism' has undoubtedly added considerable urgency and energy to efforts to curb secretiveness and exclusive, informal business–political relations. The Asian crisis has prompted other world economic commentators to criticise authoritarian political systems that promote vested business interests and, ultimately, economic and social instability. The *Economist*, for example, pronounced that '[c]ountries that are open, honest and responsive to their citizens' concerns are likely to be the ones that flourish', and went on to warn that '[i]n time…links between the rich and the powerful will have political consequences' (*The Economist*, 1997a: 13). In a series of articles which maintained focus on personalised Asian business practices, the *Economist* pointed at the way economic crisis can lead to sociopolitical crisis (*The Economist*, 1997b; 1998a; 1998b; 1998c; 1998d; 1998e; 1998h).[38] In Stevens' vision of the future

[37] The crisis nations of South-East and East Asia in September 1998 were referred to by *The Economist* (1998g: 96) as 'Asia's ex-tiger economies'. The World Bank coined the term 'East Asian [economic] miracle', recently used ironically in an analysis of the region's crisis: 'Miracle or mirage?' (Pyon and Lee, 1998). The former 'tigers' of Asia are notorious for giving rise to the term 'crony capitalism'.

[38] Iwan Azis (1998) explores the way in which the financial crisis very quickly became a social and then a political crisis in Indonesia. He writes that '[e]ventually almost everyone [became] the victim [of the financial crisis]' (Azis, 1998: 152).

of the oil industry, economies dependent on oil production—the GCC states in particular—run the risk of serious political instability if chronically volatile oil prices fall to significantly low levels for long enough (Stevens, 1996; see also Stevens, 1997).

The reasoning behind the new international emphasis on transparent, inclusive business practices, formalised business–political relations, and social and political development, is simple: powerful political and business élites too often co-operate to grant themselves economic privileges, to the exclusion of the majority of the population. This co-operation becomes entrenched and expands at the expense of the national economy. In order to protect the dealings of such networks, secrecy, opaqueness and exclusivity become features of national political and business life. This is why transparency is closely linked with issues of corruption and ultimately to 'good governance'.[39] In fact, this path of reasoning has led to the ultimate conclusion, drawn by the director of the IMF's Fiscal Affairs Department, that: 'It is unlikely that corruption can be substantially reduced without modifying the way governments operate. The fight against corruption is, thus, intimately linked with the reform of the state' (Tanzi, 1998: 590).

President Suharto was forced from power after bloody riots in May 1998. Dr Chandra Muzaffar, Deputy Leader of Malaysia's National Justice Party, publicly stated in 1999 that, '…the economic crisis which has now become a political crisis has resulted in a type of mass awakening…people have become more conscious of their rights…the importance of democratic governance, of human rights…of the need for good government' (Muzaffar, 1999). Malaysia's former Deputy Prime Minister, Anwar Ibrahim, has blamed corruption and the crony capitalism of the Prime Minister, Mahathir Mohamad, for Malaysia's financial ills. It was Ibrahim's attempts to curb such excesses which led to clashes with Mohamad—Asia's longest-serving leader since coming to power in 1981—and his sentencing to 15 years' imprisonment on dubious sodomy charges (Williams, 2000).

[39] For a concise connection of the three key issues of transparency, corruption and good governance, see *IMF Survey* (1997c). The IMF position is supported by arguments presented by *The Economist* (1999a): '…since corruption usually creates inefficiency, corrupt countries tend to lose out in the global competition for capital and aid'; and, 'corruption…is closely connected to economic malpractice'. And on sociopolitical protest against corruption, '[f]or once, protesters…are on the same side as the IMF' (*The Economist*, 1999a).

Saudi Arabia and the challenges of 'transparency' and 'good governance'.
However Saudi politics and society may be perceived, the one thing
they are not is transparent. This may not have been an issue in the
past when local traditions governed local conditions and oversaw
the formation of the modern state, but in a highly technological
and globalising world, a 'closed' society and opaque *asabiyya* capitalism can present serious problems. Illustrative of Saudi Arabia's relative lack of transparency is the absence of a publicly available IMF
Staff Country Report for the kingdom when, for example, reports
are available for Samoa, San Marino and Swaziland.[40] Unsurprisingly, Saudi Arabia is also among approximately half the world's
countries that cannot be rated on Transparency International's 'corruption perceptions index' because 'reliable data is not available'
(Eigen, 1998).[41]

What may strike an unpleasant chord with the Al Saudi relates to
another area of comparison with the crony capitalist regimes of the
Asian crisis, namely, limitations on the ability to gather and effectively use accurate economic and social information, an area linked
to issues of domestic transparency and 'good governance'. Commenting on the role of information in the Asian crisis, Katherine
Marshall (1998: 6) writes, '[p]oor information...has contributed
to important policy errors and failure to act quickly...We know
well the dangers of information gaps, distorted facts...[and] patchy
and stale quantitative information...'. The haphazard planning and
inconsistent development that followed on the destruction of
the Saudi government's information-gathering structures with the
birth of the rentier–distributive state have only been compounded
by the Saudi form of *asabiyya* capitalism and an acute lack of

---

[40] No notice of a Staff Country Report for Saudi Arabia had been posted on the
IMF Internet site as of November 2002 (http://www.imf.org/external/pubs/
CAT/scr.cfm). The IMF can only produce these reports with the co-operation
of the subject country. Writing for the *Financial Times*, Robin Allen (1999)
reveals that, without special clearance, IMF and World Bank staff are blocked
from accessing data on Saudi Arabia from their respective internal websites. The
IMF published an assessment of the kingdom for the first time in November
2001 (IMF, 2001). Searching the Internet site of the World Bank (http://
www.worldbank.org/) in November 2002 for 'Bank Reports' for Saudi Arabia
yielded only, 'No records found'.

[41] Four Arab countries—Tunisia, Jordan, Morocco and Egypt—have been listed
(see Transparency International, 2002; Tanzi, 1998: 579–80).

transparency (see Chapter 3). To a certain extent, detailed knowledge of Saudi socioeconomics eludes even the Saudi regime and its economic and social policy-makers, a situation that does not augur well for the future health of the Saudi economy; nor does it recommend the regime to the international economic community, which claims to have learned many lessons from the Asian crisis.

Saudi Arabia's lack of openness is more than a mere inconvenience as the pressure for economic restructuring gathers momentum. The linking of economic internationalisation with issues of local political economy is also gathering pace, and problems caused by the clash of domestic economic and political imperatives with those of the new global economy are likely to impede Saudi objectives for the internationalisation of their economy. They will certainly present the regime with significant challenges. For example, although Ouattara's address in Berlin focused on Africa, the principles he outlined on the intersection of politics and economic reform apply to the Arab states and to Saudi Arabia. In relation to the 'three pillars' of development—'good economic policy…a conducive legal and political environment…and attention to equitable social development' (Ouattara, 1999)—Saudi Arabia's record is not encouraging. Firstly, Saudi economic policy to date has proved flawed and generally less than successful, despite significant strides in infrastructure development.[42] Secondly, the kingdom's legal and political environment is not conducive to continuing successful development by the IMF's definition. Finally, although '[e]stablishing social justice is one of the most important doctrines in our faith', according to the 1994 secret cabinet report on the state of the kingdom's finances (see CDLR, 1995a: 54), contemporary evidence suggests in general that the standard of living is falling and inequalities in wealth distribution are growing.[43]

---

[42] Even achievements such as infrastructure development have been called into question: 'Although there has been phenomenal development in the construction of cities, freeways, and other infrastructure projects, this construction was designed and executed primarily by foreign firms using imported labor and equipment. Such construction, although essential economic development, remains an example of consumption rather than production' (Palmer, Alghofaily and Alnimir, 1984: 19).

[43] These latter issues are dealt with in greater detail below. See note 21 above and associated main text for discussion of the 1994 cabinet report (memorandum no. 9223).

A more specific example is provided by the 'paradoxical' situation emerging in Saudi Arabia (and in other Arab states) in the banking and finance industries with respect to emerging Islamic models of banking and finance—models which are broadly compatible with the 'transparency and accountability' of the 'dominant Anglo–Saxon model of capitalism' (Henry, 1999a: 12). However, and here lies the paradox, it is 'the vested interests of governing elites in existing conventional banking arrangements' that are preventing the greater formal sanctioning and domestic institutionalisation of Islamic banking and financial systems.[44] This is a situation which 'is especially ironic [in the case of Saudi Arabia] in that much of the material and moral encouragement for Islamic banking comes from Saudi Arabia' (Henry, 1999a: 4; also Henry, 1999c: 31; cf. EIU, 1997). The fact that Muslim graduates of major US business schools such as Harvard and Stanford are now developing 'financial packages that any Western banker would understand' and which are in the process of potentially bridging the gap between Muslim and Western economic cultures (Henry, 1999b), only tends to highlight the internal resistance to upsetting the status quo in existing financial and banking arrangements within states which have the power to effect reform in this sector. Once again, this situation is particularly ironical given Al Saud status as protectors of the two Holy Mosques, and the regime's preferred image as the world's Islamic government *par excellence*.[45] In the meantime, the architects of the global economy and the advocates of international economic reform have indicated that 'the cosy relationships…between businesses, banks and governments' is an area that requires some critical examination (*The Economist*, 1997b: 27–8).[46]

In fact, the link between economic and political reform (which a recalcitrant regime can pass off with a few minimal adjustments) has been widened by the IMF to include linkages between more substantial and sustained processes of social development and political

---

[44] See note 52 below for a cursory example of the interests of Saudi élites in the banking sector.

[45] See the work of Abdullah Saeed (1993, 1995, 1996, 1998) for a study of Islamic finance, and Saeed (1996: 12) for how the Saudi financial system departs from the Islamic model.

[46] The BCCI fraud scandal, broached in Chapter 3, is a case in point (see also Cave, 1999).

development. As a state in transition from a traditional–authoritarian–distributive political system to one minus the crucial distributive element, modern Saudi Arabia is gradually becoming more susceptible to wider-ranging political reform. However, many of the following 'political dimensions of economic reforms' set out by Ouattara (1999) remain unthinkable for the kingdom in the foreseeable future:

> ...certain key principles seem to be common to social development in any country:
> • the rule of law, and the establishment of a system of checks and balances;
> • participatory and representative systems of government;
> • freedom from repression and the right to express preferences for all citizens; and
> • an institutionalized sharing of power.[47]

Scholars of Arab politics are also beginning to use terms such as 'political markets' (Springborg, 1999), which reflect the application of the language of economics directly to politics, thus reinforcing the increasingly strong connections between the two spheres evident in the growing sociopolitical focus of international economic organisations. 'Transparency' and 'good governance' are political concepts and the Al Saud must address such political–economic issues in their quest to integrate their economy into the emerging global economy. To what extent they do so is another question, dealt with in greater depth below.

Saudi economic internationalisation, privatisation and asabiyya capitalism.
The developing internationalisation of state economies forms the backdrop to domestic economic reform: for Saudi Arabia, *asabiyya* capitalism presents some unique challenges if the Al Saud are to comply with the requirements of an open economy and earn the confidence of the WTO and IMF. Since the pace of economic restructuring in Saudi Arabia has been slow and has met with resistance from various sectors of the Saudi economy and society, the conclusion that structural rather than macroeconomic problems

---

[47] The issue of Saudi political development is covered in Chapter 5.

precipitated the Asian crisis (Pyon and Lee, 1998: 4) will not be welcomed in the kingdom. Without great risk of a future Asian-style economic collapse, the political–economic and socioeconomic challenges facing the Al Saud in the era of globalisation cannot be adequately met with only superficial adjustments to macroeconomic policy. Saudi Arabia, however, is not alone in the Arab world in the need to confront this dilemma.

Although it faces vastly different prospects, due to its large population and the lack of a resource comparable with Saudi Arabia's oil, the case of Egypt does help to throw some light on the struggle that will soon engulf the Al Saud and the kingdom's various, structurally entrenched, vested economic interests. The link between important, overdue structural reform of Egypt's economy and the political élites' ability—essentially willingness—to make corresponding adjustments to the state's political infrastructure, has been pointed out by up-to-date research on Egypt's political economy: '[w]hether economic markets can emerge in the absence of open political ones is a question not only for Egypt, but for other countries also seeking to accelerate rates of economic growth while retaining political infrastructure inherited from…an earlier era' (Springborg, 1999).

Egyptian élites have, in fact, 'de-link[ed]…economic and political structural adjustment', and are in a process of 'de-globalising'; current economic management is working against Egypt's integration into the world economy by, for example, failing to privatise as promised to the IMF and World Bank (Springborg, 1999). The country is also reported to be returning to the debt crisis which existed prior to the 1991 Gulf War debt-relief measures offered to Egypt as a reward for its participation in the coalition opposing Iraq. The major cause of this unwelcome development—and of the failure to progress with economic development/modernisation and economic liberalisation—according to Robert Springborg (1999),[48] is Egypt's 'crony capitalism'. Quite simply, opening the economy threatens the crony networks—centred on the Mubarak family, former military officers, and their associates—which profit from the control of key resources and of the economy in general: '…the constraints of the political system make it impossible to open the

---

[48] The author, Professor Robert Springborg, is a specialist on Egyptian politics and political economy now at the School of Oriental and African Studies, London.

economy...' (Springborg, 1999). Saudi Arabia's *asabiyya* capitalism faces a similar dilemma, although in the long term it may prove to be more flexible if only because the greater wealth of the country might allow for a loosening of élite economic control without the total loss of their wealth-generating structures.

How the opening up of the Saudi economy is going to affect the Najdi élite networks is a vital question to which there is no answer at present. In addressing 'the deconstruction of the national market' and 'the enormously disruptive effects of economic liberalization', Chaudhry (1997: 272, 294–5), posits that 'a change in the life cycle of the oil state in Saudi Arabia' may herald the formation of a 'new alliance between the Hijazi elite and the Al Saud' (Chaudhry, 1997: 299).[49] There are many precedents in Saudi history for changing allegiance if it brings political advantage; however, maintaining a Najdi socioeconomic power base after thirty years of inexorable momentum still seems advantageous to the Al Saud at this stage, especially in the absence of a firm alternative. On the other hand, a narrowing of this power base of economic élites is consistent with the globalisation process and the economic reforms it is generating, and with the current experience of greater inequality of wealth distribution and falling living standards in the kingdom (see Chaudhry, 1997: 271, 273, 273n. 9, 289, 293, 295, 297, 297n. 78).[50]

One feature of Saudi *asabiyya* capitalism that will come under pressure with the growing influence of economic internationalisation is the rigid network of élitist agents who act as obligatory middlemen for foreign businesses seeking to operate in the kingdom. The commission-driven Saudi system of agency—a lucrative source of profits for Saudi nationals—is already coming in for open if restrained criticism in the interests of economic liberalisation, notably from representatives of United States commercial interests. The following comment made at the Gulf '99 Conference in Abu

---

[49] Chaudhry points the way to the reformation of the Saudi state away from distribution, but—as with her linking of the Saudi recession with the sociopolitical unrest of 1990–5—does not provide sufficient support for her emphasis on this vital development in the making (see Chaudhry, 1997: 272, 288, 297–99, 304–7). Regarding the 'possible shift' in the Saudi political–economic alliance, Chaudhry's discussion is speculative (see Chaudhry, 1997: 298–9).

[50] These latter issues in contemporary Saudi socioeconomics are treated in more depth below (see the section, 'State subsidies and "Gulf Perestroika"').

Dhabi by the Counsellor to the US Department of Commerce, Jan H. Kalicki, is illustrative of the pressure that will increasingly be brought to bear on Saudi methods of economic management: 'We have also pointed out that companies are deterred from investing when they are less than free to choose their own commercial agent or [to] change agents...' (Kalicki, 1999). Economic opening up and the deregulation, or even eventual abolition, of such rigid controls may, in the longer term, also contribute significantly to the narrowing of the élite base by reducing the number of Saudis privileged with exclusive business arrangements under the current incarnation of *asabiyya* capitalism.

Another possibility which may prove a form of de facto realignment of the Saudi political economy is closely related to a narrowing of the élite power base, and which can most conveniently ride the wave of globalisation-induced economic restructuring, is the international privatisation drive. Privatisation in Saudi Arabia has to date been implemented only slowly and cautiously, even half-heartedly (see, for example, *The Middle East*, 1994; 1995b; 1995c; *MEED*, 1997b; also Collett, 1995). At stake are monolithic and massively profitable concerns such as SABIC.[51] Put simply, the wealthiest and best-connected of the Saudi élite are the best placed to buy into and thus take advantage of the privatisations that are likely to occur as the policy gains new momentum over the course of the next decade. A prototype of this potential shift in the profile of the élite is seen in Prince Walid bin Talal bin Abd al-Aziz, who may one day be regarded as a pioneer of a new class of corporate princes who are concerned to cultivate a legal and relatively open economic legitimacy.[52] However, privatisation implemented in a

---

[51] Private investors within Saudi Arabia and the GCC bought close to one-third of the Saudi government's stake in SABIC when these shares went to market in 1984. Despite much rhetoric, not a great deal has happened since (see Amuzegar, 1999: 102; also *MEED*, 1997b). SABIC, according to one effusive report in the Saudi media, '...is among the world's strongest companies [and is] geared up to face the challenges of the globalization of trade...a global industrial player with global standards and specifications' (Sharani, 1998).

[52] As his name suggests, Prince Walid is a grandson of Ibn Saud. He owns the Royal Investment Company, is Chairman of the Kingdom Holding Company and was Chairman of the United Saudi Bank (USB) until its merger with SAMBA in July 1999. His personal fortune is estimated at approximately

fashion designed to further the interests of a narrowing (mainly Najdi) élite base may conform to the letter of economic restructuring as dictated by the imperatives of globalisation, but is unlikely to satisfy the spirit of restructuring; nor will it promote the goal of an equitable society. In a post-Asian crisis world, it is also unlikely to impress the architects of the new global economy—the IMF, WTO and other powerful transnational financial and economic organisations—and in fact will probably be readily recognised as a continuation of *asabiyya* capitalism in a modified form.

The indications are that the privatisation process will indeed accelerate as the kingdom strives to meet the minimum requirements of an open, globalised economy. For example, privatisation as a strategic economic policy was re-affirmed by King Fahd and the Council of Ministers in August 1997 (see *Saudi Gazette*, 1997b); in a paper dated 27 November 1998, SAMBA's chief economist wrote that 'milestone[s] toward privatization' had still been reached, despite the economic difficulties caused by the 1998 crash in oil prices (SAMBA, 1998e: 1);[53] and globalisation and privatisation featured in many of the economics-oriented presentations at the 1999 international Saudi Centennial Conference.[54] F. Gregory Gause (1997: 79),

---

US$15 billion, and he has business interests all over the world, especially in the finance and tourist industries. Many of his interests overlap: for example, he holds a stake in Citibank of the US (part of the Citigroup financial services conglomerate), which itself holds a 30% stake in SAMBA; the Saudi government, in turn, held a 22% stake in USB. He also has investments in News Corporation, Apple Computer and Euro Disney. His various 'stunning investments...have made him a major player in global finance' (Schleifer, 1998). Questions are known to have been asked about the sources of his original wealth. His international corporate image is augmented domestically by traditional Al Saud patronage of worthy Islamic causes; he is known to have donated generously to Saudi charities, some of which are chaired by senior princes, and is involved in mosque-building throughout the kingdom (see, for example: Saudi Economic Survey, 1999; *Al-Quds al-Arabi*, 1999; EIU, 1999e; Reuters, 1999a).

[53] This economist, Kevin Taecker (1999, pers. comm., 26 Jan.) assured me that a new, Western-educated Saudi generation which is 'fluent in English and the language of business', is very quickly taking over the leadership of Saudi private business, and that he was optimistic about private sector growth.

[54] One speaker at the conference, a member of the Saudi Consultative Council, pronounced that the government should not play any role at all in the economy which, as the title of his paper suggested, was indeed 'a futuristic outlook' for the kingdom (al-Hulaiqa, 1999). The same session of the conference also featured

however, argues that the recent enthusiasm for privatisation which has been sweeping all the Arab Gulf states is due to the 'governing elites…[erroneously] see[ing] it as a cost-free way of dealing with fiscal problems'. Gause points out that real socioeconomic costs are likely to be paid in increased unemployment and higher prices as newly privatised companies seek to improve profits. Although these 'costs' may indeed become political liabilities, more self-interested concerns involving the precedents of transparency and the economic management aspects of governing are likely to occupy the regime in the shorter term.

Some of the transparency and 'good governance' problems associated with Saudi privatisation noted by economic commentators are reminiscent of the Egyptian predicament outlined above. They are undoubtedly not lost on the Saudi regime; the political aspects of economic opening up which accompany globalising measures such as privatisation threaten the existing structures of *asabiyya* capitalism and have almost certainly been the major cause of delay in any significant implementation:

Privatisation could throw up…unexpected problems. Such a project entails the creation of a new legal framework, transparency of ownership and public accountability. Such habits may prove hard to acquire for the family which not only rules Saudi Arabia but owns it as well. Loosening financial control without loosening its absolute political authority could prove a delicate exercise. (Evans, 1996: 9; see also *The Middle East*, 1995b; Collett, 1995)

Economists and business people associated with the kingdom, both Saudi and non-Saudi, are well aware of the delays that have plagued privatisation and economic reform in general. A senior Riyadh-based economist in the Saudi finance industry, for example, has acknowledged that the Saudis do not have a good record of moving quickly (Senior economist, 1999, pers. comm., Riyadh, Jan.).[55] The *Middle*

---

the Deputy Minister for Planning and Programmes, Ministry of Municipality and Rural Affairs, Prince Saud bin Abdullah bin Thunaiyan, who encouraged the concept of privatisation and called upon the Saudi media to promote the privatisation process (Bin Thunaiyan, 1999).

[55] This confidential source was colourfully direct in personal interview when emphasising the now pressing need for the reform of the Saudi economy. Commenting on Saudi procrastination, he said: 'They [the Saudis]…can't screw

East Economic Digest (MEED, 1997a) has pointed out that even at a time of rising revenues, 'no action' on fiscal reform has been the preferred government option. The general director of research, training and information at the Riyadh Chamber of Commerce and Industry, Abdullah al-Shidadi, has implied that the delays to date have been a less than satisfactory outcome for the Saudi economy. In commenting on the oil price crash, then at its most serious, Shidadi (1999, pers. comm., 26 Jan.) said that what at first may be seen as a crisis will actually facilitate positive changes and that the economic downturn and financial difficulties were providing the necessary environment in which to implement them: 'We have to stop and think—we needed this kind of break.' This opinion is by no means an isolated one (see Dourian, 1998; Gause, 2000).

A Reuters article, written in April 1999 after oil prices had begun their dramatic rise, pointed out that '[t]he government of Saudi Arabia…has been under pressure to reform and liberalise its economy by encouraging a more active role for the private sector…[but that] progress has been slow', and warned that 'Gulf states may squander the benefits from a recent deal to lift oil prices by cutting production if they retreat from moves to liberalise their economies and privatise state corporations' (May, 1999). Barry May (1999) quoted a Saudi economist, Beshr Bakheet, who reinforced the widely-held view expressed by Shidadi by saying that 'now oil prices had recovered, many people felt less pressure psychologically and emotionally and the pace of privatisation might be delayed' (see also *MEED*, 1997b; *The Middle East*, 1996a: 29; Collett, 1995).

The Saudi American Bank (SAMBA, 1998d: 5–6) has pointed out a number of factors it believes are inhibiting privatisation, the most important being 'almost entirely psychological', an allusion to the traditional relationship between government and population—between ruler and ruled, patriarch and people, patron and client. Deference to the royal family and the general popular submissiveness to rule derived from the Saudi traditional-authoritarian-distributive political–economic system have had as debilitating an effect on business initiative as on bureaucratic and sociopolitical initiative.

---

around any more—all the slack's been taken up' (Senior economist, 1999, pers. comm., Riyadh, Jan.).

SAMBA appears to believe that an invigoration of the local business community could help persuade the government to move more quickly on economic liberalisation; the bank's spokesman therefore gently told his business audience in Riyadh: '...if you want to know why things seem to be going too slow—look in the mirror' (SAMBA, 1998d: 6; see also *The Middle East*, 1996b: 28).[56]

The EIU (1999c) has put the situation regarding privatisation, economic reform and delays in concise perspective:

...the extent to which the government is actually prepared to allow the private sector to replace the state remains a contentious point, and little real progress has been made to date. In addition, although the government is publicly committed to joining the...WTO, the EIU remains sceptical about [Saudi] willingness or ability to implement the necessary economic liberalisation, including opening up the economy to competition from domestic private-sector and foreign companies. The legal framework for selling public assets to private investors is not yet in place, and nor have the authorities outlined the methods they will use to divest state holdings. As a result, progress on privatisation is expected to be patchy over...1999–2003, and will be concentrated mainly in the restructuring of the telecommunications and electricity sector that has already been announced, which is seen as a prelude to eventual privatisation...

Reluctant to relinquish its control over large sections of the economy and still concerned to 'manage' the development of the private sector, the kingdom is expected to continue to encourage the expansion of the private sector alongside the state sector, rather than pursue a major privatisation programme.

A leading analyst interviewed by *The Middle East* (1996b: 28) concurs, expressing doubt whether reforms will go far enough to effect the required economic transformation, even though the pace of privatisation will probably accelerate. Progress was, in fact, made during 1999, 2000 and 2001. The more significant steps include the following: the electricity and telecommunications sectors have been restructured and are being prepared for privatisation; the Saudi stock market has been opened to foreign investors, whether resident

---

[56] I should emphasise that the connection made between these comments, which were subtle and entirely business-oriented, and the less flattering aspects of the Saudi sociopolitical-economic environment is my own.

in the kingdom or not; a law allowing foreigners to own real estate in the kingdom was approved by the Council of Ministers in July 2000; and a foreign investment law was approved in April 2000, together with the mandating of the Saudi Arabian General Investment Authority.[57] However, the fundamental concerns remain, and there is good reason for questioning whether the extended regime will move far enough, efficiently enough and quickly enough to avert the series of crises that lay on the horizon.

Dealing with similar issues, although a little more positively, and adding to the mounting international pressure on Saudi Arabia, an early-1999 Deutsche Bank study reported that 'broad-based and wide-ranging structural reform, so far neglected, is becoming ever more urgent in the Gulf. Large-scale privatisations seemed likely in Saudi Arabia in the not too distant future…[but the bank] acknowledged that tax reform remains an extremely delicate political question' (May, 1999; see also Chaudhry, 1997: 273–5). Such statements underline the interaction between the various dimensions of globalisation, not only economic, but also political, social and cultural. Further delays and cynical élite manipulation of economic restructuring in the Saudi privatisation process will only increase social and political unease in the kingdom. Sociopolitical tensions sparked off by economic issues characterised a number of Asian countries during the period of financial crisis 1997–9, and it is the duplication of such turmoil in other developing countries which the current international drives for 'transparency' and 'good governance' are attempting to circumvent.

Al Saud concessions and minor adjustments to the sociopolitical status quo are quite possible—the institution of the long-promised

---

[57] The major points of the foreign investment law, as outlined by SAMBA (2000), are: a reduction in corporate tax rates; foreign businesses have the right to own land and sponsor their own employees; and privileges formerly limited to Saudi companies, such as soft loans from the Saudi Industrial Development Fund, are extended to foreign investors. The Saudi Arabian General Investment Authority (called a 'General Commission for Investment' by SAMBA in its report of April 2000) has been described as a 'one stop shop', for the approval of investment projects within 30 days and 'to facilitate interaction with government agencies' (SAMBA, 2000). SAMBA (2000) states that the 'driving force' behind the new measures to promote foreign direct investment is 'a need for stronger private sector growth and job creation'. See also IMF (2001) for a brief report on these measures.

majlis al-shura (Consultative Council) in 1993 is a case in point—but fundamental political reform is even less likely in the near future than basic economic restructuring. It is therefore not surprising that Crown Prince Abdullah should declare: 'We are open to adoption of the good aspects of globalisation and development, but we reject all those changes that appear good but go against our beliefs and social set-up' (Bin Abd al-Aziz al-Saud, (Crown Prince) Abdullah, 1998a). Further emphasising that the Saudi regime is attempting to keep economic reform and sociopolitical reform completely separate and striving to attain WTO membership with minimal economic reform in any case, is the address of the Saudi Commerce Minister, Osama bin Jafar bin Ibrahim Faqih, at the WTO ministerial meeting in Seattle at the end of 1999. Faqih is reported as saying that, 'controversial issues, such as labor and social factors, should not be included in the [WTO] talks... [that] some countries were making "unrealistic demands" during negotiations... [and] that countries should not be pressured to sign agreements to win membership.' He is also reported to have 'insisted [that] under-developed countries...be given special and preferential treatment... [which] should be one of the basic principles of these negotiations' (Faqih, quoted in *Arab News*, 1999; see also *Saudi Gazette*, 1999).

On the other hand, the architects of a new global economy have warned against 'wrong-headed policies—sometimes pompously characterized as "a national way to development"—[which are opposed by] the IMF...because they in no way serve the interests of the majority of citizens' (Camdessus, 1997). The full weight of the IMF was behind Camdessus when he uttered these words, as was the chaos of the Asian financial crisis and years of mounting pressure on the Saudi regime to liberalise and restructure the kingdom's economy.

These, then, are the battle lines being drawn, not only over what economic reforms will be implemented, but over how far they will go, and how far they will be carried over into other spheres, namely social and political. The priority for the Al Saud is to maintain social stability while economic restructuring of the rentier–distributive state is implemented gradually with a minimum of political concessions and minimal disturbance to the existing structure of Saudi *asabiyya* capitalism. To what degree these objectives can be achieved remains to be seen.

Economic reform and socioeconomic challenges in a new era

Other issues besides those discussed above are a part of the relation between Saudi economic reform and global integration. For example, the Al Saud will not be reassured to hear that economic decline 'should not be isolated from demographic and social trends', and that strong economic growth can both create and mask social tensions (*The Economist*, 1997b: 27–8).[58] On this latter point, with respect to development planning in the oil producing Gulf Arab states, Osama (1987: 33) claims that 'most of the mistakes made in decision-making are absorbed by financial abundance'. Without fundamental reform of the Saudi rentier–distributive state, the erosion of this abundance over the longer-term may herald the beginning of a cycle of decline comparable to that which has recently struck Asia not only economically, but socially and politically. Furthermore, it has been posited that unless economic globalisation is well managed, '*international economic integration* is likely to bring about *social disintegration*' (see Schulze and Ursprung, 1999: 296, authors' emphasis).

Fiscal difficulties and concerns related to the opening up of the economy, transparency and *asabiyya* capitalism are thus not the only problems confronting the Al Saud in the kingdom's dawning era of global integration, restructuring and austerity: a number of worrying socioeconomic issues also present the regime with difficulties, which again have deep roots in the rentier–distributive state and are intimately related to Saudi Arabia's economic structure. These will not be resolved without extensive basic reforms which, like the need for economic restructuring, is now becoming urgent. Among the specific problems that have faced the regime for some time are:

- The related issues of high unemployment, rapid population growth, an inadequately trained national workforce, and a dependence on imported labour and expertise;
- Subsidies for inefficient industries, and for services, public utilities, some staple foods and imports;
- Bureaucratic inefficiency;

---

[58] *The Economist* was evaluating the implications of the then unfolding Asian economic crisis, but as this section shows, the principle can and should be applied to Saudi Arabia. (See also Chapter 3.)

- The entrenchment of informal and exclusive business-political relations that are often associated with corruption and poor economic management.

Inefficiency, wastage, the complexities of *asabiyya* capitalism and 'corruption' have already been dealt with: the issues raised by the first two points will be discussed below, to illustrate the seriousness of the socioeconomic difficulties facing Saudi Arabia in the new millennium.

Population, labour force and youth unemployment. One area of potential social hardship, and perhaps of future political liability, is the combination of a relatively high rate of population growth and high unemployment. On unemployment, 'published figures' quoted in 1999 put the rate at 27%—compared with 12% five years earlier (Bashir, 1999). SAMBA (2001: 1, 2–3) estimated the 2000 unemployment rate for Saudi males at 14%, rising to 15% in 2001. Another report put the rate in 2001 at 'about 30 percent' (Fahmy, 2001). Figures ranging from 10% to 25% have been widely floated (US diplomat 1998, pers. comm., 9 Mar.). However, a senior figure at the Saudi Chambers of Commerce and Industry has stated that, 'Nobody has accurate figures' (al-Shubaili, S., 1998, pers. comm., 7 Mar.;[59] see also SAMBA, 2001: 8; Kanovsky, 1994: 80–1).

The uncertainty surrounding unemployment statistics is indicative of a systemic lack of reliable socioeconomic data and a general lack of sociopolitical–economic transparency. Using Saudi figures from the Fifth Development Plan (1990–5), Wilson and Graham (1994: 254–5) reveal unemployment rates of 45.6% for men and 94.7% for women: in fact, the Sixth Development Plan states that the 'participation rate [of Saudi nationals in the domestic labour market in the mid-1990s]…is at the internationally low level of only 30.2 percent' (Ministry of Planning, ?1994: 170).[60] Ten years

---

[59] At the time of interview, Saud al-Shubaili was the Director of the Contractors' Department and Executive Director of the Contractors' National Committee at the Saudi Chambers of Commerce and Industry.

[60] It has also been suggested to me by an independent source that the real rate of unemployment is around 40% (Business consultant 1996, pers. comm., 1 May). See also Chaudhry (1997: 275, 297).

earlier, in 1984, Saudi nationals made up 40% of total employment
(see Kanovsky, 1994: 25), indicating a deteriorating employment
environment for Saudis (see also Bashir, 1999; Palmer, Alghofaily
and Alnimir, 1984: 22).

Already-high levels of unemployment are clearly going to be
exacerbated by the rapid rate of population growth, currently running at 3.4% to 3.8% annually (see World Bank, 1999: 195; Wilson
and Graham, 1994: 12)—a figure much higher than the world average of 1.5%, and higher than the 2.5% average for the Middle East—
and is significantly outstripping economic growth.[61] Population
growth of this rate has been described as 'destabilising' because of
the 'tremendous economic pressure' it generates: i.e. it means per
capita wealth automatically decreases in the absence of extraordinarily high economic growth, and strains infrastructure and social
services (see Byman and Green, 1999b; see also *The Middle East*,
1996b: 28). In 2000, the Saudi Ministry of Planning estimated that
the number of nationals would grow by more than 90% over the
following 20 years, from 15.6 million in 1999 to around 29.7 million in 2020 (see *MEED*, 2000). These are statistics which the Minister of Planning has said 'will require significant further expansion
of our infrastructure to serve our citizens and the general economy'
(al-Gosaibi, 2000). Saudi real GDP growth averaged only 2% annually 1998–2001 (see IMF, 2002), supporting earlier EIU forecasts
cited above of zero to 2%, 1999–2003. Moreover, as of the mid-
1990s, around 60% of the Saudi population was under the age of 20
(*The Economist*, 1995), and approximately 50% of the population was
under 15 years of age (Ministry of Planning, ?1994: 170); thus, future
youth unemployment is of particular concern (see also *The Middle
East*, 1993a: 26; 1996a: 29). GDP growth estimates ranging from
stagnant to slow fall a long way short of the sustained 5% reportedly

[61] According to World Bank statistics, Saudi Arabia's average annual population
growth rate has been around 4.3% for the years 1980–97 (see World Bank, 1999:
195). Another statistic, which also sheds light on Saudi attitudes to family life and
the role of women, is the 1996 fertility rate figure of 6.2 births per woman compared with the world average of 2.8 births and the Middle East average of 4.0
births per woman. The fertility rate in Saudi Arabia, although still one of the
highest in the world is, in accordance with the world trend, declining: the kingdom's fertility rate in 1980 was 7.3 births per woman (World Bank, 1999: 203).

required even 'to compensate for earlier declines in living standards and absorb new entrants to the labour force' (Collett, 1995).[62]

The link between economic liberalisation and the posited resultant increases in productivity, efficiency, competitiveness and growth on the one hand, and socioeconomic issues such as youth unemployment on the other, has been made by a senior SAMBA representative in an economic seminar for Saudi businessmen (SAMBA, 1998d: 6): creating 'jobs for young Saudis…[is] one big answer to the question, "Why open up"… If you think that the [GCC states are] beginning to face a youth unemployment problem today, just wait five years. What is completely clear is that demographic pressures that are already there… will keep employment issues at the forefront for decades to come.' SAMBA has continued to emphasise this crucial link between economic restructuring and development, and society:

Another growth driver for the economy is the country's demographic profile with its strong youth bulge. This is currently seen more in the context of an employment challenge since the front edge of the Kingdom's 'oil boom baby boomers' are now at an age that they are entering the labor market in ever increasing numbers. If over the next several years the job creation challenge is met, then the groundwork is laid for strong domestic consumption-driven growth for many decades to come. (SAMBA, 2001: 12)

The bank states unequivocally that '[u]nemployment remains the most important challenge for the Saudi economy' (SAMBA, 2001: 3). *The Middle East* (1993a: 25) made the same point years earlier: 'less talked about [than other reasons for expanding the private sector] but of increasing concern, is that only the private sector can

---

[62] The negative effects of a high unemployment rate among Saudi nationals is made worse by the poorer economic environment and, in the view of a serving diplomat, this dilemma is further accentuated by the profound, family-based nature of Saudi society: the concept of a greater society doesn't exist, therefore the poor and disadvantaged, who, as will be noted, are increasing in number, are left to fend for themselves for lack of an adequate support mechanism outside the family (Australian diplomat 1, 1995, pers. comm., 14 July). The generally extensive safety-net of the family is also a factor in obscuring high rates of unemployment and in dampening the negative consequences that might otherwise be expected to feature more strongly in the Saudi sociopolitical landscape.

productively absorb the growing number of educated Saudis coming onto the labour market.' It has also been suggested that one motive for post-Gulf War Saudi military expansion has been to provide employment and income—and, perhaps revealingly, discipline—for the country's youth (see Kanovsky, 1994: 70–1).

Rapid population growth is by no means the only factor contributing to the Saudi unemployment problem; another, major, factor is the economy's dependence on foreign workers. The increasing urgency of the need to employ Saudi nationals rather than to continue the practice of importing a cheap workforce from poor developing countries can be seen in the way in which the issue is dealt with in successive Saudi development plans. Compared with the relatively cursory treatment in the Fourth Plan (1985–90), the Fifth Plan (1990–5) is less strident in its trumpeting of the 'Saudiisation' of the workforce and more detailed in setting forth what is required to make the process more viable (cf. Ministry of Planning, ?1984: 50–2, 83–93; Ministry of Planning, ?1989: 115–31). The Sixth Development Plan, giving the issue a note of increased urgency, has stated that 'the apparent unrestrained demand for foreign workers...regardless of calls in the Fourth and Fifth Development Plans for a reduction in non-Saudi worker numbers...will increase the difficulties in finding...jobs for poorly qualified Saudi workers, who make up such a high proportion of new entrants to the labor market' (Ministry of Planning, ?1994: 171–2).

According to the 1992 census, foreign workers numbered 4.62 million people out of a total population of 16.92 million; however, official Saudi population figures are widely believed to be 'suspect' (see Wilson and Graham, 1994: 12, 12n. 8), and are thought to be the result of a deliberate policy of overestimation of the native population and underestimation of expatriates 'in order to minimize reports of Saudi dependence on both skilled and unskilled foreign workers, without whom the economy would grind to a standstill' (Kanovsky, 1994: 47; see also Salamé, 1989: 81–3, 88n. 4, 89n. 11). Supporting such suspicions are reports that, by 1997, the number of foreign workers resident in the kingdom numbered approximately nine million, with '9 out of every 10 private sector jobs in Saudi Arabia...filled by foreigners, which is to say that though the country's phenomenal physical development was paid for with Saudi money, it occurred largely without Saudi labor' (Kronemer, 1997).[63] At times during the development boom since the oil shock of 1973–4, expatriate workers have been estimated at up to 80% of the total civilian workforce (Kanovsky, 1994: 49).

The Saudi government has probably consciously used the economic advantages of a cheap foreign workforce as 'a safety valve to assure some attainment of its more important priorities' (Looney, 1990: 36). Saudi labour is generally recognised to be more expensive in terms of wages and lower productivity, at least initially. It should also be noted that labour policy appears to be linked with *asabiyya* capitalism and that the responsibility for Saudiisation and the development of national human resources appropriate to a modern industrial state has been farmed out to companies which are not integral to *asabiyya* networks. The observation that foreign firms have been pressed to employ Saudi nationals while Saudi firms have not (Former British ambassador to Saudi Arabia 1998, pers. comm., 26 May; cf. Chaudhry, 1997: 275, 275n. 18), supports the conclusion that profits for the élite networks employing cheap foreign labour have been as much a priority as national development.[64]

Thus, although Saudiisation has been presented as a major socioeconomic goal for more than 15 years—ushered in with the words

[63] A Saudi official (pers. comm., 1999) has stated that expatriate workers in his country number nine million. Using a 1988 US Embassy estimate of a maximum of six million Saudi nationals (see Kanovsky, 1994: 48), and population growth rates of 5.2% and 3.8% (World Bank, 1999: 195; Wilson and Graham, 1994: 12), the native Saudi population in 1999 could not be more than 9.3 million—a figure that reinforces the impression that foreigners comprise at least half the people encountered in day-to-day life in the kingdom. As with other fields of data (see notes 3 and 10 above), there has been much contradictory speculation on Saudi population figures. The World Bank (1999: 195) puts the total population at 20 million as of 1997, a number reached by applying the Bank's 3.4% growth rate to the official total population (1992 census) of 16.92 million people—a calculation which applies the same rate of population growth to Saudi nationals and to foreign workers. *The Middle East* reports that the 1992 census appeared to have been 'scrupulously conducted', but that the 'number of Saudi nationals may [still] not reflect reality'; according to this source, a Saudi national population of 15.8 million is projected 'by the end of the century' (*The Middle East*, 1993a: 25–6).

[64] On the subordination of employment and other policies of economic reform to vested interests, see Chaudhry (1997: 274–5 and notes, 288–9, 297).

'a reduction…in the number of non-Saudi workers…is one of the most important targets of the [fourth] Plan' (Ministry of Planning, ?1984: 50–1; see also Kanovsky, 1994: 25)—progress has been non-existent or, at best, 'piecemeal' (*The Middle East*, 1993a: 27). There is as yet no firm evidence that this pattern is changing, despite official speeches and the convening of 'conferences and debates held to address the issue' (Bashir, 1999). While economic goals remain at least as important as ever, the social—and potentially political—consequences of burgeoning youth unemployment have assumed an importance the regime can no longer easily continue to subordinate to the profits of specific vested economic interests and of *asabiyya* capitalism in general. Genuine development of national human resources is an important element in long-term sustainable economic development, and cheap imported labour amounts to a subsidy of Saudi industry which, along with the large state sector, is not in tune with economic internationalisation under the auspices of the WTO.

Not surprisingly, the government's strategy of transferring to the private sector the absorption of new Saudi entrants into the labour market now appears to be regarded with renewed seriousness.[65] By 1994, 'only a third of the graduates from Saudi universities could find jobs in the public sector' (Byman and Green, 1999b). Saudi-isation ultimately would mean the formation of a *Saudi* labour market as part of 'the introduction of market economics' into the kingdom (Taecker, K. 1999, pers. comm., 26 Jan.). But as a strategy it still faces the vested interests of *asabiyya* capitalism in the tangible 'inbuilt obstacles' of industrial 'convenience', namely, the ready supply of appropriately trained and (in most fields) significantly lower-paid expatriates from countries such as Egypt, Pakistan, India, Bangladesh and the Philippines (*The Middle East*, 1993a: 26–7; see also al-Hegelan and Palmer, 1985: 50; Ministry of Planning, ?1989: 117, 237; Birks and Sinclair, 1982: 205; al-Nashwan, T., 1998, pers. comm., 7 Mar.;[66] al-Shubaili, S., 1998, pers. comm., 7 Mar.; Chaudhry, 1997: 275n. 18).

---

[65] As well as the Fourth, Fifth, Sixth and Seventh Development Plans themselves, see, for example, Kronemer (1997) and Avancena (1999).

[66] Mr T. al-Nashwan was the Sales Manager, Chemical & Plastic Products Division, Saudi Industrial Export Co. at the time of interview.

Despite the increasing urgency of Saudiisation, the factors which have contributed to its slow pace in the past are likely to continue for some time. Shidadi (1998, pers. comm., 7 Mar.), has stressed the complex nature of the 'many aspects and dimensions' of Saudi-isation, which include the education and training of Saudi nationals, government-industrial relations, and employer–employee relations. More recently, Shidadi (1999, pers. comm., 26 Jan.) has re-emphasised the problematic nature of the qualifications of Saudi nationals; and according to Saud al-Shubaili (1998, pers. comm., 7 Mar.), ultimately 'the demand for jobs is high, the key is qualifications.' This recognition is presumably behind recent increases in the Saudi education budget: public expenditure on education in general rose from 4.1% of GNP in 1980 to 5.5% in 1995 (World Bank, 1999: 201). And, commenting on the 1997 budget, a *Middle East Economic Digest* (*MEED*, 1997a) commentator wrote: 'In a budget statement that was short on detail, education is the largest area of specified spending. Education will get SR41,700 million (US$11,130 million), or 23 percent of total spending, which is a 51 percent increase from the previous year'.[67]

To ensure that young nationals entering the workforce are appropriately qualified, a restructuring of the education system from an emphasis on university studies to technical training is already under way. A growing emphasis on science and technology and on technical and vocational training can be seen from the Fourth to the Seventh Plan, along with progressive budget increases (for example, cf. Ministry of Planning, ?1984: 293–301; ?1989: 273–98; ?1994: 182–4, 280–97). There is also evidence that the regime is as mindful of sociopolitical as of socioeconomic considerations when it comes to the question of an educated workforce. A 1998 conference on higher education in Riyadh presented the Saudi Ministry of Higher Education with a good deal of food for thought, especially the example of Singapore's 'cautious approach [to ensure] that a situation of the "educated unemployed" does not become critical'

---

[67] The quality of Saudi education is, however, being questioned and the practice of throwing money at such problems will, as in so many other cases, not be a solution. See the section 'The sociopolitics of education in the Saudi oil state', in the preceding chapter. It should also be remembered that some defence spending occurs off-budget.

(Mani, 1998). The channelling of a greater percentage of students into polytechnics to match education to the needs of the labour force and the economy to avoid producing a surplus of highly educated university graduates, and the integration of social, economic and 'above all, political, considerations' into higher education (Mani, 1998) are other lessons from Singapore that will be of particular interest to the Saudi government. A view of higher education which would not go down well with the Saudi regime, however, was delivered by the Assistant Director General for Education of the United Nations Educational, Scientific and Cultural Organisation (UNESCO), Colin Power: namely that educating a national population is 'contributing to the process of democratization and equality' (Power, 1998).

The 'mudir syndrome'.   Saudiisation not only requires the creation of an appropriately qualified national workforce but also convincing young nationals that they really do want to work in trades and technical jobs. In practice, the task of redirecting the interest of young Saudis is a difficult one; moreover, the battle is being lost according to one well-informed observer, who pointed out that the Saudi authorities have made much of large numbers in technical training intakes but do not usually mention a large drop-out rate (Former British ambassador to Saudi Arabia, 1998, pers. comm., 26 May). The root of this particular problem appears to be the '*mudir* syndrome'—a concept of honour in employment which dictates that nothing less than a position of authority, status and respect is acceptable.

Muhammad al-Masari, the London-based dissident of CDLR notoriety, states matter-of-factly that this 'syndrome' is due to a Bedouin background (al-Masari, M., 1998, pers. comm., 20 May). One former diplomat with a great deal of experience of Saudi Arabia agreed, speaking of a 'hierarchical' view of jobs and explaining that the attitude is a Bedouin legacy which sees a man's role as that of a warrior and desert survivalist, and manual work as dishonourable (see also Kronemer, 1997). He also reported that senior Saudis are worried about the 'moral' effects of this attitude (Former British ambassador to Saudi Arabia, 1998, pers. comm., 26 May). Palmer, Alghofaily and Alnimir (1984: 20) write that 'manual labor tends to be disdained [and is] generally regarded as '*aib* or shameful by traditional norms' (see also Birks and Sinclair, 1982: 202–3). This predisposition has clearly been reinforced by the 'new rentier pattern of behavior' which has dealt 'a serious blow to the ethics of work' and is a product of 'the oil disease' which has 'contaminated' Saudi Arabia along with the other Arab oil states (Beblawi, 1987: 393), or, as Amuzegar (1999: 217) puts it, a symptom of 'a new petro-culture' which stemmed from rentier–distributive status. The legacy of slavery is cited as another factor in the persistence of the syndrome (see Wilson and Graham, 1994: 256).

The trait in question is widely acknowledged and recognised as an obstacle to progress in reducing unemployment and improving the kingdom's long-term economic prospects (al-Shubaili, S., 1998, pers. comm., 7 Mar.; Former British ambassador to Saudi Arabia, 1998, pers. comm., 26 May; Saudi nationals and Arab expatriates 1998, confidential and informal sources, Riyadh, Jan.-Mar.; Palmer, Alghofaily and Alnimir, 1984; see also Bashir, 1999; Amuzegar, 1999: 217–18; Rugh, 1973: 15; Abir, 1993: 73). The government is attempting to change these attitudes. For example, in a clear example of social engineering, the Saudi government has been promoting technical jobs and trades through a subtle and well-produced televised recruitment campaign (viewed personally in Riyadh, between January and March 1998). A fusion of documentary and advertising lasting about 15 minutes, it typically featured young Saudi men speaking about their work in the manufacturing industry. Whilst its true aim was to eventually ease young Saudis away from the *mudir* syndrome, the series of television programmes cleverly emphasised the relatively prestigious supervisory role in factories.

How effective such measures will be is not known at this stage: the 'dominant social values' do not favour technical education and, indeed, vocational training was, and probably still is, associated with failure in more prestigious fields of education (Osama, 1987: 132, 150). There are, apparently, numerous employment opportunities for those with qualifications and who are 'willing to work' (al-Shubaili, S., 1998, pers. comm., 7 Mar.)—a view shared by no less an authority than the Saudi Ministry of Planning (?1994: 179) as expressed in the Sixth Development Plan: 'All jobs currently filled by non-Saudi workers are potentially available to Saudis whose education and skills match the job requirements, provided that they are ready to accept such jobs in the locations and at the salaries on offer.'

Some commentators have optimistically suggested that the solution to the Saudiisation problem is as simple as 'de-expatriatisation'—that is, employment opportunities for approximately 2.5 million young Saudi nationals already exist even if unpalatable menial jobs are excluded (Taecker, K., 1999, pers. comm., 26 Jan.). In reality, Saudiisation programmes are not expected to reap the desired economic and social benefits for at least another ten years (al-Shidadi, A., 1998, pers. comm., 7 Mar.; al-Nashwan, T., 1998, pers. comm., 7 Mar.). Shidadi has since re-affirmed the 10-year time frame for Saudiisation, although he added that it would be a good result if achieved in that time (al-Shidadi, A., 1999, pers. comm., 26 Jan.). However, these projections may yet prove to be optimistic:

...prevailing behavior patterns in Saudi Arabia pose a serious obstacle to the government's efforts to break the rentier pattern. If most of the population remains psychologically aloof from the productive sector of the economy, no amount of capital expenditure will produce a diversified indigenous economy capable of sustaining itself at anything approaching current consumption levels without massive infusions of oil rents. Rather, increased capital expenditures will only result in increased dependence on foreign labor, a process that has already produced an indigenous labor force dwarfed by expatriate workers. (Palmer, Alghofaily and Alnimir, 1984: 33)

The patterns of a rentier state and a national population born with the first oil boom and well established in the more than 25 years since, are proving difficult to modify. More than 15 years of Saudiisation rhetoric (for a recent example of which, see Albayyat, 1998) has already yielded 'little evidence of significant progress' (see Kanovsky, 1994: 38–9, 55): The shadow of unemployment is set to loom larger in the declining days of the Saudi rentier–distributive state.

The state subsidies bind.   The rude shock delivered to Saudi budgetary planning in 1998–9 took its toll of the economy. It was the most recent example of the state's dependence on, and vulnerability to unstable world oil prices. Although these have since recovered, breaking free of this vulnerability will require the long-term commitment of the state. In the meantime, at ground level, the economics of recession provide fresh insight into the social effects of the more or less continuous fiscal difficulties discussed earlier. Stories of a limping Saudi economy abound on the streets of Riyadh, told and retold many times by both non-Arab and Arab expatriate workers. Spoken from first-hand experience, and often with the benefit of up to a decade of life in the kingdom, these narratives paint a picture of significant economic decline in recent years. Some of the resident expatriates I talked to between January and March 1998 in Riyadh were even preparing to return to their homes in Pakistan and Bangladesh because they were no longer earning sufficient money to make their sacrifices worthwhile. Most also spoke of a noticeable tightening up in the attitudes and spending habits of Saudi nationals. Others mentioned that friends working on construction sites had not been paid for up to six months (resident expatriates, 1998, informal pers. comm., Riyadh, Jan.–Mar.).

The Saudi government's practice of delaying contractual payments dates back to the recession of the 1980s—a policy of de facto default which caused much hardship and many bankruptcies (see Chaudhry, 1997: 273n. 6, 279, 297, 297n. 80; Allen, 1996; Wilson and Graham, 1994: 182–4; Kanovsky, 1994: 75). Commenting on the effect of this particular government strategy during the 1993–4 budget crisis, a *Gulf Business* writer observed that 'salaries went unpaid and contractors and suppliers were left stranded for cash for months at a time' (Bailey, 1998). Approximately US$5,900 million in arrears dating back to 1992 were only cleared with better than expected oil export revenues in 1996 (*MEED*, 1997a). In hindsight, the policy of delayed payments 'was seen to be damaging and self-defeating', and has been labelled 'the blunt axe approach' to fiscal restraint (Bailey, 1998). Although it was widely believed a serious repetition of this policy was unlikely (Bailey, 1998), it has been revisited to some extent in the most recent financial problems (see Abuljadayel, 1999; Reuters, 1999b). Taecker (1999, pers. comm., 26 Jan.), however, has noted that government contract payments, although 'slowed' in 1998 to early 1999 from three months to around six months, do not breach contractual agreements. Although perhaps legally acceptable, this gives little comfort to the workers who have left family life in their home country to earn a better wage in the kingdom. Settling many payments with the 2000 budget surplus was no doubt a welcome development for all concerned but, again, questions linger about the state's ability to avoid a similar or even worse predicament from developing in the future.

Uncertainty must remain over the future dynamics of Saudi socio-economics as the rentier–distributive state winds down and is restructured. Besides the larger 'globalisation' pressures on the Saudi regime that stem from the momentum of world economic integration itself and, therefore, from organisations such as the IMF, the wisdom of 'fiscal consolidation' is continually being pointed out to the regime by leading economists. Indeed, economists at the Saudi American Bank (SAMBA, 1997: 2) have announced that the 'main elements of Saudi Arabia's fiscal consolidation program are to reduce government spending levels, add budget discipline to the contracting process, and improve the timeliness of payments for budgeted obligations.'

This programme represents the early stages of the process whereby the government bows out of direct economic management in favour of the private sector. As indicated above, this is something that does not come naturally to the Al Saud, and progress has been slow and painful. Already, one result of the fiscal consolidation programme has been, '[s]ince 1992–93…big cuts in effective subsidies…' (SAMBA, 1997: 2). Subsidies to Saudi industry, especially, are becoming a vital issue for WTO membership—indefinitely delayed but presumably inevitable. Although one of the original goals of state subsidies was to help kick-start the kingdom's economic diversification and industrialisation, extensive subsidy programmes—of '[e]verything from date production to fishing…making new ventures risk-free and highly profitable' (Chaudhry, 1997: 151)—have ultimately proved to be of dubious benefit:

The goal of economic and especially industrial diversification was to reduce the country's overwhelming dependence on oil revenues. Instead, the massive direct and indirect subsidies required to operate many of these industries raised the overall level of state revenue needs and *increased* the country's dependence on oil—precisely the *opposite* of what the diversification program was supposed to achieve. (Kanovsky, 1994: 40, author's emphasis. See also *The Middle East*, 1993b: 27.)

Once entrenched, subsidies became an important lubricant of *asabiyya* capitalism, and vested interests have consistently—and to date mostly successfully—opposed all government attempts to reduce various subsidies (see Chaudhry: 1997: 274–5, 286, 288–9). Saudi companies—or at the very least 'some'—'feel threatened' by impending

WTO membership and the changes to subsidy and other industrial policies that will probably follow (SAMBA, 1998a: 3–4).

An example of the regime's continuing attempts to effect the strategic withdrawal of industrial subsidies came at the end of 1997, when it was proclaimed that the state-owned Saudi Aramco, together with its domestic customers, 'established an important precedent' with an agreement that the supply of natural gas to Saudi industry should rise by 50%. According to SAMBA (1997: 5, 8), this rise, 'from the very low base of $0.50 to only $0.75 per thousand cubic feet... [means] the price of Saudi natural gas remains very competitive in global terms', and would probably retain for the kingdom 'a true comparative advantage to export industries that use gas or electricity generated from gas' whilst still meeting WTO obligations on 'unfair trade practices, in particular subsidies that would artificially lower export prices' (see also *The Middle East*, 1995a). Stressing the less than clear picture of government subsidies for the power needs of Saudi industry, one source (Gulf energy expert, 2001, pers. comm., 19 Feb.) maintains that 'the price of gas is very contentious', and that, 'in terms of theory the "correct" price should equal the real opportunity cost [but] what this is in a Saudi context is highly debatable. Arguably it would be extremely low.'

These examples only tend to emphasise the extent to which Saudi industry has been subsidised and the artificially low prices Saudi consumers have come to expect for finished products and utility services. They also emphasise the natural competitive advantage that would still be enjoyed by Saudi energy consumers, even after the withdrawal of subsidies. It is the plan of the government to extend the country's gas grid and to exploit its substantial reserves of this natural resource with the aim of substituting gas for oil as a fuel and feedstock for industry and the electric power sector (SAMBA, 1997: 7–8).[68] The significance of the increase in the cost of gas has been emphasised by SAMBA (ibid., 8):

It successfully demonstrated that the price of gas *must at least cover the company's* [Saudi Aramco's] *long-term marginal costs.* Such a guideline, if applied

---

[68] Currently, most Saudi natural gas is produced as a by-product of crude oil extraction, but the country also possesses an abundance of 'non-associated' gas fields. Saudi Arabia's gas reserves have been estimated at 204 trillion cubic feet— nearly 4% of total world reserves (see SAMBA, 1997: 7).

to electricity rates, water charges, or national air fares, would go a long way toward putting all of the quasi-governmental entities onto more stable financial footings (authors' emphasis).

This statement also hints at the longer-term and broader goals of global economic rationalism in the Saudi context; the increase in the price of fuel for Saudi industry and utilities is seen by economists as the successful negotiation of one of the first obstacles on the road to eliminating government subsidies altogether. It is, though, a relatively easy obstacle to negotiate considering that the cost of energy will still remain low by world standards. Energy pricing policies raise obvious questions, such as why such subsidies were provided in the first place, and why it has taken the government so long to rein them in. The answers lie in the vested interests of *asabiyya* capitalism. However, the possible sociopolitical ramifications of a wider removal of subsidies are not totally lost on economists; SAMBA (1998b: 6–7), for example, addressing 'a great reluctance to further reduce [more direct] subsidies', refers to 'public sensitivity to water pricing issues' and to a 'strong sensitivity to political issues' on the part of farmers when it comes to government support— though the bank does suggest that 'disbursements to farmers for the current [1998] harvest could be postponed…possibly [for a year]'.

In fact, the boom-era development of the Saudi agricultural sector has been a glaring example of an extraordinarily costly and wasteful programme of industrial subsidy. According to Chaudhry (1997: 183), it has been, 'the most expensive fiasco in late twentieth-century agricultural history'. These agricultural development programmes—which also show examples of the links between subsidies, wastage and corruption—were also socially disruptive, and are still environmentally hazardous (see Chaudhry, 1997: 172–85; Nowshirvani, 1987; George, 1994; Wilson and Graham, 1994: 221–8; Allen, 1996). They also illustrate the workings of *asabiyya* capitalism (see especially Nowshirvani, 1987: 9–10; Chaudhry, 1997: 297n. 78).

Another way to rein in government spending, suggested by Taecker (1998, pers. comm., 9 Mar.), would be to defer new projects, including those in education and in the infrastructure, e.g. 'new sewers and roads': in his view it is no longer necessary for the government to fund every aspect of development in the country and the 'slack' can be taken up by the private sector. Another way the regime could save money, according to a SAMBA economics paper—while admitting the move would be 'very difficult'—would be to 'cut… government workers' pay or…the stipends that are distributed to junior princes and their households' (SAMBA, 1998b: 6). Significantly coinciding with the 1998 oil price collapse, Crown Prince Abdullah was reported to have issued 'notes' to all members of the extended royal family by early 1999 advising them of a rolling back of state-funded privileges (Finance industry sources, 1999, confidential pers. comm., Riyadh, Jan.), which represented a significant potential saving for the state given the number of princes involved.[69]

Similarly, the regime is gently 'trying to wean its people off state largesse' (Dourian, 1998). In some instances this objective is closely related to industrial subsidies, as is illustrated by impending higher utility prices for the general Saudi population as a result of the flow-on effect from the increased cost of natural gas to industry. Another form of socioeconomic subsidy related to the state's '[w]elfare-oriented staffing policies' (Palmer *et al.*, 1989: 19) is targeted for scaling back through privatisation. Commenting in 1998, a Saudi banker (quoted in Dourian, 1998) said, 'I think you will see gradual change and low oil prices will make it easier for people to understand the need for change.' This may be the case, but independent observers are less convinced that the restructuring of the Saudi rentier–distributive state will be a smooth one. Noting that spending on 'a very wide range of direct and indirect subsidies and other expenditures' rose precipitously after each of the oil shocks but was powerfully resistant to strong cutbacks when oil revenues plummeted, Kanovsky (1994 1:21) wrote:

Evidently, the Saudi authorities were (and appear to remain) wary of the internal discontent that could result from cutting producer subsidies and

---

[69] Alain Gresh (2000) reports that payments to the royal family and to 'heads of allied tribes' could be as high as 15% to 20% of the state budget. Daniel Byman and Jerrold Green (1999a: 16) give an idea of the cost to the state of the extended royal family: 'Most of Saudi Arabia's perhaps 20,000 princes and princesses receive a stipend from the Saudi state, ranging from thousands to millions of dollars per month.' Quoting royal stipend figures from the 1980s, Aburish (1995: 68) claims that a senior or high-profile prince might receive up to US$100 million annually. Wilson and Graham (1994: 20) cite more conservative figures but emphasise the avenues open to royals for often considerable supplementary incomes. See Chapter 2, note 75, for a range of estimates of the number of princes.

aggravating the problems of the business community, or cutting outlays on wages and salaries in the burgeoning public sector and causing depressed wages or even unemployment. Cutting consumer subsidies would lower living standards and add to popular disaffection. (Kanovsky, 1994: 21)

Living standards in decline and 'Gulf Perestroika'. If public spending continues to be reduced—despite the regime's demonstrated reluctance to engage in any reforms that may foster such socially undesirable developments—socioeconomic sore points such as youth unemployment, falling standards of living and increasing poverty will only be exacerbated. Various sources already concur in pointing to falling standards of living and lower expectations: Taecker (1999, pers. comm., 26 Jan.) believes the expectations of young Saudis 'are greatly diminished'—an adjustment from the boom days, encouraged by the fact that what life was like in the pre-boom days is 'in current living memory'. Mabro (1998, pers. comm., 14 May) maintains there is 'no doubt' that young Saudis today have 'lower expectations [of living standards and lifestyle]'. A Saudi executive is on record as stating that '[m]ore and more Saudis appear to be coming to terms with the harsh [socioeconomic] reality...' (see Bashir, 1999). A Saudi academic, Rayed Krimly (1999, 260–1), implies that 'almost surreal popular expectations' are gradually coming down to earth. A US diplomat has observed the twin signs of a greater incidence of poverty and a decline in conspicuous consumption (US diplomat, 1998, pers. comm., 9 Mar.). A veteran Australian diplomat who has served in Riyadh concludes that some Saudi citizens are 'sliding into poverty' (Australian diplomat 2, 1997, pers. comm., 18 June). A former British ambassador to Saudi Arabia with firm connections with the kingdom has confessed that he is 'beginning to hear of poor Saudis' (Former British ambassador to Saudi Arabia, 1998, pers. comm., 26 May. See also Khashoggi, 2002; *The Economist*, 1999b; Chaudhry, 1997: 271, 295, 297, 306; Osama, 1987: 25, 184–5; Kanovsky, 1994: 31; MIRA, 1999; Amuzegar, 1999: 216.)[70]

[70] Likewise, a confidential business contact is adamant that living standards are definitely falling in Saudi Arabia (Business consultant, 1996, pers. comm., 1 May). Saudi Arabia is not alone in experiencing the rentier-state phenomenon of sharply falling living standards in recent years. *The Economist* (2000d), for example, simply states that 'two-thirds of Venezuelans...live in poverty'; similarly, Venezuela's problem of 'dependence on oil' and the partial remedy of 'fostering

It is interesting, but not unexpected, to note that a World Bank fact sheet on Saudi Arabia presents a blank on poverty statistics for the kingdom (World Bank, 1998). Chaudhry (1997: 171–2), moreover, convincingly maintains that the 'Saudi government's distributive policies [always] lacked…any ideological commitment to equal distribution': a vital element in the formation of the kingdom's Najdi-based *asabiyya* capitalism (see also Salamé, 1989: 83–4). Amuzegar refers to 'the glaring income disparity between the ruling elites (the royal family, well-placed technocrats and other fortunate beneficiaries of the oil rent) and ordinary citizens', which he also notes is widening (Amuzegar, 1999: 153).[71] Equality of wealth distribution for Saudis is unlikely to improve in the era of economic globalisation, if the track record so far on the worldwide phenomenon of the growing divide between rich and poor is any indicator: in fact, it is acknowledged that it will be accentuated (see, for example, *The Middle East*, 1996b: 28).[72]

---

a competitive private sector' (*The Economist*, 2000d) are reminiscent of the restructuring formula being presented to Saudi Arabia by the global economic–financial community. Related to the issue of living standards in Saudi Arabia, despite government denials, is a level of inflation that is worthy of mention (Business consultant 1996, pers. comm., 1 May). A World Bank graph measuring inflation in the kingdom displays a 1991 rate of 4% falling to −3% in 1993, then rising just as steeply back to 4% by 1995 (see World Bank, 1998). SAMA statistics quote Consumer Price Index (CPI) inflation for 1993 at 0.8%, and 4.9% for 1995 (see O'Sullivan, 1996), yet the Saudi Industrial Development Fund Annual Report for 1996 lists a Cost of Living Index inflation rate for 1996 at less than 1% (SIDF, 1996: 24). Such fluctuating and conflicting statistics are typical, and further illustrate the transparency-related difficulties of obtaining reliable, up-to-date information on the kingdom.

[71] See Chaudhry (1997: 158, t. 4.4) for some interesting and revealing statistics: although Najdis made up just 26% of the total urban population in 1981, they accounted for 44% of the top household income bracket—the largest single percentage according to region.

[72] The problem is not only a widening wealth gap domestically, but also internationally, between rich and poor countries. The result is, 'a world of greater income inequality than ever before in history' (Sachs, 1998: 19). The former, longest-ever serving managing director of the IMF has himself admitted to a 'widening of income gaps' in advanced economies (Camdessus, 1997), and a paper published by the Brookings Institution states unequivocally that '[n]ations throughout the industrialized world have seen income disparities rise since the late 1970s' (Burtless, 1996), observations and admissions which cannot augur

Further evidence of economic decline and what it means for Saudi nationals is provided by Byman and Green (1999b):

The Gulf states today lack the wherewithal to satisfy their burgeoning populations. The per capita incomes of many Gulf residents have plummeted since the 1970s after the price of oil began falling in the early 1980s. From 1984 to 1994, real per capita GDP fell from... $11,450 to $6,725 in Saudi Arabia... Although all figures are skewed by poor census-taking procedures and large numbers of expatriates often included in Gulf population figures, in a general sense this figure reflects the decline of individual wealth in the Gulf states.

Supporting the scenario outlined above are figures from the Jedda-based National Commercial Bank which reveal annual per capita income in the period 1981–9 as having fallen by 55% to US$6,441 (see Allen, 1999). Moreover, a recent survey of the major cities of Riyadh, Jedda, Madina, Mecca, Dhahran, Khobar and Abha carried out by the Saudi Ministry of Public Works and Housing revealed that the income of 40% of the households in these cities is less than 6,000 riyals—approximately US$1,602—and that around 51% of the households had no fixed income (Saudi Economic Survey, 2000).[73] On the other hand, it has been reported that less than 1% of the

---

well for wealthy developing countries in which an inequality of wealth distribution is already entrenched. Evidence that inequality of wealth distribution is in fact structurally a part of economic internationalisation is presented by Schulze and Ursprung (1999: 295, 299, 300; see also Barnet, 1994). The WTO, especially during the fiascos surrounding the organisation's third ministerial meeting of November–December 1999 in Seattle, has been accused of fostering 'the concentration of wealth in the hands of the rich few [and] increasing poverty for the majority of the world's population...' (see Rowell, 1999). Even in a modern industrial state such as Australia, 'the economic divide between the rich and poor is widening' (Laurence, 1999; see also Hanna, 1999; Steketee and Haslem, 2000), a 'stark' fact acknowledged by no less a figure than the Prime Minister (see Lawson, 1999). Community groups are now also adding their voice in protest at the 'huge gap in the share of income between wealthier and poorer families [as a result of] deregulation and the integration of Australia into the global economy' (Adelaide Central Mission, 1999).

[73] The survey report distributed by Reuters does not make clear whether the figure of SR 6,000 is annual; but in light of other statistics, the figure must refer to annual income.

Saudi population had more than US$500 billion in liquid portfolio investments held in Western equity markets by September 1999 (see Allen, 1999).

Further declines in individual wealth and overall standards of living can be expected as economic reforms are, albeit gradually, implemented. A strong but respected leader who is still in touch with local traditions will be needed to push through budgetary austerity measures and new emphases in socioeconomic restructuring, especially so in the face of the ongoing reliance on oil and financial uncertainty. The pressures of globalisation as the Saudi rentier–distributive state is transformed back into a more normative extractive–re-distributional state makes the task ahead a truly daunting one, made all the more so by past delays and continuing procrastination. It is possible, however, that Crown Prince Abdullah is just such a leader: addressing the inaugural session of the December 1998 GCC summit, he is on record as announcing, apocalyptically, that 'the days of affluence are over and they will never come back' (Bin Abd al-Aziz al-Saud, (Crown Prince) Abdullah, 1998a; see also May, 1998).

In words that are pleasing economists and the international corporate and financial worlds, Prince Abdullah is speaking the language of economic internationalisation. At the same 1998 GCC summit, for example, he said: 'We must all get used to a different way of life which does not stand on total dependence on the state' (Bin Abd al-Aziz al-Saud, (Crown Prince) Abdullah, 1998b)—a reference to clear intentions to increase the role of the private sector in the Saudi economy, accelerate the privatisation process, and build up a self-sufficient private sector without the props of state subsidies. Also from the 1998 GCC summit, the de facto Saudi ruler declared that:

> ...the GCC governments could no longer afford to give their citizens everything on a silver platter. The private sector, as well as every individual, should contribute to...economic development and play an important role in capital formation, investment and human resources development... governments would continue to provide the basic amenities, but as far as industrialisation is concerned, the private sector would have to play a very important role... the private sector should also reduce drastically its

dependence on expatriate labour and employ nationals in a more meaningful manner (reported in *The Emirates News*, 1998).[74]

Prince Abdullah's statements at the summit were 'welcomed…as an historic milestone' and, following his lead, newspapers 'across the Gulf…urged citizens to play a bigger role in their economies after years of pampering by their cradle-to-grave welfare states' (May, 1998). Abdullah's comments have in some quarters been enthusiastically dubbed 'the beginning of "Gulf Perestroika"' (see May, 1998). It is, however, a 'perestroika' that is not being applied to government: Gulf Arab media have not urged citizens to play a bigger role in politics. Even in the economic sphere, it is a 'perestroika' that has been a long time coming and which, despite relatively radical language, still has a long way to go as the vested interests of *asabiyya* capitalism are renegotiated.

Conclusion

Despite the temporary fiscal relief that may be provided by upturns in world oil prices, such as was seen from mid-1999 to mid-2001, the era of Saudi Arabia's fabulous oil wealth is at an end. Financial difficulties which have plagued the kingdom in a see-saw fashion for more than a decade and a half only emphasise the vulnerability of an economy still dependent on the oil sector. Such persistent difficulties also point to an unsustainable economic structure based on the rentier–distributive model which developed extremely rapidly with the 1973–4 oil boom. Infrastructure development and lavish industrial and socioeconomic subsidies reflected the boon of new-found wealth but were also adapted politically by the regime to serve the legitimacy of largesse. The boom era also facilitated the further entrenchment and political–economic power of a mainly

---

[74] Similar sentiments were expressed by the Kuwaiti Minister of Finance, Yussuf al-Ibrahim, almost exactly three years later. Referring to the difficulty his government was experiencing in passing a bill to facilitate privatisation in the shaikhdom, the minister said, 'How can we link our destiny to oil prices when they are out of our control? We need economic reform, we have to start it immediately, we cannot continue in this way' (Ibrahim, quoted in MacDonald, 2001).

Najdi bureaucratic and business élite and gave rise to an expanded *asabiyya* capitalism.

When the boom turned sour in the mid-1980s, the Saudi distributive state could not adapt and the failure to reform is now haunting the kingdom: the 1999 budget deficit represented the seventeenth consecutive deficit; foreign reserves have been run down; total public debt stands at around 100% of GDP; and economic growth is stagnant. Brief relief in the 2000 fiscal year did not solve any of the kingdom's underlying economic problems. Unemployment, although unquantifiable, is extremely high and is a potentially disruptive social problem. This is especially so in light of the kingdom's rapid rate of population increase. Difficulties with appropriate education and skills, combined with the *mudir* syndrome and the economy's continued reliance on cheap, expatriate skilled and unskilled labour present multifaceted obstacles to expanding the national labour force and socioeconomic restructuring. A bloated and inefficient bureaucracy and a lack of effective development planning exacerbate the problems.

Macroeconomic manipulation, like reshuffling deckchairs as a *Titanic* slowly goes down, is not going to secure a prosperous future: a fundamental restructuring of the economy, no less, is required. The functionality of the rentier–distributive state is not only unsustainable, but is in fact already impaired—the task now facing the regime is to initiate a new phase in the life of the state. The urgency of basic reform is increasing, but entrenched structures—and vested interests, both of élites and of the general population—are not easily reformed. Clashes with the established order of *asabiyya* capitalism, and with the Al Saud's own strategy of the legitimacy of largesse, add to the sociopolitical difficulties associated with basic economic restructuring.

The internationalisation of state economies forms the backdrop to domestic economic reform. Saudi Arabia now sees its own future as intimately tied to greater integration into a rapidly evolving world economy. However, *asabiyya* capitalism presents many challenges for Saudi compliance with the requirements of an open economy. The Al Saud must also earn the confidence of organisations such as the WTO and IMF, especially since the major international economic organisations are increasingly turning their attention to social and political issues, with transparency and 'good governance' the principal areas of attention.

None of the new focus on the social and political extensions of economic reform and global integration will please the Al Saud. *Asabiyya* capitalism is clearly antithetical to the economic openness, sound economic management and political–economic transparency of the new global economy: the very foundations of the Saudi political economy need to be renegotiated to conform to these ideals. Some renegotiation is likely and is already detectable, but this process will usher in new problems. Falling standards of living and unequal wealth distribution are set to continue and are likely to be the hallmarks of a narrowing of the mainly Najdi bureaucratic–business élite. Moreover, the Saudi political economy can no longer afford—and will eventually not tolerate—royal passengers, but the creation of a new category of corporatised princes by those royals astute enough to read the economic future should provide ready means for the maintaining of privilege.

Minimal economic restructuring and the manipulation of reforms in order to preserve the essential nature of *asabiyya* capitalism—the course of action thus far chosen by the kingdom's rulers—will not address the increasingly urgent challenges faced by the Al Saud. They will also not impress the international economic community in a post-Asian crisis world, and will be seen for what they would be: an attempt to perpetuate the system of *asabiyya* capitalism. In the longer term, perversions of the restructuring process will exacerbate sociopolitical tensions in the kingdom—precisely the effects seen in financially stricken Asian countries in 1997–9 and that current international economic opening up, pro-transparency and anti-corruption drives are attempting to avoid in the future.

The pattern of 'globalisation' is thus becoming clearer as it progresses: economic internationalisation is opening the door to other reforms in the political and social spheres. Sooner or later in the globalising process, Saudi Arabia will come under increasing pressure to implement reforms other than economic, so that economic reforms can indeed be consolidated on secure foundations. The status quo in Saudi Arabia has been buoyed by oil wealth; despite financial difficulties, this wealth has been sufficient to maintain economic and sociopolitical calm. But a glimpse of a bleaker destiny was caught during the oil price crisis of 1998–9 and, whatever the fortune of oil prices in the near future, the Al Saud have been warned that time is running out to put their house in order if more serious problems are to be avoided. Since in the Saudi case the loss of economic sovereignty also to some extent represents a loosening of absolute sovereignty in the political sense, the methods the regime employs to maintain a firm grip on power, and its potential weaknesses, will be a measure of Al Saud survivability, questions examined in the following chapter.

5

INSTABILITY WITHIN STABILITY

DOMESTIC POLITICAL OPPOSITION AND REGIME RESPONSES

As the rulers of Saudi Arabia set their sights on WTO membership and increasing integration into the global economy, the economic reforms required to achieve these goals are being implemented only very slowly and in some cases half-heartedly. While fundamental economic restructuring has thus far been avoided to preserve the infrastructures of *asabiyya* capitalism and the legitimacy of largesse, the international economy and the culture of globalisation have been making inroads into the kingdom.

Balancing religiopolitical legitimacy, domestic sociopolitics and the *umma* on the one hand, and managing global economic integration and serious domestic socioeconomic reforms on the other hand, is already proving to be a difficult task for the Al Saud. It will increase in difficulty as contradictory priorities and vested interests compete for time, money and a place in the public consciousness—increasingly precious resources for the troubled Saudi rentier–distributive state. The traditional Al Saud strategy of procrastination and the lengthy sociopolitical–cultural process of consensus-building do not augur well for the increasingly urgent, economically driven challenges faced by the regime. Effective remedial action in meeting these challenges is complicated because the regime is instinctively attempting to minimise the political ramifications of socioeconomic reform, a recipe that is only likely to intensify sociopolitical tensions in the longer term.

The perennial problems of religiopolitical legitimacy and succession to the throne are now merging with new problems of economic and even cultural management as economic internationalisation and the global spread of—mainly Western—cultural and lifestyle influences come in on the back of the communications and information revolutions of the 1990s.

Thus, for the Al Saud, the more familiar thorny issues of political dissent and alliance with the United States are now merging with new controversies such as the growing influence of Western culture, rising youth unemployment and drug use. These issues have taken on new meaning and urgency in the aftermath of 11 September 2001: the Saudi regime's involvement in the wars in Afghanistan and its support for the Taliban regime have indeed come back to haunt it. Osama bin Laden may officially be a renegade, but evidence suggests he enjoys a semi-underground folk-hero status with many in the kingdom—and not just among the some 15,000 Saudi nationals who participated in the *jihad* in Afghanistan. All of these problems, however, now have to be faced in light of the economic restructuring dictated not only by supranational financial and economic organisations such as the IMF and WTO but also by the ultimate dysfunctionality of the Saudi rentier–distributive petrostate.

Daunting though the immediate future may be for the Al Saud, the mechanisms the regime has developed for survival have been impressive. All challenges have to date been met with varying degrees of success and this record suggests a measure of adaptability sufficient to cope with future challenges. The regime is already sailing in uncharted economic and socioeconomic waters: rolling back the rentier-distributive state is a far more difficult, delicate, lengthy and painful process than was its creation. This chapter examines the 'survivability' of the Al Saud, specifically, the sociopolitical forces at work in the kingdom today, how they might combine with a changing socioeconomic environment, and how the Saudi regime has dealt—and is dealing—with political opposition, dissent and socioeconomic challenges to its authority.

Problems: post-Gulf Crisis sociopolitics

The rising dissent of the Gulf War period. The dramatic events of 1990–1 need little introduction. On 2 August 1990, Saddam Hussein's Iraq invaded Kuwait; four days later, the US Secretary of

Defence, Dick Cheney, was in Saudi Arabia persuading King Fahd to accept US troops in his kingdom. The king agreed immediately, and on 8 August President George H.W. Bush announced what was already becoming 'the largest and fastest mobilisation of troops and military equipment in history' (Globalvision, 1993). Just over five months later, on 17 January 1991, the 'Desert Shield' of the Gulf Crisis had become the 'Desert Storm' of the Gulf War: a US-led coalition of nations crushed the Iraqi army as the Middle East experienced another watershed comparable to the founding of the modern state of Israel in 1948 and the June 1967 'Six Day War'. Saudi Arabia had also become a state garrisoned by US troops as the United States implemented its policy of 'dual containment' of Iraq and Iran. This series of events had similarly dramatic consequences for domestic Saudi Arabian sociopolitics, though of a much lower global profile—at least until the 1995 Riyadh and 1996 Khobar bombings and the 11 September 2001 airliner suicide attacks on New York and Washington.[1]

As the 1990 Gulf Crisis dragged on into 1991, unease over King Fahd's policies began to spread in the kingdom. Despite assurances from diplomatic sources that the massive Western military presence in Saudi Arabia was effectively insulated from domestic life in the kingdom (Austrian, M., 1995, pers. comm., 13 July; Australian diplomat 1, 1995, pers. comm., 14 July), there is little doubt that the 1991 Gulf War made a deep impression on significant segments of Saudi society.[2] Dekmejian, for example, believes opposition to the presence of foreigners and foreign influence reached a level of

---

[1] American investigators have established that up to 15 of the 19 hijackers involved in the 11 September attacks were Saudi citizens.

[2] Austrian (1995, pers. comm., 13 July) offered his opinion that most Saudis were 'scared shitless' after the Iraqi invasion of Kuwait and were content to host Western military forces. However, he also said that the fact that the kingdom needed these foreign forces 'raises other questions of legitimacy', such as how was it that after years of massive defence expenditures, the Saudi military was not capable of defending the country—indeed, would have been 'no match' for the Iraqis (Austrian was a former senior US Middle Eastern diplomat of extensive experience). Whether Saudi Arabia is in any better position a decade later to meet another, similar threat is questionable. On the issue of the insulation of Western troops from Saudi society, a note in the 1995 country report commissioned by the CDLR (CDLR, 1995a: 26n. 20) states: 'The main problem is the presence of the foreign forces themselves which was, and still is highly objectionable.'

'heightened xenophobia' after the Gulf War, a symptom of an 'identity warp' caused by, among other factors, declining living standards, eroded socioeconomic standing, rapid modernisation, Western cultural influences, conflicting Al Saud policies, and the military weakness of the kingdom (Dekmejian, 1994: 629–30). Fandy (1999: 102) also refers to 'moral and patriotic…xenophobia' in the discourse of Islamist dissent that rose with the Gulf Crisis: a fusion of 'Sa'udi nationalism' and wounded *muwahhidi* religious sentiment.

The explosion of dissenting voices being raised against the regime at this time did not of course materialise from nowhere. Saad al-Fagih, in his history of dissent against the Al Saud, presents a fuller historical perspective. Fagih depicts a sociocultural and political landscape in which the Islamist discourse was dominant but low profile, a situation which led to 'the alienation…of the political leadership from the nation', creating tensions between society and the state. Thus the Gulf Crisis was able to provide 'the cultural shock' and the 'historic event which pushed [these] tensions…to manifest [themselves]…politically in an open manner' (al-Fagih, 1998: ch. 2).

'Neo-fundamentalist theologians' and 'non-conformist' ulama began campaigning against the regime and the presence of foreign troops and, with the launching of the war against Iraq, even the 'liberal elites' could no longer hold back criticism of 'Al Saud double standards, corruption and nepotism' (see Abir, 1993: 172–189; see also Fandy, 1999: 48–72, 84–121, 158–9, 189[3]). Surprisingly, it was the latter, minority, segment of Saudi society who first took advantage of the opportunities—however slight—offered by the crisis to initiate political reform: in late January 1991, they petitioned the king in an open letter.[4] Widely circulated in the kingdom and published

[3] See especially Fandy, who provides a very close and up-to-date analysis of the post-Gulf Crisis 'politics of dissent' in the kingdom. His analysis is a postmodern one which emphasises the unique sociopolitical environment of Saudi Arabia in the context of the global revolution in information and communications technologies.

[4] Fandy (1999: 33) posits that 20% of the Saudi population is liberal, 20% is conservative, and 60% is 'pragmatic', although sources and statistical support for these figures are not provided. Instead, this breakdown appears to be drawn from Fandy's personal communication with Saudi nationals over an extended period of time. Although the broad categories and percentages presented by Fandy may be roughly on target, any details on the orientation of the population must be, at best, an educated guess considering the absence of such scientific data on Saudi

in the Arab world, the document, signed by '43 moderate liberal businessmen and intellectuals', reflected a 'resignation' to 'minimal reforms acceptable to the regime'; it was, 'in fact, a watered-down version of a set of demands, never presented to the monarch, which circulated among the Hijazi intellectuals in Jedda during the autumn of 1990.' The letter also requested reforms that 'were far less meaningful than those demanded by the liberal elites in the early 1980s' (Abir, 1993: 188–9).

After the war, the regime and its United States ally faced a diffuse Islamist movement which was more demanding than that of the 'liberals'. The Islamists' reform campaign began in accordance with tradition, that is, with a letter—in the form of advice—presented quietly 'to the authorities' by a highly respected professor at Imam Muhammad bin Saud Islamic University, Shaikh Abdullah al-Tuwaijri, early in 1991. It was 'signed by nearly 200 ulama, academics, lawyers and other leading persons in society' (al-Fagih, 1998: ch. 6). Although, as usual, the details conflict, another, 'far more astounding', petition was presented to King Fahd in mid-May 1991 (Abir, 1993: 189–90).[5] Accounts of the official supporters of this document vary, but its impact was no doubt due to the fact that it was signed by around 400 ulama, judges, university professors and other leading scholars. Indeed, the first page of the petition, known as the 'Letter of Demands', displayed the seals of 52 primary signatories, many of whom were senior and establishment ulama (see al-Fagih, 1998: chs 6–7; Fandy, 1999: 159; Abir, 1993: 189–90; cf. Dekmejian, 1994: 635–6). Fandy (1999: 119) is cautious in his coverage of this document: the 'letter of demands…appeared independently and not as a response to the liberal forces'; it 'addressed various issues ranging from bureaucratic corruption, to legal codification, to Islamic human rights'; and it 'was signed by many Saudi Islamists and intellectuals.' Even the state's head *alim*, Shaikh Abd al-Aziz bin Baz,

---

society: even the basic population statistics of the kingdom are in doubt and are hotly disputed (see Chapter 4, note 63). It is also noteworthy that Fandy (1999: 32) relies on outdated and unreliable official figures for the number of expatriate workers in the kingdom (cf. Chapter 4, note 63 and associated main text).

[5] Abir writes that the petition was presented on 30 April; Dekmejian (1994), Fandy (1999: 119) and, significantly, Fagih (1998) definitively give May.

endorsed a draft version of the letter (al-Fagih, 1998: chs 6–7; Fandy, 1999: 119, 159; cf. Abir, 1993: 192).[6]

The significance of this petition, even though Bin Baz soon issued a memorandum toning down his support, is summed up by Abir (1993: 191) as follows:

On the surface it seemed that King Fahd had opted to follow the time-honoured Saudi practice of doing nothing... Yet, the '400 ulama's petition' seriously shook the monarch and most Sauds because it signified the emergence of a broad-based coalition between the different streams in the ranks of the ulama. It also represented a departure from the traditional alliance between 'state and church' within the framework established by Ibn Saud after 1930 and, therefore, a threat to the regime's authority and legitimacy.

According to Fagih, the chief of the security service was 'severely reprimanded' for failing to detect the activity surrounding the preparation of the letter. The security chief later 'intimated to one opposition figure that the shock created by the letter to the King was greater within the ruling family than the shock of learning of Iraq's invasion of Kuwait' (al-Fagih, 1998: ch. 7). The Letter of Demands was the first major document of the Saudi Islamist reform movement, and was the basis of the more comprehensive petition, the 'Memorandum of Advice', which followed in 1992.[7] The demands contained in the Letter are as follows.[8]

---

[6] Shaikh Baz was at this time head of the Council of Senior Ulama, not Grand Mufti as Fandy implies (see, for example, Fandy, 1999: 51, 119, 120, 159). See Chapter 2, note 57 on the re-institution of the position of Grand Mufti in May 1993.

[7] Two cassette tapes, produced secretly in August and September 1991 linked the Letter of Demands and the Memorandum of Advice in both time and content. These two tapes were produced by one sub-group of the broad and diffuse Islamist movement inside the kingdom at the time. The cassettes were allegedly widely distributed throughout the kingdom and created a significant impact, particularly the first of the two which became known as 'The Supergun' (see al-Fagih, 1998: ch. 8).

[8] The full text of the letter, which comprises these 12 demands and a short but respectful introductory paragraph addressed to King Fahd, is presented on MIRA's website as an appendix to Fagih's history of dissent in Saudi Arabia (see Letter, 1991). Fagih was a member of the secret opposition grouping which produced the Letter of Demands.

1. The establishment of a consultative council to decide on internal and external affairs. The members of this body should be selected so as to include individuals of diverse specialisations, and who must be know[n] for their sincerity and upright conduct. The council must be fully independent and free from any pressures which could affect the discharging of its full responsibilities.
2. Examining all political, economic and administrative laws and regulations to ascertain their conformity to Shari'a. This task should be conducted by fully-mandated, competent and trustworthy Shari'a committees. All laws not conforming to Shari'a should then be abrogated.
3. Ensuring that all state officials and its representatives internally and abroad must be competent and suitably specialised. They must also be dedicated, upright and honest. Failure to fulfill any of these requirements must be deemed as betrayal of trust and a major threat to the country's interest and its reputation.
4. Achieving justice and equality for all individuals in society, safeguarding full rights and exacting duties without preferment to the privileged or condescension towards the disadvantaged. It should also be realised that taking advantage of one's influence to shirk one's duties or usurp the rights of others could cause the disintegration of society and lead to the dire fate against which the Prophet (peace be upon him) had warned.
5. Subjecting all officials without exception, and especially those in key posts, to rigorous accountability, and removing anyone found to be corrupt or incompetent, no matter who he may be.
6. Ensuring fairness in the distribution of public wealth between all classes and groups within society. All taxes should be cancelled, and all levies which became a burden to the people should be reduced, while the resources of the state must be protected from wastage and exploitation. Priority should be given to expenditure in areas where need is more pressing, while illegal monopolies must be ended and improperly acquired assets reclaimed. The ban on Islamic banks must be ended, and all private and public banking institutions must be purged from usury, which is equivalent to waging war on God and his prophet [*sic*], and is a cause for the loss of God's favour and blessing.
7. The building of a strong and integrated armed forces [*sic*], fully equipped from diverse sources. Special attention should be paid

to the development of military industries. The aim of the army should be to protect the country and its sacred values.

8. Reconstructing the media to bring them in line with the Kingdom's policy of serving Islam. The media should reflect the values of society and enhance and advance its culture, and they must be purified from all that contradicts the above goals. Freedom of the media to educate and inform through the propagation of true stories and constructive criticism must be safeguarded in accordance with the legitimate safeguards.

9. Directing foreign policy to safeguard the interests of the nation, away from illegitimate alliances. The state must champion Muslim causes, while the status of our embassies abroad must be rectified to reflect the Islamic character of this country.

10. The development of religious and missionary institutions in this country, and providing them with all the necessary human and material resources. All obstacles preventing them from fulfilling their tasks properly must be removed.

11. Unifying judicial organs, according them full and real independence, and ensuring that the authority of the judiciary extends to all. An independent body must be set up to follow up the implementation of judicial decisions.

12. Safeguarding the rights of individuals and society, and removing any trace of restrictions on the will of the people and their rights, safeguarding human dignity in accordance with the proper legitimate safeguards.

Repressive measures were taken against the signatories and the most active among them were harassed and in some cases imprisoned; the regime also resorted to the legitimacy of largesse to 'mitigate the population's dissatisfaction' (see Abir, 1993: 192–3; Fandy, 1999: 60). As senior ulama distanced themselves from the petition, it became clear the religious establishment in the kingdom was not homogeneous. Well before the Gulf Crisis, it was posited that the 'rubber stamp' nature of the role of the establishment ulama was indicative of their marginalisation from political power, which 'may suggest they no longer represent religious elements in the Saudi population…[a] gap [that] might produce a "revival movement" in Saudi Arabia not unlike similar such movements in other Middle

Eastern nations' (see Bligh, 1985: 47, 49). The birth of a broad Islamist sociopolitical movement divorced from the officially sanctioned religious establishment and opposed to an allegedly pseudo-Islamic state is indeed what occurred in Saudi Arabia in 1990–1.

Clearly determined to take risks and press on with their programme for reform, the Islamist opposition regrouped during 1992 and, in July, a committee associated with staff at King Saud University (Riyadh) delivered a 45-page 'Memorandum of Advice' (*muthakkara al-nasiha*) to Shaikh Baz. According to Dekmejian (1994: 633), the Memorandum 'contained an elaboration of the May 1991 letter and advanced a new set of more radical demands'. This document bore the signatures of more than 100 petitioners: 'ulama, university professors and prominent figures' (al-Fagih, 1998: ch. 9). Significantly, most signatories were affiliated with the conservative Najd region (cf. Dekmejian, 1994 and Fandy, 1999: 59, 65, 255n. 43).[9] The document reflected the traditional *muwahhidi* context of Saudi Arabia, although modernist and progressive attitudes were also discernible. Fagih (1998: ch. 8) believes the Memorandum 'was no more than a restatement of the content' of two cassette tapes recorded and widely distributed by the opposition in the months following the release of the Letter of Demands; he also states that it must 'be considered among the most important achievements of the Islamic revivalist movement in Arabia' (al-Fagih, 1998: ch. 10).[10]

Although the petitioners 'refrained from directly attacking the royal family', the divided reaction of the establishment ulama indicates that the opposition's efforts to present a unified Islamic front for reform led to 'a partial victory' (Dekmejian, 1994: 634):

...seven of the seventeen senior 'ulama' declined to sign the denunciation issued by Ibn Baz's Supreme Authority, which prompted their dismissal by King Fahd in December 1992 and their replacement by ten pro-government 'ulama'. This was a clear indication that the young Islamists enjoyed considerable support among a large minority of establishment 'ulama', who were prepared to resist the regime's dictates.

---

[9] The fragmented evolution of this and other opposition documents leaves some details, such as the exact number and identity of signatories, in doubt; 107–109 signatories to the Memorandum, have been variously quoted. See Dekmejian (1994: 635–6) for statistics pertaining to his 'profile of the Islamist elite'.

[10] See note 7 above. Fandy (1999: 50–60) analyses the full text of the document.

Importantly, the Memorandum focused on and called for reform in the kingdom's socioeconomic and political–economic structures. Issues that required addressing, according to the Memorandum's authors, included: commission farming, bribery and corrupt practices generally; nepotism and favouritism; commercial monopolies; an inefficient and unfair state bureaucracy; the waste of national résources; wasteful state spending and the lack of strategic planning; the absence of accountability and transparency in government; and rising unemployment and a growing population (see al-Fagih, 1998: ch. 10; Fandy, 1999: 50–60).[11] Thus, it was an attack on the regime's structures which 'legitimated administrative and financial corruption…sanctioned injustice, despotism, wide-spread corruption and nepotism' (al-Fagih, 1998: ch. 10). That is, it was largely an assault against the Saudi system of *asabiyya* capitalism, which was condemned broadly as anti-Islamic.

Equally discernible in this Gulf War period of dissent is a reaction against reckless modernisation which is perceived as having damaged the religiocultural character of Saudi society and, more specifically against alien—mainly Western—cultural and lifestyle influences. Generally, both the Letter of Demands and the Memorandum of Advice reflect a perceived decline in the moral and Islamic stature of the Saudi state, seen as signs of the even more complete 'corruption' of the Al Saud. In these respects, the demands put by these two documents evoke Juhaiman al-Utaibi's at the Great Mosque 12 years earlier (see Chapter 3). In particular, the Memorandum remains central to the Sunni Islamists' platform for reform in the kingdom (see Fandy, 1999: 19, 22, 50, 147, 161, 171, 255n. 38).

Thus, although the roots of contemporary dissent lie deep in Saudi and *muwahhidi* history and tradition, the tensions that had been building up as a result of the tremendous societal changes since the oil boom—glimpsed briefly but tragically in the 1979 siege of the Great Mosque—found a catalyst for their more general release in the turbulent period of the Gulf Crisis. From these early days of post-Gulf War calls for reform sprang the attempts of the mid-1990s to organise dissent. A number of dissident organisations

---

[11] Many issues are closely linked; for example, the call for an effective and expanded defence force is interrelated with issues of corruption, wastage, transparency and accountability (see al-Fagih, 1998: ch. 10).

were formed, some of which achieved a relatively high profile and gained some notoriety both inside and outside the kingdom, including the Advice and Reformation Committee (ARC) associated with Osama bin Laden.[12] But foremost among these organisations was the Committee for the Defence of Legitimate Rights (CDLR), a good example of the relatively successful early attempts at dissident organisation and effectiveness, and of the regime's response and the opposition's fragmentation.

The CDLR: the first attempt at opposition organisation and regime response. The existence of the CDLR was announced in Riyadh on 3 May 1993. The regime responded by coercing the Council of Senior Ulama to condemn the fledgling organisation. The establishment ulama duly issued a condemnation on 11 May—a measure tantamount to an official ban, and which paved the way for the repression that followed. On 15 May the CDLR's international media spokesman, Muhammad al-Masari—a professor of physics at King Saud University and a signatory to the 1992 Memorandum—was arrested. Within days around 20 CDLR supporters on the university staff had been arrested. More prominent senior CDLR associates were subjected to other means of pressure by the regime. More imprisonments followed; among those arrested was Saad al-Fagih, one of the leading Islamist activists and a founder of the

---

[12] The rich and influential Bin Laden family of Saudi Arabia migrated from (south) Yemen in the 1960s, earned a place in the élite *asabiyya* circle of the Al Saud, and was a notable beneficiary of the kingdom's boom-time *asabiyya* capitalism; it is particularly prominent in the construction industry. Osama himself played a significant personal and financial role in Arab involvement in the war in Afghanistan after the Soviet invasion in 1979. When the communist regime in Kabul fell in April 1992, the *jihad* continued for Osama and many 'Arab Afghans'. Opposed to the Al Saud regime and the United States he was disowned by his family and stripped of his Saudi citizenship in 1994, lived in Sudan for some years and, when expelled from there in May 1996, returned to Afghanistan, eventually finding a haven with the Taliban movement when it triumphed later that year. He is suspected of involvement in—if not 'masterminding'—terrorism against Americans worldwide, including bombing the US embassies in Kenya and Tanzania in August 1998 and the attacks of 11 September 2001, after which he became the primary target of US military action in Afghanistan from October 2001. His personal wealth has been estimated at US$200–$400 million. In 2000 he was in his mid-40s.

CDLR. The regime also took repressive measures against the two principal young ulama who were speaking publicly and unflatteringly on issues of concern and embarrassment for the Al Saud, shaikhs Safar al-Hawali and Salman al-Auda.[13]

Those who were arrested were eventually released; Fagih and Masari, among others, fled the kingdom and established themselves in exile in London, where the CDLR was refounded in April 1994. As the organisation's secretary-general and spokesman, Masari adopted a very high profile and proved adept at conducting a clever public relations campaign in the (mainly British) media. The CDLR thus quickly came to represent two things the Saudi regime both feared and loathed: organised opposition, and publicity. Publicity was particularly embarrassing for the regime when it included the circulation of inside information on Saudi affairs.

As the CDLR endeavoured to create some kind of structure for non-violent dissent, the organisation became a two-way conduit for regime-damaging sociopolitical and economic information moving into and out of the kingdom by way of fax, e-mail, and toll-free telephone numbers. CDLR propaganda activity was prolific and became a source of agitation for both the Al Saud and the British establishment. For example, *The Economist* (1994: 71) reported that the CDLR faxed 800 copies of its newsletter into the kingdom on a weekly basis, to be further copied and distributed there. Commenting on the effect of up to 1,000 faxes per week to the kingdom, Masari said, 'Perhaps 150,000 people see what we write and perhaps 80 per cent of people oppose the government…10,000 of them are activists…' (al-Masari, 1996; see also Fandy, 1999: 10–12, 126–35). Fagih has estimated that more than 120 phone calls a day offering comment and information from the kingdom were received by the CDLR at the height of its notoriety (al-Fagih, S., 1998, pers. comm., 28 May).

Responding to heavy pressure from the Saudi government, in November 1994 the British Home Office formally denied political asylum to Masari, which would have meant his deportation to the

---

[13] See Fagih (1998: chs. 12, 13) for a general, insider's account of these events. Masari's specific story is well told by Leslie and Andrew Cockburn (1994). See Fandy (1999: 61–113) for a detailed account and analysis of the activities of Hawali and Auda.

country of his escape route, Yemen.[14] In March 1995, the British Immigration Appeals Tribunal upheld Masari's appeal, but continued pressure from the Saudi government and British arms manufacturers led the Home Office to virtually circumvent British law by ignoring the Tribunal's decision and attempting once again to deport Masari, this time to the Caribbean island-state of Dominica. This second case received wide publicity from early January to April 1996—the time of the Saudis' axing of the BBC's Arabic Television service (see Victor, 1996; Snoddy and Gardner, 1996; Bowcott and Hirst, 1996)—and developed into near scandal in which, among other revelations, 'the symbiotic relationship between the [British] arms firms and various branches of [the British] government' was exposed (Milne and Black, 1996a).

Writing for the *Guardian*, Seumas Milne and Ian Black (1996a) revealed: that the chief executive of the armaments firm Vickers, Sir Colin Chandler, was a former head of arms exports at the Ministry of Defence (MoD); that Vickers' director of international relations was also a former MoD official; and that the new British ambassador-designate to Saudi Arabia, Andrew Green—a senior Middle East expert in the Foreign Office—was a non-executive director of Vickers Defence Systems (see also Beavis, Barrie and Norton-Taylor, 1996). The *Guardian* exposed communication between these three men and senior executives of two other British arms manufacturers, British Aerospace and Giest, Keen and Nettlefold, and between all of them and the British government, over Masari's activities. The arms firms executives had reportedly discussed the concerns of American and British intelligence agencies—the CIA and MI6—about Masari's activities, and had referred to 'direct Saudi intervention...to stifle [Masari] personally'. Revelations also abounded over the dramatic 300% increase in British aid to Dominica at the time.

---

[14] See P. Cockburn (1994) and Bishop (1994) for examples of the coverage in the British press of this attempt to deport Masari. See also Binyon (1994), who reported: 'The [Masari/CDLR] case was raised by King Fahd in recent meetings with both [the then British Prime Minister] John Major and Douglas Hurd, the Foreign Secretary.' Evans (1994) pointed out that '[t]he kingdom is Britain's largest defence customer and an important export market.' Masari himself (1995, pers. comm., 6 July) said the Al Saud were 'extremely outraged' and 'extremely concerned' by his activities, and that a diplomatic crisis was brewing 'behind the scenes' between the Saudi and British governments over the CDLR.

The British Foreign Office defended the government's stance and role in the Masari affair and government–arms firms links (see Hotten and Brown, 1996; Rose, 1996a, 1996b; Brown *et al.*, 1996; Beaumont, 1996; Jury, 1996; Brown and Sheridan, 1996; Hotten, 1996; Milne and Black, 1996b; *Independent*, 1996).

The second attempt to deport Masari, however, also failed on appeal, and resulted in severe embarrassment for the Saudi and British governments: the judge who presided over the case, David Pearl, found that the British government had attempted 'to "circumvent for diplomatic and trade reasons" its obligations under the UN convention on refugees' (see report in Lichfield, 1996). Soon after Masari was granted leave to remain in Britain, he and Fagih parted company, with Fagih founding a new organisation in London in March 1996, the Movement for Islamic Reform in Arabia (MIRA).

Greater success greeted efforts to halt the activities of the Advice and Reformation Committee (ARC) with the September 1998 arrest of Khalid al-Fauwaz. Fauwaz, another Saudi exile, had established an ARC office in London—also in April 1994—to carry out functions similar to those of the CDLR, but from a more radical position. His arrest followed on a US extradition warrant and was made by the British police Special Branch in co-operation with MI5 and the FBI. Fauwaz is wanted in the United States in connection with the August 1998 bombings of the US embassies in Kenya and Tanzania and on the basis of links between the ARC and Osama bin Laden. According to Fauwaz (1995, pers. comm., 21 Sept.), Bin Laden was 'a very important [ARC] member', but was not the organisation's leader—i.e., it was a loose association in keeping with the diffuse nature of Saudi Islamist opposition (see also MIRA, 1998b).[15]

The end result of these events in Britain was that the CDLR continued to exist more in name than in practice, with Masari as its head; MIRA, a new, reasonably well-funded and relatively professional organisation led by Fagih came into being, and the always marginal presence of the ARC dried up.

---

[15] For British media reports and comments on these reports, see MIRA (1998c, 1998d, 1998e); see also Weiser, 1998a; *Electronic Telegraph* (1998b). Fauwaz, from an English gaol, was still fighting against extradition in November 2002; see Hopkins and Norton-Taylor (2001) and Johnston and O'Neill (2002) on various aspects of the legal case against Fauwaz.

The spread and intensification of dissent: the liability of the Saudi–US relationship

Violent messages: the 1995 Riyadh and 1996 Khobar bombings. In Saudi Arabia, campaigners affiliated with the CDLR and members of Masari's family had meanwhile become a target of repression. Suspected dissidents were arrested by the hundreds in the kingdom in 1994–5, with the net cast far beyond the CDLR by this stage. Hawali and Auda were arrested in 1994; the arrest of the latter in September sparked off demonstrations, described by the opposition as an 'uprising', in the Qasimi shaikh's home city of Buraida.[16] A cycle of violence appeared to have been set in motion when, in mid-August 1995, a CDLR-associated dissident was executed and, almost exactly three months later, in mid-November, the bombing of a US-run Saudi National Guard installation in Riyadh killed seven people, including five Americans.[17] There was little doubt that Americans were the target in the last case—the bombing was not just retaliation against Al Saud repression but was also aimed at the regime's 'special relationship' with the United States.

The Saudi–US relationship is not without some significant problems; historically, it starts from a position of Saudi weakness and US strength and is centred on oil, arms and military infrastructure (see, for example, Halliday, 1982). The bases of this relationship have been publicly questioned in both countries since the events of 11 September 2001, but nowhere more bluntly than in a *New York*

---

[16] The event was secretly captured on video and sent to the CDLR in London. Footage of an anti-Saudi demonstration in London on 30 September 1994—as well as what is apparently a professionally produced narration—were subsequently added, and a VHS video tape, 'Buraidah Uprising', was released by the CDLR to publicise the reality of dissent in Saudi Arabia. See Fandy (1999: 91) for an *asabiyya*-centred explanation of why the Buraida disturbances failed to inspire similar incidents elsewhere in the kingdom.

[17] For background on the US company Vinnell Corp., which was contracted to train the National Guard in 1975, see Hartung (1996; see also Halliday, 1982: 140). Among many other issues, including the suggestion that Vinnell personnel assisted Saudi forces during the 1979 siege of the Great Mosque, the Hartung article reports doubts raised in a US Congressional hearing on Vinnell's contract that a commission of US$4.5 million out of a contract value of US$77 million may have been paid to a 'middleman'.

Times editorial, which referred to 'America's deeply cynical relationship with Riyadh':

> Over the decades, the United States and Saudi Arabia have benefited from the cold-blooded bargain at the core of their relationship. America got the oil to run its economy and Saudi Arabia got the protection of American military might whenever the kingdom was threatened by its violent neighbors, including Iraq and Iran. (*International Herald Tribune*, 2001; see also Hoagland, 2001)

In fact, Saudi–US relations today have striking parallels with pre-World War II Saudi–British relations and, whatever its problems, the Saudi–US link continues to testify to Al Saud astuteness in cultivating a powerful ally.[18] The current 'special relationship', which proved so effective during the Gulf War, can be traced back to 1943 when US President Franklin D. Roosevelt declared Saudi Arabia— because of its oil resources and the interests of US companies in exploiting those resources—to be of vital strategic interest to the United States (see, for example, Library of Congress, 1992). The first US military mission was dispatched to the kingdom in 1943. A mutual defence agreement was formalised in 1951.[19]

The 'special relationship' provided the basis for Saudi Arabia's US-built military infrastructure which, between 1947 and 1990, had cost the Saudis approximately US$48,000 million and had kept the US Army's Corps of Engineers busy for 23 years from 1965 to 1988 (see Library of Congress, 1992).[20] Included in this monumental

---

[18] See the sections 'The British, the First World War and post-Ottoman Arabia', and 'Hijaz conquered, kingdom proclaimed' in Chapter 2.

[19] Sources on Saudi–US relations are numerous. For a glowing overview of the relationship, see the special edition of *Middle East Insight* (1995) to mark '50 years of US–Saudi partnership'; see also, for example, Hart (1998); Peterson (1986); Safran (1985: 295–308, 398–419); Quandt (1981: 137–59, 162–3); and Part 3, 'US political–military response', in the volume on US strategic interests in the Gulf edited by Olson (1987).

[20] Other sources have cited the sale of five US Airborne Warning and Control Systems (AWACS) planes to the kingdom in 1981 as marking the beginning of a military build-up that would be worth US$156,000 million by 1992—'the largest armaments system that the world has ever seen in any region of the world', according to the programme's researchers (Globalvision, 1993). US arms manufacturers were not the only ones to benefit from Saudi military modernisation;

military infrastructure are major ports, 'dozens of airfields all over the kingdom' and, most imposing of all as a symbol of the special relationship, King Khalid Military City—one of five interlinked military control centres and bases (Globalvision, 1993). The Khalid centre was built in secrecy at Hafar al-Batin, in the desert near the Iraqi border, around 380 kilometres north of Riyadh. It is a self-contained, self-sufficient city for 65,000 military and civilian personnel. Its features include ballistic missile silos and nuclear-proofed underground command bunkers and, by 1984, it had cost around US$8,000 million (Globalvision, 1993; Library of Congress, 1992; see also Armstrong, 1991).

Although paid for with Saudi money and remaining under official Saudi sovereignty, this infrastructure was built with US technology to US specifications and can be put to very effective use by US forces when required, as the 1991 Gulf War amply demonstrated. In fact, the 'huge scale of the Saudi base complexes and the inter-operability of equipment' proved to be 'indispensable' to the US war effort against Iraq in 1990–1 (Library of Congress, 1992). Prince Sultan Air Base at al-Kharj, approximately 100 kilometres southeast of Riyadh, was constructed for the security of US forces after the 1996 Khobar bombing. It hosts more than 4,000 US military personnel and around 100 strike and support aircraft (see Jehl, 1996; Myers, 1997; Graham, 1998). It is a high-technology command and control centre for US air operations and, although offensive missions were—officially at least—not permitted by the Saudis, it played an important command role in the anti-Taliban and 'anti-terrorism' Afghan campaign of late 2001 (see, for example, Schmitt and Dao, 2001).

The military alliance that exists between the United States and the Gulf Arab states, particularly Saudi Arabia, means that the US is in a position to exercise regional power almost at will.[21] The scale of this military infrastructure suggests the US may have transferred some of its global command functions to Saudi Arabia. It at least

---

British and French companies were also major beneficiaries. The Al-Yamamah arms contracts with British companies from 1986 were alone worth in excess of US$28,100 million (see Norton-Taylor and Pallister, 1999).

[21] Kuwait and Bahrain in particular are notable for their hosting of US air and naval forces; Bahrain is home to the US Navy's 5th Fleet.

points to a long-term US strategic commitment to military intervention, not only in the Middle East, but in Central Asia and Africa. Despite the difficulties presented when it fails to obtain Saudi permission to make full use of the facilities, this US regional strategic commitment has been demonstrated by the continuing enforcement of 'no-fly zones' and periodically intensified action against Iraq, and by US military operations in Afghanistan from 7 October 2001. This combination of infrastructure and US personnel and equipment based in the kingdom also means the US will also be on hand to offer assistance to friendly regimes, such as the Saudi royal family or the Mubarak government in Egypt, should they be seriously threatened by any internal upheaval.

Thus the November 1995 Riyadh bombing, although an act representing only a relatively small number of committed radicals in the kingdom, was an act of resistance against what many Saudis had come to see as a de facto US occupation of their country. As the fear and tension of the Gulf Crisis eased, even non-political Saudis began to doubt the motives of the continued US presence in their country and the motives of their own government in allowing such a presence to continue. The view that the holy land of Islam was, and remains, effectively occupied is no longer the preserve of the followers of outspoken young ulama such as Hawali and Auda and more radical opponents of the Al Saud such as Osama bin Laden. At the time of the 1990–1 crisis, the majority of Saudis believed the 'propaganda' that Iraq would have invaded Saudi Arabia, but this belief had worn thin by 1993. Now, 'ninety-five percent' of Saudi citizens believe the war was 'a well staged plan' for the United States to insert a greater presence in the kingdom and the Gulf region generally (Saudi nationals 1998, confidential and informal sources, Riyadh, Jan.–Mar.; see also Fandy, 1999: 71–2, 87, 189; Fagih, 1998: ch. 3). Common terms for the Gulf War inside the kingdom today are 'the Gulf Show' and 'the Gulf Massacre'. Many citizens also believe that Saudi media references to Western/US forces in the kingdom represent an attempt by the regime to condition the population to accept de facto 'occupation' (Saudi nationals 1998, confidential and informal sources, Riyadh, Jan.–Mar.).[22]

---

[22] One Qasimi source (Saudi national, 1998, pers. comm., Riyadh) quoted his 70-year-old father—generationally and regionally the very epitome of old, conservative

This underground national narrative continues. According to informal sources, the Gulf War and its aftermath left the Saudi population 'simmering' and provided the environment for Auda and Hawali to emerge to prominence—the regime was forced to act against them because they were bringing the simmering to the boil. The massive crackdowns of 1994 were largely effective, but the underlying dissatisfactions remained and led to bomb attacks in 1995 and 1996 (Saudi nationals 1998, confidential and informal sources, Riyadh, Jan.–Mar.). The notorious Osama bin Laden did not, of course, confine his anti-Al Saud and anti-US sentiments to underground activity and he has consequently been accused by the United States of being at the centre of a global network of terrorism. Speaking while Bin Laden was being vigorously hunted by US forces in Afghanistan, the former head of the Saudi intelligence service, Prince Turki al-Faisal, reflected on the path of Bin Laden's radicalisation; he believes there is 'no doubt' the catalyst 'that led to what he is now' was the arrival of US troops on Saudi soil in 1990 (al-Faisal, cited in Reuters, 2001b).[23] Opposition to the 'US occupation' of the land of the two holy mosques and, by extension, opposition to the Al Saud, was not confined to the kingdom but soon took on an international dimension, making itself known and spreading throughout the Muslim world via the new media

---

Saudi traditions and attitudes—on 'finally knowing what it is like to be occupied by a foreign imperial power'. The source also described how his father came to express 'disagreement' with the senior establishment *alim*, Shaikh bin Baz, and 'agreement' with the radical young *alim*, Shaikh Salman al-Auda. Byman and Green lend support to the conclusion that popular anti-US feeling is growing in Saudi Arabia, Bahrain and the UAE, although they imply this feeling is largely unfounded: 'many Gulf citizens credit the United States with exaggerated influence over domestic politics, as well as over events in the region in general' (Byman and Green, 1999a: 25). They also draw a distinction between popular feeling and action: 'Despite the atmosphere of discontent...few individuals in the Gulf actively oppose the ruling families or the U.S. presence, and even fewer use violence to advance their agendas' (Byman and Green, 1999a: 41).

[23] Prince Turki, a son of the late King Faisal and brother to the Saudi Foreign Minister, Prince Saud al-Faisal, took up his post in 1977. He stepped down suddenly in August 2001, shortly before the 11 September attacks against the United States.

technologies (see, for example, *Muslimedia International*, 1996a, 1996b).[24] In these global treatises, links have been drawn between economic internationalism and the politics of the concept of US 'occupation' of Saudi Arabia and the Gulf region (see Marwan, 1998).

In the meantime, the cycle of violence inside the kingdom continued to intensify. On 31 May 1996, four Saudi nationals were beheaded for the 1995 Riyadh bombing. Three of the four, all Sunnis, are reputed to have been veterans of the Afghan war (see Fandy, 1999: 1–3). Only a few weeks later, on 25 June 1996, a massive truck bomb was detonated next to a US Air Force barracks at Khobar, near the eastern city of Dhahran, killing 19 USAF personnel and wounding more than 300 others, many seriously. The Khobar bombing triggered intense intelligence and security activity, with a wave of arrests and FBI involvement. In the general Saudi and US eagerness to blame Iran for the bombing, hundreds of Saudi Shiites were arrested. Efforts to implicate Iran (see, for example, CNN, 1996c; Lancaster, 1998) resulted in Iran going on to high military alert as a precaution against US military 'retaliation' (see Wright, 1996). A controversy developed around the Saudi Shiite dissident, Hani al-Sayegh, who was extradited from Canada to the United States in June 1997, only to have all charges of involvement in terrorist activities against Americans, including links with the Khobar bombing, dropped three months later because of lack of evidence.[25]

After the Khobar bombing, Osama bin Laden expressed his support in principle for the act—although he denied direct involvement, as he did in the case of the bombings of the US embassies in Kenya and Tanzania, and as he did with the 11 September attacks against New York and Washington. More significantly, Bin Laden

[24] An entire section of Muslimedia archives is devoted to articles dealing with 'the occupied Arab world' during the period 1996–8 (see the Muslimedia website at: http://www.muslimedia.com/archives/oaw98/oaw98.htm).

[25] The Khobar bombing and its aftermath was the subject of widespread coverage in the media at the time and for months afterwards. See Vicini (1997) for a report on the outcome of the Sayegh affair in the United States. Sayegh was deported to Saudi Arabia in October 1999 by the United States. He was arrested upon arrival in the kingdom, amidst Amnesty International (AI) concern for his well-being (see AI, 1999). The United States has been implicated in attempts to coerce Sayegh (see HRW, 1998).

made clear and very public his opposition to the presence of non-Muslim forces—namely Western and mainly US—in Arabia in a series of interviews with Western journalists, framing his objections in the historical and global context of Western anti-Islamic antagonism (see, for example, Fisk, 1996a, 1996b). In August 1996 from his refuge in Afghanistan, Bin Laden issued his notorious declaration of a *jihad* 'against the Americans occupying the land of the two holy places' (Bin Laden, 1996).

Almost two years after the event, in May 1998, the Saudi Interior Minister, Prince Na'if bin Abd al-Aziz, announced that the Khobar bombing was committed by Saudi citizens acting from within the kingdom without foreign involvement (see, for example, CNN 1998a; Lancaster 1998). Regime statements at this time may have admitted the bombers were Saudis, but in typically vague fashion they did not admit they were Sunnis, implying that only *direct* foreign involvement could be ruled out. The possibility has thus been left open that the bombers were Shiite Saudis who may or may not have enjoyed the indirect assistance of a foreign power—that is, Iran. The regime is still not prepared to acknowledge openly that the bombers were Sunnis from the Saudi heartland, which would be tantamount to admitting the existence of a serious internal security problem emanating from the *muwahhidi* majority; that this is in fact the case is all but a certainty. Despite the indictment by the United States in June 2001 of 13 Saudi nationals who were allegedly members of the clandestine Saudi Arabian branch of the Shiite Hizbullah organisation, and despite evidence the United States claimed to possess that linked Iran to the bombing, definitive and public proof that the bombers did not come from the *muwahhidi* mainstream does not exist.[26] After 11 September 2001, it is clear that radical—and anti-Shiite—Sunni Saudi dissidents associated with Bin Laden would have had the organisational and practical skills, the means and the motivation to have executed the Khobar bombing.[27] The Saudi regime had already linked Bin Laden to the

[26] See note 44 below and associated main text and references regarding the US indictments for the 1996 Khobar bombing.

[27] The most committed Saudi 'Afghans'—those most likely to have developed associations with Bin Laden's network—were staunchly anti-Shiite. The involvement of Saudi Arabians in Afghanistan was a de facto extension of official Saudi

1995 Riyadh bombing (see, for example, Schneider, 2001a); the likelihood that the Khobar bombing was conducted by individuals in sympathy, if not connected with the Riyadh bombers, and that the Khobar bombing was motivated at least in part by revenge for the execution of the Riyadh bombers not four weeks earlier, is too strong to ignore.[28]

Osama bin Laden and the effects of 11 September 2001.   Although mainstream Saudis may have regretted 'the means of delivery' represented by the 1995 and 1996 bombings, many openly professed that they 'liked the message' (see Hirst, 1996)—a sentiment of worrying significance for the regime. It is clear that a lack of popular support for radical action does not mean an absence of sympathy for many of the concerns expressed by the perpetrators of such acts. In this respect the general feeling in the kingdom, post-Gulf War, resembles the feeling surrounding the 1979 siege of the Great Mosque, namely that Juhaiman al-Utaibi's rebels were expressing legitimate complaints but chose the wrong target.[29] However, post-Gulf War political opposition, in a broad sense, enjoys a good deal more popular sympathy than did Juhaiman's narrowly based rebellion and, by comparison, the radicals among today's dissenters are choosing the right targets. This observation is supported by statements on the Khobar bombing made by prominent advocates of non-violent reform in the kingdom: '...the bombers had an "intellectually very strong" case for their action. "As long as [US administrations] protect an oppressive regime and occupy our territory, then America can be regarded as the enemy"' (Masari, reported in the *Guardian Weekly*, 1996); and from MIRA (1998a): 'While we in MIRA as well as all Muslim elite [*sic*] in the kingdom are with Bin

---

government foreign policy to counter the influences of revolutionary Iran and Shiism as much as those of the Soviet Union and communism (pers. observ., 1988–9, Peshawar, Jalalabad, Islamabad). See also Fandy (1999: 172–3, 195–228) and Rasheed (1998) for evidence of the tension, if not hostile feeling, between Saudi Arabia's Sunni political opposition and Shiites.

[28] In an article providing background to the series of pre-11 September bombings in the kingdom which targeted Westerners from November 2000 to May 2001, *Guardian* writers present as a given fact that the 1996 Khobar bombing was the work of Bin Laden's supporters (see Pallister, Kelso and Whitaker, 2002).

[29] See Chapter 3, 'The 1979 siege of the Great Mosque of Mecca'.

Laden in that the American presence is not acceptable in the peninsula, we believe that the effort should be directed to the removal of
the foundation of their presence. The problem is more in the
regime and the official religious establishment which provide this
foundation.'

The above observation is also supported by reports of a number
of foiled bomb plots against US targets and the Saudi regime since
the Khobar bombing (al-Fagih, S., 1998, pers. comm., 28 May; see
also Davies, 1996). Fagih believes only some of these foiled plots
were planned by followers of Bin Laden. He also claims there has
been at least one successful attack against regime figures that was
completely covered up, with no information whatsoever being leaked
to the Saudi public or to the foreign media; it reportedly killed 'at
least' eight Ministry of Interior personnel in 1996 (al-Fagih, S., 1998,
pers. comm., 28 May). Whether linked with Bin Laden or not, it is
probable that Saudi veterans of the Afghan war were behind most if
not all of them. Fagih reported that 60 Afghanistan veterans were
arrested by Saudi authorities in March 1998, and that secret cells of
'Arab Afghans' were still being discovered in the kingdom, principally as a result of information gained through the April 1997 defec-
tion to US authorities of 'a senior Bin Laden confidante' (al-Fagih,
S., 1998, pers. comm., 28 May; see also Weiser, 1998b). CNN (1996a)
has also reported on the smuggling of explosives into the kingdom
by Saudi citizens. Domestic bombing campaigns and their cover-up
by the regime are by no means unprecedented in modern Saudi
history; in November 1966, for example, at least three bombs targeted regime and US facilities, including 'the private residence of
Prince [now King] Fahd' (Man, 1966b). The British ambassador to
Saudi Arabia at the time, Morgan Man, wrote, 'There has of course
been nothing in the local press and very few people seem to know
about these explosions so far. It is interesting that the Saudis blame
the Yemenis—it would of course not do to admit that Saudis might
be involved!' (Man, 1966b).

Man's words of 1966 are brought to mind by the attempts to
implicate non-Saudis in the 1996 Khobar bombing, and again in
the case of at least seven bombings targeting Westerners in Riyadh
and Khobar from November 2000 to June 2002. A British engineer
was killed in the first bombing in Riyadh, a British manager for

Coca Cola and an American chiropractor were seriously maimed in the Khobar bombings of 15 December 2000 and 2 May 2001, seven others were wounded in two other bombings on 23 November 2000 and 15 March 2001, and a British banker was killed by a car bomb in Riyadh on 20 June 2002. All the victims were civilians. After the first bombings the Saudi Interior Ministry took custody of 14 Westerners, mostly Britons, claiming they were liquor bootleggers bombing each other as a result of a 'turf war'. Although six subsequently 'confessed' to illegal activity and the bombings, both Saad al-Fagih and British government officials believe that Bin Laden supporters were behind the bombings and that the Saudi government was deliberately attempting to conceal an escalating internal security problem. The research conducted by the *Guardian* into the case revealed that '[n]o concrete evidence exists of a "turf war". None of the blast victims had any connection to the alcohol trade, and the accused men are all friends' (Kelso *et al.*, 2002; see also *Guardian*, 2002; Kelso and Pallister, 2002; Pallister, Kelso and Whitaker, 2002; Norton-Taylor and Pallister, 2002; Pilkington and Kelso, 2002. And see also Chapter 1, note 11).

The aftermath of 11 September has added new fuel to grass-roots Saudi antipathy to the United States. The US-led 'war against terrorism' has been a significant development which has antagonised religious and nationalist feelings in the kingdom. This global 'war' without defined limits began in Afghanistan in October 2001 by targeting Bin Laden for capture or death and brought down the Taliban regime formerly recognised by Riyadh; the campaign also revealed evidence of an unofficial US policy of extermination directed at the mostly Arab fighters associated with Bin Laden in Afghanistan.[30] These events have combined with pre-existing

[30] The Taliban regime enjoyed the official recognition of only three countries: Pakistan, the United Arab Emirates, and Saudi Arabia. Saudi Arabia withdrew its recognition in September 2001, after the 11 September attacks against the United States. For evidence that the United States was deliberately scuppering surrender negotiations with pro-Bin Laden, mainly Arab, foreign fighters in the mountains of eastern Afghanistan in order to 'annihilate' them, see Ricks (2001). For an indication of the misgivings felt in the Arab world over the plight of their nationals in Afghanistan, and abhorrence of any policy of annihilation, see the *Daily Star* (2001a; 2001b). The United States subsequently became embroiled in scandal over the treatment of captured Taliban and non-Afghan fighters

suspicion of US designs and resentment of US behaviour to build-up a level of anger that will have repercussions for many years to come and is a source of concern to the Saudi government. Saudi citizens who were involved in some way in the wars in Afghanistan over the course of two decades have been 'conservatively estimated' at around 10,000, but probably number around 15,000 (al-Fagih, S., 1998, pers. comm., 28 May) and reportedly according to 'royal Saudi intelligence' sources, possibly even up to 25,000 (see Jehl, 2001b). This represents a potentially significant pool of sympathy for past causes and former comrades-in-arms which could manifest itself in a renewed commitment among their number.

Besides the Arab Afghans themselves, reports abounded of popular sympathy, even if largely by default, for Bin Laden and a greatly heightened anti-Americanism in the kingdom at the time of the United States' Afghan campaign. For example, another dissident young shaikh, Hamud bin Uqla al-Shuaibi surfaced in Buraida, describing the United States as 'an enemy of Islam' (see Nuesse, 2001); a high-profile member of the establishment ulama, the retired but still respected former member of the Council of Senior Ulama, Shaikh Abdullah bin Abd al-Rahman bin Jibrin, issued a *fatwa* calling on Muslims to support the Taliban (see DPA, 2001); demonstrations and protests were reported in Sakaka and in Mecca against the US Afghan campaign (see Nuesse, 2001); and Saudi school teachers were reprimanded for praising Bin Laden in their classes (Reuters, 2001d). Jamal Khashoggi (2001a), a Saudi political analyst and the deputy editor of Saudi Arabia's *Arab News* daily newspaper, wrote that 'there are very few people in Saudi Arabia who are prepared to criticize Bin Laden, especially among the more religious (after all, he had become a symbol of confrontation with the United States)…'. In one remarkable report from Riyadh, the director of Saudi intelligence, Prince Nawaf bin Abd al-Aziz, 'acknowledged that the vast majority of young Saudi adults felt sympathy for the cause of [Bin Laden] after Sept. 11, even though they rejected the attacks in New York and Washington.' Evidence was

---

allegedly linked to Osama bin Laden. Of at least 158 of these prisoners held at the US military base at Guantanomo Bay in Cuba, more than 100 were reported to be Saudis (see Whitaker, 2002). For an account of the prisoner furore, see the *International Herald Tribune*, 2002b.

also presented in this report that, of the kingdom's nationals aged between 24 and 41 surveyed by Saudi intelligence, 95% were found to be supportive of Bin Laden's cause (see Sciolino, 2002).[31]

The publicity given in US media to the direct role of Saudi nationals in the 11 September suicide attacks, thought to number 15, the demonisation of Osama bin Laden, regarded by a significant minority in his homeland as a committed Muslim and war hero, and the fierce US media accusations directed against the kingdom as a veritable well-head of 'terrorists' have done nothing to endear the United States to Saudis in general. Statements such as those made by the British foreign secretary, Jack Straw, in which he likened Bin Laden's followers to Nazis and referred to Bin Laden as 'psychotic and paranoid' (see Reuters, 2001c), will likewise not help Britain's image in the kingdom, and will only foster grass-roots belief that a Western alliance is bent on attacking Muslims.

Moreover, official Saudi representatives have all but admitted that, over the longer term, the stationing of large numbers of US forces on Saudi territory has become a political liability for the Saudi regime and a security hazard for US personnel (al-Rawaf, 1998; see also Byman and Green, 1999a: 25–8, 97–8). Domestic security concerns have, in turn, contributed to strains in the strategic alliance with the United States. According to Othman al-Rawaf, a King Saud University professor of politics and former member of the Saudi Consultative Council, cumulative tensions involving various regional issues have resulted in the Saudi–US relationship 'becoming more and more difficult' (al-Rawaf, 1998; cf. Cordesman, 1997: 192–6). A member of the Consultative Council, Saudi businessman Abd al-Rahman al-Zamil, wrote a piece in November 2001 for the London-based Saudi pan-Arab daily newspaper *Asharq al-Awsat* which verged on a damning of the United States. Zamil was responding to what was perceived in the kingdom as unjustifiably

---

[31] See also MacFarquhar (2001) for reports of popular sympathy for Bin Laden among Saudi professionals in Jedda, and Pincus (2001) for similar reports from Khobar, ranging from a 19-year-old student to a 50-year-old businessman. Saudi Arabia was by no means the only country witnessing support—muted or otherwise—for Bin Laden's motivations and objectives, if not necessarily for his methods; see MacFarquhar (2002) for an account of Bin Laden's 'folk hero' status in Egypt, and Hedges (2001) on the identification with Bin Laden on the part of French citizens of North African background.

harsh criticism of Saudi Arabia on the part of the US political and media establishments in the wake of the 11 September attacks. He asserted that the Saudi government only tolerated a US military presence in the kingdom because of post-Gulf War commitments to the United Nations, and stated that such a presence is 'a political burden on the kingdom's government rather than a stabilizing factor, because many people have reservations about it' (al-Zamil, quoted in the *Daily Star*, 2001c).

Examples of recent strains in the relationship came to notice when US officialdom clashed with the Saudi regime over its conduct of the investigations into the 1995 Riyadh and, especially, the 1996 Khobar bombings. The four Saudis convicted of the Riyadh bombing were beheaded before they could be questioned by US authorities. During the early stages of the still unresolved Khobar investigation, '[t]he top two law enforcement officials in the United States... launched a public assault on Saudi Arabia for withholding information... Attorney General Janet Reno and FBI director Louis Freeh say that since the bombing, U.S. investigative efforts have been rebuffed—Saudi officials keeping federal agents outside the inner circle of information' (CNN, 1997). FBI investigators were reportedly even refused access to 'ordinary Saudis' in the community (Davies, 1996). Consequently, according to many reports, in 1996–8 Saudi–US relations went through a period characterised by 'mutual distrust' and 'ill-feeling' (CNN, 1998b; see also CNN, 1996b; Byman and Green, 1999a: 6).

Saudi–US tensions that resulted from the investigation of the 1996 Khobar bombing were, however, minor in comparison with the storm that brewed up over the post-11 September investigations. The fact that Bin Laden's roots were Saudi, that his informal *jihadi* network had a wide, albeit diffuse base of support in Saudi Arabia, and that 15 of the 19 suicide-hijackers of 11 September were believed by US investigators to have been Saudis, made the kingdom an object of suspicion and criticism in many quarters of the United States. The Saudi regime was depicted in the US media as the embodiment of obstinacy and lack of co-operation (see, for example, Perlez, 2001). A *Washington Post* editorial went further, asserting that, despite the official Saudi-US alliance, the kingdom 'is rapidly becoming an obstacle' in the campaign against 'terrorists', and 'risks evolving into an adversary'. The editorial went as far as to state that 'Saudi political policies have become…a genuine menace to the United States (see *International Herald Tribune*, 2002a). A prime example of the US media campaign against Saudi Arabia and its people is the *New York Times* editorial published on 14 October 2001 (reprinted in the *International Herald Tribune*), which was particularly strident and succeeded in causing great offence in the kingdom. Scathing of the basis of the US relationship with Saudi Arabia, the piece focused on 'Saudi Arabia's tolerance for terrorism', the 'malignant behavior' of the Saudis, 'Riyadh's acquiescence' in helping 'create and sustain Osama bin Laden's terrorist organization', the Saudi royal family's 'passive attitude toward terrorism' and 'Saudi Arabia's tangible connections to Islamic fundamentalist terrorism' (*International Herald Tribune*, 2001; see also, for example, Schneider, 2001b).

These charges were met in the kingdom with official outrage and ripostes in the Saudi media (see, for example, Saudinf, 2001b; Jehl, 2001a; Parker, 2001a; 2001b; Isa, 2001a; the *Daily Star*, 2001c; Khashoggi, 2001b). Saudi offence was followed by statements from Washington that the US administration was, in fact, 'very satisfied' with Saudi co-operation in anti-terrorism investigations—but the satisfaction did not cancel out a perceived need to send a high-level delegation to the kingdom to 'discuss' the role the Saudi government was expected to play in countering alleged terrorist affiliations in and with the kingdom. The delegation, consisting of US Treasury, FBI, State Department and National Security Council officials, left for Riyadh on 6 December 2001 (see Reuters, 2001f; Mohammed, 2001; AFP, 2001c). In an interesting turn of phrase, a White House official, who insisted on anonymity, described the mission as 'a great example of the spirit of cooperation and the dialogue between our two countries' (senior US official, quoted in AFP, 2001c).

The delegation's list of topics for discussion with the Saudi regime no doubt included the 6 October 2001 bombing in a shopping district in Khobar that killed an American oil industry engineer. The other person killed was the bomber, identified in mid-November by the Saudi Interior Ministry as a Palestinian dentist based in Riyadh (see Saudinf, 2001a). The bombing was very likely related to the events following 11 September and rising anti-American sentiment in the kingdom on the eve of the US military operations in Afghanistan which began on 7 October 2001. Presuming that regime charges of bootlegging by Westerners are bogus, this bomb attack may, or may not, have been carried out by an accomplice of those involved in the campaign of bombings against Westerners which began in Riyadh on 17 November 2000. Considering that the attacker was a Palestinian and that he has been described as a suicide bomber (*Guardian*, 2002; Pallister, Kelso and Whitaker, 2002), it also seems likely that anti-American sentiment spurred by the growing perception of expanding US regional hegemony was combined with resentment of continuing US support for the Israeli occupation of the Palestinian territories.

Regional issues interrelated: US 'double standards'.   The October 2001 Khobar bombing thus provides evidence for the way in which Saudi Arabia is being drawn into a wider arena of political dispute and dissent as a result of its close association with the United States. The overlap between Saudi foreign policy and domestic sociopolitics extends beyond the localised problems of this relationship and the presence of the US military on Saudi soil. Other, related issues, such as the ongoing stand-off with Saddam Hussein, are relevant to Saudi internal security and regime stability. The post-Gulf War, US-enforced weapons inspection programme and UN sanctions against Iraq have provided no shortage of drama. Major confrontational crises between the two protagonists, the United States and Iraq, occurred in 1994, and in February and then December 1998, and have necessarily involved Saudi Arabia. These events—in addition to continuous lower level tension and incident—have had a great impact in the Arab world, including Saudi Arabia. The Saudi population, for example, has been feeling increasing empathy for the Iraqi people, as opposed to the regime of Saddam Hussein (Saudi nationals 1998, confidential and informal sources, Riyadh, Jan.–Mar.; also Saudi prince 1998, pers. comm.). Even economic analysts noticed this popular feeling in the kingdom, and thought it important enough to record officially. The author of a SAMBA briefing paper on the Saudi economy at the time of the February 1998 crisis wrote that, '[l]eading up to the [Kofi Anan] agreement it became clear that the Saudi public feels deep sympathy for the Iraqi people' (SAMBA, 1998c).

The Saudi government supports the US stance against the Iraqi regime despite its consequences for the Iraqi people; hence, this aspect of Saudi foreign policy provides an ongoing point of contention with the vast majority of the Saudi population. The Iraqi dilemma is merging with Saudi perceptions of the US occupation of their country, and together these issues are fuelling the build-up of anti-American sentiment in the kingdom. This sentiment is neither new nor narrowly based. Since (the then Crown Prince) Fahd's promotion of pro-American policies after King Faisal's death in 1975, 'in essence, anti-Western sentiments were widely shared as well by the conservatives and by most new elites in Saudi Arabia' (Abir, 1993: 72). Diplomats and observers of Saudi affairs have widely believed for some time that, in order to diffuse this hostility, the Al Saud would prefer the United States to maintain an 'over-the-horizon' military presence—that is, to be at instant call in time of need and effectively invisible in the meantime. A US diplomat serving in the Political Section of the US Embassy in Riyadh admitted that the February 1998 Iraq crisis was indeed a significant event in the process of 'distancing' that has occurred in the Saudi–US relationship since 1994. According to this source, the Saudis are now less co-operative, but continue to see the United States as an important part of their defence strategy—but in the 'invisible' way referred to above (US diplomat 1998, pers. comm., 9 Mar.).

That the importance the United States attaches to Gulf Arab alliances is owed to oil and geostrategics rather than to love for the Gulf Arab regimes and peoples is a fact of life with which many Saudi nationals are, often cynically, fully cognisant (Saudi nationals and Arab expatriates, 1998, confidential and informal sources, Riyadh, Feb.). Even a member of the royal family, although generally in favour of an alliance with the United States, has stated that the Saudi–US relationship has been 'too close' and even 'abnormal' considering the two countries are basically ideologically and culturally opposed (Saudi prince, 1998, pers. comm.).

Another contentious regional issue that is, in the perception of the Arab world, intimately linked with US Middle Eastern hegemony and the US–Iraq confrontation is that of Israel–Palestine.

The popular Arab perception that the United States applies double standards in its treatment of Israel on the one hand, and Palestinian and Iraqi issues on the other, is shared by the vast majority of Saudi citizens. For example, a hostile view on the US stance and its 'double standards' was tangible at grass-roots level in Riyadh during the February 1998 Iraq crisis among both Saudi nationals and Arab expatriates (pers. observ. and informal pers. comm., 1998, Riyadh, Feb.; Saudi prince, 1998, pers. comm.).[32] The tensions revealed during the various crises with Iraq and their relationship to other regional issues such as that of Israel-Palestine are not confined to popular sentiment but have also deeply and genuinely affected Saudis up to the highest levels of the regime. US Middle East and Gulf policies, including the pressure that Washington has applied on Riyadh to support more fully and overtly the current, fatally flawed Israeli–Palestinian 'peace process', have been cited as a source of uneasiness in the alliance (al-Rawaf, 1998; see also Khashoggi, 2001b). According to Rawaf this concentrated pressure on Riyadh is due to US recognition that 'Saudi Arabia is the leader of the Muslim states', although he maintains similar pressure to normalise relations with Israel is being applied to all countries of the GCC (al-Rawaf, 1998).

These pressures and tensions are likely to make themselves felt in the broad economic sphere over the longer term, as was indicated by a senior Riyadh-based economist in the Saudi finance industry interviewed at the time of the February 1998 Iraq crisis. He drew many links between economics and politics in Saudi Arabia and believed a difficult situation was made more so by US 'posturing' during the crisis (Senior economist, 1998, pers. comm., Riyadh, Mar.). Concerns about the ability of acute political developments in the region to affect business at ground level in Saudi Arabia were also expressed institutionally at the time. The Saudi American Bank, for example, put these in writing as follows: 'Our concern, if

---

[32] Saudi Arabians, and Arabs and Muslims generally, are not the only ones to have levelled this accusation at the United States. Shortly after US President George W. Bush's aggressive 2002 State of the Union address in which he described Iraq, Iran and North Korea as an 'axis of evil', the Russian Defence Minister, Sergei Ivanov, claimed that the West's US-led 'war on terrorism' revealed the existence of 'double political standards' (see Chalmers, 2002).

it gets to [US military] strikes [against Iraq], would be a possible wave of anti-American sentiment which could result in violence' (SAMBA, 1998c; see also Cordesman, 1997: 192–3).

Events since 11 September and the subsequent US military campaign in Afghanistan have also interacted with the second Palestinian *intifada* against Israeli occupation. Beginning in September 2000, it refocused the attention of the Arab world on the still unresolved issue of Palestinian independence after eight years of a deadlocked 'peace process'. By mid-2001, and especially after the right-wing government of Israeli Prime Minister Ariel Sharon adopted a harsher military line against Palestinians in the Occupied Territories, the United States was seen in the Arab world to be reinforcing its image as the Jewish state's primary benefactor. As the largely US-equipped Israeli army was given a freer hand in the last months of 2001— with American backing after a spate of Palestinian suicide bombings in Israel was likened to the 11 September attacks on New York and Washington—Saudi resentment of Israel and the United States was very much to the fore of Arab opinion.[33] Once again, charges of double standards and hypocrisy have been levelled against US policies by prominent Saudi citizens in touch with popular feeling in the kingdom. Jamal Khashoggi (2001b), for example, saw fit to write in the following terms:

The distance between us and the United States is growing ever wider. It appears that Israel and its supporters in Congress have succeeded in exploiting Sept. 11 to their own advantage, after the Americans apparently agreed to belittle their own suffering by allowing the likes of [former Israeli Prime Minister] Binyamin Netanyahu and [Israeli Prime Minister] Sharon to equate it with Israel's so-called 'suffering'. There is no way that a terrorist act against innocent people who have not occupied and subjugated anyone can be compared to the alleged suffering of a country that has usurped the lands of others and banished the original owners to refugee camps.

Yet despite the great difference between the two cases, Bush finds no compunction in saying that his country and Israel share the same values! Is the occupation of other people's lands an American value? I wonder. The problem is how we can say 'good-bye' to the Americans.

---

[33] For an example of this opinion, presented by the director of Saudi intelligence, Prince Nawaf bin Abd al-Aziz, see Sciolino (2002).

In Washington in November 2001, the Saudi Foreign Minister, Prince Saud al-Faisal, was asked '[w]hy so many young, affluent Saudis answer bin Laden's call to exterminate Americans...' and in response, 'claimed that U.S. support for Israel was the key factor...' (see Hoagland, 2001). Even before 11 September and the 'vitriolic American media campaign against the kingdom' (Khashoggi, 2001b), Crown Prince Abdullah responded to popular sentiment by sending a letter to President George W. Bush in August 2001 in which he warned him that American support for Israel was challenging the viability of the Saudi–US relationship. The letter went on: 'We are at a crossroads. It is time for the United States and Saudi Arabia to look at their separate interests' (quoted in Isa, 2001a). In late October, Abdullah read the letter to 'prominent Saudis' (see Isa, 2001a) in order to re-affirm officially and publicly the regime's displeasure at being so closely associated with a country which supported Israel all but unconditionally. The mood had not changed by 2002, when Professor Othman al-Rawaf wrote that if the United States began favouring Israel any more than it already does, 'then it would be natural for Saudi Arabia to seek another partner' (quoted in Hanley, 2002).

Solutions: The mechanisms of state stability

Fragmented opposition and the strategy of divide and rule. Contemporary opposition to the Al Saud began to find a greater voice from the time of the 1990 Gulf Crisis, when the kingdom hosted hundreds of thousands of Western troops. This opposition was non-violent until the November 1995 Riyadh bombing. Despite this and the 1996 Khobar bombing, what remains of post-Gulf War dissent is still mainly non-violent. Aside from the public speeches of a relatively small number of very vocal young religious scholars such as Hawali and Auda and the circulation of cassettes, the upsurge in dissent took the form of letters, petitions and 'advice' to King Fahd and Shaikh Baz. Their authors ranged from businessmen and intellectuals to university staff of all levels and disciplines and to both young religious scholars and establishment ulama. However, the alignment of these various groupings, which did indeed worry the regime, was always tenuous and co-operation between them soon began to break down.

Opposition in Saudi Arabia since the Gulf Crisis has, with the possible exception of the kingdom's Shiite minority, been heterogeneous, fragmented, disorganised and unprepared. Although this has long been recognised by Saudi dissidents, it is unlikely to change in the foreseeable future (see al-Fagih, 1998: ch. 3; Fandy, 1999: 160; see also Byman and Green, 1999a: 48–53). Religiously-based opposition has presented by far the greatest challenge to the Al Saud. However, opinions run strong where ideology is concerned, and compromise in the greater interest of unity in a common cause appears to elude those who might otherwise regard each other as colleagues, even within the Islamist movement itself. The splitting of the CDLR in March 1996 is a classic case; the two principal figures in the organisation, Masari and Fagih, fell out over what the CDLR ultimately stood for and how its campaigning should be operated and focused. Until the split, the CDLR had been the most organised and professional Saudi political opposition group. Masari was allowed to keep the CDLR name but, once cut off from Fagih, who was the principal organiser and networker, he was officially declared bankrupt and has been relatively ineffective since the split. Fagih, on the other hand, formed MIRA, which is much more low-key than the old CDLR but still very active, with an office and several full-time workers. Not unusually for political activists, the two former colleagues now harbour a certain amount of bitter feeling for each other (al-Masari, M., 1998, pers. comm., 20 May, 26 May; al-Fagih, S., 1998, pers. comm., 20 May, 28 May; see also Fandy, 1999: 141, 150–1, 162, 244).[34]

The split up of the CDLR and the tension between Fagih and Masari do not augur well for future co-operation, co-ordination

---

[34] Although the two former colleagues were restrained in their criticism of each other in personal interview, the antagonism between them was apparent. Masari's bankruptcy and MIRA's relative prosperity all but prove that Fagih was the one with the backing of financial supporters, testimony to his long association with Islamist societies in the kingdom. Fagih was reluctant to discuss details, saying that funding was an obviously sensitive topic which necessitated a general reply: MIRA has the support of individuals inside and outside the kingdom, and the organisation does not ask questions as long as the money is donated without conditions. Fagih could not reveal the identity of donors or the means of fund transfer, saying only that MIRA 'accounts for every pound' and that 'we never break the law'. Providing a clue to the extent of MIRA funding, Fagih said 'half a million dollars is a lot for us' (al-Fagih, S., 1998, pers. comm., 20 May).

and effectiveness within the collective Saudi opposition. It is also a significant indication of 'the loose nature of the [Saudi] Islamic organizations' that the split 'did not result in any visible cracks in the opposition inside the kingdom'—an observation which supports the conclusion that 'these groups are not as connected with or knowledgeable of each other as many would have supposed' (Fandy, 1999: 150–1, 181). Indeed, Fandy (1999: 116, 161–2, 193) suggests that the CDLR, MIRA and the more shadowy ARC, are fragmented even in their focus.[35] Other observers testify to the absence of organised political opposition, noting that in a government-promoted 'fractured' society, individual Saudi citizens are prepared to criticise, but do little (Australian diplomat 1, 1995, pers. comm., 14 July). More recently, Fagih (quoted in Fandy, 1999: 167) has confirmed that this is still the case: 'Horizontally we are strong. There are thousands who support us. Support that requires sacrifice, however, is very weak.'[36] Using the example of traditional religious conservatives versus modernisers who are calling for more democratic reforms, another authority believed that opposition within the kingdom was 'coming from different directions' and that it was—even in 1995—limited (Austrian, M., 1995, pers. comm., 13 July). Also testifying to the intangible nature of Saudi dissent, a Middle Eastern analyst for the BBC believes there are no opposition movements as such, and that 'vague words' are required to describe the Saudi opposition (BBC Middle East analyst, 1998, pers. comm., 26 May), a fact borne out, for example by Fandy (1999) in his constant use of terms such as 'the group' and 'grouping' to refer to various elements of the Saudi opposition.

The history of the CDLR even before the split testifies to the fragmentation of the broader opposition and of its focus and bases of support. By wearing a number of hats it may have enhanced its overall appeal to the major segments of Saudi society, but in the short term, attempting to appeal to a broad spectrum of socio-political orientation resulted only its reflecting the 'fractures' of the society it wished to represent. Some observers believe the organisation lost its direction—if it ever had one—early in life (Australian

---

[35] A conclusion I pointed towards in 1995 (Champion, 1995: 41–64).

[36] Refer also to the observations of Byman and Green (1999a: 25, 41) quoted in note 22 above.

diplomat 1, 1995, pers. comm., 14 July). While pursuing consensus the CDLR was not backward in criticising other opposition movements and in ways indicative of its own position. For example, the ARC—with whom the CDLR was in open and extensive communication—was described as 'immature' in its political thought and activities (al-Masari, M., 1995, pers. comm., 6 July). The Saudi neo-Ikhwan ideology epitomised by Juhaiman al-Utaibi's movement was described as 'classical Wahhabism, but revolutionary', and as 'rejectionist'; with 'no program…no clear ideas' about a constitution, human rights and the like, they were 'a little bit better than the present government, but not much' (al-Masari, M., 1995, pers. comm., 3 July). Similar sentiments have been expressed by Fagih (see Fandy, 1999: 154). Such criticisms helped to clarify the CDLR's position on political opposition, but not its own specific programme for reform.

The fragmented nature of Saudi opposition has been emphasised repeatedly by Fagih himself, who wants to use MIRA to create a 'vertical structure' among Islamists working for reform in Saudi Arabia. He admitted to the existence of many individuals and groups, but said that they were 'spread horizontally' (al-Fagih, S., 1998, pers. comm., 20 May; see also Fandy, 1999: 165, 166, 167). Before the split, Masari also agreed with the CDLR's attempting to position itself as the middle ground for opposition by providing a focus, and that it was therefore developing policies that would appeal to the whole spectrum of opposition (al-Masari, M., 1995, pers. comm., 5 Aug.). He still feels that this remains a major task and that 'the underground is fragmented', that 'there is no leading figure', and that it 'takes time' to develop a serious and credible opposition movement that can achieve results—'four years is not long'. On political opposition within the kingdom, Masari believes that 'without day-to-day guidance, they are headless', and that 'the main handicap…is lack of organisation' (al-Masari, M., 1998, pers. comm., 20 May).

Masari's comment, 'there is no leading figure', provides a clue to his falling out with Fagih. While Fagih and MIRA are working relatively quietly to build a 'vertical structure'—that is, concentrating on the institutionalisation and co-ordination of the specifically Saudi Arabian opposition—Masari is a believer in the strategy of a charismatic leader and the linking up of Islamic struggles world-wide. Masari was being promoted as such a figure during the time of the original CDLR, by both himself and Fagih, as a deliberate policy to appeal to the Arabian cultural tradition of personalised politics and the larger-than-life charismatic leader who is both patri-arch and patron to his people. Fagih believes the strategy gained the CDLR much beneficial early publicity and popularity but ultimately proved to be a mistake (al-Fagih, S., 1998, pers. comm., 20 May).

A further important insight into the CDLR split is provided by Fagih's insistence that MIRA is not an opposition movement: 'We are not the opposition. We are in harmony with the history of the Arabian peninsula and we represent the mood of the society. If there is an opposition to the values of Saudi society, it is the state' (al-Fagih, quoted in Fandy, 1999: 163).[37] Fagih also maintains that MIRA 'serves as a media arm and office for the needs of the nation as com-municated from within [Saudi Arabia]', and that MIRA may be compared in this regard with the African National Congress (ANC) in its struggle with the apartheid government of South Africa (al-Fagih, S., 1998, pers. comm., 20 May; see also Fandy, 1999: 163–6).

Besides dissenting ulama like Hawali and Auda and nominally organised opposition such as the CDLR and MIRA, political opposition to Al Saud rule has other faces. The Riyadh and Khobar bombings, at the very least, prove there are maverick groups uncon-nected with the more 'moderate' fronts, and which may be associ-ated with the notorious Saudi dissident in exile, Osama bin Laden. But here again, even Bin Laden moves within a 'diffuse, decentral-ized network' of international Islamists (Fandy, 1999: 185; see also Roy, 1998). If the ARC ever meant anything as an organisation rather than a collection of loosely affiliated individuals, that has been undermined with the closing of its London office and Bin Laden's positioning as number one on the United States' interna-tional list of most-wanted persons suspected of terrorist activities. For all practical purposes, the ARC—at least in its open, Western-based, in-exile form—can be regarded as defunct.

---

[37] Fandy (1999) consistently, and inexplicably, implies that MIRA is Fagih's per-sonal organ in his quest to become 'an alternative to the Sauds'; see, for example, pp. 152, 157–8, 163.

There has also been another kind of opposition to the Al Saud, the presence of which has been felt only on the Internet. The only organised Saudi political opposition that has existed exclusively in this form was the Committee Against Corruption in Saudi Arabia (CACSA), mentioned briefly in Chapter 3.[38] Once again, 'organisation' must be used cautiously. CACSA's website certainly gave the impression of being a collective effort with resources behind it, as opposed to the fleeting cyber-presence of individuals hostile toward the Al Saud. Article 1 of CACSA's mission statement (CACSA, 1999b) made clear the orientation of the US-based organisation:

CACSA is a peaceful organization whose sole purpose is to change the Saudi Arabian status quo using the Internet as a worldwide campaign tool. CACSA is not associated or affiliated with any political or religious group. CACSA condemns violence, fundamentalism, and extremism and supports the interests of both the United States and Saudi Arabia.

It is also interesting to note CACSA's emphasis on traditions and Islam, considering that the organisation was the odd one out in fostering an avowedly liberalising political and social agenda. For example, Article 2 of the CACSA mission statement read:

CACSA is committed to identifying alternative leadership in Saudi Arabia that will govern the country without corruption and malice. This alternative leadership needs to include independently-minded businessmen, intellectuals, and other Saudis who wish to bring Saudi Arabia into the twenty-first century without disrupting Saudi societal mores nor its Islamic roots.[39]

Apparently resurrected in 2002 after vanishing in late 1999, CACSA appears to be 'an example of the so-called virtual opposition to the [Al Saud]' (al-Fagih, S., 1999, pers. comm., 19 Mar.). Although the organisation is mysterious, its Internet site is well designed and constructed and, at least until its three-year disappearance into cyberspace, offered a wealth of detailed information in many well-written articles: 'I met many people of many backgrounds and nobody

---

[38] See Chapter 3, note 32.

[39] CACSA's revamped website revises the wording of its mission statement. Of enormous significance is the substitution of 'tribal roots' for 'Islamic roots' (see CACSA, 2002a).

knows who [is] behind it. The site is…served properly and is full of information' (al-Fagih, S., 1999, pers. comm., 19 Mar.; see also Fandy, 1999: 230). CACSA also appers to be a relatively rare example of an (apparently) organised and highly visible (in Internet terms) group of dissidents which was opposed to the current Saudi leadership but not to the United States.[40]

The fragmentation of dissent in Saudi Arabia also has a sectarian element. Saudi Arabia's Shiite minority, concentrated in the kingdom's Eastern Province and traditionally discriminated against, has been a source of unrest.[41] Violent riots by Shiites in 1979 touched off nearly a decade of disturbances, principally at the time of the annual *hajj*. The more hierarchical structure of Shiite Islam and the greater independence and autonomy of Saudi Shiites forced on the community by state discrimination have made the Saudi Shiites more effective clandestine organisers of dissent than their Sunni counterparts (see Byman and Green, 1999a: 50, 50n. 12, 51–2). The disturbances of the 1980s occurred against the backdrop of the Iranian Revolution and the eight-year Iran–Iraq war, but acute Saudi suspicion and intolerance of Shiites, driven principally by a fear of Iran and by *muwahhidi* religious zealotry, ran through and even beyond the 1990–1 Gulf Crisis. More recent Saudi concern about its Shiite population has been linked to severe civil disorder involving the Shiite majority in Bahrain.

Saudi treatment of the Shiites demonstrates the regime's astute divide-and-rule policy that exploits existing social divisions. In a programme amounting to a campaign of coercion through largesse, the regime has, since 1979, steadily worked at defusing Shiite sources of instability (see Kechichian, 1990: 5; Fandy, 1999: 195–201). The

---

[40] Many questions need to be asked about CACSA. Its new website compares very unfavourably to the old one; its 'archives' section, for example, was empty in late 2002. See Fandy (1999: 1–20) for a discussion of the study of political opposition to the Saudi regime in the age of the Internet.

[41] Saudi suspicion and intolerance is both religiously and politically motivated, and can be carried to extreme. For example, in a 1990 *fatwa*, Shaikh Abdullah bin Jibrin, then still a member of the Council of Senior Ulama, proclaimed that Shiites 'deserve to be killed' (AI, 1993b: 16; see also Dekmejian, 1994: 639). When processing newly-arrived Iraqi refugees after the 1991 Gulf War, Saudi officials reportedly asked, 'Are you Sunni or *kafir*?' (Shiite Iraqi refugees, 1996, pers. comm., 21 Apr.).

Gulf War provided further impetus to the need for the Al Saud to reconcile the community; in 1993, a low-key 'deal' was struck between the regime and prominent Shiite dissidents abroad which resulted in an amnesty and 'political concessions' in return for the cessation of anti-Saudi propaganda (*Impact International*, 1993: 14; *Facts on File*, 1993; see also al-Rasheed, 1998: 135–8; Fandy, 1999: 198; Lockwood, 1996). The settlement was, according to Masari, a 'masterly stroke' by King Fahd to ease pressure on the regime at a time of increasing calls for reform from the Sunni mainstream (al-Masari, M., 1998, pers. comm., 26 May; see also al-Rasheed, 1998: 129–30, 134, 136–8; Fandy, 1999: 200).[42] Nevertheless in this context, it was important for the regime to cut off any possibility, however unlikely, of this wide fissure in the political opposition being bridged. It is interesting to note that in 1995 Masari paralleled this about-turn in Saudi policy by affirming that the CDLR advocated freedom of speech and expression for all citizens, including Shiites (and non-Muslims), which would effectively end their alienation from mainstream society (al-Masari, M., 1995, pers. comm., 6 July; Alohaly, A.R.N., 1995, pers. comm., 13 July).[43]

The fragmentation of the opposition lends itself to the Al Saud strategy of divide and rule, but this demands constant and careful attention and updating (cf. Fandy, 1999: 174). For example, the 'truce' between the regime and the Shiites was reported to have broken down by mid-1996 (see Lockwood, 1996; also al-Masari, M., 1998, pers. comm., 26 May). Evidence of strained relations and continuing distrust was provided in the wake of the June 1996 Khobar bombing; although certainly the work of radical Sunnis, hundreds of Saudi Shiites were arrested in 1996 and 1997 in the search for those responsible (Lockwood, 1996; BBC Middle East

[42] Detailed discussions with a Saudi national indicated that politically astute Saudis are well aware of their government's practice of cyclic divide and rule of the opposition according to which kind of ideology presents the most acute threat at any particular time (Saudi national, 1998, confidential pers. comm., Riyadh).

[43] Alohaly was then serving as Saudi Arabia's ambassador to Australia. To what extent Masari's views actually represented the CDLR position is doubtful in light of the organisation's split. For a fuller treatment of the Saudi Shiites in the contemporary politics of the kingdom, including tension between the Shiites and the more moderate mainstream of the Sunni political opposition as represented by—or, rather, through—MIRA, see Fandy (1999: 172–3, 195–228); also Rasheed (1998).

analyst, 1998, pers. comm., 26 May; al-Fagih, S., 2000, pers. comm., 16 June). Although this situation may point to renewed trouble with the Shiite minority in the future, Shiite opposition is unlikely of itself to represent a serious threat to the regime. Improving Saudi–Iranian relations under Crown Prince Abdullah since 1997 also make any threat from the Shiites over the coming decade less likely, and when the *majlis al-shura* ('Consultative Council') was expanded by 50% to 90 members in July 1997, new appointees included representatives from the Shiite minority (see, for example, Reuters, 1997b). Despite these manoeuvrings, the Islah Islamic movement in the Arabian peninsula is calling attention to the continuing discrimination against, and neglect of Saudi Shiites— and one observer, whilst believing there is no Saudi Hizbullah underground at present, thinks there may well be in the near future (BBC Middle East analyst, 1998, pers. comm., 26 May). Masari, however, maintains that a Saudi Hizbullah has existed for many years but is dormant (see also Fandy, 1999: 198).[44] He also dismisses the alleged potential Shiite 'threat', saying that Shiism is exhausted as an effective political ideology (al-Masari, M., 1998, pers. comm., 26 May), a view shared by Fagih (al-Fagih, S., 2000, pers. comm., 16 June).

While the 'fractured' nature of Saudi society may be stealthily encouraged by the regime for political purposes, it also testifies to the country's pluralism, as well as to the dramatic effects of rapid modernisation and development. Social diversity, often overlooked in studies of the kingdom,[45] is reflected in the disunity of the political opposition which the Al Saud obviously would prefer to see continue. At an official level, however, the regime sees the benefit of promoting 'the unique nature of the unity of the Kingdom of Saudi Arabia' (al-Rubiyya, 1999).[46] The January 1999 celebrations to

---

[44] Hani al-Sayegh, the Shiite Saudi arrested in Canada and extradited to the US in connection with the 1996 Khobar bombing, reportedly admitted to having been a member of Saudi Hizbullah (UPI, 1997). Although other Saudi nationals indicted by the United States in June 2001 were allegedly members of Saudi Hizbullah, the Saudi government has denied that such an organisation exists (see Abeidoh, 2001; also Valinejad, 2001).

[45] See Chapter 3, 'The rise of Najdi *asabiyya* capitalism'.

[46] Dr Muhammad al-Rubiyya was speaking at the closing session of the Centennial Conference, as vice-president for postgraduate studies and scientific research at Imam Muhammad bin Saud Islamic University, Riyadh.

mark one hundred years of the modern kingdom provided ample evidence that the regime is aware of the value of a state-defined patriotism. The unity of the kingdom and the concept of the natural and historical existence of the Saudi state, and of the Al Saud as the natural and legitimate rulers of this state, were extolled throughout the celebrations. For example, in depictions of Saudi history at the King Faisal Foundation pavilion during the Janadriyya cultural festival in January of that year, the purported founder of Diriyya c. 1446—Mani al-Muraidi—was described as the 'early ancestor' of the Al Saud. The narration then went on to present the first two Saudi realms as 'states': 'after the first Saudi state was crushed, a number of efforts were made to *reunite the country...*', and '[Faisal bin Turki]...was soon able to *reunite* all the regions which had been under his father'; then, visitors could read that the Saudi capture of Riyadh in 1902—the main focus of the centenary—'represented 'Abdul-'Aziz's first step towards *the reunification of the country* under his rule' (pers. observ., 1999, Janadriyya, 24 Jan.; my emphasis, in quotations from the official narration). An official history is also being bolstered by the writings of Saudi historians who, for example, refer to 'the unifying influence of the Saudis' from the time of the first realm (see Omer, 1978: 275).[47]

The unity, stability and security of the kingdom were emphasised throughout the Centennial Conference, and repeatedly in the closing session.[48] Thus, the construction of a national history can be seen to be fusing with the imperatives of state security. The fact that unity, stability and security were given such emphasis suggests that all three are more tenuous than the Al Saud care to admit openly, and require reinforcing. However, the Saudi Foreign Minister, Prince Saud al-Faisal, has all but publicly admitted to their tenuous state in the country. Discussing regime reform, he told a *Washington*

[47] Interestingly, however, Omer (1978: 275) also refers to a 'policy of conquest'. See 'The first Saudi realm, c. 1744–1819', 'The second Saudi realm, c. 1824–91' and 'Ibn Saud on the march', in Chapter 2 for an historical account of these events.

[48] The closing session was hosted by the governor of Riyadh Province, Prince Salman bin Abd al-Aziz, one of the Sudairi Seven and possibly third or fourth in line to the throne. Prince Salman praised the 'scientific and scholarly conference' and the 'profound nature' of the topics studied and discussed (Bin Abd al-Aziz al-Saud (Prince) Salman, 1999). See 'The sociopolitics of education in the Saudi oil state', Chapter 3, for discussion of other aspects of the conference.

Post writer that, 'We will not take chances with the cohesion of our country... We are not willing to do what happened in many African countries where democracy was imposed on a tribal society and it broke down into civil war' (Prince Saud al-Faisal, quoted by Hoagland, 2001). It is, of course, desirable from the regime's point of view to persuade the population to subscribe to the official narrative of Saudi history and rule and to the notion of national unity. But, in the event that persuasion does not entirely succeed, and it clearly has not, there are other means by which the Al Saud can ensure that their authority, and stability, prevail over their subjects.

Primary internal security: the importance of public opinion. Keeping a finger on the pulse of the population is a key strategy of the Saudi regime at which it has become adept. Knowing what is the general feeling on the issues of the day assists the regime's public position, if not its actual policy, on any particular issue. It also reinforces the traditional patriarchal function of the ruler in a general sense, and bolsters the image of some degree of responsiveness and public participation. This approach to population management is a primary part of internal security since its objective is to minimise the risk of any heightening of public feeling which could lead to more serious expressions of dissent.

While the domestic socioeconomic information gathering methods of the Saudi state suffered a setback with the advent of the rentier–distributive state in the 1970s, the traditional–authoritarian regime of the Al Saud has maintained its informal sociopolitical intelligence gathering mechanisms. These are not scientific, but rely principally on traditional structures and methods; they are also not without fault, as the shocks of the 1979 Juhaiman revolt and the more recent Riyadh and Khobar bombings demonstrated. In the absence of scientific methods of gauging public opinion, such as surveys and polls, the royal family utilises informal networks of informers 'with links to academics, businessmen, tribesmen and other sections of the community' to keep in touch with feeling at a grass-roots level (al-Fagih, S., 1998, pers. comm., 7 Sept.; see also US State Department, 2000: sections 1.f, 2.a; *Middle East Report*, 1993: 20). The state security apparatus is also involved in monitoring public opinion, with a special branch of the professional intelligence service dedicated to gathering information on anything that may have political connotations, including 'whatever is said in general discourse including…jokes about the king and [senior] princes' (al-Fagih, S., 1998, pers. comm., 7 Sept.).

An example of this in action was seen in the Saudi response to the February 1998 Iraq crisis over UN weapons inspections, a forerunner of the stand-off that provoked Operation Desert Fox on 17 December 1998, the heaviest military assault against Iraq since the 1991 Gulf War. During the February crisis, the Saudi government—aware that most Saudis and Arabs from other countries opposed US military strikes—refused to permit the United States to launch strikes from Saudi bases (see, for example, Graham, 1998; Myers, 1998).[49] The domestic public relations value of the regime's position was emphasised by the wide coverage it was given in the Saudi media at the time, since nothing is publicised in the Saudi media that does not meet the approval of the regime (Saudi television, pers. observ., 1998, Riyadh, Feb.). What was not given wide publicity, however, was the fact that the regime had not refused the United States permission to use Saudi bases in a support capacity. The fact that US forces would not have needed the use of these bases in any attack short of war on a Desert Storm scale only emphasises the value to the regime of being seen to refuse the Americans permission to use Saudi bases.[50]

However, within this broad framework there exists the seeds of potential instability. In a society where privacy, patron–client relations and the tradition of informal, personal links are so highly valued, the reliability of informants—especially those associated with the personal networks of individual princes—can be compromised. For example, by wishing to curry favour with their patrons, many informants make themselves the bearers only of good news. In addition, many informants are denied access to 'many circles' in Saudi society, both because they are known to be linked to a prince,

---

[49] This public stance was taken again, even more prominently, during the US campaign in Afghanistan in 2001 (see, for example, *Guardian Unlimited*, 2001a; 2001b; Tyler, 2001).

[50] The US Secretary of Defence at the time, William S. Cohen, stated that his country had enough warplanes stationed in Kuwait and Bahrain, and on aircraft carriers in the Gulf, and operating out of the Indian Ocean island of Diego Garcia, to carry out any offensive against Iraq (see Graham, 1998).

and thus to the regime, and because their status—often official—as a companion/friend/dependent of a prince (*khawi*), is shunned as being lowly and of dubious personal honour. In fact, the personalised *khawi* networks surrounding Saudi princes—which are also coupled to the broader Saudi political–economic system of *asabiyya* capitalism—form a microcosmic sociopolitical (and economic) system that mirrors the traditional values of the greater society (al-Fagih, S., 1998, pers. comm., 7 Sept., 12 Sept.; 1999, pers. comm., 22 Oct., 24 Oct.; Fandy, 1999: 35).[51]

In sum, perceptions of honour and shame, the deference paid to senior royals, and the patron–client relations that exist even between royalty and professional agents of the state often results in intelligence of widely varying accuracy and utility (al-Fagih, S., 1998, pers. comm., 12 Sept.; 1999, pers. comm., 22 Oct. and 24 Oct.; Former British ambassador to Saudi Arabia, 1998, [seminar paper] 1987/88). The combination of these informal networks of informers and professional intelligence services—now bolstered by Internet and electronic mail surveillance[52]—creates another efficient means of ensuring regime security, namely, that of insidious intimidation and fear. Intimidation and fear are part of the more active, 'secondary' internal security strategy which reinforces the primary measures designed to prevent instability from becoming manifest in the first instance. Primary and secondary security strategies are, however, linked by the regime's censorship policies aimed at manipulating public opinion. In the era of globalisation, censorship is an increasingly important and problematic issue for the Saudi regime; the information and communications revolutions have presented the Al Saud with unique challenges—and solutions—which are receiving high priority in the maintenance of state authority.

Censorship in the kingdom. Falling between the passive security measures of monitoring public opinion and active security enforcement, the mechanisms of state censorship and propaganda seek to mould the psychology of the Saudi population. These non-physical means

---

[51] Fandy (1999: 21–50) provides important background for the understanding of the Saudi social system of personal relations. Fagih, although critical of Fandy's analysis in the book, thinks the 'context' chapter is 'fairly sensible' (al-Fagih, S., 2000, pers. comm., 16 June).

[52] See 'Information policy globalised: The Internet', below.

of coercion are employed by the regime to ensure that 'incorrect' attitudes do not find expression and should therefore be included among what may be termed the primary resources of the regime's state security.

Censorship in the kingdom is now well established and is synonymous with the closed, repressive nature of Saudi society. The Al Saud attitude toward unbiased news, analysis and criticism is one of extreme intolerance, and reflects insecurities as to their image and legitimacy. The Saudi royal family simply cannot bestow the luxury of liberal expression upon its captive population because to do so would unleash political forces which would soon coalesce and apply even more pressure for political reform than has been seen thus far in the post-Gulf War period. In this respect, the Al Saud are on the defensive, and the importance of censorship and propaganda dissemination is evident. Saudi Arabia, however, is not alone among the Gulf monarchies. Thus Naqeeb (1990: xx) conveys a sense of the mood pervading the Arab Gulf on the free flow of information, ideas and expression:

Many matters connected with regimes of government…take on a sensitive character owing to the censorship which the regimes impose upon themselves and others…the governing systems in the Arab Peninsula have been known historically for their excessive fear of *all* criticism arising from objective research…

…matters of a sensitive nature connected with the system of government…are almost taboo subjects, not open to discussion (author's emphasis).

In Saudi Arabia, monitoring of the media became an official task of the state apparatus in 1962 with the establishment of the Ministry of Information; power over the kingdom's print media has since been vested mainly in the Ministry (see Ministry of Information, 1993b: 193–202). Policies introduced in 1964 'drastically restricted the right to start a periodical and accorded the ministry [of Information] the right to shut down newspapers and veto editorial candidates or demand their resignation' (Salameh, 1980: 20). These policies are set forth in the 'National Press Establishment Law', which became effective in the twilight period of King Saud's reign.[53]

---

[53] Approval of the law was signed by King Saud in early 1964 (24/08/1383H), although his half-brother Faisal, then prime minister, and soon to be successor in

It gave the regime the absolute right to determine who owned and operated the kingdom's newspapers, as is made especially clear in Articles 3, 8(c) and 28(c), which state that: '...[t]he Ministry of Information may reject any...of the applicants who apply for a press establishment' (Article 3); 'The presence and the privilege of the [press] establishment shall expire...[w]hen the Ministry of Information has reason to believe that the public interest of the country will be better served by withdrawal of the press privilege and liquidation of the establishment...' (Article 8c); 'The [tenure] of the... editor-in-chief [of any press establishment] will expire...[w]hen the Ministry of Information has reason to believe that he is unable to carry out his job in a manner which meets the public interest' (Article 28c) (see Ministry of Information, 1993b: 196–7, 201).

According to a British diplomat based in Jedda during this period, '[i]n practice the [Saudi government's] control is still wider-reaching than in theory because many of the members of the [privately-owned] newspaper corporations also hold senior positions in the Government' (Cranston, 1966).[54] The reality of bureaucratic-business networks in the print media, and the personalised and discretional nature of state regulation represented in the 1964 press law, also suggest this law may have had its roots in early *asabiyya* capitalism as much as in censorship policies.

To extend the role of the Ministry of Information, a royal decree was issued in 1970 to establish the Saudi News Agency (SNA) (Ministry of Information, 1993b: 111). Operational in 1971, the SNA 'is considered to be the main source of the news transmitted by...[Saudi] radio and TV' (Ministry of Information, 1993b: 111); an alternative interpretation of the SNA's task is that it exists 'to feed the media "selected" material' (Salameh, 1980: 20). British diplomatic despatches once again provide a fascinating historical perspective which supports the view that the Saudi regime has, since the early days of media development in the kingdom, and thus predating the SNA, actively sought to control domestic media:

As in other fields in Saudi Arabia, the Government exercises its hold over the press firmly but very much behind the scenes. Newspaper men here

---

less than harmonious circumstances, played an important role in its formulation (see Ministry of Information, 1993b: 193–5).

[54] W.P. Cranston was Counsellor at the British Embassy in Jedda.

will not admit that they receive instructions from the Government on what to print, but there is no other way of explaining the fact that all news items on sensitive subjects are virtually identically worded, in the newspapers as well as in the bulletins of the Government Radio Service. Comment is very scarce and where it occurs is limited to vapid treatment of well-worn themes. Only in minor items of purely local interest is there any variety of content. (Cranston, 1966)

In 1982, the regime further tightened its control over the dissemination of information in the kingdom with the 'Press and Publication Law' and the kingdom's official 'Information Policy' (see Ministry of Information, 1993b: 155–80).[55] Reinforcing the link between information and censorship policies and regime perceptions of state security is the fact that the Interior Minister, Prince Na'if bin Abd al-Aziz, as Chairman of the Supreme Information Council, played an important role in the formation of information policies (Ministry of Information, 1993b: 155–6), and that the head of foreign intelligence also serves on the Supreme Information Council (*Mideast Mirror*, 1994). The Supreme Information Council was established in 1981; Prince Na'if, who has been Interior Minister since 1975, has headed the Council since its establishment. Among many other tasks, the Council 'is authorized to supervise all the materials presented by radio and TV, and the contents of books, magazines, newspapers, films, cassettes, bulletins and announcements and all government and private related information inside and outside the Kingdom...' (Ministry of Information, 1993b: 123).

The result of such state control of information has been summed up by Abd al-Bari Atwan, the editor of the independent, London-based, pan-Arab daily newspaper, *Al-Quds al-Arabi*: '[the Al Saud] definitely want to cover up their domestic affairs. The Saudi press doesn't discuss anything about Saudi Arabia. No-one has any sense of how many people are in prison or any statistics on road accidents for fear that such reporting might be construed as a criticism of the king or his government' (Atwan, 1996; see also World Press Freedom Review, 1997, 1998). Commenting on Saudi Arabia, World

---

[55] See especially Articles 6–8, 11, 13–16, 28, 33 of the Press and Publication Law for prohibitions on domestically printed material and state control over publishing in the kingdom, and on what material is prohibited from being brought into the kingdom (Ministry of Information, 1993b: 173–8).

Press Freedom Review (1999) has stated that '[p]ress freedom violations are not reported so they technically do not exist.'

All domestic radio and television stations are owned and directly controlled by the government. This is unlikely to change in the near future. Despite the general, globalisation-driven push to privatise state concerns, the Saudi Minister of Information, Fu'ad al-Farsi, has dismissed the possibility of the privatisation of the regime's electronic mass media operations: these were, he said, 'a manifestation of sovereignty' (al-Farsi, quoted in World Press Freedom Review, 1999). A Saudi media professional has admitted to an overt censorship policy in television and described the way it works in relation to foreign programmes: a list of topics, scenes and behaviour likely to trespass on Saudi political, religious or cultural sensitivities is presented to those responsible for programming, and programmes are accordingly rejected or edited before going to air on domestic channels (Saudi media professional, 1998, pers. comm., Riyadh). Such a policy is in direct accordance with the 'Press and Publication Law' and 'Information Policy' of 1982.

The value of the Saudi media as a source of meaningful news and information is thus severely compromised. A mostly bland Information Ministry product is disseminated domestically and internationally, through the SNA, by the various media. International distribution is secured through media exchange agreements with a number of global news agencies (Ministry of Information, 1993b: 115), as in the following three typical examples gleaned from the Reuters news agency:

On May 11, the Consultative Council held its first meeting of 1418H under the chairmanship of Sheikh Muhammad Bin Jubair, and approved a resolution regarding the situation of the Ports Authority. This resolution will shortly be submitted to the Prime Minister. The council also approved... (IPR, 1997a)

Riyadh (SPA)—The chief of staff, General Saleh bin Ali Al-Mohaya received here Wednesday the general commander of the American central command, General J.H. Benford. During the meeting, they discussed issues of mutual interest. The meeting was attended by a number of senior commanders of the armed forces and a number of US Defense ministry's officials. (*The Riyadh Daily*, 1997a)

Jiddah, 12th July: The Servant of the Two Holy Places, King Fahd Bin Abd al-Aziz Al Sa'ud, received a telephone call tonight from his brother

HE Lt-Gen Ali Abdullah Salih, president of the sisterly Republic of Yemen.

During the call they exchanged common courtesies and reviewed bilateral relations to serve their common interests. (Saudi Press Agency, 1997a)

In the first example cited above, neither the 'situation of the Ports Authority' nor the Consultative Council's resolution is communicated in the article; in the second example, no clue is given as to the nature of the 'issues of mutual interest'; the third example reveals nothing other than that the two heads of state spoke with each other by telephone. These examples epitomise the 'information' that is available from official Saudi sources (see also Cranston, 1966). The principal purpose of such material is to attempt to keep under tight control the spread of news and current affairs affecting the kingdom. By maintaining the pretence that 'news' is indeed on offer from the government on domestic affairs, the regime appears to believe that superficial scraps of information—useless as far as anything of real meaning is concerned—may satisfy the Saudi population and the international media. On the other hand, the domestic media can be directed to present a particular interpretation of events affecting the lives of Saudi citizens, including in the economic sphere. Examples of this proactive censorship occurred during the recession of the 1980s (see Wilson and Graham, 1994: 182, 230n. 35), and is occurring now, with local media being called upon to promote economic and socioeconomic restructuring on behalf of the regime.[56]

Serious news is also often entirely absent from the Saudi media. Among the most dramatic examples of censorship by complete omission is the failure for five days to report the Iraqi invasion of Kuwait in 1990 (al-Fagih, S., 1998, pers. comm., 20 May; Tusa, 1996). Another example is the failure for several days to make any mention of the 1997 *hajj* fire in which hundreds of pilgrims died (see Lockwood, 1997; Amayreh, 1997). A confidential Saudi source—a

---

[56] At the 1999 Centenary Conference, the Deputy Minister for Planning and Programmes, Ministry of Municipality and Rural Affairs, Prince Saud bin Abdullah bin Thunaiyan, appealed to the media to support a privatised Saudi Arabia: see Chapter 4, 'Saudi economic internationalisation, privatisation and *asabiyya* capitalism'. For reference to Bin Thunaiyan's conference presentation, see Chapter 4, note 54.

professional skilled in media, information and language—has described the Ministry of Information in unflattering terms and its output as 'propaganda' carried out by pro-regime people who 'have
little shame' (Saudi professional, 1998, pers. comm., Riyadh). To
underline the contempt felt by the general population for newspapers so tightly controlled that they can only be regarded as organs of
the state, the same source said that many Saudi citizens only buy
domestic newspapers for the sports pages (Saudi professional, 1998,
pers. comm., Riyadh).

More overt acts of censorship are for example, the banning of
publications or deletion of articles within a publication which are
deemed to be potentially threatening to the security of the regime
or to the image of the royal family. A representative act of this form
of censorship was the destruction in 1996 of 9,000 copies of the
Reader's Digest[57] because the magazine contained an article critical
of the Saudi royal family—in a magazine published in English and
for the consumption of United States military personnel stationed
in the kingdom.[58] This event was reported by Trevor Fishlock
(1996), who commented: '[t]here is rigorous censorship of the press,
strictly limited free speech and no freedom of assembly in the kingdom'.[59]

Another, dramatic example of active censorship that reflects the
regime's determination to curb any mention of domestic political
dissent was the confiscation of the 12 May 1997 edition of the

---

[57] Carried out in accordance with Articles 13, 14 and 16 of the 1982 Press and
Publication Law (Ministry of Information, 1993b: 175).

[58] The offending article in the July 1996 edition of the *Reader's Digest* was 'Alarm
bells in the desert', by Fergus Bordewich. I also collected a number of foreign
magazines from my two visits to Saudi Arabia in which various advertisements
had been blacked out by hand before going on sale. The offending advertisements were typically for alcoholic drinks and for women's products which
featured, in the opinion of the censors, inappropriately attired women. Occasionally, entire articles had been torn out of magazines. This kind of censorship is
in accordance with Article 15 of the Press and Publication Law (see Ministry of
Information, 1993b: 175).

[59] Public assembly is regarded as potentially subversive, and is therefore a suspicious
activity in the eyes of the regime. Except for predictable, ostensibly non-
threatening, pre-sanctioned events such as congregation for the fulfilment of
religious duties or for sporting events, unauthorised public assembly is unlawful,
and is almost unheard of in the kingdom.

London-based Pan-Arab daily newspaper *Al-Hayat* for carrying an interview with Osama bin Laden. Copies of the paper were seized before they reached news stands. Reporting the event, the international Associated Press news agency wrote: 'The Saudi press is strictly censored and articles on Saudi dissidents are banned' (Associated Press, 1997; see also World Press Freedom Review, 1997). Commenting on the seizure, MIRA stated in its regular *Arabia in the Media* Internet publication that, '[t]he article itself was anti-Bin Ladin…but it seems that all articles on dissidents, be they for or against, are banned' (MIRA, 1997). This conclusion has been indirectly supported by at least one Saudi diplomat: when questioned about the kingdom's political opposition, the former Saudi Arabian ambassador to Australia, A. Rahman N. Alohaly, responded sharply and conclusively: 'We don't have any opposition' (Alohaly, A.R.N., 1995, pers. comm., 13 July). Ambassador Alohaly's successor has (informally) presented a similar front. As suggested by Naqeeb, however, these same 'taboo' attitudes apply generally throughout the Arab Gulf. For example, in July 1997, Bahrain expelled a German journalist 'for publishing a report containing fallacies and offences to the state of Bahrain' (cited in DPA, 1997). The journalist's offence was to quote an exiled opposition group in her article—an echo of the Saudi wish to deny and silence any acknowledgement of, or reference to the existence of political dissent.

Also occupying a higher priority since the post-Gulf Crisis disturbances incited by young ulama such as Auda and Hawali, is the censorship of the Friday *khutba*: 'Speeches in the 11,000 mosques are pre-censored by administrative officials' (*Saudi Arabia Index*, 2000b). If any *alim* insists on speaking in a manner perceived as politically provocative, he is dismissed, a system that has led to self-censorship in the mosque, one of the few remaining legal places of public assembly (see Boustany, 1994).

The influence of Saudi Arabia's media policies extends beyond the borders of the kingdom. Editorial decisions of foreign publications, especially Arabic ones, are also heavily influenced by the desire to avoid offending the Al Saud because of the potential negative repercussions of such offence, including the threat of being banned in the kingdom, and loss of advertising. Advertising is a powerful indirect tool of control since, according to a former editor of *Al-Hayat*, 'almost all advertising in the Arab world is concentrated [in Saudi Arabia]' (Khazen, 1996).[60] However, Saudi influence goes far beyond the press. The current era of international Arabic media has been described as 'the Saudi age of media production' (see World Press Freedom Review, 1999; cf. Atwan, 1996 and Khazen, 1996). According to Atwan (1996), 'Saudi Arabia dominates 95 per cent of the Arabic-language newspapers and magazines, radio and television stations in the Arab countries and abroad'; and the 1995 CDLR-commissioned 'Country Report' points to:

...the substantial influence of the Saudi regime on the British and American media. During the past ten years or so the regime was able to control most of the Arabic immigrant press and media, and has acquired substantial interests in some of the major non Arabic news media, including such prestigious names...as Reuters. (CDLR, 1995a: 47n. 1)

Information policy globalised: satellite television. Besides dominating the newspapers, magazines and radio of the Arab world, prominent Saudis from among the *asabiyya* capitalist élite, including members of the royal family, control technologically advanced satellite media ventures such as the Middle East Broadcasting Centre (MBC), Arab Radio and Television (ART) and the Orbit Communications Corporation (see Schleifer, 1998; World Press Freedom Review, 1999; Fandy, 1999: 235–6). World Press Freedom Review (1999) has elaborated on the ownership of the three most important Saudi-owned international Arabic media enterprises, the MBC, ART and Orbit, as follows:

...the [MBC was] set up by...King Fahd's brother [in-law]...[Shaikh] Walid Al Ibrahim [and] has become central to Arab broadcasting throughout the

---

[60] Occasionally, even media associated with Saudi Arabia fall victim to the harsh censorship measures applied by other Arab states. In September 1997, '[a]n Egyptian [criminal] court sentenced two publishers of the [London-based Arabic-language] Saudi daily *Al-Sharq al-Awsat* and three others to a year in prison with hard labour for defaming President Hosni Mubarak's sons by advertising that a sister publication would implicate them in corruption—although the latter article was never published' (*South China Morning Post*, 1997; see also Committee to Protect Journalists, 1997).

region. A similar role is played by the Saudi-owned [ART] and Orbit which beam throughout the Middle East and are also closely connected to the royal family. The former is partly owned by a nephew of the King while the latter is owned by [Prince Khalid bin Fahd] bin Abdallah bin Abdel Rahman Al Saud who is related to the King. (See also Fandy, 1999: 235–6)

ART was established by the Saudi entrepreneur, Shaikh Salih Kamil, who was also a founder of MBC. Kamil has since been joined in partnership at ART by Prince Walid bin Talal, the nephew of the king referred to above.[61] Kamil owns Dallah al-Baraka, '...a vast holding company successfully involved in Egypt, Saudi Arabia, and other Arab countries in trading, Islamic banking, supermarkets, food product manufacturing, publishing, real estate and many other ventures' (Schleifer, 1998). Prince Khalid bin Fahd is a younger brother-in-law of King Fahd; he is also the son of one of King Fahd's cousins, from the line of Abd al-Rahman bin Faisal bin Turki al-Saud—the father of Ibn Saud (see Diagram 2.1). The former editor of *Al-Hayat*, Jihad Khazen, has commented in what would appear to be an accurate assessment, that 'limited financial resources...have resulted in a system of patronage' (Khazen, 1996). *Al-Hayat* is itself owned by Prince Khalid bin Sultan, Commander of Joint Forces during the 1991 Gulf War and son of the Saudi Defence Minister (Associated Press, 1997).

MBC in particular has quickly gained a prominent place in Arabic satellite television. Established in 1991 in London (and now UAE-based), it is a free-to-air operation inspired by, and modelled on the US Cable and News Network (CNN). ART began transmission in January 1994 and now carries more than 20 channels; it has a policy of 'no news' (Schleifer, 1998). Orbit, a Rome-based subsidiary of the Saudi Al-Mawarid investment group, began transmission in May 1994. Orbit's subscribers have access to more than 40 television and radio services, some provided exclusively by Star-TV.[62]

The 'Saudi age of media production' has also seen attempts to influence the Arabic television service of the BBC. Saudi socio-politics and regime censorship policies were at the heart of the

---

[61] See Chapter 4, 'Saudi economic internationalisation, privatisation and *asabiyya* capitalism'; see especially note 52 on Prince Walid bin Talal.

[62] Star-TV is owned by Rupert Murdoch.

fiasco which led to the closing of the service in 1996. BBC Arabic Television was launched in June 1994 with funding from Al-Mawarid and with transmission carried by Orbit. The TV service was thought by all parties involved to be mutually beneficial and was intended to build on the success of the 'hugely admired' BBC World Service Radio's Arabic Service, which attracted a regular listenership of around 14 million and was 'arguably the most powerful media force in the Arab world' (Richardson, 1997).[63]

Saudi sensitivities soon led to differences over the BBC's editorial independence and resulted in the Orbit announcement on 4 April 1996 that it was terminating its 10-year, £100 million contract with the BBC. A guarantee was given to the BBC for an 'orderly wind-down' of the service; however, the BBC channel was switched off permanently without warning, at the close of transmissions on 20 April 1996 (Richardson, I., 2000, pers. comm., 25 Oct.; Richardson, 1997; Bowcott and Hirst, 1996; Snoddy and Gardner, 1996). According to BBC Arabic Television's managing editor, Ian Richardson, the service had 'barely got on the air before the Saudis started trying to push back on the boundaries' of editorial style and content (Richardson, I., 1998, pers. comm., 20 May).[64] Political issues affecting the kingdom were the main points of contention. The ongoing Masari deportation case in Britain, in particular, was a point of friction, with Orbit's satellite relay station in Rome reported to have 'blacked out' the BBC's coverage of the 1995–6 Masari affair (see, for example, Victor, 1996; Snoddy and Gardner, 1996; Bowcott and Hirst, 1996; Schleifer, 1998; also Richardson, I., 1998, pers. comm., 20 May). In addition, the Ministry of Information is reported to have ordered at least one leading hotel in Riyadh to cease broadcasting Orbit at this time (Victor, 1996). Although

[63] The Arabic television service was seen by the BBC's commercial arm (now BBC Worldwide Television) as a means to compensate for Star-TV's termination of BBC broadcasts to China after Star's purchase by Murdoch. The BBC's liaison with Saudi interests was not without its critics inside the organisation (Richardson, 1997; Tusa, 1996).

[64] Richardson is a professional journalist who worked for the BBC World Service News 1968–96. He was project manager for the BBC's Arabic Television service and became its managing editor once it was operational; he resigned from the BBC in August 1996 to establish his own broadcasting consultancy and production company.

clashes over style and content occurred almost from the beginning of the service, the conclusive confrontation resulted from the BBC's coverage of human rights issues in the kingdom:

While it is likely that Orbit had decided that the BBC contract had no future because of Masari and other issues, the last straw—publicly at least—was the BBC's insistence on broadcasting an edition of the flagship current affairs program 'Panorama' that accused Saudi Arabia of widespread abuses of human rights and included scenes of a public beheading. (Richardson, I., 2000, pers. comm., 25 Oct.; see also Snoddy and Gardner, 1996; Bowcott and Hirst, 1996)

Besides human rights and the Masari affair, discussion of King Fahd's health and royal succession were specific topics that angered the Al Saud (Richardson, 1997; Snoddy and Gardner, 1996). The Al Saud, however, were not the only ones who were unimpressed with the BBC's coverage of Saudi affairs: British diplomats and other government figures, and British businessmen, were also 'hostile' (Richardson, 1997; see also Snoddy and Gardner, 1996; Tusa, 1996). Orbit's argument against the BBC centred on the cultural insensitivity of much of the BBC's product (see Snoddy and Gardner, 1996), an argument supported by Abdallah Schleifer (1998).[65] The case against BBC Arabic Television should, however, also be assessed in the context of a history of Al Saud dissatisfaction with BBC World Service Arabic radio. John Tusa, managing director of BBC World Service (radio), 1986–92, has revealed that complaints against the BBC centred on then current Arabian peninsula and Gulf political affairs were issued directly from the Saudi government. The resultant

---

[65] Even Richardson (1998, pers. comm., 20 May) agreed with some Saudi criticism of inappropriate BBC use of Masari; however, his opinion on the affair is: '[Orbit's] guarantees of editorial independence proved to be a sour joke, only barely obscured by a thin smokescreen about the BBC's alleged failure to observe "cultural sensitivities"–Saudi code for anything not to the Royal Family's liking…it was only a matter of time before there would be a final parting of the ways' (Richardson, 1997). In a 1998 interview, Orbit's president, Alexander Zilo, proclaimed that working with a partner in news programme production was difficult and inappropriate, that 'from our own experience…editorial integrity is sacrosanct with control', and that his 'priority [at the time of interview]…is to produce Arabic entertainment programming, which will not run the risk of being politically offensive' (Zilo, 1998).

'series of detailed monitoring exercises...established beyond question that Saudi charges of direct or indirect bias or distortion were totally untrue' (Tusa, 1996).

The Orbit–BBC affair did not end with the termination of the BBC's Arabic Television contract. Secret preliminary negotiations were held 'within days' between the BBC and 'several potential alternative backers [who] had emerged', but the talks 'came to nothing' (Richardson, 1997). Richardson (1997) offers two reasons for the failure to resurrect a BBC Arabic television service at this time: (1) 'The Saudis let it be known that they would make life difficult for alternative backers, who inevitably needed Saudi goodwill to maintain their other commercial interests in good health' (cf. Atwan 1996; Khazen, 1996); and (2), 'None of the potential backers appeared to have any better concept of BBC editorial freedom than Orbit.'

A beneficiary of the collapse of the Orbit–BBC partnership was the MBC, which 'no longer has to ponder the problem of explaining why certain sensitive stories are judged to be of no interest to its viewers' (Richardson, 1997).[66] The Orbit–BBC affair remains a prime example of Saudi censorship and information policy projected internationally, and it exemplifies the struggle the Saudi state has had—and is still having—in coping with the globalising effects of the information and communications revolution.

Saudi concern over satellite television is, in theory, irrelevant because the ownership of satellite dishes has been banned in the kingdom since June 1994. In reality, the ban is not enforced and satellite dishes proliferate (see, for example, Butter, 1995; Schleifer, 1998; also pers. observ., 1998, 1999).[67] This contradiction appears to

---

[66] The BBC, on the other hand, was 'certainly not a winner', according to Richardson (1997): 'The corporation's God-like image in the Arab world was seriously tarnished by getting into bed with the Saudis to produce what some sections of the Arab press sneeringly called "the BBC's Petrodollar Channel"...[t]he abrupt closure provoked widespread jeers of "we told you so".' Richardson (1998, pers. comm., 20 May) said the BBC's 'unique selling point is total independence and editorial integrity...[the] Saudis believe everyone has his price...the BBC was a unique experience for them.' He also said that soon after his articles on the Orbit–BBC affair were published in 1997, an attempt was made to 'buy [him] off' and that those involved were linked to the Saudi Embassy in London (Richardson, I., 1998, pers. comm., 20 May).

[67] As early as 1992, the number of private satellite dishes in the kingdom was estimated at between 16,000 and 20,000 (Hardy, 1992: 32). The ban on ownership

stem from the regime's overriding concern that the Saudi population be denied access to political news and debate, which it equates with security. Hence the effort to control and censor content rather than to enforce the ban on dishes. Since some offending entertainment content can still be carried into Saudi homes on satellite television, the (unenforced) ban on dishes appears to be a policy designed to placate to a minimal degree the demands of the more conservative religious and traditional elements of Saudi society. This contradiction is a point of grievance against the regime on the part of Islamists of all persuasions, from young radicals to progressive modernisers to the establishment ulama.[68]

Any contradiction over the banning of dishes, however, will largely be a thing of the past with the widespread employment of new broadcasting technologies. Saudi Arabia is in the process of introducing a country-wide Multichannel Multipoint Distribution Service (MMDS, also known as 'wireless cable'), and is leading the Arab world in doing so. For security-conscious states, the MMDS system presents distinct advantages over direct-to-home satellite systems. The advantage lies in domestically-based terrestrial signal control:

Whether the programming to be transmitted by MMDS is generated locally or pulled down from satellite and retransmitted, the critical factor is the employment of a local broadband delivery system to individual locations from a central transmission point; a high-power microwave transmitter delivers a multichannel signal to individual standard television receivers, either directly or through a series of repeaters... (Schleifer, 1998)

Control over the transmitters means control over every television channel carried on the system; in Saudi Arabia's case, the system is likely to offer 60 channels. It is 'an incredibly sophisticated and expensive...system [which] has been implemented by the private sector with government financing under the guidance of the Saudi

---

was ordered by the Interior Ministry. The import or manufacture of dishes was banned earlier, in March 1994. The reason given for the bans was the threat to 'religious and social values' posed by satellite television (*Independent*, 1994).

[68] Opposition to satellite- and other media-borne Western cultural influences is treated below in the section, 'Socioeconomic issues in Saudi politics'.

Ministry of Information' (Schleifer, 1998). The private companies involved are MBC and its sister enterprises in Saudi Arabia. Any news programming carried on the system will remain inoffensive to the Saudi regime; most programming will be entertainment oriented. Schleifer explains in some detail how new communications technologies are providing the Al Saud with solutions for population control as well as problems:

Although the intention is to provide only programming that is acceptable to the Saudi Ministry of Information, a precautionary design has been developed to ensure complete control over the content of television signals received in the kingdom through the MMDS system. Editorial control is exercised through the access control system when the specifics of program content are known in advance. Where a specific undesirable program presentation is known of ahead of time, the access control system in Riyadh issues control signals to the addressable decoders, and the access control system will substitute that program with other viewing material available on a stand by basis. When the undesirable program content is not known ahead of time, an editor has access to a real-time control mechanism which will interrupt the transmission and replace the segment of undesirable programming with a previously prepared teletext message.

This will be accomplished with a Manual Override Switch Server (MOSS), which permits an editorial control specialist or censor to monitor each channel and immediately interrupt the television signal by activating a switch that will block that channel throughout the kingdom. The interrupted program will be automatically replaced with a previously prepared teletext type message. (Every channel will have teletext capacity.) The editorial specialist will restore the original program when he is satisfied that unacceptable program content has ended, by again using the push-button switch control. Since a five-second delay has been inserted in each television channel at each MMDS head-end, the editor has up to five seconds to react to interrupt each program. (Schleifer, 1998)

Hence the problems that dogged the Orbit–BBC relationship in the early years of Saudi satellite television are unlikely to feature in the kingdom's future. Such sophisticated, leading-edge technology comes at a price and is another example of the way the state's oil rents are utilised in the control of the population. Innocuous entertainment is welcomed by the Saudi state into the homes of the Saudi populace; hard news and anything else the regime considers politically risky, is not.

Information policy globalised: the Internet.   While satellite television—one aspect of the globalisation of information and entertainment—is on the way to being tamed in Saudi Arabia, the Internet, introduced in the kingdom in early 1999, is proving to be a more difficult challenge, but one basically similar to that posed by satellite television: namely how to introduce domestic Internet access whilst ensuring that sensitive material would not be available online. To risk becoming a technological, economic and educational laggard by attempting to ban access indefinitely was not an option for the regime.[69] Economic internationalisation—a key long-term objective of the kingdom's economic planners (see Chapter 4)—is increasingly relying on the flow of electronic information and commerce (e-commerce). Multinational companies operate sophisticated information technology systems and any company, wherever based, wishing to do business on a global scale must do likewise (see Fuchs and Koch, 1996: 165–6). Questions have already been asked about the global viability of the Saudi economy because of the kingdom's late connection to the Internet—it was the last Gulf state to allow domestic access. Internet banking and a legal framework for e-commerce, for example, were still not available in Saudi Arabia as late as the year 2000 (Whitaker, 2000; Gardner, 2000).

To delay Internet access much beyond 1999 might have risked economic damage that would have outweighed any threat to socio-political security from an earlier introduction. In any case, thousands of Saudis were already connecting to Internet Service Providers (ISPs) in Bahrain and the UAE after the Internet was introduced in those countries from 1995. According to the president of the King Abd al-Aziz City for Science and Technology (KACST), Salih al-Adhil, the government was prepared to wait until the technology was available to filter out access to 'material that corrupts or that harms our Muslim values, tradition, and culture' (al-Adhil, quoted in Whitaker, 2000). The blocking of pornographic and other sites

---

[69] This dilemma is not restricted to Saudi Arabia. On the role of telecommunications in the era of globalisation, Gerhard Fuchs and Andrew Koch (1996: 163) have the following to say: 'There is a growing discrepancy between the [world's] states' desire to regulate telecommunications activity in the pursuit of security and economic stability and the ability of the states to generate the power necessary for such ends.'

that may offend *muwahhidi* sensibilities has received much publicity (see, for example, Gardner, 2000; Whitaker, 2000; EIU, 1999i). As a number of commentators have suggested (see Whitaker, 2000), an effective Internet filtering mechanism was important for the regime to preserve its religious credentials with conservative bases of support while it pressed ahead with a globalising innovation that was as inevitable as it was necessary for the future economic prosperity of the kingdom. In this respect, the introduction of the Internet recalls the historical precedents of the controversial introduction of radio and television into the kingdom.[70]

Pornography, however, is not the only issue at stake for the regime. The attempt to control what Saudi citizens may access on the Internet has been approached by the regime with a heavy-handedness typical of its dealing with free-flowing information of any kind. The magazine *Gulf Business*, just before the introduction of Internet access, reported that 'actual implementation will be far more restrictive than previously thought...[with] a censoring mechanism which is even more tightly controlled than that in the UAE and Singapore, currently the two most restrictive countries outside China' (Preisler, 1998). The organisation Reporters sans Frontières has listed Saudi Arabia among 20 countries it regards as 'enemies of the internet because they control access totally or partially, have censored web sites or taken action against users' (Reporters sans Frontières, 1999).

The measures that have been taken to control domestic Internet access are remarkable. Once again, while the advance of technology causes problems for the Al Saud with the very existence of such a postmodern, globalising phenomenon as the Internet, it is also helping to provide the Saudi regime with solutions to Internet censorship. Unlike other Internet-restricting countries which filter access to Internet sites, such as the UAE and Singapore, Saudi Arabia has effectively banned every site until officially approved (Preisler, 1998). This is achieved by a 'unique...[and] unconventional approach' to the technical infrastructure for Internet service (EIU, 1999i), namely a 'three-tier' system which depends on: (1) a single, government-controlled, centrally-managed international connection to the Internet for the entire kingdom; (2) a single, government-

---

[70] See Chapter 3, 'Islam, traditional values and development'.

owned company charged with managing the kingdom's own
domestic Internet infrastructure; and, (3) privately owned and
operated ISPs to provide consumer access to the underlying government-controlled domestic Internet system (see EIU, 1999i).
The first tier, i.e. the international connection, is centred in the
KACST—the kingdom's 'Internet gatekeeper'; the Saudi Telecom
Company (STC) manages the second tier; and around 30 private
ISPs comprise the third tier (EIU, 1999i).[71] ISPs are awarded a five-
year renewable licence which obliges them to submit a bank guarantee to insure the payment of fees, and to 'commit to the stringent
moral standards set by the government' (EIU, 1999i).

This system, at the ISP/consumer end of the Internet, gives the
impression of a wide range of choice, which is in fact an illusion
since Internet access is all but totally controlled by the regime: 'The
structure...[is] centralised to the point where the service providers
are nothing more than access points to the network, with everything else being managed centrally' (Preisler, 1998). Technically, the
Saudi system of control is sophisticated:

...the Saudis' system works in two ways. First, it caches all approved web
pages in a 500-gigabyte storage system. Users get these sites from the
[KACST] computer in Riyadh rather than the original source on the web.
This means that frequently-used pages can be accessed quickly without
the system having to check their suitability each time. Requests for pages
that are not stored in the cache are passed to the second stage of the system,
supplied by a US-based company, Websense, which lists and can filter out
30 categories of potentially unsuitable sites. (Whitaker, 2000)

Given such an advanced information technology system, it is
unsurprising that the Saudi regime should engage in political as
well as cultural censorship. Saad al-Fagih has vouched for the efficiency and pervasiveness of the Saudi Internet system, claiming that
millions of sites have been effectively banned from access, including
'all the hot political sites, such as Amnesty International' (Fagih,
quoted in Whitaker, 2000). Electronic mail is also being targeted by
the regime's censors, with ISPs effectively being manoeuvred by the

---

[71] The exact number of ISPs was still unsettled by mid-2000 due to licensing com-
plications and mergers (see Preisler, 1998; EIU, 1999i; Whitaker, 2000).

regime into acting as monitoring agents of the state and informing on their customers (see Preisler, 1998). Indeed, political censorship is almost certainly the principal motivating factor behind such an elaborate system of Internet control: when a sex shop chain is being given permission to open a branch in Mecca (see Alderson and Syal, 2000), the Saudi regime's proclaimed anti-pornography motives for Internet censorship have to be called into question.[72]

Problems of Internet control, of course, remain for the regime. Direct satellite connections and connecting through ISPs in neighbouring countries will continue to circumvent the Saudi censorship net. The exponential growth and change in the Internet will, in all likelihood, also result in censorship measures—regardless of the level of sophistication—remaining 'half a step behind' (see Whitaker, 2000; also Gardner, 2000). Furthermore, a hobbled Internet is not going to be capable of delivering to the kingdom the kind of technological, economic and educational future that most states are aiming to achieve. Filtering systems 'are very difficult to administer and are likely to over-censor—for example cutting out information about breast cancer or Aids in order to exclude sex sites' (anonymous computer industry expert, quoted in Whitaker, 2000). Some commentators believe Saudi Arabia will be unable to develop e-commerce with such stringent restrictions on the Internet, and that a difficult decision awaits the Al Saud in the near future: '...a choice between surrendering control and being shut off from the electronic future' (anti-censorship campaigner, quoted in Whitaker, 2000; see also Gardner, 2000).

Secondary internal security: Coercion and repression.   When the primary mechanisms of state security fail to achieve the desired result and grievance against the regime becomes open protest and dissent, the Al Saud resort to direct, physical methods of coercion and repression. At this stage, the more overt organs of population control such as the police, *mutawwaeen* (*muwahhidi* 'religious police'), national guard, and the various domestic security intelligence organisations, including *Al-mabahith al-amma* ('General Investigations'), are called

---

[72] The opening of an Ann Summers branch in Mecca is, among other incursions into the kingdom of aspects of Western culture, treated below, under 'Socioeconomic issues in Saudi politics'.

upon to ensure that any kind of dissent is quashed. The *mabahith*, in particular, has been described as 'feared' (Abir, 1993: 70; al-Fagih, S., 2000, pers. comm., 30 Oct.; see also Kelso and Pallister, 2002), and is regularly mentioned in Amnesty International (AI) reports on repression and human rights violations in Saudi Arabia.

The Saudi regime is not known for its light treatment of those who challenge its social or political norms. AI has noted a steady rise in the number of executions since the 1991 Gulf War: 15 executions were recorded for 1990, 29 for 1991, 66 for 1992, 88 for 1993, and 'at least' 53 for 1994, and the trend appears to be continuing (AI, 1995a; see also AI, 1993a; 1995d: 253). Although the number of executions in the kingdom can vary considerably from year to year, 1995 saw at least 192 people put to death—the highest number in recent years. In 1999, AI recorded 'at least' 103 executions; by December 2001, '[a]t least 75 people' had been executed in that year (see AI, 1993a: 10; 1995c; 1996; 2000a; Reuters, 2001e). In fact, Amnesty International reports that 'Saudi Arabia has one of the highest rates of executions in the world. In the past 20 years 1,163 people are known to have been executed. The true figure is probably much higher' (AI, 2000a). The international human rights monitoring organisation has elaborated on the nature of the death penalty, and on 'the intense fear and secrecy' connected with its imposition in the kingdom:

Those facing execution are rarely told in advance the date of execution. Sometimes prisoners are not even aware that they have been sentenced to death. The death penalty is frequently imposed following summary and secret trials. None of those executed has had access to a lawyer. Some have been convicted solely on the basis of 'confessions' extracted by torture.

Saudi Arabia's increasing use of the death penalty flies in the face of the worldwide trend towards abolition. The scope of the penalty has been widened and covers many non-violent crimes. People have been executed for apostasy… 'witchcraft', adultery, 'highway robbery' and drug offences, as well as for murder. The death penalty is mandatory for the vaguely defined offences of 'acts of sabotage and corruption on earth', which have been used to punish those exercising their right to freedom of expression. In addition, there appear to be no legal safeguards to ensure that juvenile offenders aged under 18 are not sentenced to death. (AI, 2000a)[73]

[73] A great many Saudi Arabians, both connected and unconnected with the regime, are highly sensitive to criticism of the kingdom's reputation in the field

Most executions are of foreign nationals, but the practice acts as an effective warning for Saudi nationals since the regime does not hesitate to execute its own citizens as it sees fit. Together with the insidious surveillance and censorship of the primary level of state security, public executions, virtually on a weekly basis—usually by beheading on Fridays—have proved to be the ultimate reminder of the absolute authority of the Saudi state.[74]

The victims of most executions carried out in the kingdom are alleged criminals; however, a significant milestone in the modern history of Saudi dissent was passed on 12 August 1995 with the execution of Abdullah al-Hudhaif, a political prisoner. Hudhaif was accused of attacking a security officer with acid and sentenced to 20 years' imprisonment. AI reports that it 'does not know how his prison sentence was increased to the death penalty as the trial has been, and remains, shrouded in secrecy'.[75] The same AI bulletin

---

of human rights. It is not the intention here to pass judgement on the Saudi system of justice and penal code, which the government officially states is in accordance with Islamic practice and indigenous cultural values. The intention is, rather, to outline how the regime makes use of its justice and penal system as an arm of state security, politically, rather than as a means of social regulation.

On the other hand, there is some substance to Saudi claims that a self-righteous, moralising Western world makes political use of human rights issues when convenient, while human rights abuses—albeit often of a different nature— are also prevalent in Western countries. It is needless to point out here that Saudi Arabia is not the only country in the world to use the death penalty.

[74] Just such a reminder was given during the February 1998 Iraq crisis, when Saudi domestic television reported the execution of a Saudi national who had been convicted of murder. The report concluded with a warning from King Fahd that anyone engaged in activities designed to undermine the stability of the kingdom could expect 'maximum punishment' (pers. viewing, 1998, Riyadh, 9 Feb.). There was nothing political about the murder or the standard punishment for such a crime, but a chillingly clear and conscious political message was attached to the execution carried out on a Monday, and at a time when US military forces in the region were being reinforced in preparation for a strike against Iraq. Although it is not unprecedented for executions to be held on days other than a Friday, the timing of this execution gave greater edge to the accompanying warning, which recalled the one issued by the Interior Ministry after the 1995 political execution of Abdullah al-Hudhaif.

[75] The US State Department (2000: section 1.e) has reported that the Saudi regime 'does not provide information on [political prisoners] or respond to inquiries about them…the Government conducts closed trials for persons who may be

reports that four others were sentenced for assisting to plan the 'attack' on the security officer, three of whom received prison terms of 15 years; the fourth, Abd al-Rahman al-Hudhaif, was given 18 years and 300 lashes. Five others were sentenced to between three and eight years' imprisonment for providing refuge to Abdullah al-Hudhaif and assisting in his abortive attempt to flee the country, and for holding dissident (CDLR) meetings and receiving dissident (CDLR) leaflets (AI, 1995b).[76] After Hudhaif's execution the Interior Ministry issued a statement which contained the following warning: '...such will be the fate of anyone who breaches any aspect of our religion...or endangers the security enjoyed by this country' (see AI, 1995b; 1997: 13).

A CDLR spokesman emphasised the importance of the Hudhaif execution as a political landmark, due, he said, to Hudhaif's being the first Islamic activist to be publicly executed for purely political reasons without his having committed any act of violence or armed opposition against the regime—'the first [totally] unjustifiable execution' (CDLR spokesman, 1995, pers. comm., 20 Sept.). The spokesman said the regime had initiated bloodshed with this execution, and that this had had a great effect on many young dissidents

---

political prisoners and in other cases has detained persons incommunicado for long periods while under investigation.' Additionally, the regime '...does not allow impartial observers of any type access to specialized Ministry of Interior prisons, where it detains persons accused of political subversion' (US State Department, 2000: section 1.c; also section 4; see also HRW, 1998). Considering the Saudi–US 'special relationship', it is interesting that the United States should publish as candid an assessment of the state of human rights in Saudi Arabia as the one contained in the State Department's annual 'Country Reports on Human Rights Practices'. As another non-governmental international human rights organisation, Human Rights Watch (HRW), has pointed out, it is also revealing that having produced 'a fairly comprehensive overview of the range of human rights abuses in Saudi Arabia, its criticisms seemed to have little or no impact on U.S. policy, and [US] public statements on Saudi Arabia throughout the year rarely [include] human rights concerns' (HRW, 1998). This is, no doubt, what the *Washington Post* writer Jim Hoagland would regard as part of the two-way 'Faustian bargain' made between Washington and Riyadh (see Hoagland, 2001).

[76] The CDLR claimed that three of the accused had, in fact, been in prison 'for between two and three months at the time of the alleged offence' (CDLR, 1995c).

by breaking a 'psychological barrier'. The spokesman also predicted, reasonably accurately as it turned out, violent retaliation against the regime 'within the next two months'. The 1995 bombing of the US-operated Saudi National Guard facility in Riyadh took place on 13 November.[77]

As well as execution, detention and arrest are widely used. Despite the non-violent nature of dissent in the immediate post-Gulf War period, the Saudi regime reacted harshly. In the weeks following the banning of the CDLR in 1993, for example, although no violent act had been committed, the regime initiated waves of arrests, creating an atmosphere of intimidation and confrontation (al-Fagih, 1998: ch. 13).[78] The unprecedented public displays of support for young, dissenting ulama and of dissatisfaction with the regime that occurred in 1994 precipitated the series of massive security crackdowns noted above as significant events in post-Gulf War dissent in the kingdom.[79]

The regime had made clear that it intended to pursue a policy of repression. What the regime fears most is organisation. While grievances may be tolerated and even entertained at the level of the individual—provided they are expressed within the prescribed limits of the royal patronage system—the Al Saud does not tolerate the slightest vestige of organisation that is suspected of a political bias. Charity and religious organisations are closely monitored. According to Fagih, there are 'hundreds of thousands of people' in many, (totally) 'secret' underground movements which, for the most part, do not have any political agenda, but are instead devoted to the promotion of Islamic values. Even so, he maintains, the regime would

[77] The CDLR spokesman was predicting violence, not threatening it. The CDLR (1994b; 1994d) has consistently denounced violence as a means of bringing about political reform in Saudi Arabia. Aziz Abu-Hamad, of Human Rights Watch for the Middle East, has said that '...no one has ever accused [the CDLR] of advocating violence. They are a peaceful group' (quoted in Cockburn and Cockburn, 1994: 56).

[78] The CDLR was, as already noted, a non-violent organisation. Likewise, MIRA remains non-violent: its continuing objective, according to its London head, is 'not to topple the regime, but to topple the regime in the minds of the people' (al-Fagih, S., 1998, pers. comm., 20 May).

[79] See above, 'Problems: Post-Gulf Crisis sociopolitics', and especially the section 'The spread and intensification of dissent'.

crush these movements if it could (Fagih, S. 1998, pers. comm., 20 May; see also Byman and Green, 1999a: 50). Although its security measures are effective and often harsh, the Saudi state has not demonstrated 'the grand-scale human rights violations...that are common in postcolonial Arab states' (Fandy, 1999: 246). The Al Saud do not, and do not need to resort to 'excessive violence' to maintain their authority; the regime knows and respects its limits 'in relation to society', according to Fandy (1999: 246, 248). There is, however, no guarantee that its relative restraint will continue if the political opposition does manage to improve its organisation, or if there is a renewal of open and widespread protest against Al Saud strategic policies such as domestic socioeconomic restructuring or alliance with the United States. Such restraint may prove difficult to maintain as economic reforms take effect and the distributive state retracts.

Saudi state security operations are not necessarily restricted to home soil. Throughout the period of Masari's two deportation cases, for example, fears were expressed that Saudi intelligence organisations were not beyond attempting to harm him while he was resident in London (see Cohen and Fisk, 1996; Rose, 1996b; al-Masari, M., 1995, pers. comm, 6 July; CDLR, 1995b; Bishop, 1994).[80] Even if Saudi dissidents resident in Western countries may be relatively safe, their families in the kingdom are not, and persecution or the threat of persecution of dissidents' families has been a tactic employed by the regime (see HRW, 2000; Cordesman, 1997: 40; Evans, 1994; AAASHRAN, 1994; Cockburn and Cockburn, 1994).[81]

Repression is not, however, the sole preserve of the Al Saud among the Gulf Arab states, nor is its potential consequences:

Except in Kuwait, the Gulf ruling families are quick to suppress most forms of political expression. Particularly in Bahrain and Saudi Arabia,

---

[80] See the discussion on the UK Masari affair above. It should be said that, despite the speculation, Masari was not harmed, but also that, if any such intention ever was entertained, the Saudi regime would not have been the first to have considered taking action against dissident nationals resident abroad.

[81] Saudi dissidents, and their families, if the threats allegedly made by Saudi Interior Ministry personnel have any substance, are not the only ones at risk. For an account of abuse in detention and alleged threats against the families of Western men arrested in relation to the series of bombings in the kingdom from November 2000 to May 2001, see Kelso and Pallister (2002).

even oppositionists seeking fairly benign reforms, such as greater respect for civil liberties and more government accountability, are subject to potentially brutal regime countermeasures. As a result, reformers as well as radicals have at times had to go underground or to flee abroad—actions that make them more susceptible to becoming a clandestine movement that would use violence in lieu of peaceful protest. (Byman and Green, 1999a: 44)[82]

Despite 'credible reports that the authorities abused detainees' (US State Department, 2000: section 1.c; see also Kelso and Pallister, 2002), the rule of (Islamic) law is important to the image that the Al Saud wish to propagate. On this count, the Saudi judicial system has been widely criticised by international, non-governmental human rights organisations for, among other weaknesses, its lack of independence from the regime. Human Rights Watch (HRW) has assessed the Saudi legal system and found that '...the king [can] appoint and dismiss judges and...create special courts... [and that] principles of Islamic law were subject to reinterpretation by government-appointed religious leaders' (HRW, 1998; see also ibid., 1999). According to AI (2000b), the Saudi judiciary is, in practice, 'subordinated' to the regime—and to the Interior Minister and the Justice Minister in particular. A US State Department report on human rights practices worldwide has observed that the Saudi judiciary 'is generally independent', but has also acknowledged that the system is open to executive and royal influence (US State Department, 2000: introduction, section 1.e).

AI's conclusion, although far from unique to Saudi Arabia, is that the kingdom's criminal justice system 'is designed to cater primarily for the might of the state', and therefore displays a 'complete disregard for international standards regulating arrest and trial' (AI, 1997: iii, 29). Like the form of capitalism that is a feature of the Saudi political economy, it reflects the dominant ethos of Arabian *asabiyya*:

---

[82] It is worth recalling at this point the words of one Saudi national on the feeling of personal vulnerability in the face of the regime's displeasure: '...the government really goes too far, they destroy him [the offender]' (Saudi national, 1998, pers. comm., Riyadh)—see the section, 'General note on confidential sources', in 'Sources and further reading'. For a succinct summary of all the measures of regime security in the Arab Gulf states, see also Byman and Green (1999b).

centralised yet personalised control '[encourages] arbitrariness in sentencing and [allows] great scope for manipulation of the justice system by well-connected interested parties' (HRW, 1998, 1999). Liberty for the Muslim World (1993), in a lengthy report on the judiciary and human rights in Saudi Arabia, has charged that:

The Judiciary has virtually become an organ of the Executive, which is practically the only authority in the Kingdom...too many lateral contradictory judicial committees have been formed upon the instructions of various members of the Royal Family. Courts have lost credibility due to the unwarranted regular interventions of Royal Family members and influential Government officials.[83]

Similarly, the US State Department (2000: section 1.e) has reported that, '[i]n general, members of the royal family, and other powerful families, are not subject to the same rule of law as ordinary citizens...For example, judges do not have the power to issue a warrant summoning any member of the royal family'.[84]

---

[83] Liberty for the Muslim World was founded in 1992 as an independent organisation specialising in the defence and promotion of human rights and civil liberties in Muslim countries. It was based in London and many of its reports were distributed by a number of non-mainstream electronic news services (such as MSANews, the news/information service of the US Muslim Students' Association) as well as being available on the organisation's own Internet site. It appears to have become defunct in 1998 and has assumed the qualities of a cyber-ghost. The document cited here is a relatively rare example of a report by a Muslim non-governmental organisation focusing specifically, and with some attention to detail, on human rights issues in Saudi Arabia. An effort appears to have been made by the organisation to present a sound report; the authors state that, 'The report has been compiled by the Liberty's Research and Field Studies Section in cooperation with a team of dedicated human rights advocates inside the Kingdom. To my knowledge, the information [provided in the report] is accurate and authentic.' Much of the detail of the document does indeed appear to be from Liberty's own, unique and confidential sources. Mainstream Western organisations are clearly not able, or in some cases not willing, to publish such details; however, the Liberty report is supported in general by such organisations as AI, HRW, and even by the US State Department (in its 'Country Reports on Human Rights Practices').

[84] Liberty for the Muslim World has published an exposition of a 'class of influential individuals...[which] has emerged in...Saudi society...[and which includes] members of the Royal Family and their associates...who consider themselves to

The Saudi government, of course, denies that its security policies are overly harsh or that its legal system is not both sound and fair. The regime's position on human rights issues and justice centres on the unique role that Islam and tradition play in the life of the kingdom, a position now being forcefully defended in the public domain. The Saudi Foreign Ministry, for example, issued a statement in April 2000 in response to an AI report on the kingdom: '...Saudi Arabia values the noble principles held by Amnesty International, but it often lacks accuracy and correctness of information...' (Saudi Foreign Ministry statement, quoted in Reuters, 2000b; see also Nebehay, 2000; Reuters, 2001e). The Saudi rebuttal of AI in this case was officially supported by the other Arab Gulf states of the GCC (see, for example, Reuters, 2000c).[85] On the Internet site of the Saudi Embassy in London, the Western concept of human rights is criticised and the Saudi position is explained in terms well designed to appeal to an educated Western reader (Royal Embassy of Saudi Arabia, London, 2000).

Working in tandem with state security measures such as execution, arrest, indefinite imprisonment and abuse in detention is a parallel policy of reconciliation. A striking example of this kind of political expediency is the Saudi regime's 1993 'deal' with Shiite Saudi dissidents which led to an amnesty in exchange for the cessation of political activity (see above, under 'Fragmented opposition and the strategy of divide and rule'). On an individual basis, political

---

be above the law.' This 'class', according to Liberty, is known as *al-mutanaffidhin* ('the influentials', sing. *mutanaffidh*) (Liberty for the Muslim World, 1993).

[85] The joint statement of the foreign ministers of all six GCC states emphasised Saudi Arabia's position as the home of Islam's two holiest sites in Mecca and Madina, as well as the kingdom's commitment to human rights based on *sharia*. In a condemnation reminiscent of the Saudi charges of cultural insensitivity directed against the BBC over its Arabic Television service, the GCC statement proclaimed that:

Amnesty International recently launched an unjustified campaign against the Kingdom of Saudi Arabia lacking objectivity or neutrality and that is because the kingdom applies the just Islamic sharia law... The council condemns the unjustified position by Amnesty International and calls on Amnesty International and other non-governmental organisations to be accurate, objective and respect the beliefs and cultures of peoples.... (GCC foreign ministers' statement, quoted in Reuters, 2000c)

detainees are often released without charge upon signing a commitment to desist from offensive behaviour, or by publicly repenting, or denouncing other dissidents (see, for example, AAASHRAN, 1994; CDLR, 1994c; US State Department, 2000: section 2.a). Refusal to sign guarantees of good conduct has been the reason offered for the long detention—without charge or trial—of Auda and Hawali, while their final acquiescence to this demand led to their release in June 1999, nearly five years after their arrest (al-Fagih, S., 2000, pers. comm., 30 Oct.). This Arabian variation on the carrot and stick approach to dissent and rebellion is an entrenched tradition. Notable repentants may even be embraced, or re-embraced into the *asabiyya* circle of the élite. An eminent example is that of Prince Talal bin Abd al-Aziz al-Saud, the leader of the Nasserite 'Free Princes' movement which advocated sweeping political reforms and a constitutional monarchy in the late 1950s and early 1960s. Prince Talal returned to Riyadh from exile in 1964 and promptly made a public statement of repentance (see, for example, Lacey, 1981: 340–2, 353; Wilson and Graham, 1994: 48–52).[86]

Reconciliation where feasible is not the only benign face of Al Saud authoritarianism. Occasionally, the ruling royals have judged it prudent to institute minor political reforms, or more exactly, conservative adjustments to the facade of Al Saud traditional–authoritarian rule. These have often been described as 'evolutionary' steps, however small and slow, toward greater political liberalisation.

An absolute monarchy: traditional–authoritarian rule entrenched. The Saudi royal family exercises absolute power. Political participation

---

[86] Ghazi al-Gosaibi, who is from a notable family loyal to the Al Saud, is another example. He was dismissed c. 1983 for writing a poem that was indirectly critical of King Fahd's coterie of advisers. At the time, he was a rising popular figure, serving simultaneously as Minister for Industry and Electricity and (acting) Minister of Health. After some years in the political wilderness during which he served in the relatively lowly position of ambassador to Bahrain (appointed 1984), having proved his loyalty to the Saudi regime, he was brought back into the fold in 1992 and made ambassador to Britain. For examples of historical Saudi precedents, see the outline of Faisal bin Turki al-Saud's second imamship in Chapter 2, 'The second Saudi realm, 1824–91'; the reconciliation of some of the *araif* after their failed coup against Ibn Saud in 1912 (Chapter 2, 'Ibn Saud on the march'); and the account in Lacey (1981: 163) of Ibn Saud's treatment of Muhammad bin Talal of the Al Rashid after the conquest of Ha'il in 1921.

has been very restricted in the past, and mainly limited to traditional tribal and élite representation and petition, often labelled
'desert democracy' (see, for example, Wilson and Graham, 1994:
82; Abir, 1993: 7, 28; Niblock, 1982: 89; Helms, 1981: 57). In
practice, however, the opportunity to raise and discuss issues with
the king did not mean active participation in the decision-making
process; rather, the historical *majlis* system may be seen as a traditional public relations exercise—generally accepted in the Arabian
context—on behalf of the king and, by extension, of the royal family. It gave weight to specific decisions, the royal decision-making
process in general, and Al Saud legitimacy overall, by nurturing an
image of consultation, discussion and consensus and providing the
king and senior royals with the opportunity to act as benevolent
patrons and patriarchs (see Niblock, 1982: 88–91; Wilson and
Graham, 1994: 86n. 131; al-Rasheed, 1996b: 368–71).

This is the sociopolitical legacy the Al Saud are expected to
uphold today. Historically informal and non-institutional in comparison with any Western system of rule, the processes of discussion
and consensus-building remain important elements of legitimacy
and stability for the regime that precede any significant policy changes.
The *majlis* system provides a forum for the exchange of views, but
in which the ruler always presides and which he uses to explain
decisions and persuade élite representatives—and through them the
general population—of the need for any changes. This process draws
on the state's information-gathering and security mechanisms and
may itself be considered a primary security measure designed to
minimise the risk of dissent forming in opposition to government
policies. At the same time, it is still the major factor in the very slow
rate of policy development and implementation in the kingdom.
Senior royalty have to be perceived to be acting in the best interests
of the people, and the people must feel that they have had some input,
however minimal and indirect, into the decision-making process.

By and large, according to the former British ambassador to
Saudi Arabia already quoted, the Saudi political system has not
altered significantly since the time of Ibn Saud. Speaking from his
personal experience, he described two methods by which decisions
in the kingdom are reached. The first is through the Council of
Ministers, which may be equated with the cabinet of a Western-

style government: 'In theory policies and measures are discussed by the Council and approved or disapproved. In practice, such is the authority of the King and the deference paid to him that frank debate is hardly possible.' The second method '...is the King's personal fiat, usually after discussion within a small circle of advisers, in private and informal session' (Former British ambassador to Saudi Arabia, 1998, [seminar paper] 1987/88). A senior British government Middle East analyst with more than three years' service in the kingdom has confirmed that Saudi policy—which is debated, but not in public—is made by a 'handful' of senior figures in the royal family: a 'very restricted process' which is 'from the top down' (British analyst 1, 1998, pers. comm., 1 June).[87]

However, the ex-ambassador, evoking the image of desert democracy, observed that '[i]t is not true to say that there is no democracy at all, for the King and Government take much account of public opinion';[88] this, together with an 'attach[ment] to the idea of social democracy', despite having 'no belief in institutional democracy', he claimed, provided the traditional, attitudinal context for the establishment of the Consultative Council (*majlis al-shura*) in 1993. The immediate political context for the inauguration of such a Council was the rise in calls for reform in the kingdom associated with the Gulf Crisis and the flow-on effect of intense popular pressure on Kuwait's Al Sabah ruling dynasty to re-institute the Kuwaiti parliament, dissolved in 1986 and reconvened in 1992 following elections. These last developments in Kuwait disturbed and drew criticism from the Al Saud (see Wilson and Graham, 1994: 73–4, 76–7).

The circumstances of the establishment and nature of the Saudi Consultative Council may be summed up as follows:

- The intention to establish a Consultative Council within six months was announced to the Council of Ministers in an

---

[87] Another political analyst has described the nature of Saudi rule in less reverential terms: 'The top echelons of government are ruled by nepotism and cronies while their policies are applauded by a seraglio of eunuchs' (Political analyst, 2000, pers. comm., 25 Jan.). Downplaying the 'very restricted process' of decision-making and rule, one member of the royal family maintains that 'the king is not an absolute ruler—power is diffused...the government is not a one-man show' (Saudi prince, 1998, pers. comm.).

[88] Taking account of public opinion is not necessarily motivated by altruism but is, as indicated, linked to the state's security mechanisms.

extraordinary session at the end of February 1992. The Council's chairman was appointed in late 1992, though the Council was not inaugurated until 30 August 1993.

- Council members—increased in July 1997 from the original 60 to 90, and again in May 2001 to 120—were to serve for four years in an advisory capacity only, and to be appointed and dismissed by royal decree.
- The king retained the right to dissolve the Council and to restructure it—the same power granted to the king with respect to the Council of Ministers.

The contemporary Consultative Council is essentially the formalisation and institutionalisation of the traditional *majlis* system of tribal consultation. As such, it is a concession to, or a gesture toward the modernisation of governmental processes. Where such a gesture may ultimately lead remains in the realm of speculation; some optimistic views have been voiced, although these come from predictable, sympathetic sources. A US diplomat, for example, has portrayed the new *majlis al-shura* and the Basic Law of Government as genuine steps toward wider participation in decision-making, significant in the Saudi context and as representative of progress toward the institutionalisation of government (US diplomat, 1998, pers. comm., 9 Mar.). Others are more sceptical: for example, an Australian diplomat expressed the belief that the Council was established when it was so that the royal family could 'spread the blame' when the time came to institute unpopular financial and socioeconomic reforms (Australian diplomat 1, 1995, pers. comm., 14 July).

The Basic Law of Government, a document constitutional in style but not in fact, is integrally associated with the *majlis al-shura*; its reference point is one of three royal decrees announced to the Council of Ministers by King Fahd on 29 February 1992, the first two of which included guidelines for the establishment of the Consultative Council. The three original decrees were: the Basic Law of Government, the Law of the Consultative Council, and the Law of the Provinces.[89] The king's absolute powers over the Consultative

---

[89] See Wilson and Graham (1994: 71–4) for an account of the introduction of these three 'statutes'. See also Rasheed (1996b: 363–5) for an insightful analysis of the statutes, together with a brief survey of Western reaction to these political 'reforms'.

Council and the Council of Ministers are set forth most clearly in Articles 57, 58, 68, of the first decree and Article 3 of the second: they make clear that both the Council of Ministers and the Consultative Council are absolutely beholden to royal decree. Emphasising the purely 'consultative' aspect of the Consultative Council, even in foreign policy, Article 70 of the Basic Law of Government states that 'Laws, treaties, international agreements and concessions shall be issued and modified by Royal Decrees' (Basic Law of Government, 1992: Articles 57, 58, 68, 70; Majlis Ash-Shura Law, 1992: Article 3; see also Mutabbakani, 1993: 26–7, 29; *Saudi Arabia Index*, 2000a).

Whether sympathetic or sceptical about recent adjustments to the Saudi political system, all observers are agreed that progress is so slow that it is 'almost imperceptible' from an outsider's point of view (US diplomat, 1998, pers. comm., 9 Mar.). At the very least, the Saudi government is recognised as 'cautious' and 'reactionary'; it is 'not innovative' and it 'moves slowly' (US diplomat, 1998, pers. comm., 9 Mar.; also Former British ambassador to Saudi Arabia, 1998, pers. comm., 26 May; British analyst 1, 1998, pers. comm., 1 June; Joffé, G., 1998, pers. comm., 27 May). In this respect, it is noteworthy that promises of greater political participation, as represented by the *majlis al-shura* of the 1990s, have been made since the reign of King Faisal (r. 1964–75). Even close allies of the Saudis recognise that delay has been a hallmark of Al Saud rule and that this particular aspect of the regime's *modus operandi* may be regarded as a weakness; a favoured policy is 'not to do anything and hope it goes away—sometimes it works, sometimes it doesn't' (US diplomat, 1998, pers. comm., 9 Mar.). Anthony Cordesman is more specific: '…the Saudi government's present approach to change is often more regressive than evolutionary. The Saudi royal family often seems to be in a state of denial in dealing with critical problems or moves so slowly that the growth problem outpaces the impact of the chosen solution' (Cordesman, 1997: 44). Abir (1993: 191) refers to 'the time-honoured Saudi practice of doing nothing'; others have made a point of 'the something will turn up attitude' (*The Middle East*, 1993b: 27) and of the tradition by which '…good intentions are often expressed but immediately abandoned' (Islami and Kavoussi, 1984: 15).

Political change, according to those who have known the kingdom professionally and are prepared to say that occasional reforms are not entirely imaginary, is 'evolutionary rather than revolutionary' (former British ambassador to Saudi Arabia, 1998, pers. comm., 26 May; also British analyst 1, 1998, pers. comm., 1 June; British analyst 2, 1998, pers. comm., 1 June). Clearly, the nature and method of Al Saud rule do not augur well for the increasingly urgent economic reforms discussed in the preceding chapter; they are even less favourable for genuine political reforms and socio-political harmony. Madawi al-Rasheed (1996b) argues convincingly that the three statutes of 1992 were not true reforms at all, but measures designed to formalise and institutionalise existing political practices and reinforce the traditional Al Saud religiopolitical, patron–client relationship between ruler and ruled. As seen in the preceding chapter, it is the distributive aspect of the traditional–authoritarian–distributive Saudi system of rule that is under threat: the two other elements are as firmly entrenched as ever. There is little that is uncertain about the Al Saud's style of rule except, perhaps, for the issue of succession to the throne, which has been a much discussed source of potential trouble for the dynasty.

The problem of succession: family unity and regime stability.   The question of succession to the throne is a core issue for the stability of the regime, the seriousness of which is not lost on the contemporary royal family. Nor is it lost on observers of the kingdom, who see in Saudi history a precedent for potentially fatal internal disruption. The Saudi dynasty, not unlike others of the Arabian peninsula, has throughout its history been riven by periods of internal dissension over leadership. That history is steeped in the devastating consequences of family feuds leading, most notably, to the fall of the second Saudi realm in the late nineteenth century. Even more than the first, the second Saudi realm was marked by intrigue, internal dissent, acts of fraternal and tribal treachery and civil war.[90] The modern era of the kingdom has also not been without its leadership and

---

[90] See Chapter 2, especially the sections, 'The first Saudi realm, c. 1744–1819', 'The second Saudi realm, c. 1824–91' and 'The royal family and the throne'. See note 31 there for an account of fratricide within the rival Rashidi dynasty of Ha'il.

succession crises. Serious royal rivalry occurred during the reign of King Saud (r. 1953–64), who, after many years of court intrigue, was eventually deposed by his half-brother, Faisal. The crisis of this era, at the height of Nasserism and intensifying conflict in Yemen, presented a real threat to the Saudi regime.[91] A blood feud within the family then led to the assassination of King Faisal in 1975.[92] If the dynasty needed a reminder of the dangers of internal conflict, then the Saud–Faisal era provided one. Although speculation and rumour have abounded, the issues of leadership and succession have not seriously ruffled the calm of the Al Saud—at least not publicly—since the death of King Faisal. Yet the process of succession remains essentially unresolved.

The task of analysing Al Saud family politics is fraught with perils of its own, however, since the secretive nature of the regime is greater still on the issue of leadership; the internal machinations of the senior echelons of the royal family are a closed, family affair and a mystery to outsiders. In the words of a prince of the royal family: 'There's not much information about this issue and lack of information creates speculation' (Saudi prince, 1998, pers. comm.)[93] Although the royal family has 'historically been rife with rivalries and contention…it assiduously shuns publicity and always seeks to maintain an outward appearance of unanimity' (Long, 1996: 64). Bligh (1985: 41) states that the Saudi ulama have been 'a party to efforts by leading Saudis to cover up disputes and to maintain a united front against…political threats'. On this question, Aburish (1995: 57) has written: '…what matters most in the improvised

---

[91] British diplomatic despatches refer to 'the Saud faction' and 'the insanity fair and disgrace abounding of the Saud reign and the resultant dangers to the very dynasty itself' (Man, 1966a). The intrigue of Saud's reign was extensive and complicated. For a brief account with references, see Chapter 3, note 58 and associated main text.

[92] See Chapter 3, 'Islam, traditional values and development'. As early as 1966, there were substantial rumours of an apparently unrelated plot against King Faisal's life by four conspirators who were subsequently arrested (see Brenchley, 1966). It is also relevant to note that bitter feuding is not limited to the upper echelons of the family (see Royce, 1991).

[93] Analysis of Saudi leadership and succession issues necessarily involves a fusion of scholarly research and speculation. See, for example, Long (1996), Henderson (1994), and Bligh (1984): together, these three works provide a detailed exposition on the succession issue utilising historical analysis, extrapolation and informed speculation.

succession process is neither seniority nor talent but who is going to protect the unity of the family'.[94] The policy of unanimity and the strategy of privacy and discretion have rarely been breached since the time of King Faisal.

Discretion is not always easily maintained given the size of the royal family. The number of Saudi princes is currently estimated at between 6,000 and 10,000, and it would be surprising if some of them were not ambitious.[95] However, the grimmest prediction—that the royal family will tear itself apart from within and bring about the collapse of the regime—is exaggerated. Although events that induce instability could of course occur at almost any time, the chances of regime implosion are remote in prevailing conditions, domestically and regionally. Ultimately, the wisdom of presenting a united front in the best interests of the dynasty—whatever bitter differences may occur behind closed doors—cannot be lost on the senior royals. However, '[m]ost observers of Saudi Arabia agree that the succession to [Prince] Sultan will be a crisis point' (Former British ambassador to Saudi Arabia 1998, pers. comm., 26 May).

Sultan bin Abd al-Aziz (b. 1927) is the eighteenth son of Ibn Saud and is currently second in line to the throne after Crown Prince Abdullah (b. 1923), who is the thirteenth son of Ibn Saud. Most recently, the Internet intelligence/news agency, Stratfor.com (1999), has provided a speculative update on the Saudi succession, the conclusion of which is that, 'Abdullah's all but certain ascent to the throne will mark only a brief period of stability in one of the world's most important nations; what follows will most certainly be a period of distinct instability.' Put simply, Sultan is widely believed to be the last viable candidate for the throne among the aging sons of Ibn Saud; at some stage the royal family will have to pass power to the second, or even the third, generation of princes. With no institutionalised succession procedure in place, the potential does exist for chaos to reign rather than a firmly based king in the period after

---

[94] This basic tenet of the family's self-preservation instincts has, according to reports in the mid-1990s, been challenged by King Fahd with ambitions 'to create a House of Fahd' (Aburish, 1995: 66). On Fahd's alleged desire to create a dynasty within a dynasty, see also Bhatia (1995); Abir (1993: 106) has referred to 'the "Fahd clan"'. Such ambitions, if they ever existed, appear to have faded.

[95] See Chapter 2, note 75, for a range of estimates of the number of princes.

Sultan, should he come to the throne after Abdullah as is generally expected.

If the views of one young prince carry any credence, however, 'the differences [between senior royals] are not substantial enough to cause [serious] friction'—like any 'board of directors', there will be differences of opinion, 'but they will not allow these differences to undermine the company' (Saudi prince, 1998, pers. comm.). This sound family-political strategy will, according to the prince, take care of stability in the near future, while in the longer term—that is, over the course of 'the next 100 years'—some kind of formally-instituted succession process will have to evolve (ibid.). His confidence may not be unbiased, but the consequences of not following this pragmatic course should be obvious to every member of the royal family, extensive though it is.

One London-based analyst, however, posits what he sees as an obvious future scenario: that is, a prince staking out a serious claim to the throne on the basis of 'political Islam' (BBC Middle East analyst 1998, pers. comm., 26 May). If this were in fact to occur, the world might see—and the Western world would surely watch in consternation—Saudi domestic and foreign policies undergo dramatic developments which would most probably not be of a favourable kind from the Western viewpoint. This could be one way in which the nature of Saudi rule might change, and there are also other possibilities, but at this stage the emphasis must be on the potential for Al Saud rule to change—i.e. evolve—rather than on the (currently) improbable prospect that it will be abolished or destroyed. Short of such an unlikely collapse of the regime, it is doubtful whether present Saudi policies in any sphere will be subjected to radical revision under a change of leadership since there are 'differences in style but not too much difference in substance' between the leading princes (Saudi prince, 1998, pers. comm.; see also Long, 1991: 11).

Mainstream political analysis of the ongoing Saudi succession crisis presents the view that 'threats against Saudi internal stability appear to be manageable', and that '[t]here is more likelihood of a change in leadership than a change in regime' (Long, 1991: 11)—at worst, perhaps, a palace coup.[96] A variation of this scenario suggests

[96] See Chapter 2, note 25 for a recent precedent in the 1995 Qatari coup.

that all the current senior contenders for the throne will be bypassed as the next generation, 'differ[ing] more in tone than in general policy direction' (Long, 1991: 11), comes to power. According to this perspective, official preparation for this transition has already begun, although 'problems' are still expected, and 'royal family politicking is virtually certain to occur no matter what formal regulations are in force' (Long, 1996: 63, 65).

Well-informed sections of the Saudi dissident movement agree with the prediction of 'problems', but disagree over the ability of the royal family to cope:

Talk of skipping them [the now aging sons of Ibn Saud] and going to a second generation [of] younger prince[s] is wishful thinking. The deteriorating situation within the Kingdom excludes considering others and there are no mechanisms in place to effect this without creating more problems than they would solve. (MIRA, 1996)

But the advocates of a basically steady–as–she–goes forecast present the compelling argument that the instinct for self-preservation will prevail within the royal family:

Because the survival of the regime depends on reaching consensus on an heir apparent, it is difficult to conceive that the family will not coalesce around a candidate from the new generation when the time comes. When this occurs, there is every reason to believe that a new set of ground rules will arise to guide the succession through the next generation. (Long, 1996: 65)[97]

At the point of generational transition, the difficulties involved in the selection and crisis-management processes could feasibly lead to other, more radical changes in Saudi rule, although speculation on what these changes might be would serve little purpose. It is sufficient to note that the possibilities range from a flawless transition to a new generation, with no other change to the basic Al Saud style of rule, to the total collapse of the regime. Whatever the short-term outcome, the Saudi succession to the throne will be one of the most important events in the kingdom's future and must eventually result

---

[97] David Long, a former US diplomat and academic at the US Coast Guard Academy, is representative of the intense US interest in the Saudi succession process.

in change in the nature of the kingdom's sociopolitical structure, although this will probably be later rather than sooner, and not before extensive socioeconomic restructuring is well advanced.

Socioeconomic issues in Saudi politics

The absolutism of the monarchy, although presented by the Al Saud as in harmony with Saudi history, traditions and religious obligation (see Chapter 2; see also al-Rasheed, 1996b), will nevertheless pose a number of political problems for the regime as basic reform of the economy proceeds. These problems are directly related to the mounting socioeconomic dilemmas highlighted in the previous chapter; the links between the kingdom's economy, society and politics in the era of globalisation will confront the Al Saud over the coming years in ways which will challenge the regime's resilience.

One crucial issue which the regime will have to address is the dichotomy between economic and social restructuring on the one hand, and the absence of political development on the other. The associated problems will be exacerbated by the youthfulness of the Saudi population.[98] A new generation of educated and unemployed Saudis will almost certainly have greater political expectations as the Saudi economy (and society) is progressively opened up and internationalised. Saudis are gradually accepting that the comfortable and lucrative era of the oil boom is over, and the resultant lower socioeconomic expectations may yet lead to widespread pressure on the government to provide some form of compensation in the shape of greater political participation. The relative importance of socioeconomic as against political expectations is likely to be reversed as the distributive state—and with it the Al Saud's legitimacy of largesse—is rolled back. In other words, the Saudi 'social contract' which, since the 1973–4 oil boom, has seen the Al Saud provide a generous 'welfare state' in return for political quietism, is facing change.

The sociopolitical liabilities of these developments are accentuated by the combination of a high rate of population growth and

---

[98] Around 60% of the Saudi population is under the age of 20, and approximately 50% is under 15 years of age according to estimates dated to the mid-1990s. See 'Population, labour force and youth unemployment', Chapter 4.

high unemployment—especially youth unemployment (see 'Population, labour force and youth unemployment', Chapter 4). Masari maintains that it is already only the state's 'social net' which is preventing a revolution in the kingdom, by supporting highly-educated, unemployed young graduates (al-Masari, M., 1998, pers. comm., 26 May). Masari was no doubt deliberately exaggerating the potential for 'revolution', yet far more conservative voices with vested interests in the kingdom's stability are only marginally more measured. One Riyadh-based US diplomat, for example, has confided that the Al Saud know they are 'sitting on a population time bomb' regarding demographics and unemployment patterns (US diplomat, 1998, pers. comm., 9 Mar.; see also Cordesman, 1997: 44–6).

Another, significant, agent of social change with political implications is the cultural incursion of the Western world. This nonphysical Western presence is increasingly being felt in Saudi Arabia, as it is in other countries of the globe. Satellite television is now a major medium of Western culture. Debate verging on social conflict is already occurring in the kingdom over what is undoubtedly becoming an onslaught of Western cultural influence.[99] Even the Saudi-owned, Arabic satellite television services of ART and Orbit are 'testing the waters' with more controversial, Western-inspired, Arabic-language programming (in the case of ART) and with greater Western programming (in the case of Orbit), as a consequence of the sheer mass projection and marketing powers of the West's global media (see Schleifer, 1998).[100]

---

[99] *Mutawwaeen* have been known to shoot at satellite dishes with their rifles (Australian diplomat 1, 1995, pers. comm., 14 July). The Great Mosque rebels of 1979 were very much concerned with Western influence; their first demand was: 'The adoption of socio-cultural values which are based on just Islamic values rather than corrupt Western emulations, and the breaking of diplomatic relations with Western states which are exploitative in nature' (see Chapter 3, 'The 1979 siege of the Great Mosque of Mecca').

[100] Schleifer (1998) provides specific examples:

> ART has increased its number of public affairs talk shows, some of which, like Ya Hala, hosted by the well-known Egyptian journalist Hala Sirhan, involve audience participation and tackle controversial, and by Arab cultural standards, daring social issues for public dialogue such as divorce, premarital sex, male impotence and drug use...

What is more, the United States is reported to be 'demanding' that cinemas be introduced into the kingdom as a part of WTO-related negotiations; some Saudis believe that WTO membership will, by itself, 'open the way to a cultural invasion' (Gresh, 2000). Domestic Internet access will accelerate the process of cultural incursion, despite elaborate regime attempts to censor what is perceived to be the most undesirable aspects of Internet-borne foreign culture and information. Officially, according to reports from Reporters sans Frontières (1999), the Internet is regarded as 'a harmful force for westernising people's minds'. Fandy (1999: 248) seriously broaches the prospect of 'virtual colonialism'.

While imams in Mecca condemn 'the anti-Islamic propaganda [and] "the poison"' of satellite television (see World Press Freedom Review, 1998), pilgrims—facing the silhouette of the Mecca Hilton—are able to stroll across the imposing plaza of the Great Mosque, straight from prayer, to patronise a Kentucky Fried Chicken outlet. For the second consecutive year, in 2000 the US global media corporation, CNN-TV, aired reports and live images of the *hajj*—'truly confirmation that the haj has become a modern business' (EIU, 2000b). With the regime's recent loosening of restrictions on Internet access, Internet cafés were seen for the first time in Mecca in 2000 (EIU, 2000b) and, soon (see above), a branch of the Ann Summers international sex shop chain will open in the Mecca International Mall (Alderson and Syal, 2000).[101]

The increasing openness—or, perhaps, vulnerability—to Western culture has also introduced more tangible new elements to Saudi society which the regime has little experience in addressing.

Orbit...has been able to deliver an extraordinary amount of programming because of its willingness to use far more non-Arabic language programming than either [MBC or ART]. Orbit's own network includes the Disney Channel, Orbit-ESPN Sports, America Plus (which features U.S. TV series such as Friends and Seinfeld), Super Movies (an HBO-type channel), Orbit News (a composite of programming provided by NBC, ABC and CBS), the Hollywood Channel (which focuses on U.S. fashion and entertainment), CNN International and the Fun Channel for children.

[101] Even if permission for the shop is withdrawn at the last minute—which would be neither surprising nor out of character for the capricious Saudi leadership—the fact would remain that such an establishment was seriously considered as a viable proposition for, of all places in the kingdom, the holy city of Mecca.

Drug use, for example, is becoming more prevalent; the consumption of heroin and cocaine in particular is reported to be rising (CIA, 1997, 2000). An anti-drugs campaign already runs on Saudi television, and drug traffickers—mostly expatriates—are well represented in the annual tally of executions in the kingdom (see, for example, MIRA, 1997).[102]

An indication of the social dichotomies beginning to manifest themselves between traditional attitudes and a new youth orientation is the fact that drug use, especially that of heroin, is actually recognised as a growing problem in a conservative society where the traditional *muwahhidi* position even on tobacco can be extremely negative. Since little information on the topic is available from Saudi sources, a measure of the growing drug problem in the kingdom may be gleaned from a recent report on Kuwait. Drug use, 'once a taboo subject [in Kuwait]...is now a national issue'; the shaikhdom was described as 'awash with illegal narcotics'; the number of drug offenders in prison has risen ten times in as many years; and, there are reportedly more than 26,000 addicts in Kuwait (SBS-

---

[102] The issue of trafficking and what is clearly becoming a substantial and largely unhindered flow of illegal drugs into the kingdom raises political questions of another kind: the possibility of the involvement of regime figures in drug smuggling. Opposition groups—for example, the CDLR in its 'Prince of the Month' bulletin series, and CACSA on its 'Who' Internet page (both now defunct)—accused certain sons of senior members of the Al Saud of drug trafficking. MIRA (1997) has written:

It must be remembered that those who are executed are at the very bottom of the pecking order and are, indeed, but runners for the big fish who are never 'caught'. All the published stories of smugglers being caught and executed...are but a facade of justice, a sop for the inquisitive. There are many more 'grandees' who are 'outside the law' and who bring in far greater quantities through 'official' channels and, of course, may not be 'caught'.

Fagih (2000, pers. comm., 7 Nov.) claims that the extended 'crony networks' of the many princes of the royal family, together with virtual legal immunity for royals, are at the root of the kingdom's drug smuggling problems. (See note 84 and associated main text above on the de facto legal immunity enjoyed by the royal family.) In at least partial support of some of these claims, a UK-based professional consultant on Middle Eastern affairs independently believes some influential members of the royal family are indeed involved in trafficking (Middle East consultant 1998, pers. comm., 13 May; also AFP, 2002). See also *Middle East Report* (1993: 20) for similar charges regarding the smuggling of alcohol into the kingdom.

TV, 2000). Indeed, the focus of a Saudi–Iranian 'security pact' negotiated in July 2000 was the fight against crime and drug trafficking
(Reuters, 2000d).[103] Hospitals for the treatment of addicts are reported to have been established in Saudi Arabia (see MIRA, 1997).

Western cultural influences are visibly opening gaps between
generations. Preliminary research in Riyadh into Westernising influences in the Arab Gulf states has drawn a conclusive link between
satellite television and the behaviour of the region's youth: the
research found that up to 50% of young people desired to emulate
the behaviour they see in Western programmes carried by satellite
television services (*Arab News,* 1997). Anthropological research on
the Saudi middle and upper class youth of Jedda is revealing that
behaviour common everywhere in the developed world is beginning to be seen in the kingdom (see Wynn, 1997). An urban youth
culture—as far as the restrictive social environment of Saudi Arabia
currently allows—is developing, although it appears to be more
advanced in the relatively more relaxed and cosmopolitan urban
centres of Jedda and the Gulf coast.[104] Lisa Wynn (1997) has indicated the direction in which a significant segment of Saudi youth is
already moving:

Using a commodity-mediated space to evade or resist the control of the
state, religious and familial authorities, upper and middle class urban youth

---

[103] Iran is reported to be 'a key route for drug trafficking' from Afghanistan and
Pakistan to the Arab Gulf states and Europe (Reuters, 2000d).

[104] Youth culture in the Najd region, unsurprisingly, seems to be more inhibited. In
Riyadh, the most visible examples of a fledgling youth identity can be observed
in males below the age of 20. I personally observed (Jan.–Mar., 1998) the occasional small band of young males in Riyadh wearing Nike baseball caps back-
wards and baggy Western-style trousers, and playing rap music on their ghetto-
blasters. Saudis in their late 20s and 30s confirmed the growth of this kind of
behaviour and expressed to me their concern about such influences and developments and the effects they may have on cultural traditions and national heritage (informal pers. comm. 1998, Riyadh, Jan.–Mar.). I am not suggesting that a
youth-culture revolution is about to sweep the kingdom; rather, that there are
signs that certain social changes—or phenomena, or aberrations—are beginning to occur below the surface and around the fringes of Saudi society which
are probably not going to be short-term or transitional. It is difficult to see how
the effects of these social—and, ultimately, psychological—breaks from the (traditional) past can *not* eventually filter into other aspects of the kingdom, including politics.

thus expand their social networks from groups primarily determined by kin contacts and school friends to those centered around a class-based consumerism. In the act of creating a youth culture which subverts dominant gender, generational and moral norms, the elite youth in Jiddah affirm their loyalty to a culture of commodity consumption.

The cumulative effect of alien cultural incursion, augmented by travel and studies in Western countries, could easily lead to social dislocation in the future. Some of these young people who have been amenable to Western influence and who, as a consequence, are somewhat less attached to tradition than previous generations, will, at some stage, come to occupy positions of influence in Saudi society, the economy and bureaucracy. This development will contribute to change from within the society as the traditional perspectives upon which much of the current social system is based are challenged by these younger representatives of the regime. Young members of the royal family are no less likely to be among this number than other Saudi youth.

On the other hand, exposure to Western culture can also inspire unfavourable reactions—as was amply demonstrated in the Gulf Crisis era—and a certain proportion of educated and under-employed youth is bound to oppose the regime on religious and traditionally conservative grounds. This possibility is real, considering the Al Saud are now proactively embracing economic internationalisation, and since hostility toward the US military presence in the kingdom remains tangible. Some of this group of disaffected youth may very well revisit the use of violence to bring pressure on the regime to halt the accelerating Western forces of globalisation. Violence, as has been noted, is by no means unprecedented in the kingdom. Hence, in the interests of short-term political stability as much as for religious and cultural integrity, the Al Saud consider it appropriate to regulate the kingdom's exposure to globalising influences of a cultural kind. In the longer-term, greater Westernisation—as long as it is implemented gradually—should reduce the risks to the regime of concerted political opposition based on conservative religious and social values. But by the same token, greater Westernisation should also increase pressure for more liberal political reforms than have been seen to date in the kingdom. Speaking on the eve of his official ascent to the throne, Crown Prince Abdullah outlined the preferred strategy of the regime: '...globalisation is at our doorstep with its scientific and technical power. We must work very hard to modernise our economic and social system...[but] [w]e must not abandon the true character of our conservative society' (Abdullah bin Abd al-Aziz al-Saud, quoted in Gresh, 2000).[105] The regime will find balancing these volatile socioeconomic–political forces a difficult challenge. A political analyst, speaking to me in January 2000, said:

> Above all other socio-political non events in the country in this century, is its 'lost generation'. The lost generation (1980–2000) was denied its past, presented with a futile and sterile present, which had all the accruement of meaningless wealth, pomp and circumstance, but no meaningful education. It seems to have existed in a vacuum, inured to nothingness... It is likely that it will be the generation that will fight the present establishment, and foreign influence. (Political analyst, 2000, pers. comm., 25 Jan.)

The 'lost generation' may, perhaps, be re-dubbed 'the 11 September generation'. However, the radically differing make-up of young potential malcontents only serves to illustrate further the fractured nature of opposition to the Al Saud. This is a trend which favours the regime and is likely to continue well into the future, although decreasing wealth and even increasing poverty among Saudi nationals may act as sociopolitical coagulants that will reduce barriers between the different segments of the Saudi population and give a more common cause to potential protest movements. Progress in this sociopolitical direction would appear to be inevitable as socioeconomic restructuring accelerates and the Saudi distributive–welfare state is reined in over the coming years.

Conclusion

During the early- and mid-1990s, Al Saud rule appeared to be heading for a sustained period of instability. Gulf Crisis-related political dissent openly confronted the regime from 1990, financial crisis hit the country in 1993–4, and 1995 ushered in a cycle of

---

[105] See Chapter 3, 'Islam, traditional values and development' (especially note 56) for background to the Saudi modernisation–cultural integrity struggle; see also Chapter 4, especially the section, 'Saudi economic internationalisation, privatisation and *asabiyya* capitalism'.

political violence which was marked by active repression by the regime, the execution of dissidents and the bombing of US personnel and installations in Riyadh and Khobar. The CDLR, established in exile in London in 1994, provided a focus of opposition that added a new dimension and renewed vigour to dissent both inside and outside the kingdom—the pressure for political reform appeared to be building up. However, by 1997 the political opposition had been muzzled, although not eliminated, through repression domestically and various means of pressure internationally, in collusion with Western governments, agencies and multinational interests. As the dust of the 1996 Khobar bombing settled, a relative calm descended over the kingdom; Saudi Arabia had also regained some measure of financial stability by 1997 and prospects were once again beginning to look brighter for the Al Saud, at least until a series of small-scale bombings beginning late 2000 merged with the events of 11 September 2001.

A number of factors contributed to the dynasty's recovery from the low period of dramatic dissent in 1990–6. These are likely to remain important lynchpins of the monarchy's stability. First, time has played its part in establishing the Al Saud as traditional rulers in a land where tradition is revered. The religious aspect of Al Saud legitimacy is also a well-entrenched tradition, bolstered over the last 75 years by its custodianship of the holy sites of Mecca and Madina and the co-optation of the state's conservative religious establishment. The Al Saud take their religious status seriously and it is an important pillar of their rule (see Chapters 2 and 3). Second, oil wealth has enabled the Al Saud to institute the legitimacy of largesse. To be patriarchs and patrons to their people is a respected role for leaders in Arabian tradition and in fulfilling this role, the Al Saud have been able to, in effect, purchase a great deal of domestic sociopolitical stability (see Chapters 3 and 4).

The third major factor in the resilience of the contemporary Saudi regime is that political opposition in the kingdom is incorrigibly fragmented, meaning that there is no viable alternative to the Al Saud. Fourthly, Saudi Arabia is a repressive state. At the first, or primary level of state security, the regime skilfully tracks and responds to the nuances of public opinion, a strategy which not only provides intelligence for the state security apparatus but helps the government both to develop policies and to build broad consensus for their policies before their implementation. Another aspect of this level of security is media censorship which, in the era of globalisation, is becoming increasingly problematic; the regime has to draw a fine line between political censorship and placating still-powerful conservative opinion, and the long-term need to integrate the kingdom into global information, financial and economic systems. At the second level of state security, the Al Saud have devised an infrastructure of active coercion and repression which effectively combines a traditional policy of harsh punishment of dissenters and reconciliation for repentants which keeps opponents in check.

Lastly, and overlapping with the factors above that touch on regime stability, is the absolutist nature of Al Saud traditional–authoritarian rule. Despite the official political 'reforms' of 1992–3, the Saudi system has made no real concessions to political development: an élite inner circle of the most senior members of the royal family continues to rule almost as it chooses. This system has served the Al Saud well since the modern state was founded in 1932, although the unresolved matter of succession to the throne continues to raise questions about the future stability of the regime. Whatever debate and conflict exists within the family has, for the most part, been kept from public view; the unity of the family and therefore of the regime is a priority in Al Saud deliberations.

Family unity will need to be maximised in the years ahead, as the regime implements unpopular economic reforms aimed at integrating the Saudi economy into the emerging global economy. As noted in the preceding chapter, fundamental economic restructuring requires the dismantling of the Saudi distributive–welfare state. The Al Saud will attempt to achieve this, while at the same time checking any political reform that could lead to a loosening of their authoritarian rule. Yet, there are those in the kingdom who believe that '[e]conomic reform is impossible without political reform' (anonymous Saudi newspaper editor, quoted in Gresh, 2000). The IMF, the World Bank and the WTO agree. Moreover, economic reform is not possible without social reform, and herein lies the Al Saud's greatest challenge.

The Saudi regime is presiding over rising unemployment, falling living standards, increasing poverty and the withdrawal of social

services and benefits. At the same time, it does not allow any meaningful political participation and, indeed, resorts to active repression to prevent any expression of even mildly divergent political
opinion. The Saudi 'social contract' is being re-cast and the ramifications of this in the context of a high level of population growth
and rising unemployment are as serious as they are apparent. An
increasing pool of educated, unemployed youth with no political
voice can only add to the ranks of the discontented as the forces of
social transformation gather momentum. Increasing exposure to
Western cultural influence is not only a point of great contention
but has the potential to spark both social conflict and political
reform. Western sociocultural influences are now making significant inroads into the kingdom via satellite television, the Internet,
and through economic internationalisation. On the one hand, such
influences may contribute to a climate more accommodative of
political reform in the longer term as the educated youth of today
who are more conversant with global culture contribute to change
from within Saudi society. On the other hand, Western influences
are passionately opposed by a significant proportion of the conservative population and, especially in the short term, can clearly stir
opposition to a regime which is perceived to be allowing Saudi
traditions to be eroded by outside, anti-Islamic and 'corrupting',
influences. There is an established base of dissent from which fresh
anti-regime campaigns may be launched, ranging from the open
and purely political on the part of exiled dissidents, to the militant
on the part of clandestine groups within the kingdom.

The regime, of course, continues to present piety as one of its
core values and is continually making gestures which promote
muwahhidi conservatism. In contrast to the official stance, however,
are such everyday policies as ignoring the ban on satellite dishes,
permitting Western fast-food and sex shop chains to open stores in
Mecca, and executing petty drug runners while the youth drug
problem continues to burgeon unabated. Analysis of regime policies on foreign cultural influence indicates that the Al Saud are
highly concerned with censoring information and news of a political nature, whilst not being overly concerned with religiocultural
issues above what is necessary to maintain an acceptable public profile. Apart from the politically necessary censoring of the more

obvious and sensational aspects of cultural incursion, such as pornography, the Al Saud may well be taking the view that Western cultural influences, the development of a Western-style Saudi youth culture and, in general, a 'mosque-on-Fridays' approach to Islam, will ultimately serve the regime well by dampening the enthusiasm of the kingdom's youth for political activism.

However, with sweeping socioeconomic reform now firmly on the agenda and given the serious problems now visible below the surface of the kingdom's social fabric, the likelihood of future political unrest cannot be ignored. As long as the Al Saud pursue domestically unpopular foreign policies such as their Western political–military–economic alliance and continue their hesitant and clumsy approach to socioeconomic restructuring while maintaining an exclusive, authoritarian and repressive regime, they will face domestic opposition, some of which will manifest itself violently. Radical acts of dissent are not, therefore, isolated occurrences that can be dismissed as aberrations but represent the secret underbelly of resentment and determined, at present unstructured and uncoordinated opposition to the central policies of the royal family.

The Riyadh and Khobar bombings of 1995 and 1996, and the bombing campaign launched in November 2000 which, after 11 September, coincided with a swell of pro-Osama bin Laden feeling, are ominous and very real warnings that all is not calm under the surface of contemporary Saudi society. The kingdom's close relationship with the United States became a liability for the Saudi regime in the years following the Gulf War; post-11 September, that liability has considerably intensified. As the United States presses ahead with its 'war against terrorism', the potential for further serious anti-US disturbances in the kingdom cannot be denied. This will remain so for as long as the United States continues to maintain a significant military presence in the Arab Gulf states and to menace Arab Iraq and Islamic Iran, while at the same time ignoring Al Saud religiopolitical legitimacy by continually signalling its more or less unconditional support for Israel.

The Saudi–US relationship suffered a very serious setback in 2001. Compounded with earlier setbacks such as those that occurred during the Iraq crises of 1998, these have soured Saudi–US relations at an official level, but the effect on the Saudi population in general has been profound: any future political protest in the kingdom will have as one of its core issues the Al Saud alliance with the world's ubiquitous superpower. The regime will be forced to respond with foreign policy adjustments that will not please any US administration, but the alliance will not be threatened in the medium term, if only because, for the Al Saud, there is no suitable alternative to its military–economic partnership with the United States.

Sporadic acts of violence targeting Western, and especially US interests, can be expected to be a feature of the Saudi sociopolitical landscape into the foreseeable future, but these will not be enough to shake the overall stability of the regime. On current analysis, as long as an astute, socially responsive Saudi leader is exercising firm control over the kingdom's affairs, the Al Saud will be well equipped to deal with such occasional challenges to its stability, even if they increase in frequency and intensity.

6

CONCLUSION

Saudi Arabia has come a long way since Ibn Saud's proclamation of the kingdom in 1932. An undeveloped, tribal society that could barely lay claim to nation-state status, the kingdom's most distinguishing feature was the fact that the holiest sites of Islam fell within the realm of the Al Saud. Forging the institutions of state as well as a national economy, whilst attempting to develop the kingdom's physical infrastructure and human resources, proved to be drawn-out and difficult processes: at the same time, they were the means by which the Al Saud and their domestic allies and clients established themselves as ruling, bureaucratic and business élites in a relatively poor country. With some notable family exceptions, the members of these élites were mainly natives of the central Najd region of the Arabian peninsula, the conservative heartland of the Al Saud and of *muwahhidi* Islam.

In the earlier years of the kingdom, state budgets were drawn mainly from revenues derived from the then modest exploitation of oil, the pilgrimage trade, and the extraction of taxes and duties from the population and the economy. This normative, extractive structure changed dramatically with the oil boom of 1973–4. After a very short time, few vestiges of the pre-boom state remained: the Saudi rentier economy had been born. The purpose of this 'new' state was to gather the income from oil production and distribute it throughout the economy and society, a function which harmonised well with traditional Arabian values, allowing the Al Saud to enhance their unique blend of religious and political ruling legitimacy with a comprehensive system of largesse through patronage widely known as 'the Saudi social contract'. This unwritten 'contract' committed the state to taking charge of the welfare of its population in return for acceptance of the established political order. Thus the Saudi oil state became quite openly a distributive–welfare state, and the Al Saud further entrenched their traditional–authoritarian rule as an absolute monarchy.

Boom-time wealth funded an accelerated programme of modernisation and development; the kingdom, as regime spokesmen were fond of repeating, had entered the new millennium ahead of time. Now that the new millennium has actually arrived, the structural flaws of the Saudi rentier–distributive state and the exaggerated optimism of the boom era have been revealed in all their startling reality. Saudi Arabia may indeed have come a long way since 1932, but it has a very long way to go before a sound and sustainable economic structure can be presented by government spokesmen as a genuinely accomplished fact. The fact is that the Saudi economy is still absolutely dependent on the petroleum sector. After more than two decades of pursuing economic diversification and industrialisation, this sector alone still accounts for around 75% of the state's budget revenues. Moreover, it still relies heavily on imported technology and expertise and on imported unskilled labour, and in this respect, differs little from the majority of the other sectors of the Saudi economy. The leaden hand of the Saudi state, which virtually owns the economy, is also a major factor contributing to poor performance. The inherent structural imbalances of the economy make the long-term development and prosperity of the kingdom problematic.

If the task facing the kingdom's rulers were purely economic, the years ahead would prove less challenging than they promise to be. If the problems were simply dealing with the sluggish growth of GDP and of balancing budgets, the Al Saud could look to the future with greater confidence; but, as the preceding chapters have indicated, the problems facing the regime are also deeply embedded in the socioeconomic and political–economic structures of the kingdom. Both the regime and the society in general have become dependent on the distributive function of the state and have vested interests in its maintenance. These interests, however, are focused on the short term. The Saudi distributive–welfare state cannot be sustained; it has been dysfunctional since the mid-1980s and the longer-term integrity of the entire Saudi socioeconomic system depends on fundamental reforms that will change the way most Saudi nationals have known life for the last quarter-century. These reforms can be resolutely implemented in a timely and orderly fashion, or haltingly and half-heartedly in a way that could jeopardise their effectiveness. To date, every indication points to the latter course. The legendary inertia of the Al Saud in dealing with serious problems of any kind has been clearly demonstrated in the field of socioeconomic reform.

A crucial element of the state's inertia in this area is the Saudi political–economic system of *asabiyya* capitalism which has its roots in the traditional Arabian ethos of personal relations based on kinship, regional and patron–client ties and *wasta* that characterised the increasingly Najdi-dominated pre-boom state. As the kingdom's political economy and socioeconomic structure were transformed during the oil boom, the Saudi *asabiyya* networks flourished, expanded and became entrenched. A rentier–distributive economy in an era of plenty offered wealth, power and prestige for the élite circles of the regime and for those with the right connections. Strategic but informal political–bureaucratic–business networks were formed and, by the late-1970s, *asabiyya* capitalism had been all but formally institutionalised. As a result, favouritism and exclusive business practices became an everyday feature of state and business affairs, leading to bureaucratic inefficiency and wastage; they cost the state dearly and also laid the regime open to charges of corruption.

The social stresses that resulted from this period of rapid development and socioeconomic upheaval combined with extreme *muwahhidi* conservatism to muster sporadic challenges to regime policies; occasionally, the very legitimacy of the ruling family was disputed. The 1979 siege of the Great Mosque of Mecca testified dramatically to the existence of a substratum of radical opposition to the kingdom's leadership. The Mecca rebels drew attention to the excesses of *asabiyya* capitalism and Western influence, and put the regime on notice that socioeconomics could, in the modernising Saudi milieu, combine with religion and politics to challenge the right of the Al Saud to rule. When the price of oil collapsed in 1986, the kingdom was launched on a new era of reform that would see the continuing convergence of economic, social, religious and political forces. Only in the mid- to late-1990s, after the political crisis of the Gulf War and another financial crisis in 1993–4, did the Al Saud acknowledge the extent of the reform being contemplated, that indeed is required to put the kingdom's economic and socioeconomic structures on a sound footing for sustainable development and prosperity. At present, these structures are not sustainable and have not been since recession struck the Saudi economy in 1982–3. The future of the kingdom's prosperity—and, potentially, its political stability as well—is therefore in jeopardy.

In fact, the kingdom's economic and socioeconomic predicament was already clear by the early 1990s, and by the late 1990s an alarm was being sounded. The budget had been running in deficit since 1983, foreign reserves had been seriously depleted, and in 1998 the public debt surpassed 100% of GDP. Another collapse in oil prices in 1998 led to a heightened sense of impending crisis. However, Saudi Arabia spurred OPEC into concerted action and co-ordinated production cuts resulted in a dramatic recovery in oil prices in 1999–2000. Although representing a very welcome turnaround in the short-term fiscal outlook, the oil price recovery only highlighted Saudi Arabia's continued dependence on the petroleum sector and did nothing to address the chronic imbalances in the kingdom's economy. The need for serious reform is now urgent and will become ever more so as the combination of advancing technology and the discovery of new, commercially exploitable oilfields reduce the world's dependence on the Gulf oil producers.

Structural economic reform is indeed being contemplated—of state subsidies to industry and business, utility services, consumer staples and even royal family stipends. In other words, the very foundations of the Saudi rentier–distributive state are being reassessed. For the Al Saud, this will mean the eventual curtailment of the legitimacy of largesse and reversion to a form of traditional–authoritarian rule stripped of its distributive aspect. This will be a politically hazardous path for the monarchy given that the kingdom's economy is as dependent on foreign labour as it is on oil, while the national population is rising at a rapid rate and national unemployment is running at anywhere from 20% to 40%. In addition, per capita income has plummeted in recent years, living standards have declined and the incidence of poverty is rising. The process of socioeconomic reform is going to hurt the Saudi population and is, hence, a political challenge for the Al Saud regime. The vested interests of *asabiyya* capitalism are firmly established; renegotiating the kingdom's political economy will be a major undertaking, the outcome of which may not necessarily be beneficial for the prosperity of the nation. While the average Saudi citizen is becoming poorer, a new generation of corporate Saudis is already beginning to take advantage of the processes of deregulation and privatisation that are slowly being initiated in the kingdom. Saudi Arabia is set to follow the global trend of increasing inequalities of wealth distribution; as the distributive–welfare state is reined in, and as the Saudi economy becomes more integrated into the emerging global economy, the gap between the haves and the have-nots in the kingdom will increase.

Economic reform in the kingdom has long been advocated by the International Monetary Fund, and some measure of such reform must be implemented before the Saudi regime can realise the coveted goal of full membership of the World Trade Organisation. While economic reform in the Saudi case does not necessarily mean economic liberalisation, the Al Saud are clearly prepared to make concessions to the IMF and the WTO. However, these powerful advocates of economic internationalisation are now drawing links between economic and sociopolitical reform: 'transparency', 'accountability', 'good governance' and a commitment to fight corruption are being actively promoted. It is this new sociopolitical and political–economic emphasis in international economic restructuring that the Al Saud are resolutely resisting. Economic reform— and, where necessary, the associated socioeconomic reform—is on the Saudi agenda, but more fundamental social and political reform remains anathema to the Al Saud.

The fact that the Al Saud will resist political change was proved in the aftermath of the 1991 Gulf War when unprecedented public displays of political protest were suppressed by the regime. Post-Gulf War dissent represented a new phase in political opposition in the kingdom. Earlier violent clashes, such as the Mecca siege of 1979 and the Shiite protests of the 1980s, gave way to political campaigns on the part of a new breed of dissidents. Contentious issues in Saudi society include those associated with the rise of *asabiyya* capitalism, such as favouritism and exclusive business practices, the kingdom's alliance with the United States, and Western cultural incursion. An increasingly well-educated and informed population has emerged from the 1980s and seized on these issues to construct a more penetrating criticism of the Al Saud and regime policies. For the dissidents of the 1990s, the regime's traditional–authoritarian–distributive system of political legitimacy has not been persuasive. In response has come a more repressive society in the sociopolitical sphere, and this is likely to become further entrenched as globalisation-related socioeconomic restructuring gathers momentum in the new millennium.

The Saudi state's security systems are insidious and all-pervasive. Both overt and covert mechanisms of monitoring, manipulating and repressing the population are employed, ranging from social surveillance and media censorship to mass arrest, abuse in detention and execution. The argument here has been that, above all, the Al Saud fear and strive to prevent anything resembling political organisation—and in prevention the regime has been largely successful. Repression, however, has driven dissent deeper underground. When the peaceful post-Gulf War opposition in the shape of speeches and petitions was cut short by the Al Saud, and especially when a non-violent dissident was executed in 1995, a message to the Saudi citizenry that no divergent political expression or protest, even of a peaceful kind, would be tolerated and that any political reform would be at their rulers' discretion. Opposition since late-1995 has thus often been expressed violently, in line with an established pattern: the 1995 Riyadh and 1996 Khobar bombings should be seen in the context of other past eruptions of violence against the Al Saud which testify to a subterranean world of discontent beneath the usually calm surface of Saudi society.

The problem for the regime is that the policies of the United States, vengeful after 11 September 2001 and buoyant after a stunning initial victory in Afghanistan, will make the Saudi–US relationship even more of a liability for the Al Saud than it has already become, and that militant anti-regime and anti-US/anti-Western action by clandestine groups in sympathy with the cause of Osama bin Laden will become more frequent and more concerted. It is possible that the aftermath of 11 September has irreparably damaged Saudi–US relations; however, if the alliance is sustained, the religiopolitical legitimacy of the Al Saud stands to be even more vigorously challenged in coming years, both inside the kingdom and from exile, by violent and non-violent dissidents alike.

Occasionally, as seen with the three 1992 statutes of government and the 1993 inauguration of the Consultative Council, concessions have been made to popular feeling. However, the Al Saud will do all in their considerable power to ensure that any such concessions are, firstly, as contained as possible and, secondly, in practice serve to reinforce the existing order. Despite any 'concessions', and despite Saudi insistence to the contrary, the existing political order in the kingdom is not as stable as the regime would wish: the political and religious legitimacy of the Al Saud was not, and is not, constructed on a solid bedrock. The still unresolved process of succession to the throne is a source of future problems. Although the Al Saud have, with occasional difficulty, maintained the basic integrity of the dynasty in the modern era, this issue remains a chink in the monarchy's armour that could easily be exploited in combination with other forms of crises. Judging by the record of the Al Saud in the modern era, a succession question alone is unlikely to present the dynasty with an irresolvable problem. However, a real threat to the continuance of Saudi sovereignty would follow from a conjunction of other possible crises, which might be domestic, i.e. financial or socioeconomic, and/or a regional political or geostrategic crisis. The last of these may, in the immediate post-11 September world, be in the process of forming as the United States pursues its open-ended 'war against terrorism'.

In the meantime, the Al Saud are maintaining a firm grip on political power and sociopolitical control, despite areas of potential instability in the sociopolitical–economic system. From the economic policies and political strategies employed by the Al Saud, two observations can be made about the nature of the regime and the ways in which it is dealing with the challenges of the new era of reform. First, the regime is reactive and the implications of being one step behind events may prove to be serious, suggesting that further socioeconomic and sociopolitical domestic disturbances will develop before their root causes are effectively addressed. Second, the regime is in any case not dealing with the core socioeconomic and sociopolitical problems which are leading to dissent that threatens its stability; in other words, it is not proceeding with economic and political liberalisation but is dealing with the economy's structural weaknesses in a piecemeal and incomplete manner, and with popular political aspirations through censorship, political authoritarianism and repression.

Overall, as traditional rulers in a conservative society, the Al Saud are forced to proceed slowly and cautiously with change. Socioeconomic reform has been conceded as necessary by the regime and one of the pivotal problems faced by the Al Saud is how to implement such measures without opening the door to political reforms. Maintaining security, stability and the prevailing political status quo is as much a priority for the kingdom's rulers as ensuring future domestic economic vitality in a globalised economy. The momentum of the process is thus clearly defined. Significant and fundamental reforms will eventually work their way through the Saudi economy and society and the titan that was the Saudi rentier–distributive state will ultimately be consigned to a bygone era.

The dynasty that moulded the modern state and gave it its name has entered a turbulent period. But whatever challenges the Al Saud face, they will have at their disposal all the mechanisms of state security that have been used and honed since Ibn Saud established the kingdom. There will be fluctuations in the effectiveness of these mechanisms but all else being equal, these are likely to occur within an environment of political continuity. There will be many anxious moments, but the survivability of the Al Saud should remain robust in the examinable future. However, the nature of that 'examinable future' changed after 11 September 2001. In the name of creating a safer world, free of terrorism, an already omnipresent United States is threatening to become even more hegemonic in the Gulf sub-region and in the Middle East generally. Such a development, if it comes about, will exert tremendous pressure on the Saudi regime in the face of inevitable popular protest against the Al Saud's 'special relationship' with their superpower partner. The potential conjunction of a regional crisis precipitated by the United States or by the Israel–Palestine conflict on the one hand, and Saudi socioeconomic and succession crises on the other, would force the Al Saud to make decisions with uncustomary speed. If these decisions are wrong, or if the regime remains mired in its inertia, the world may yet witness a political crisis in the kingdom unprecedented since the modern state's foundation, with entirely unpredictable consequences.

SOURCES AND FURTHER READING

Sourcing information in a 'closed' society

Saudi Arabia has always presented difficulties for researchers. Inform-ation is a tightly controlled asset in the Arab world, and a robust concept of privacy makes it doubly so in Saudi Arabia. Where doc-uments, statistics and other data exist, they are notoriously difficult to access, and are frequently full of gaps and lacking in detail, reli-ability often ranging from the doubtful to the extremely dubious. This situation was spelled out in a 1995 country report commissioned by the London-based Saudi dissident organisation, the Committee for the Defence of Legitimate Rights (CDLR, 1995a: 7):[1]

Aside from North Korea, Saudi Arabia is one of the most closed countries in the world. Information is difficult to obtain... Reliable economic data tends to be out of date (by at least 18 months)... Essentially, Saudi Arabia remains wrapped in a shroud, in part much maligned, in part inaccessible, and especially incomprehensible, to western—even Arab—observers and analysts.

The report later states that '...Saudi Arabia is one of the most secre-tive societies in the world', and goes on to explain the 'fruitless exercise' of attempting to analyse Saudi budget any and other eco-nomic data (CDLR, 1995a: 31–2; see also Gause, 1997: 81n. 10). On more than one occasion when speaking with Saudi citizens whilst I was in the country on field work, Saudis themselves matter of factly described their own society as 'closed' (Saudi nationals 1998, confidential and informal sources, Riyadh, Jan.–Mar.). Arab

---

[1] This report represents independent research. Its analysis and conclusions tally, by and large, with those of other independent researchers.

expatriates also made the same point but were less benign in their views on it (Arab expatriates 1998, confidential informal sources, Riyadh, Jan.–Mar.).

The official Saudi stand on any particular issue, if expressed publicly, is usually confined to minimalist statements notable for their lack of elaboration and detail and, often, for their vacuousness. In most cases, interviewing government officials—and they are usually not available for interview—will yield little, if anything, more than the basic information already publicly available. Specific questions and requests for detail are not welcome, usually not expected, and often regarded as a breach of etiquette if ventured. More accessible junior government officials are generally not privy to detailed information on political and economic affairs, and would not dare to reveal any such information if they were.

The legendary 'closed' nature of the kingdom is widely acknowledged and lamented by scholars. From the academic world, words such as 'taboo' (Salameh, 1980: 13), '*terra incognita*' (Abir, 1988: xiii), and '...inscrutable, elusive...' (al-Naqeeb, 1990: ix), are frequently found in the work of other scholars of the kingdom. Fred Halliday (1994: 691, 692) believes that it 'remains virtually inaccessible to independent or in-depth research', and that 'all who study Saudi Arabia have to rely on a combination of fragments, muffled sounds, and intuitions', while Anthony Cordesman (1997: 197) emphasises that sources '...are at least in partial conflict' and that there is 'no consensus' on major areas of data concerning the kingdom.

The experience of Alexander Bligh (1984: 2) can also be noted: 'The researcher must face a number of problems apart from scarcity of sources...', and '...the Saudis themselves prefer to keep the world ignorant of their internal politics. Non-Saudi political and economic figures with special access to such information tend to keep their knowledge private.' Even Saudi academics, who might be expected to enjoy a relatively privileged position regarding research on their own country, complain that 'reliable information was sometimes scarce, inaccessible or unavailable' (Osama, 1987: 3, 31–4). Not much has changed since these words were written. A Saudi official (informal pers. comm., 1999) mentioned to me that even he could not gain access to more senior officials and to other information in the course of his own university degree research; when he did manage to see another official, meaningful information was not forthcoming.

Illustrating how pervasive is this culture of privacy taken to the point of secrecy is the fact that IMF and World Bank staff can access public finance information on all member states except Saudi Arabia, for which special clearance is required (see Allen, 1999). The year 2001 was notable in that it saw, in November, the IMF's first ever economic assessment of the kingdom—a five-page overview issued in the public domain. But the overwhelming message coming from all researchers of Saudi Arabia is that even if Saudi sources of data can be obtained, they must be regarded with some reservation and that any analyses and conclusions drawn from the extensive use of Saudi sources must to some extent be compromised.[2]

A leading Saudi dissident, Saad al-Fagih, has suggested that '[Saudi] policies can be read through observation of actions'—only the acquisition of firm economic or social figures, for example, presents problems (al-Fagih, S., 1998, pers. comm., 20 May). This is a discovery soon made by most scholars of the kingdom; however, even observation can be difficult. I was fortunately able to visit Saudi Arabia twice during the course of my study. The first field research trip, of nearly two months' duration (January–March 1998), was invaluable and an experience that has not been afforded to many others. Mordechai Abir (1993: xi), for example has articulated his frustration at not being able to conduct field work in Saudi Arabia, or even to communicate with Saudi academics; he attributes his research hardships to his Israeli nationality. However, Halliday (1994: 691) writes that:

[Abir's] difficulties are common to all who write on the kingdom, Saudi and non-Saudi, Arab and non-Arab, alike. Everyone seems reduced to writing of one particular part of the whole of which they have reasonably confident, direct, knowledge. Those who know more, and in some cases much more, are reticent about what they reveal.

The reticence mentioned by Halliday was encountered as a matter of course in my own field work, especially in the kingdom itself. All my requests for access to government officials were denied, sometimes by armed Saudi National Guardsmen at the entrance to

---

[2] For more detail see Chapter 3, note 1; Chapter 4, notes, 3, 10, 14, 63.

ministry buildings. A Riyadh-based US diplomat I interviewed was not surprised to hear of these trials, telling me that gaining access to Saudi officials even by US Embassy staff and by high ranking and important American visitors presents a problem (US diplomat, 1998, pers. comm., 9 Mar.).

While the exploits involved in attempting to gain access to Saudi government officials could provide the substance of another book, it was this first trip in 1998 that paved the way for the substantive economic and socioeconomic focus of the present work, with the chance of many interviews with non-government economic and financial professionals. The only notable exception to the rule of Saudi silence was encountered at the Saudi Chambers of Commerce and Industry in Riyadh, where I gained a great number of valuable insights into the Saudi economy and social trends and government policy on unemployment, education and training.[3] One interviewee confirmed what had already become familiar first-hand experience: 'As you know, information is very restricted here...' (Saudi industrial spokesman, 1998, pers. comm., Mar.). By uttering these words, he also reconfirmed that Saudi citizens are well aware of the national habit of keeping information a tightly controlled asset. In an interview at the Chambers almost a year later, the Riyadh institution's general director of research, training and information, Dr Abdullah al-Shidadi, suggested that I might know more about the (negative) state of Saudi national finances—then bearing the full brunt of the oil price collapse—than he did (al-Shidadi, A., 1999, pers. comm., 26 Jan.).

The timing of my first visit was, on the one hand, unfortunate because the February 1998 Iraq crisis considerably reinforced the usual difficulty of access to officials. However, as already indicated, it is very doubtful whether such interviews would have proved significant. On the other hand, being in Riyadh during the crisis provided a rare opportunity to gauge the feeling 'on the street' of Saudi nationals and of expatriate Arabs. The impression gained from conversations during this period has combined with other data, including the actions of the Saudi government during the crisis, to confirm

---

[3] The Saudi Chambers of Commerce and Industry is a body created and privately funded by Saudi industry in the interests of economic advancement and better business.

that the US–Saudi relationship—seven years after the Gulf War and almost two years after the 1996 Khobar bombing—was still a source of domestic discontent in the kingdom. Nothing has changed in the meantime to provide relief on this front for the Al Saud.

The Saudi dissidents based in London were, of course, willing to speak openly and at length; thus, at the opposite end of the secrecy spectrum, this prompted questions about source reliability, a problem recognised by the CDLR-commissioned researchers, who note that 'western observers and journalists…are frequently victims of dis- and mis-information planted by interested parties' (CDLR, 1995a: 7), a situation as true today—and in fields of research other than Saudi Arabia—as it has ever been. However, I might add at this point that in nearly six years of communication with the UK-based Saudi dissidents, I have found many of their insights and assessments reasonably accurate. Nevertheless, the researcher needs to be acutely aware of the interests and connections of his or her sources, whether they be linked to Saudi dissidents, to the Saudi government, or to the British or US governments, or to specific corporate or commercial organisations.

My second trip to Saudi Arabia was a year later, in January 1999, to attend the kingdom's centenary celebrations. I was there as a guest of the Saudi government to present a paper at the Centennial Conference. I was able to catch up with contacts made during the first trip, to re-interview a number of finance and economy professionals, and to gather important statistical and other economic data from the Saudi Arabian Monetary Agency (SAMA), the kingdom's central bank. Attending both the conference and various centenary celebration events naturally afforded the opportunity to conduct research of a more discreet nature and, indeed, to make once-in-a-lifetime observations of this unique occasion in Saudi history.

Overall, a difficult research topic—and the enigma that is Saudi Arabia fits this description—can either be consigned to the 'too hard' basket and avoided, or taken as a challenge and an opportunity to shine a light on something that receives all too little illumination. This book is the result of the latter course.

General note on confidential sources. Saudi Arabia is hypersensitive about privacy and image, and those dealing in information face the prospect of retaliation in one form or another. During field research, current and former diplomatic service personnel, journalists, and even some academics, routinely requested the interview be 'off the record'—one former US ambassador to Saudi Arabia, now working as a private Gulf region consultant, flatly refused to have any dealing with me in the interests of what he claimed was discretion. Other contacts, even after cordial and fruitful relations, regularly dropped away; still others, especially—and ironically—academics, ignored attempts at contact from the very beginning. These experiences only stress the importance of protecting those sources who were willing to share insights, experience and expertise and to provide information of a sensitive nature.

In many instances, sources specifically stipulated that anonymity be maintained. Some were simply exercising what they deemed to be a prudent prerogative; others wished to protect specific business or professional interests. In other cases, common sense—as with diplomats currently serving in Saudi Arabia and in other Middle Eastern countries—led me to regard their interviews as confidential, even though no such specific request for confidentiality was made. One specific case needs some explanation: a former British ambassador to Saudi Arabia presented a seminar on the kingdom in 1987/88 (the paper was undated and the ambassador could not remember exactly when he delivered it). The years cited in this reference, 1987/88, refer to the date of the paper, not to the years of ambassadorship.

In the case of Saudi nationals and foreign expatriates working in the kingdom who are more directly exposed to retaliation, a responsible attitude toward their welfare or even their safety, dictate that names and dates of conversations be reserved.[4] One Saudi national specifically requested that all details by which the regime might identify him be suppressed; this person said that when someone (he was referring to Saudi citizens) incurs the wrath of the regime, 'the government really goes too far, they destroy him' (Saudi national, 1998, pers. comm., Riyadh). For these reasons, the identity of a number of sources must remain strictly confidential.

[4] This work makes limited use, in a supportive role, of sometimes significant information gained from often substantive conversations with Saudi nationals and expatriates in the kingdom. These personal communications are cited as 'informal' and, because the contact took place outside the more formal interview context, have not been listed in the bibliography. Identifying these sources would in any case compromise many of them.

This book in the context of existing literature

Writing on contemporary Saudi Arabia is marked by two events of global significance: the 1973–4 oil boom and the 1990–1 Gulf Crisis and War. A third event, the 1979 Iranian Revolution (and the subsequent Iran–Iraq war), linked the milestone years of 1973 and 1990. Saudi Arabia's importance before these events was of a much lower profile. As far as readily accessible (and mainly European) works are concerned, it was a period in which a fascination with the idea of a 'Wahhabi desert kingdom' prevailed. This earlier era generated a body of writing which has been described as a 'treasur[y] of facts, descriptions and impressions, but…no [substitute] for academic or analytic accounts' (Bligh, 1984: 1). This kind of treatise on the kingdom is epitomised by the writings of H. St. John Philby (1922, 1928, 1952, 1957, 1968). Other examples of this form of 'classic' literature include the volumes by Charles M. Doughty (of *Arabia Deserta* renown), and by T.E. Lawrence. In the same vein, and finding a place in the historical background included in this work, is the writing of Sir John Bagot Glubb (1959, 1960). The fairly extensive use of Philby's writing by Bligh (1984), for example, testifies to the historical value of this body of literature.

Biographies of modern era Saudi rulers, with a focus on Ibn Saud, also peppered the earlier literature (see, for example, Armstrong, 1934; Howarth, 1964; de Gaury, 1966[5]). Oil was a topic, and even Philby (1964) paid attention to it; but, unsurprisingly, it did not enjoy the significance that it assumed after 1973. This category of early literature is a natural companion to more modern and scholarly historical studies, some of which were also undertaken before the oil boom.

Purely historical studies of early- and pre-kingdom (Saudi) Arabia, such as the core works of R. Bayly Winder (1965), Gary Troeller (1976), Christine Moss Helms (1981) and Joseph Kostiner (1993) are, of course, not concerned with the two global events of 1973 and 1990. For deeper background on contemporary Saudi Arabia, an exhaustive historical study of the kingdom which extends into the modern era—through the oil boom and beyond, and encompassing

---

[5] De Gaury is also the author of a number of Doughty- and Philby-like travel/personal experience books; Howarth is a general historian.

politics and economic development—may be undertaken with the aid of the books by Helen Lackner (1978), Alexander Bligh (1984), Mordechai Abir (1988, 1993) and Kiren Aziz Chaudhry (1997).[6] To these may be added the book by Peter Wilson and Douglas Graham (1994), which is a catch-all survey of the modern kingdom. Wilson and Graham provide very useful supportive evidence and research leads in a number of fields, and capture the mood of a period of uncertainty surrounding the kingdom in the immediate aftermath of the 1991 Gulf War. All these works may be supplemented by those of David Holden and Richard Johns (1981), and Robert Lacey (1981). These two books present interesting perspectives which are less academic and, certainly in the latter's case, more personal. To some extent they represent examples of bridging works between those of the very early period of writing on Saudi Arabia and the more recent, formal academic studies.

With the 1973–4 oil boom came an increased concern with the internal dynamics and, especially after the Iranian Revolution, with the security and stability of the now crucially important kingdom. Three books already mentioned in a historical context, Lackner (1978), Bligh (1984) and Abir (1988), are good examples of this period of scholarly awakening to the need to know more about Saudi sociopolitics (Bligh and Abir) and about the Saudi political economy (Lackner). They were at the leading edge in contemporary study of the kingdom in their day; today there is an important historical aspect to the work of this era, and they should be regarded as essential reading in any detailed study of the development of the boom-time kingdom.

The oil boom gave rise to a new emphasis on political economy and development, a trend well represented, for example, in the works by Ragaei el-Mallakh (1982), A. Reza, S. Islami and Rostam Kavoussi (1984) and Robert E. Looney (1982, 1990). Another aspect of the kingdom's political economy—Saudi bureaucratic culture—has been treated in articles by Monte Palmer, written in collaboration with various other scholars and bureaucrats, notably Abdelrahman

---

[6] Chaudhry's book is a study of the modern Saudi and Yemeni political economies in juxtaposition, but it also presents much that is of great value historically, especially in chs. 2 and 3 (Chaudhry, 1997: 43–136). This book occupies an important place in the present work and is discussed in more detail below.

al-Hegelan, a Saudi (al-Hegelan and Palmer, 1985; Palmer *et al.*, 1989). They provide revealing insights into bureaucratic (in)efficiency and the environment of *asabiyya* capitalism, reconfirmed in this book. The burgeoning interest in Saudi domestic affairs is also reflected in other journal articles of the period, for example, Rugh (1973), Salameh (1980), Bligh (1985) and Kechichian (1986, 1990).

The field of Saudi security and stability was dominated by a United States-oriented, big-picture perspective, as represented by works such as those by William B. Quandt (1981) and Nadav Safran (1985). Explaining his attempt to break out of the prevailing mould of this period, John Peterson (1986: ix) wrote, 'Not surprisingly... [Gulf security] literature deals only with the period since 1979 or so and is primarily or exclusively concerned with US (and, to a lesser extent, Western European) national interests and political, economic and military policy options.' (Peterson is here referring to the impact of the Iranian Revolution.) The study of Gulf security in general at this time did, however provide a wider framework for the Saudi-specific works like Peterson's and the volume edited by William J. Olson (1987). Safran's approach falls somewhere between Quandt's security focus and Abir's sociopolitical studies (1988, 1993). Quandt and Olson in particular are good examples of a US establishment position which presents an overtly US-centric analysis.[7]

The latest period of scholarly analysis of Saudi Arabia is that which followed the 1991 Gulf War, although a number of major themes, such as the kingdom's oil-driven global economic importance and political security, overlap with the pre-Gulf War period. Anthony H. Cordesman's most recent work on Saudi Arabia (Cordesman, 1997) is an example of this overlap, and may be regarded as an update of the earlier, security-oriented offerings from Quandt and Safran. Cordesman brings a formidable reputation as a military and strategic analyst to his study of the kingdom and presents a more comprehensive definition of security than his predecessors.

---

[7] Quandt joined the Brookings Institution after two periods on the staff of the US National Security Council (1972–4, 1977–9). He was also involved in negotiations leading to the Camp David Accords and the Egyptian–Israeli Peace Treaty. Olson was a regional security affairs analyst at the Strategic Studies Institute, US Army War College, when his book was produced.

US-centrism, however, is still clearly discernible in his work[8] and, despite some detailed presentation of facts, generally sound conclusions spring from arguments that are relatively thinly presented. For the purposes of the present work, the three chapters of Cordesman's book dealing with the kingdom's internal challenges and with—mainly US and mainly geostrategic—relations with the West, proved most relevant (Cordesman, 1997: 21–76, 181–96).

Just as Cordesman (1997) can be described as an update of Quandt (1981), F. Gregory Gause (1994) is a post-Gulf War update of Safran (1985), with the focus broadened to include all the Gulf Cooperation Council states. Gause's book also represents an important step in an ongoing reassessment of the linkages between domestic politics and oil economics. Gause, like Safran, reads less like an overt policy resource for US administrations than do Quandt, Olson and Cordesman; the Washington perspective of the latter three writers needs to be taken into consideration when this body of literature is used for any fresh analysis of the kingdom.

The 1990–1 Gulf Crisis and War is now well-ploughed land, as is the period 1990–6—that is, from the Iraqi invasion of Kuwait to the Khobar bombing. In dealing with the sociopolitical issues of this period in Chapter 5, notably the rise in Saudi domestic political dissent, the major works by Abir (1993)[9] and Fandy (1999) proved very helpful—as did the fascinating insider's account of the 'rise and

---

[8] See, for example, the assessment that the 'primary [external] threats to Saudi security come from…Iran and Iraq' (Cordesman, 1997: 21). In the face of an Iraq crippled by the Gulf War and by subsequent United Nations sanctions, and of the massive US military commitment to the Gulf, the question that must be asked is how long can such assessments go on being made given the non-materialisation of such threats. Gause (1997: 61) provides a contrast; even before Saudi–Iranian relations began improving around mid-1997, he concluded that Iran and Iraq are not viable threats. Cordesman's brief biographical note states that he 'has served in senior positions in the office of the [US] secretary of defense, NATO and the U.S. Senate' (Cordesman, 1997: 220).

[9] Abir's 1993 book is a revised and extensively updated version of his 1988 work. In accommodating his analysis of Saudi sociopolitics in the immediate aftermath of the Gulf War, Abir has edited out from his 1988 book much good material that is still relevant to a study of Saudi Arabia. Writing for the later book, however, was completed before significant milestones in post-Gulf War Saudi dissent were reached, such as the 1992 Memorandum of Advice and the 1993 launching of the CDLR.

evolution of the modern Islamic reform movement' in Saudi Arabia provided by Saad al-Fagih (1998), formerly of the CDLR and probably now the kingdom's most active and effective, non-violent dissident. Madawi al-Rasheed and Joseph Kechichian are two scholars whose ongoing work on Saudi Arabian sociopolitics is regularly published in major journals and their articles are always enormously enlightening. Together with Cordesman (1997), and with the broader, Gulf region context-setting volumes by Gause (1994), and Sick and Potter (eds, 1997), these works present as up-to-date and thorough an analysis as possible of the essential issues in Saudi sociopolitics and security.

The Saudi post-Gulf War economy is thoroughly analysed in the monograph by Eliyahu Kanovsky (1994). His study falls into the sub-period of uncertainty over the kingdom's future c. 1991–5 that characterised the immediate aftermath of the war. This period, mentioned above in relation to Wilson and Graham's broad and in part historical survey of the kingdom, saw the publication of a number of more concise but equally pessimistic articles, such as that by Mohamedi (1993).[10] Although mainly economically-oriented, Kanovsky and Mohamedi ventured into the fields of political economy and socioeconomics and made reference to the political consequences potential of a seriously unbalanced economy. Although the direst forecasts—e.g. Wilson and Graham's 'coming storm'— have not been realised, the warning sounded by all these works was that the structural weaknesses of the Saudi economy were an ongoing problem that was only likely to grow worse. This assessment remains valid and is taken up in this book in the context of economic globalisation. The work of Paul Stevens (1996; 1997) also adds substance to this view of Saudi Arabia's continuing economic dependence on the petroleum sector.

A different category of literature which spans all periods is that which deals with the purely economic issues although, as noted in this work, the economic discourse is beginning to take on strong overtones of the socioeconomic and even the sociopolitical. IMF and Economist Intelligence Unit (EIU) sources and articles from *The Economist*, the *Middle East Economic Digest* (MEED) and *The*

---

[10] The pessimism of this time extended to all of the Gulf Arab rentier states, as evidenced in Collett (1995) and the *Middle East Monitor* (1995).

Middle East provide as sound a basis as any for the analysis of the
Saudi economy and of important economic trends, both domestically
and globally, as they affect, or may in future affect, Saudi Arabia.
This is particularly true when these sources are used in conjunction
with material from the Saudi Arabian Monetary Agency and
directly from the financial industry inside the kingdom, namely, in
my case, the Saudi American Bank (SAMBA). I draw extensively
on these sources in Chapters 3 and 4 to present such an analysis,
regardless of laments over the 'fruitless exercise' (CDLR, 1995a: 32)
of attempting to come to grips with Saudi budget and other economic data.

This study traverses and knits together what are possibly the two
most original and significant books on the kingdom to appear in
recent years: those by Chaudhry (1997) and Fandy (1999), studies in
political economy and sociopolitics, respectively. Chaudhry's book
is a meticulously documented and absorbing history of the Saudi
political economy presented in the context of a study of institutionalisation and juxtaposed with a parallel study of the Yemeni political
economy. Fandy's sociopolitical study goes a long way toward
unravelling the mystique of the Saudi political opposition and is
essentially a history of recent and current dissent in the kingdom
seen in the framework of the global–local dialectic of postmodern
forms of resistance (see Fandy, 1999: 6–10).

The groundwork for the analysis based on the concept of *asabiyya*
capitalism developed in this book was provided by Chaudhry's
exploration of '...the rise of a new Nejdi private-sector elite'
(Chaudhry, 1997: 315). This business élite—'a client private sector...created [by] the fiscally autonomous Saudi oil state...in an
effort to build a stable base of political support'—rapidly attained
enormous influence over the state's economic decision-making (see
Chaudhry, 1997: 316)[11] Chaudhry's main argument is that because

---

[11] It should be noted that the word 'policy' denotes too ordered a process to be
comfortably employed in describing the Saudi state's approach to economic
management: 'decision-making' more accurately portrays an often whimsical
process. Bligh (1984: 2) is just one example of those who have concluded that
observers of the kingdom 'cannot really trace any organized decision-making
process ... national goals are determined on an ad hoc basis'. See also Osama
(1987: 33). Amuzegar (1999: 48) also refers to an 'often *ad hoc* manner' of oil rent
allocations in OPEC countries in general.

favouritism, informal business–political relations and exclusive business practices became institutionalised during the oil boom years when Saudi Arabia became a distributive state, the results cannot be categorised as nepotism, cronyism and corruption.

Chaudhry recognises the significant roles of favouritism and of practices widely termed 'corrupt'; she especially recognises that (Najdi) bureaucratic–business and professional–social alliances during the boom years 'produced an extreme form of clan organization'. But, unlike Fandy (1999: 30–1), she denies that these are evidence of 'established patterns of patronage writ large' or of 'sheer corruption'.[12] In fact, she posits that one of the three major factors which explain the nature of the contemporary Saudi political economy is 'the preexisting composition of the bureaucracy...the organization and composition of the institutions that govern the economy' (Chaudhry, 1997: 191). As Chaudhry herself has amply demonstrated, this was the result of established patterns of patronage and traditional loyalties (see Chaudhry, 1997: 155, 160, 162–3, 162 n. 68, 170–2, 190–1). The institutionalisation of kinship allegiances and personalised business networks does not negate them, or change them into something other than what they are at root level. These state–business links are the basis of a 'pact [which] persists' (Chaudhry, 1997: 316): the fabric of *asabiyya* capitalism. Chaudhry's more overt ventures into contemporary Saudi politics, however, are less convincing (see Chaudhry, 1997: 293–9, 304–19); it is here that a bridge between Chaudhry's work and that of Fandy is required. Although the most recent publications of Gause (1997, 2000) go some way in supplying this vital link, a more substantial, Saudi-specific study was clearly required.

Fandy's book is both substantial and Saudi-specific but, in sharp contrast to Chaudhry, Fandy plays down the economic dimension of Saudi sociopolitics.[13] Although one of Fandy's principal themes

[12] Fandy (1999: 31), elucidating the Saudi politico–socioeconomic system, states that he does 'not...condone corruption', but seeks to avoid any value-judgement by writing, 'I merely seek to explain how money and power are allocated within the Saudi system'. The topic of what may or may not be construed as 'corruption' in the Saudi context is an involved and thorny one, and is an issue broached in Chapter 3 of this book.

[13] Fandy's principal arguments for adopting this approach are outlined in the section 'Oil, resistance, and the political economy of signs' (Fandy, 1999: 25–31).

is globalisation, its most tangible manifestation—economic internationalisation—is virtually ignored. Scholars of the kingdom must indeed 'look beyond the rentier model when analyzing Saudi resistance' (Fandy 1999: 29), but the role of economics and, more importantly, of socioeconomics in the era of globalisation cannot be marginalised in a truly balanced study of Saudi sociopolitics. Fandy's cursory dismissal of 'the rentier model' of analysis (see Fandy, 1999: 25–30), whilst also occasionally appearing to acknowledge its relevance (ibid., 145, 245), does not do justice to his overall analysis; in addition, his historical background is minimalist and omits much of consequence (see Fandy, 1999: 41–3). However, Fandy's concepts of a Saudi 'familialism' and '*qaraba* society' are vitally important (ibid., 22–5, 30–1) and make sound common sense in the Saudi context; they are also concepts which have hitherto not received the acknowledgement they warrant. They are, of course, the basic components of the informal 'pact' which underwrites the Saudi sociopolitical–economic system of *asabiyya* capitalism.[14]

In summary, this book picks up where Chaudhry ends by extending analysis of the Saudi political economy into the era of globalisation and, much more overtly, into the sociopolitical realm. In doing so, it fills the gaps left by Fandy and by other politically-oriented analysts. It is in its exploration of the substance of the relationships between the kingdom's economy, society and politics in the twilight era of the Saudi welfare state and the dawn of the kingdom's economic internationalisation that this book strives to make a contribution to knowledge on contemporary Saudi Arabia.

---

[14] Fandy (1999: 23) defines *qaraba* as 'closeness both in space and social relations'. These concepts are introduced in Chapter 2 in this book as background to *asabiyya* capitalism.

BIBLIOGRAPHY

Saudi sources: Government and dissident[1]

Al-Qimam (1997a). 'Mina fire expertly controlled', 5 May. Distributed by the Muslim Students Association electronic news service (MSANews, e-mail delivery).

Al-Qimam (1997b). 'Prince Nayef declares Mina fire accidental', 6 May. Distributed by the Muslim Students Association electronic news service (MSANews, e-mail delivery).

Basic Law of Government (1992). Royal Order of King Fahd No. A/90, dated 27/8/1412H (29 Feb/1 Mar., 1992). Reproduced in *Highlights of Development in Saudi Arabia*. Riyadh: Dar al-Ufuq/Saudi Ministry of Information (n.d.), pp. 91–110.

Bin Abd al-Aziz al-Saud, (Crown Prince) Abdullah (1998a). Quoted in 'Prince Abdullah calls for action on oil prices', *Emirates News*, 9 Dec. 1998.

Bin Abd al-Aziz al-Saud, (Crown Prince) Abdullah (1998b). Quoted in Barry May (1998), 'Gulf Arabs end summit with oil cut pledge', Reuters news service, 9 Dec.

Bin Abd al-Aziz al-Saud, (King) Faisal (n.d.). Quoted in Fouad Abdul-Salam Al-Farsy (1980), 'King Faisal and the First Five Year Development Plan' in *King Faisal and the Modernisation of Saudi Arabia*, ed. Willard A. Beling. London: Croom Helm, pp. 60, 61.

Bin Abd al-Aziz al-Saud, (Prince) Salman (1999). Address at the Closing Session of the Centennial Conference of the Kingdom of Saudi Arabia, Riyadh, 28 Jan.

Bin Laden, Osama (1996). *i'lan al-jihad 'ala al-amrikiyyin al-muhtalin li bilad al-haramain* ('Declaration of war against the Americans occupying the land of the two holy places'). A Message from Osama bin Muhammad bin Laden, Friday, 9/4/1417 A.H. (23/08/1996 AD), Hindukush Mountains, Khorasan, Afghanistan.

[1] Question marks accompanying a reference date or publisher in this section indicate that full publishing details were not provided in the original source and that the cited details are the probable ones.

Bin Thunaiyan, (Prince) Saud bin Abdullah (1999). 'Privatization: Its essence, dimensions and implementation in the Kingdom'. Paper presented in the 45th Session, Kingdom of Saudi Arabia Centennial Conference, Riyadh, 24–28 Jan.

CACSA (1999a). 'al-Yamamah scandal'. Committee Against Corruption in Saudi Arabia. Internet site.

http://www.saudhouse.com/al-yamam.htm (when active)

(CACSA home page: http://www.saudhouse.com/ (reactivated 2002))

CACSA (1999b). 'Our mission'. Committee Against Corruption in Saudi Arabia. Internet site.

http://www.saudhouse.com/ (when active pre-October 1999)

CACSA (2002a). 'Mission'. Committee Against Corruption in Saudi Arabia. Internet site.

http://www.saudhouse.com/mission.asp

CACSA (2002b). 'Al-Yamamah contract'. Committee Against Corruption in Saudi Arabia. Internet site.

http://www.saudhouse.com/stories/article.asp?idr=24

CDLR (1994a). *Hadj: The Saudi Performance.* Report, Committee for the Defence of Legitimate Rights (London), 25 June.

CDLR (1994b). Press Release, Committee for the Defence of Legitimate Rights (London), 14 Sept.

CDLR (1994c). Press Release, Committee for the Defence of Legitimate Rights (London), 19 Sept.

CDLR (1994d). Statement of Objectives and Policies, Committee for the Defence of Legitimate Rights (London), Nov.–Dec.

CDLR (1995a). *Saudi Arabia: A Country Report. The Political and Economic Situation.* Report commissioned by the Committee for the Defence of Legitimate Rights (London), 3 Jan.

CDLR (1995b). 'The meeting of betrayal', *CDLR Monitor*, no. 41 (31 Mar.). Weekly bulletin of the Committee for the Defence of Legitimate Rights (London).

CDLR (1995c). 'Saudi judicial murder marks beginning of new stage in the confrontation between regime and its opposition', Press Release, Committee for the Defence of Legitimate Rights (London), 13 Aug.

CDLR (1995d). 'King's illness and seriousness of stage ahead', Communiqué no. 42 (11 Dec.), Committee for the Defence of Legitimate Rights (London).

CDLR (1997). 'Shame on the House of Saud!! Fire killed and injured over 13,500', Communiqué no. 48 (20 Apr.), Committee for the Defence of Legitimate Rights (London).

al-Fagih, Saad (1998). *The Rise and Evolution of the Modern Islamic Reform Movement in Saudi Arabia* (revised edn). Posted on the MIRA Internet site. http://www.miraserve.com/HistoryOfDissent.htm

[First published as 'History of Dissent' (serialised, 1996), in the MIRA monthly publication *Arabia Unveiled*.]

al-Farsy, Fouad (1990). *Modernity and Tradition: The Saudi Equation*. London: Kegan Paul International.

al-Gosaibi, Khalid bin Muhammad (2000). Quoted in, 'In brief: Al-Gosaibi addresses MEED conference', *Middle East Economic Digest*, 7 Apr. Distributed electronically by Reuters (Business Briefing Select), n.d.

al-Hulaiqa, Ihsan bin Ali (1999). 'Contributions of the private sector to the Saudi economy: A futuristic outlook'. Paper presented in the 45th Session of the Kingdom of Saudi Arabia Centennial Conference, Riyadh, 24–28 Jan.

Ibn Saud (1929a). Public statement condemning the Ikhwan, early April. Quoted in Christine Moss Helms (1981), *The Cohesion of Saudi Arabia: Evolution of Political Identity*. London: Croom Helm, pp. 258–9.

Ibn Saud (1929b). 'Translation, speech of King Abd al-Aziz to the Utaiba at Duwadami', 9 July 1929. Quoted in Christine Moss Helms (1981), *The Cohesion of Saudi Arabia: Evolution of Political Identity*. London: Croom Helm, pp. 114, 265.

Letter (1991). 'Letter of Demands'. First major document of the Saudi Islamist opposition, presented to King Fahd in May 1991. Full text posted on the MIRA Internet site: http://www.miraserve.com/appendix.html

Majlis Ash-Shura Law (1992). Royal Order of King Fahd No. A/91, dated 27/8/1412H (29 Feb./1 Mar., 1992). Reproduced in *Highlights of Development in Saudi Arabia*. Riyadh: Dar al-Ufuq/Saudi Ministry of Information (n.d.), pp. 123–31.

al-Masari, Muhammad (1996). Quoted in Christopher Lockwood, 'Dissident tries to topple rulers by fax', *Electronic Telegraph*, 22 Feb. http://www.telegraph.co.uk:80/et?ac=000148889415120&rtmo=aTa5u5aJ&atmo=99999999&pg=/et/96/2/22/nsaudi22.html

al-Masari, Muhammad (1997). Interviewed by the *Middle East Times* (Egypt). Posted on the *Middle East Times* Internet site for censored articles as 'An embarrassment in exile'.

http://metimes.com/cens/c6.htm

(*MET* home page: http://metimes.com/cens/censored.htm)

Ministry of Information (1993a). *At the Service of Allah's Guests*. Riyadh: Dept. of Information Affairs, Saudi Ministry of Information.

Ministry of Information (1993b). *The Saudi Media: Evolution and Progress*. Riyadh: Dept. of Information Affairs, Saudi Ministry of Information.

Ministry of Information (1997). *The March of Nation Building*. Riyadh: Dept. of Information Affairs, Saudi Ministry of Information.

Ministry of Information (1998). *This is Our Country.* Riyadh: Dept. of Information Affairs, Saudi Ministry of Information.

Ministry of Information (n.d.). *The Kingdom of Saudi Arabia.* Riyadh: Dept. of Information Affairs, Saudi Ministry of Information.

Ministry of Planning (?1984). *Fourth Development Plan: 1405–1410 A.H./ 1985–1990 A.D.* Riyadh: Ministry of Planning Press.

Ministry of Planning (?1989). *Fifth Development Plan: 1410–1415 A.H./ 1990–1995 A.D.* Riyadh: Ministry of Planning Press.

Ministry of Planning (?1994). *Sixth Development Plan: 1414–1420 A.H./ 1995–2000 A.D.* Riyadh: Ministry of Planning Press.

MIRA (1996). 'Royal succession potential source of destruction'. *Arabia Unveiled* (monthly news letter of the Movement for Islamic Reform in Arabia), May (no. 1). MIRA Internet site.

http://www.miraserve.com/arabia.htm

(MIRA home page: http://www.miraserve.com/)

MIRA (1997). *Arabia in the Media*, no. 2 (11–19 May). Internet site of the Movement for Islamic Reform in Arabia.

http://www.miraserve.com/pressrev/eprev02.htm

MIRA (1998a). 'Bin Laden's war', *Arabia in the Media*, no. 48 (26–31 May). Internet site of the Movement for Islamic Reform in Arabia.

http://www.miraserve.com/pressrev/eprev48.htm

MIRA (1998b). 'Arrest of Khaled al-Fawaz', Communiqué no. 6 (26 Sept.), Movement for Islamic Reform in Arabia (London). Attached to 'London arrests', *Arabia in the Media*, no. 64 (21–27 Sept.). MIRA Internet site.

http://www.miraserve.com/pressrev/eprev64.htm

MIRA (1998c). 'London arrests', *Arabia in the Media*, no. 64 (21–27 Sept.). Internet site of the Movement for Islamic Reform in Arabia.

http://www.miraserve.com/pressrev/eprev64.htm

MIRA (1998d). 'Al Fawwaz', *Arabia in the Media*, no. 65 (28 Sept.–4 Oct.). Internet site of the Movement for Islamic Reform in Arabia.

http://www.miraserve.com/pressrev/eprev65.htm

MIRA (1998e). 'Khaled Al-Fawwaz', *Arabia in the Media*, no. 73 (31 Nov.– 6 Dec.). Internet site of the Movement for Islamic Reform in Arabia.

http://www.miraserve.com/pressrev/eprev73.htm

MIRA (1999). 'Hardship', *Arabia in the Media*, no. 108 (9–15 Aug.). Internet site of the Movement for Islamic Reform in Arabia.

http://miraserve.com/pressrev/eprev108.htm

Mutabbakani, Saleh (1993). *Saudi Arabia: Modern Economy, Traditional Society.* Riyadh: Saudi Ministry of Information publication(?).

al-Rawaf, Othman Yassin (1998). 'Saudi Arabia and the stability of the Gulf'. Paper presented at the 17th Annual Conference of the Australasian

Middle East Studies Association, The Australian National University, Canberra, 18–19 Sept.

Royal Embassy of Saudi Arabia, London (1997). *The Kingdom of Saudi Arabia: A Welfare State*. Publication of the Royal Embassy of Saudi Arabia, London (Sept.).

Royal Embassy of Saudi Arabia, London (2000). 'Saudi Arabia: Questions of human rights'. Publications section, Internet site of the Royal Embassy of Saudi Arabia, London.

http://www.saudiembassy.org.uk/publications/questions-of-human-rights/questions-of-human-rights-1.htm

(Saudi Embassy, London, home page: http://www.saudiembassy.org.uk/)

al-Rubiyya, Muhammad bin Abd al-Rahman (1999). Address at the Closing Session of the of the Kingdom of Saudi Arabia Centennial Conference, Riyadh, 28 Jan.

SAMA (1998). *Saudi Arabian Monetary Agency: Thirty-Fourth Annual Report, 1419H (1998G)*. Riyadh: SAMA Research and Statistics Department, Oct.

SAMA (2001). Statistics—Annual Report. Internet site of the Saudi Arabian Monetary Agency (Dec.).

(SAMA home page: http://www.sama-ksa.org/)

Saudi Economic Survey (1999). 'AlWaleed donates SR 12.5m', 12 May. Distributed electronically by Reuters (Business Briefing Select), 18 May 1999.

Saudi Economic Survey (2000). 'Saudi families income', 29 Mar. Distributed electronically by Reuters (Business Briefing Select), 3 Apr. 2000.

Saudi Press Agency (1997a). Original broadcast in Arabic, 1850 GMT, 12 July. Text of report, SPA news agency (Riyadh), issued by BBC Monitoring Summary of World Broadcasts (Middle East), 14 July. Distributed electronically by Reuters as, 'Saudi King Fahd receives phone call from Yemeni president' (Reuters Middle East News Briefs, article ref. no.: 001060172279), 14 July 1997.

Saudi Press Agency (1997b). '478 kgs of relief supplies sent to Azerbaijan', SPA news agency (Riyadh), 2 Aug. Reported in *Arab News*, 3 Aug. Distributed electronically by Reuters (Business Briefing Select), 13 Aug. 1997.

Saudi Press Agency (1997c). Original broadcast in Arabic, 1540 GMT, 4 Aug. Excerpts from report, SPA news agency (Riyadh), issued by BBC Monitoring Summary of World Broadcasts (Middle East), 6 Aug. Distributed electronically by Reuters (Business Briefing Select) as, 'King tells ministers kingdom will never deviate from Islamic course', 6 Aug. 1997.

Saudinf (2001a). 'Bomb blast culprit named', Saudi Arabian Information Resource (Riyadh)/SPA news agency (Riyadh), 14 Nov. http://www.saudinf.com/main/y3361.htm

Saudinf (2001b). 'False accusations against Kingdom regretted', Saudi Arabian Information Resource (Paris)/SPA news agency (Riyadh), 15 Nov. http://www.saudinf.com/main/y3373.htm

SIDF (1996). *Saudi Industrial Development Fund: Annual Report 1996 (1416/1417)*. Riyadh: Ministry of Finance and National Economy (Legal Deposit No. 16/3419, ISSN: 1319-5530).

Yamani, Hashim bin Abdullah bin Hashim (1997). Quoted in, 'Saudi to start bilateral WTO talks next year', Reuters news service, 5 Aug.

Interviews and other personal communication

Alohaly, A. Rahman N. (1995). Personal interview (Royal Embassy of the Kingdom of Saudi Arabia, Canberra), 13 July.

Aslimy, Fahd M. (1998). Personal interview (Saudi Export Development Center, Riyadh), 7 Mar.

Australian diplomat 1 (1995, 14 July). Personal interview (Dept. of Foreign Affairs and Trade, Canberra).

Australian diplomat 1 (1995, 17 Aug.). Telephone interview (Sydney–Dept. of Foreign Affairs and Trade, Canberra).

Australian diplomat 2 (1997). Informal conversation (Canberra), 18 June.

Australian diplomat 3 (1998). Informal conversation (Australian Embassy, Riyadh), 23 Feb.

Austrian, Michael (1995). Personal interview, 13 July (The Australian National University, Canberra).

BBC Middle East analyst (1998). Confidential personal interview (London), 26 May.

British analyst 1 (1998). Confidential personal interview (Foreign and Commonwealth Office, London), 1 June.

British analyst 2 (1998). Confidential personal interview (Foreign and Commonwealth Office, London), 1 June.

Business consultant (1996). Confidential telephone communication (Sydney–Canberra), 1 May.

CDLR spokesman (1995). Telephone interview (Sydney–CDLR office, London), 20 Sept.

al-Dawood, Nasser (1997). Invitation from the Secretary-General of the Conference Committee to submit a paper for the Kingdom of Saudi Arabia Centennial Conference, 29 July (1/4/1418H).

al-Fagih, Saad (1998, 20 May). Personal interview (MIRA office, London).

al-Fagih, Saad (1998, 28 May). Personal interview (MIRA office, London).

al-Fagih, Saad (1998, 7 Sept.). E-mail communication (MIRA office, London–Canberra).

al-Fagih, Saad (1998, 12 Sept.). E-mail communication (MIRA office, London–Canberra).

al-Fagih, Saad (1998, 16 Sept). E-mail communication (MIRA office, London–Canberra).

al-Fagih, Saad (1999, 19 Mar.). E-mail communication (MIRA office, London–Canberra).

al-Fagih, Saad (1999, 25 May). E-mail communication (MIRA office, London–Canberra).

al-Fagih, Saad (1999, 25 Aug.). E-mail communication (MIRA office, London–Canberra).

al-Fagih, Saad (1999, 22 Oct.). E-mail communication (MIRA office, London–Canberra).

al-Fagih, Saad (1999, 24 Oct.). E-mail communication (MIRA office, London–Canberra).

al-Fagih, Saad (2000, 16 June). Telephone interview (MIRA office, London–Adelaide).

al-Fagih, Saad (2000, 30 Oct.). E-mail communication (MIRA office, London–Adelaide).

al-Fagih, Saad (2000, 7 Nov.). Telephone interview (Adelaide–MIRA office, London).

al-Fauwaz, Khalid (1995). Telephone interview (Sydney–London), 21 Sept.

Former British ambassador to Saudi Arabia (1998). Confidential personal interview (London), 26 May. [Reference is also made to a confidential seminar paper delivered in the late 1980s as 'Former British ambassador to Saudi Arabia, 1998 [seminar paper] 1987/88'.]

Gulf energy expert (2001). E-mail communication (UK–Canberra), 19 Feb.

Joffé, George (1998). Personal interview (Royal Institute of International Affairs, London), 27 May.

Kopietz, Hans-Heino (1999). Facsimile communication (London–Canberra), 8 Dec.

Mabro, Robert (1998). Personal interview (Oxford Institute for Energy Studies, Oxford), 14 May.

al-Masari, Muhammad A.S. (1995, 3 July). Telephone interview (Sydney–CDLR office, London).

al-Masari, Muhammad A.S. (1995, 6 July). Telephone interview (Sydney–CDLR office, London).

al-Masari, Muhammad A.S. (1995, 5 Aug.). E-mail communication (CDLR office, London–Sydney).

al-Masari, Muhammad A.S. (1998, 20 May). Personal interview (London).

al-Masari, Muhammad A.S. (1998, 26 May). Personal interview (London).

Mitchell, Debra (1999). Personal interview (Economics Program, Research School of Social Sciences, The Australian National University, Canberra), 23 June.

al-Nashwan, T. (1998). Personal interview (Saudi Industrial Export Company, Riyadh), 7 Mar.

Piscatori, James P. (1998). Personal interview (Oxford Centre for Islamic Studies, University of Oxford), 15 May.

Political analyst (2000). Confidential correspondence (London–Canberra), 25 Jan.

al-Rasheed, Madawi (1998). Personal interview (London), 22 May.

Richardson, Ian (1998). Personal interview (London), 20 May.

Richardson, Ian (2000). E-mail communication (London–Adelaide), 25 Oct.

al-Rubiyya, Muhammad bin Abd al-Rahman (1997). Personal letter from Dr Rubiyya, Chairman of the Centennial of Saudi Arabia Conference Committee, 8 Nov. (17/7/1418H).

Saudi industrial spokesman (1998). Confidential personal interview (Riyadh), Mar.

Saudi media professional (1998). Confidential personal communication (Riyadh).

Saudi national (1998). Confidential personal interview (Riyadh).

Saudi official (1999). Informal conversation (confidential).

Saudi prince (1998). Confidential personal interview.

Senior Australian diplomat (1999). Confidential personal interview (Canberra), Feb.–Mar.

Senior economist (1998). Confidential personal interview (Riyadh), Mar.

Senior economist (1999). Confidential personal interview (Riyadh), Jan.

al-Shidadi, Abdullah (1998). Personal interview (Saudi Chambers of Commerce and Industry, Riyadh), 7 Mar.

al-Shidadi, Abdullah (1999) Personal interview (Saudi Chambers of Commerce and Industry, Riyadh), 26 Jan.

Shiite Iraqi refugees (1996). Personal group interview (Sydney), 21 Apr.

al-Shubaili, Saud (1998). Personal interview (Saudi Chambers of Commerce and Industry, Riyadh), 7 Mar.

Taecker, Kevin (1998). Personal interview (SAMBA HQ, Riyadh), 9 Mar.

Taecker, Kevin (1999). Personal interview (SAMBA HQ, Riyadh), 26 Jan.

UAE Embassy (1997). Telephone communication with the embassy of the United Arab Emirates, Canberra, 11 Dec.

US diplomat (1998). Confidential personal interview (US Embassy, Riyadh), 9 Mar.

Books, articles and other sources

AAASHRAN (1994). 'Saudi Arabia: Arrest and detention of professor of agriculture', American Association for the Advancement of Science Human Rights Action Network, 4 Nov. (Case no. SA9429.ALW).

Distributed by the Muslim Students Association electronic news service (MSANews, e-mail delivery).

(AAASHRAN home page: http://shr.aaas.org/aaashran.htm)

Abdullah, Mahmoud (1997). 'Renovation of Al-Azhar Mosque progressing well', *Arab News*, 6 Aug. Distributed electronically by Reuters (Business Briefing Select), 14 Aug. 1997.

Abeidoh, Rawhi (2001). 'Riyadh fumes over Washington's Khobar indictments', *Daily Star* (Beirut), 27 June, 5. (Reuters news agency, 26 June)

Abir, Mordechai (1988). *Saudi Arabia in the Oil Era: Regime and Elites; Conflict and Collaboration*. London: Croom Helm.

———— (1993). *Saudi Arabia: Government, Society and the Gulf Crisis*. London: Routledge.

Abuljadayel, Sarah (1999). 'Workers still await salaries', *Arab News*, 14 July. Distributed electronically by Reuters (Business Briefing Select), 28 July 1999.

Aburish, Saïd K. (1995). *The Rise, Corruption and Coming Fall of the House of Saud*. London: Bloomsbury.

Adelaide Central Mission (1999). 'Life getting tougher for low income families', Media release, 24 June.

AFP (2001a). 'OPEC eager to head off crude price drop', *Daily Star* (Beirut), 4 Dec., 8. (Agence France Presse news agency, 3 Dec.)

AFP (2001b). 'Saudi Arabia is set to end year with $3.2bn deficit', *Daily Star* (Beirut), 5 Dec., 8. (Agence France Presse news agency, 4 Dec.)

AFP (2001c). 'US sends officials to Saudi Arabia', Agence France Presse news agency, 6 Dec.

AFP (2001d). 'Oil on the slide as OPEC cutback deal still proving elusive', Agence France Presse news agency, 7 Dec.

AFP (2002). 'French arrest Saudi drugs ring suspect', Agence France Presse news agency, 17 Dec.

AI [Amnesty International] (1993a). 'Saudi Arabia: An upsurge in public executions', Report, 15 May (AI Index: 23/04/93).

AI (1993b). 'Saudi Arabia. Religious intolerance: The arrest, detention and torture of Christian worshippers and Shi'a Muslims', Report, 14 Sept. (AI Index: MDE 23/06/93).

AI (1995a). 'Alarming increase in number of executions', Urgent Action bulletin, 20 Apr. (AI Index: MDE 23/01/95).

AI (1995b). 'Execution/flogging/legal concern', Urgent Action bulletin, 15 Aug. (AI Index: MDE 23/05/95).

AI (1995c). 'Alarming increase in number of executions', Urgent Action bulletin, 16 Aug. (AI Index: MDE 23/06/95).

AI (1995d). 'Saudi Arabia', *Amnesty International Annual Report 1995*. London: Amnesty International Publications.

AI (1996). 'Human rights violations in the Middle East and North Africa, January to December 1995: Summary', *Amnesty International Annual Report 1996* (Internet edn). London: Amnesty International Publications. http://www.amnesty.org/ailib/aireport/ar96/index.html#middle east (AI home page: http://www.amnesty.org/)

AI (1997). *Saudi Arabia. Behind Closed Doors: Unfair Trials in Saudi Arabia.* Report, Nov. (AI Index: MDE 23/08/97).

AI (1999). 'Amnesty International plans to attend trial of Hani el-Sayegh', News Service 192/99, 13 Oct. (AI Index: MDE 23/11/99).

AI (2000a). 'Saudi Arabia defying world trends: Death penalty', Theme leaflet no. 5, 12 June (AI Index: MDE 23/09/00).

AI (2000b). 'Saudi Arabia', *Amnesty International Annual Report 2000*. London: Amnesty International Publications (AI Index: POL 10/001/00). http://www.web.amnesty.org/web/ar2000web.nsf/ f5ea2b18926bc708802568f500619c95/ dff7967be13bbf6c802568f200552964!OpenDocument

Ajami, Riad (1987). 'The Saudi economy in transition: Prospects and bottlenecks' in William J. Olson, ed., *US Strategic Interests in the Gulf Region*, Boulder, CO: Westview Press.

Albayyat, Saeed (1998). 'Private firms register high compliance of Saudization', *Saudi Gazette*, 29 Nov. Distributed electronically by Reuters (Business Briefing Select), 9 Dec. 1998.

Alderson, Andrew and Rajeev Syal (2000). 'Ann Summers to open sex shop in Mecca', *Electronic Telegraph*, 27 Aug. http://www.telegraph.co.uk:80/et?ac=000148889415120&rtmo= lnkAPvQt&atmo=rrrrrrvs&pg=/et/00/8/27/wmecc27.html

Al-Hawadith (1997). 'Council of Ministers sets basic rules for privatization'. Excerpt from report by *Al-Hawadith* (London), 27 Aug. BBC Monitoring Service: Middle East, 2 Sept. Distributed electronically by Reuters (Business Briefing Select), 2 Sept. 1997.

Ali, Abdullah Yusuf (1938). *The Holy Qur'an: English Translation of the Meanings and Commentary.* Lahore: Sh. Muhammad Ashraf.

Allen, Robin (1996). 'Saudi debt move gets mixed response', *Financial Times*, 4 Apr., 4.

———— (1998). 'Oil price crash forces Saudis to seek $5bn bail-out', *Financial Times*, 4 Dec., 4.

———— (1999). 'Secretive Saudis start to admit economic realities', *Financial Times*, 1 Dec., 13.

Al-Quds al-Arabi (1999). Reported as 'Daily highlights princes' reported power struggle' (*Al-Quds al-Arabi*, 23 June, 1). BBC Monitoring Service (Middle East), 25 June. Distributed electronically by Reuters (Business Briefing Select), 25 June 1999.

Amayreh, Khalid (1997). 'Mina Fire Overshadows Hajj', *Palestine Times* (Internet edn), issue 71, May.
http://www.ptimes.com/issue71/articles.htm#anchor308281

Amuzegar, Jahangir (1999). *Managing the Oil Wealth: OPEC's Windfalls and Pitfalls*. London: I.B. Tauris.

Anjaria, Shailendra J. (1999). 'The IMF: Working for a more transparent world. How new technology and the IMF are beginning a new openness to new financial markets', *Journal of Information Policy*, 11 Jan. [Reproduced with permission by the IMF External Relations Department, IMF Internet site.]
http://www.imf.org/external/np/vc/1999/011299.HTM

Arab News (1997). 'Satellite TV corrupting young people—Study', 27 July. Distributed electronically by Reuters (Business Briefing Select), 6 Aug 1997.

Arab News (1999). 'WTO negotiations should be completed rapidly—Faqeeh', 4 Dec. Distributed electronically by Reuters (Business Briefing Select), 17 Dec 1999.

Armstrong, Harold Courtenay (1934). *Lord of Arabia: Ibn Saud, An Intimate Study of a King* [first publ. 1924]. London: Arthur Barker.

Armstrong, Scott (1991). 'Eye of the storm', *Mother Jones*, 16 (6), (Nov.–Dec.), 30–5, 75–6.

Asad, Muhammad (1984). *The Message of the Qur'an* [English transl. of the Quran with commentary and essays]. Gibraltar: Dar al-Andalus.

Ashrawi, Hanan (1999). 'The Middle East Peace Process'. Centre for Arab and Islamic Studies/ANU public lecture, The Australian National University (Canberra), 6 July.

Associated Press (1997). 'Authorities seize Saudi newspaper', Associated Press news agency, 13 May.

Atwan, Abd al-Bari (1996). Interview, *Index on Censorship*, Feb. edn. Available online at: http://www.indexoncensorship.org/issue296/saudi.html
(*IoC* home page: http://www.indexoncensorship.org/index.html)

The Australian (1999). 'Brent crude tops $US21 as cuts bite' (syndicated from *The Times*). 23 Aug., 39.

Avancena, Joe (1997). 'Al-Zamil urges Saudi firms to get ready over WTO precepts', *Saudi Gazette*, 27 Aug. Distributed electronically by Reuters (Business Briefing Select), 4 Sept. 1997.

———— (1999). 'N'aimi stresses Saudization in private companies of oil sector', *Saudi Gazette*, 12 Mar. Distributed electronically by Reuters (Business Briefing Select), 19 Mar. 1999.

al-Awaji, Ibrahim (1989). 'Bureaucracy and development in Saudi Arabia: The case of local administration', *Journal of Asian and African Studies*, 24 (1–2), 49–61.

Ayubi, Nazih N.M. (1982–83). 'The politics of militant Islamic movements in the Middle East', *Journal of International Affairs*, 36 (Fall–Winter), 271–83.

Azis, Iwan J. (1998). 'Transition from financial crisis to social crisis' in proceedings of the conference: *Social Implications of the Asian Financial Crisis* (Seoul, 29–31 July), eds Elizabeth Pyon and Hyehoon Lee (EDAP Joint Policy Studies, no. 9). Published by the Korea Development Institute.

Bailey, Robert (1998). 'How will Saudi Arabia handle low oil prices?', *Gulf Business* (Internet edn), Aug.

http://www.gulfbusiness.com/issues/sept98/august_issue/saudi.html (back issues past Dec. 1998 no longer available on-line) (*GB* home page: http://www.gulfbusiness.com/cgi-local/index.cgi)

The Banker (1995). 'Saudi set to see red', Dec., 59–60.

The Banker (1999). 'Riding the storm', July, 124.

Barber, Benjamin (1996). *Jihad vs. McWorld*. New York: Ballantine Books.

Barnet, Richard J. (1994). 'Lords of the global economy', *The Nation*, 19 Dec., 754–7.

Bashir, Abdul Wahab (1999). 'Creating jobs is a challenge for planners', *Arab News*, 23 July. Distributed electronically by Reuters (Business Briefing Select), 4 Aug. 1999.

Beaumont, Peter (1996). '20 billion reasons for greed', *Observer*, 7 Jan., 11.

Beavis, Simon, Chris Barrie and Richard Norton-Taylor (1996). 'Web that links weapons and Whitehall', *Guardian*, 6 Jan., 2.

Beblawi, Hazem (1987). 'The rentier state in the Arab world', *Arab Studies Quarterly*, 9 (4), (Fall), 383–98.

Bhatia, Shyam (1995). 'Saudi soothsayers start royal uproar', *Observer*, 5 Mar.

Bill, James A. and Robert Springborg (1994). *Politics in the Middle East*, 4th edn. New York: Harper Collins.

Binyon, Michael (1994). 'Saudis persuade Britain to expel Islamic fundamentalist', *The Times*, 28 Nov., 2.

Birks, J.S. and Clive A. Sinclair (1982). 'The domestic political economy of development in Saudi Arabia' in Tim Niblock, ed., *State, Society and Economy in Saudi Arabia*. New York: St. Martin's Press.

Bishop, Patrick (1994). 'Saudi dissident "in danger"', *Daily Telegraph*, 29 Nov., 17.

Bligh, Alexander (1984). *From Prince to King: Royal Succession in the House of Saud in the Twentieth Century.* New York University Press.

Bligh, Alexander (1985). 'The Saudi religious elite (ulama) as participant in the political system of the kingdom', *International Journal of Middle East Studies*, 1, 37–50.

Borowiec, Andrew (1995). 'Crucial ally's economy seems lost in the desert', *Insight on the News* , 26 June. Carried by Northern Light Technology LLC Internet news service: Special Collection (document ID: ZZ19970430010162949).

Boustany, Nora (1994). 'Traditional Saudis take dim view of attempts to modernize Islam', *Washington Post*, 24 Aug., A22.

Bowcott, Owen and David Hirst (1996). 'Fallout with Saudis forces BBC off air', *Guardian Weekly*, 14 Apr., 1.

BP Amoco (1999a). '1998 in Review', *BP Amoco Statistical Review of World Energy 1999* (Internet edn, June.)

http://www.bpamoco.com/worldenergy/review/index.htm (when BP Amoco)

(BP home page: http://www.bp.com)

BP Amoco (1999b). 'Oil prices: Spot crude prices', *BP Amoco Statistical Review of World Energy 1999* (Internet edn).

http://www.bpamoco.com/worldenergy/oil/index.htm (when BP Amoco)

BP (2001). 'Oil prices: Spot crude prices', *BP Amoco Statistical Review of World Energy 2001* (Internet edn).

http://www.bp.com

Brandreth, Gyles (2000). 'Farewell to riches of the earth', *Electronic Telegraph*, 25 June. http://www.telegraph.co.uk/et?ac=000148889415120&pg=/home.html

Brenchley, Thomas Frank (1966). Letter ('confidential') to Morgan C. G. Man, British Embassy, Jedda, 7 June (no ref.); FO 371/185477.

Brown, Colin and Michael Sheridan (1996). 'Saudi threats forced Britain's hand', *Independent*, 5 Jan., 2.

Brown, Colin, Patrick Cockburn, Steve Crawshaw and Phil Davison (1996). 'Secret deals in arms and bananas that condemned a man to exile', *Independent*, 5 Jan., 1.

Brummer, Alex (1999). 'BAe shares tumble over fears for Saudi arms deal', *Guardian Unlimited*, 19 Feb. Internet site of the *Guardian* and *Observer.*

http://www.guardian.co.uk/Archive/Article/0,4273,3824257,00.html

Buchan, James (1981). 'The return of the Ikhwan, 1979' in David Holden and Richard Johns, *The House of Saud.* London: Sidgwick & Jackson.

Burtless, Gary (1996). 'Worsening American income inequality: Is world trade to blame?', *The Brookings Review*, 14 (2), (Spring), 26–31. Brookings Institution Internet site.

http://www.brookings.edu/press/review/burtsp96.htm

Butter, David (1995). 'Battling for Arab satellite space', *Middle East Economic Digest*, 10 Nov., 4–5.

Byman, Daniel L. and Jerrold D. Green (1999a). *Political Violence and Stability in the States of the Northern Persian Gulf.* Santa Monica, CA: RAND publication MR-1021-OSD, 1999.

———— (1999b). 'The enigma of political stability in the Persian Gulf monarchies', *Middle East Review of International Affairs*, 3 (3), (September).

http://www.biu.ac.il/SOC/besa/meria/journal/1999/issue3/ jv3n3a3.html

Camdessus, Michel (1997). 'Camdessus calls for actions to make globalization work for workers'. Excerpts of address to the World Confederation of Labor, Bangkok, 2 Dec., *IMF Survey*, 15 Dec., 391–2.

———— (1998). 'Toward a new financial architecture for a globalized world'. Transcript of address at the Royal Institute of International Affairs, London, 8 May. IMF Internet site.

http://www.imf.org/external/np/speeches/1998/050898.HTM

Cave, Andrew (1999). 'Saudi forced to pay $1.1bn over BCCI', *Daily Telegraph* (UK), 25 June, 33.

CGES (2001). Summary of *Oil Market Prospects*, 6 (11), (Nov.). Internet site of the Centre for Global Energy Studies.

(CGES home page: http://www.cges.co.uk)

Chalmers, John (2002). 'U.S., Russia at odds over war on terrorism', Reuters news service, 3 Feb.

Champion, Daryl (1995). 'The House of Saud: Legitimacy and the contemporary Islamic challenge', unpublished Honours thesis, Department of Politics, Macquarie University (Sydney).

Chandler, Clay (1994). 'Desert shock: Saudis are cash-poor', *Washington Post*, 28 Oct., A1.

Chaudhry, Kiren Aziz (1997). *The Price of Wealth: Economies and Institutions in the Middle East.* Ithaca NY: Cornell University Press.

CIA (1997). *World Factbook, 1997* (Internet edn). Annual publication of the CIA Directorate of Intelligence.

World Factbook home page:

http://www.odci.gov/cia/publications/factbook/index.html

(CIA home page: http://www.cia.gov/index.html)

CIA (1999). *World Factbook, 1999* (Internet edn). Annual publication of the CIA Directorate of Intelligence.

CIA (2000). Country Profiles: Saudi Arabia ('Transnational issues'), *World Factbook, 2000* (Internet edn). Annual publication of the CIA Directorate of Intelligence.
http://www.odci.gov/cia/publications/factbook/geos/sa.html

CNN (1996a). 'FBI director revisits Saudis to check on bombing probe', *CNN Interactive*, 13 July. Cable & News Network Internet service.
http://www.cnn.com/WORLD/9607/13/saudi.bombing/index.html
(CNN home page: http://www.cnn.com/)

CNN (1996b). '"Frustrated" FBI pulls out of Saudi blast probe', *CNN Interactive*, 1 Nov. Cable & News Network Internet service.
http://www.cnn.com/WORLD/9611/01/fbi.saudi/index.html

CNN (1996c). 'Saudis allege Iran behind bombing', *CNN Interactive*, 12 Dec. Cable & News Network Internet service.
http://cnn.com/WORLD/9612/12/saudi.iran/index.html

CNN (1997). 'Reno, Freeh critical of Saudi bombing probe', *CNN Interactive*, 23 Jan. Cable & News Network Internet service.
http://www.cnn.com/WORLD/9701/23/saudi/index.html

CNN (1998a). 'Saudi official says countrymen responsible for Khobar Towers bomb', *CNN Interactive*, 22 May. Cable & News Network Internet service.
http://www.cnn.com/WORLD/meast/9805/22/khobar.towers/

CNN (1998b). 'U.S. probe of blast in Saudi Arabia falling apart', *CNN Interactive*, 21 June. Cable & News Network Internet service.
http://www.cnn.com/WORLD/meast/9806/21/saudi.khobar/index.html

Cockburn, Leslie and Andrew Cockburn (1994). 'Royal Mess', *New Yorker*, 70 (39), (28 Nov.), 54–72.

Cockburn, Patrick (1994). 'Britain denies leading Saudi dissident asylum', *Independent on Sunday*, 27 Nov., 3.

Cohen, Nick and Robert Fisk (1996). 'Saudis plotted to kill me, says dissident', *Independent on Sunday*, 7 Jan., 1.

Collett, Naomi (1995). 'The stark economic choices facing the Gulf states', *Middle East International*, no. 508 (8 Sept.), 17–18.

Committee to Protect Journalists (1997). Letter from the Committee to Protect Journalists to Egyptian president Hosni Mubarak, 17 Sept. Distributed electronically by MSANews as 'CPJ condemns prosecution of journalists', 18 Sept.
MSANews home page: http://www.mynet.net/~msanews/

Cooper, John (1995a). 'The new face of the Saudi state', *Middle East Economic Digest*, 18 Aug., 2–3.

——— (1995b). 'First steps on the road to recovery', *Middle East Economic Digest*, 3 Nov., 34–8.

Cordesman, Anthony H. (1997). *Saudi Arabia: Guarding the Desert Kingdom.* Boulder, CO: Westview Press.

Cranston, W.P. (1966). Letter ('confidential') to A.B. Urwick, British Embassy, Amman, 22 Aug., (sender's file ref. 1027/22/8); FO 371/185514.

Curtiss, Richard H. (1995). 'Four years after massive war expenses Saudi Arabia gets its second wind', *Washington Report on Middle East Affairs*, Sept., 48–52.

al-Dabbagh, Taher (1999). Quoted in 'Saudi assets abroad at around 420 bln-economist', Reuters, 21 Feb. Distributed electronically by Reuters (Business Briefing Select), 21 Feb. 1999.

Daily Star (2001a). '"Arab Afghans" to the slaughter?', Arab Press Review, 23 Nov., 6.

Daily Star (2001b). 'Sympathy and loathing for the foreign fighters', Arab Press Review, 27 Nov., 6.

Daily Star (2001c). 'Stern Saudi warning to America', Arab Press Review, 28 Nov., 6.

Davies, Hugh (1996). 'Saudis "are blocking US inquiry into Riyadh blast"', *Electronic Telegraph*, 16 July.

http://www.telegraph.co.uk:80/et?ac=000148889415120&rtmo=lnHlbuPt&atmo=FFFFFFFX&pg=/ixworld.html

Dekmejian, R. Hrair (1985). *Islam in Revolution: Fundamentalism in the Arab World.* Syracuse University Press.

—— (1994). 'The rise of political Islamism in Saudi Arabia', *The Middle East Journal*, 48 (4), (Autumn), 627–43.

Donner, Fred McGraw (1981). *The Early Islamic Conquests.* Princeton University Press.

Dourian, Kate (1998). 'Low oil price seen forcing Saudi reform', Reuters news service, 14 Oct.

DPA (1997). 'Bahrain expels German agency reporter for article', Deutsche Presse Agentur. Distributed electronically by Reuters (Middle East news briefs, article ref. no.: 001053426425), 1 July 1997.

DPA (2001). 'Saudi cleric issues fatwa for Muslims to protect Taleban', *Daily Star* (Beirut), 5 Oct., 5. (Deutsche Presse Agentur news agency, 4 Oct.)

The Economist (1994). 'Challenge to the House of Saud', 8 Oct., 71.

The Economist (1995). 'Saudi Arabia's future: The cracks in the kingdom', 18 Mar., 21–7.

The Economist (1997a). 'South–East Asia in denial', 18 Oct., 13.

The Economist (1997b). 'The blind, the deaf and the dumb', 18 Oct., 27–8.

The Economist (1998a). 'The old man of Java', 10 Jan., 21.

The Economist (1998b). 'Korean glums', 10 Jan., 22.

The Economist (1998c). 'Asia's coming explosion', 21 Feb., 13.

The Economist (1998d). 'East Asia's new faultlines', 14 Mar., 13–14.

The Economist (1998e). 'Suharto's family values', 14 Mar., 27–8.

The Economist (1998f). 'Towards a new financial system: The perils of global capital', 11 Apr., 62–4.

The Economist (1998g). 'Two kinds of openness', 12 Sept., 96.

The Economist (1998h). 'Indonesia: Cleared out', 26 Sept., 31.

The Economist (1999a). 'A global war against bribery', 16 Jan., 21–3.

The Economist (1999b). Abdullah and the ebbing tide', 23 Jan., 43–4.

The Economist (1999c). 'Sick patients, warring doctors', 18 Sept., 81–2.

The Economist (2000a). 'Globalising'. Business this week, 5 Feb.–11 Feb. (e-mail edn, 10 Feb.).

The Economist (2000b). 'Globalisation'. Business this week, 6 May–12 May (e-mail edn, 12 May).

The Economist (2000c). Business this week, 1–7 July (e-mail edn, 6 July).

The Economist (2000d). 'Venezuela on a gusher' (Internet edn), 23–29 Sept.

Eigen, Peter (1998). Statement on the role of the Corruption Perceptions Index, Transparency International (Internet site). Berlin, 22 Sept.

http://www.transparency.de/documents/cpi/cpi-role.html

EIU (1997). 'Saudi Arabia investment: New impetus in privatisations', *Country Alert*, Economist Intelligence Unit (EIU Electronic). Distributed electronically by Reuters (Business Briefing Select), 14 Aug. 1997.

EIU (1999a). 'Saudi Arabia: Crude prices undermine budget and growth', *Country Report*, Economist Intelligence Unit, 11 Mar.

EIU (1999b). 'Saudi Arabia: A riyal battle', *Business Middle East*, Economist Intelligence Unit, 1 Apr.

EIU (1999c). 'Saudi Arabia economy: Policy towards private sector investment', *Country Briefing/Country Forecast*, Economist Intelligence Unit, 9 Apr.

EIU (1999d). 'Saudi Arabia finance: Oil price rise barely boosts budget', *Country Briefing*, Economist Intelligence Unit, 3 May.

EIU (1999e). 'USB-Samba bank merger thrown into doubt', *Country Briefing/Business Middle East*, Economist Intelligence Unit, 20 May.

EIU (1999f). 'Saudi Arabia: 5-year forecast table', *Country View/Country Forecast*, Economist Intelligence Unit, 14 July.

EIU (1999g). 'Saudi Arabia: Country forecast summary', *Country View*, Economist Intelligence Unit, 14 July.

EIU (1999h). 'Saudi Arabia economy: Recovery seen next year', *Country Briefing*, Economist Intelligence Unit, 16 July.

EIU (1999i). 'Saudi Arabia Industry: Internet growth lagging', *Country Briefing*, Economist Intelligence Unit, 28 July.

EIU (1999j). 'Saudi Arabia economy: Little prospect of positive GDP growth in 1999', *Country Briefing*, Economist Intelligence Unit, 9 Aug.

EIU (1999k). 'Saudi Arabia: Country Outlook', *Country View*, Economist Intelligence Unit, 20 Aug.

EIU (1999L). 'Saudi Arabia: Quarterly Economic Indicators', *Country Background/Country Report*, Economist Intelligence Unit, 20 Aug.

EIU (1999m). 'Real GDP growth around the world (%)'. Economist Intelligence Unit, 14 Dec.

EIU (2000a). 'Saudi Arabia: Country risk summary', *Country View*, Economist Intelligence Unit, 3 Apr. Distributed electronically by Reuters (Business Briefing Select), 3 Apr. 2000.

EIU (2000b). 'Saudi Arabia: The haj business', *Country Briefing/Business Middle East*, Economist Intelligence Unit, 12 Apr.

Electronic Telegraph (1998a). '100 Muslim pilgrims die in stampede at bridge', 10 Apr.

(*ET* home page: http://www.telegraph.co.uk)

Electronic Telegraph (1998b). 'Arab suspect remanded at extradition hearing', 29 Sept.

Emirates News (1998). 'Prince Abdullah calls for action on oil prices', 9 Dec. Distributed electronically by Reuters (Business Briefing Select), 9 Dec. 1998.

Esposito, John L. (1991). *Islam and Politics*, 3rd edn. Syracuse University Press.

Evans, Kathy (1994). 'Saudi refugees fear for families', *Guardian*, 26 Apr., 12.

——— (1996). 'Shifting sands at the House of Saud', *The Middle East*, 253 (Feb.), 6–9.

Fabietti, Ugo (1982). 'Sedentarisation as a means of detribalisation: Some policies of the Saudi Arabian government towards the nomads' in Tim Niblock, ed., *State, Society and Economy in Saudi Arabia*. New York: St. Martin's Press.

Facts on File (1993). Item on 'reconciliation accord' between the Saudi regime and the Shiite Reform Movement. 18 Nov., 859.

Fagan, Mary (2000). 'Sheikh Yamani predicts price crash as age of oil ends', *Electronic Telegraph*, 25 June.
http://www.telegraph.co.uk/news/
main.jhtml;$sessionid$K2EDKGPLKMDLJQFIQMFCFGGAVCBQ
YIV0?xml=%2Fnews%2F2000%2F06%2F25%2Fnoil25.xml

Fahmy, Miral (2001). 'Saudi budget deficit seen rising on weak oil', Reuters news service, 5 Dec.

Fandy, Mamoun (1999). *Saudi Arabia and the Politics of Dissent*. New York: St. Martin's Press.

Fischer, Stanley (1998). 'Reforming world finance: Lessons from a crisis', *The Economist*, 3 Oct., 19–23.

Fishlock, Trevor (1996). 'Saudis destroy article critical of royal rulers', *Electronic Telegraph*, 19 July.
http://www.telegraph.co.uk:80/et?ac=000148889415120&rtmo=aqdaKh5J&atmo=FFFFFFFX&pg=/et/96/7/19/wsaud19.html

Fisk, Robert (1996a). 'Arab rebel leader warns the British: "Get out of the Gulf"', *Independent*, 10 July, 1.

———— (1996b). 'Why we reject the West—by the Saudi's fiercest Arab critic', *Independent*, 10 July, 14.

Fuchs, Gerhard and Andrew M. Koch (1996). 'The globalization of telecommunications and the issues of regulatory reform' in Eleonore Kofman and Gillian Youngs, eds, *Globalization: Theory and Practice*. London: Pinter.

Gardner, Frank (2000). 'Saudis "defeating" internet porn', BBC News Online, 10 May.
http://news6.thdo.bbc.co.uk/hi/english/world/middle_east/newsid_742000/742798.stm

de Gaury, Gerald (1966). *Faisal: King of Saudi Arabia*. London: Arthur Barker.

Gause, F. Gregory (1994). *Oil Monarchies: Domestic and Security Challenges in the Arab Gulf States*. New York: Council on Foreign Relations Press.

———— (1997). 'The political economy of national security in the GCC states' in Gary G. Sick and Lawrence G. Potter, eds, *The Persian Gulf at the Millennium: Essays in Politics, Economy, Security, and Religion*. New York: St. Martin's Press.

———— (2000). 'Saudi Arabia over a barrel', *Foreign Affairs*, 79 (3), (May/June), 80–94.

George, Alan (1994). 'Water scandals', *The Middle East*, 238 (Oct.), 30.

Globalvision (1993). *The Arming of Saudi Arabia* (video documentary), 'Timewatch', SBS-TV (Aust.), 25 Oct.

Glubb, Lt.–Gen. Sir John Bagot (1959). *Britain and the Arabs: A Study of Fifty Years, 1908 to 1958*. London: Hodder & Stoughton.

———— (1960). *War in the Desert: An R.A.F. Frontier Campaign*. London: Hodder & Stoughton.

Graham, Bradley (1998). 'U.S. to avoid strikes from Saudi bases', *Washington Post*, 9 Feb., 1.

Gray, Joanne (1999a). 'Camdessus resignation sparks fierce race in EU', *Australian Financial Review*, 11 Nov., 1.

———— (1999b). 'Leader departs an IMF that still has much to learn', *Australian Financial Review*, 11 Nov., 14.

Gresh, Alain (2000). 'The world invades Saudi Arabia', *Le Monde Diplomatique*, Apr. edn (*Guardian Weekly*, supplement), 4–5.

Guardian Unlimited (2001a). 'Saudi Arabia: No US attacks from our air bases', 23 Sept. Internet site of the *Guardian* and *Observer*. http://www.guardian.co.uk/Archive/Article/0,4273,4262918,00.html (*Guardian Unlimited* home page: http://www.guardian.co.uk/)

Guardian Unlimited (2001b). 'Saudi Arabia refuses to be US strike base', 3 Oct. Internet site of the *Guardian* and *Observer*. http://www.guardian.co.uk/Archive/Article/0,4273,4269682,00.html

Guardian Unlimited (2002). 'A year of attacks on expats', 30 Jan. Internet site of the *Guardian* and *Observer*. http://www.guardian.co.uk/Archive/Article/0,4273,4345721,00.html

Guardian Weekly (1996). 'Saudi blast kills 19 US servicemen', 7 July, 3.

Habib, John S. (1978). *Ibn Sa'ud's Warriors of Islam: The Ikhwan of Najd and Their Role in the Creation of the Sa'udi Kingdom, 1910–1930*. Leiden: E.J. Brill.

Habiby, Margot (1999). 'Major producers say oil output cut figure final', *Economic Times* (India), 17 Mar. Distributed electronically by Reuters (Business Briefing Select), 17 Mar. 1999.

Halliday, Fred (1982). 'A curious and close liaison: Saudi Arabia's relations with the United States' in Tim Niblock, ed., *State, Society and Economy in Saudi Arabia*. New York: St. Martin's Press.

———— (1994). Book Review: *Saudi Arabia: Government, Society and the Gulf Crisis* by Mordechai Abir (London: Routledge, 1993), *Middle Eastern Studies*, 30 (3), 691–2.

Hanley, Charles J. (2002). 'America and Saudi Arabia: They've made it work, but for how much longer?' Associated Press news agency, 28 Jan.

Hanna, Jim (1999). 'More wealth held in fewer hands', *Canberra Times*, 24 Sept., 21.

Hardy, Roger (1992). *Arabia after the Storm: Internal Stability of the Gulf Arab States*. Middle East Programme report. London: Royal Institute of International Affairs.

Hart, Parker T. (1998). *Saudi Arabia and the United States: Birth of a Security Partnership*. Bloomington: Indiana University Press.

Hartcher, Peter (1999). 'Camdessus pulled fund through intact', *Australian Financial Review*, 11 Nov., 14.

Hartung, William D. (1996). 'Inc. mercenaries: How a US company props up the House of Saud', *The Progressive*, 60 (4), (April), 26–8.

Hedges, Chris (2001). '"Bin Laden!" becomes rallying cry for France's dispossessed', *International Herald Tribune*, 17 Oct., 9.

al-Hegelan, Abdelrahman and Monte Palmer (1985). 'Bureaucracy and development in Saudi Arabia', *The Middle East Journal*, 39 (1), 48–68.

Helms, Christine Moss (1981). *The Cohesion of Saudi Arabia: Evolution of Political Identity*. London: Croom Helm.

Henderson, Simon (1994). *After King Fahd: Succession in Saudi Arabia* (WINEP Policy Paper no. 37). Washington, DC: Washington Institute for Near East Policy.

Henry, Clement M. (1999a). 'Guest Editor's Introduction', *Thunderbird International Business Review*, 41 (4), (July/Aug.), 1–12.

——— (1999b). 'Islamic finance and globalisation: Potential variations on the "Washington consensus"'. Paper presented at the 18th Annual Conference of the Australasian Middle East Studies Association, The University of Sydney, 23–24 July.

——— (1999c). 'Islamic finance in the dialectics of globalisation: Potential variations on the "Washington consensus"', *Journal of Arabic, Islamic and Middle Eastern Studies*, 5 (2), 25–37.

Hiro, Dilip (1993). 'Saudi dissenters go public', *The Nation*, 28 June.

Hirst, David (1996). 'Dangers of supping with the Americans', *Guardian Weekly*, 7 July, 12.

——— (1999). 'Fall of the house of Fahd', *Guardian Unlimited*, 11 Aug. Internet site of the *Guardian* and *Observer*.
http://www.guardianunlimited.co.uk/Archive/Article/0,4273,3891425,00.html

Hoagland, Jim (2001). 'The true cost of Arab oil is more than Americans can afford', *International Herald Tribune*, 26 Nov., 12 (from the *Washington Post*).

Hodgson, M.G.S. (1974). *The Venture of Islam: Conscience and History in a World Civilization* (3 vols). Chicago University Press.

Holden, David and Richard Johns (1981). *The House of Saud*. London: Sidgwick & Jackson.

Holderness, T.W. (1914). India Office memorandum, 16 April, no. 1396/1914; L/P & S/10, 2182/1913, Pt. II. Quoted in Gary Troeller (1976), *The Birth of Saudi Arabia: Britain and the Rise of the House of Sa'ud*. London: Frank Cass, p. 58.

Hopkins, Nick and Richard Norton-Taylor (2001). 'Faulty intelligence', *Guardian Unlimited*, 29 Nov. Internet site of the *Guardian* and *Observer*.
http://www.guardian.co.uk/Archive/Article/0,4273,4309593,00.html

Hopwood, Derek (1982). 'The ideological basis: Ibn Abd al-Wahhab's Muslim revivalism' in Tim Niblock, ed., *State, Society and Economy in Saudi Arabia*. New York: St. Martin's Press.

Hotten, Russell (1996). 'Riyadh pressured defence firm', *Independent*, 5 Jan., 2.

——— and Colin Brown (1996). 'Vickers director our man in Saudi', *Independent*, 6 Jan., 1.

Hourani, Albert (1990). 'Conclusion: Tribes and states in Islamic history' in *Tribes and State Formation in the Middle East*, eds P.S. Khoury and J. Kostiner. Berkeley and Los Angeles: University of California Press.

———— (1991). *A History of the Arab Peoples*. London: Faber and Faber.

Howarth, David (1964). *The Desert King: A Life of Ibn Saud*. London: Collins.

HRW [Human Rights Watch] (1998). 'Saudi Arabia: Human rights developments'. *World Report, 1998*.

http://www.hrw.org/hrw/worldreport/Mideast-08.htm#P975_166296 (HRW home page: http://www.hrw.org/hrw/index.html)

HRW (1999). 'Saudi Arabia: Human rights developments'. *World Report, 1999*.

http://www.hrw.org/hrw/worldreport99/mideast/saudi.html

HRW (2000). 'Saudi Arabia: Human rights developments'. *World Report, 2000*.

http://www.hrw.org/hrw/wr2k/Mena-08.htm

Hudson, Michael C. (1977). *Arab Politics: The Search for Legitimacy*. New Haven: Yale University Press.

———— (1995). 'Regime responses to political Islam'. Paper presented at the 14th Annual Conference of the Australasian Middle East Studies Association, Macquarie University (Sydney), 22–23 Sept.

Hussain, Thomas (1998). 'Gulf's oil industry's slick strategies', *Gulf Business* (Internet edn), Sept.

http://www.gulfbusiness.com/issues/sept98/gulf.html

Hutchcroft, Paul D. (1998). *Booty Capitalism: The Politics of Banking in the Philippines*. Ithaca, NY: Cornell University Press.

Huyette, Summer Scott (1985). *Political Adaptation in Saudi Arabia: A Study of the Council of Ministers*. Boulder, CO: Westview Press.

Ibn Khaldun. *The Maqaddimah: An Introduction to History*, trans. Franz Rosenthal (3 vols), 2nd edn (1967). Bollingen Foundation Series no. 43. Princeton University Press.

Ignatius, David (1981a). 'Royal payoffs: Some Saudi princes pressure oil firms for secret payments', *Wall Street Journal*, 1 May, 1.

———— (1981b). 'Royal payoffs: Big Saudi oil deal with Italy collapses after fee plan is bared', *Wall Street Journal*, 4 May, 1.

IMF (1999a). *International Financial Statistics* (June). Washington DC: International Monetary Fund Statistics Department.

IMF (1999b). *International Financial Statistics* (July). Washington DC: International Monetary Fund Statistics Department.

IMF (1999c). SDR/Fund Rates. Internet site of the International Monetary Fund.

http://www.imf.org/external/np/tre/sdr/sdr.htm

IMF (2000a). *International Financial Statistics* (February). Washington DC: International Monetary Fund Statistics Department.

IMF (2000b). *International Financial Statistics* (March). Washington DC: International Monetary Fund Statistics Department.

IMF (2001). 'IMF concludes 2001 Article IV consultation with Saudi Arabia', Public

Information Notice (PIN) No. 01/119, 7 Nov.

IMF (2002). 'IMF concludes 2002 Article IV consultation with Saudi Arabia', Public Information Notice (PIN) No. 02/121, 25 Oct.

http://www.imf.org/external/np/sec/pn/2002/pn02121.htm

IMF Survey (1997a). 'World Bank development strategy targets corruption, environment, and institution-building', 26 May, 162–3.

IMF Survey (1997b). 'Forces of globalization must be embraced', 26 May, 153–8.

IMF Survey (1997c). 'Denver summit highlights global cooperation and integration', 7 July, 204–5.

IMF Survey (1997d). 'Corruption linked to capital spending can slow growth', 1 Dec., 375–7.

IMF Survey (1998). 'Comprehensive strategy is needed to fight global corruption', 8 June, 182–3.

IMF Survey (1999). 'Improvements in global financial system hinge on transparency and management of risk', 5 Sept., 110.

Impact International (1993). 'Shi'i dissidents to return home', 12 Nov.– 9 Dec., 14.

Independent (1994). 'Saudi Arabia bans all satellite dishes', 29 June, 12.

Independent (1996). 'Saudis step up pressure over Masari', 1 Apr., 2.

International Herald Tribune (2001). 'Saudis and terrorism', 15 Oct., 8. (Editorial reprinted from the *New York Times*, 14 Oct.)

International Herald Tribune (2002a). 'Out of Saudi Arabia?', 22 Jan., 6. (Editorial reprinted from the *Washington Post*, 21 Jan.)

International Herald Tribune (2002b). 'Taliban prisoners', 26–27 Jan., 4. (Editorial reprinted from the *Washington Post*, 25 Jan. With extract by Robert Fisk, 'Other comment: Prisoners at Guantanamo', reprinted from the *Independent*, London.)

IPR (1997a). 'Recent Consultative Council meeting', IPR Strategic Business Information Database, 20 May. Distributed electronically by Reuters (Middle East News Briefs, article ref. no.: 001031466873), 20 May. 1997.

IPR (1997b). 'Inauguration of the King Fahd Islamic Center in Gibraltar', IPR Strategic Business Information Database, 13 Aug. Distributed electronically by Reuters (Business Briefing Select), 13 Aug. 1997.

IPR (1997c). 'King Fahd Islamic Center in Malaga', IPR Strategic Business Information Database, 13 Aug. Distributed electronically by Reuters (Business Briefing Select), 13 Aug. 1997.

IPR (1997d). 'Saudi Arabia: Full membership in the World Trade Organization just in the year 2002', IPR Strategic Business Information Database, 17 Sept. Distributed electronically by Reuters (Business Briefing Select), 17 Sept. 1997.

IPR (1997e). 'Imam of the Grand Mosque in Makkah visits the United States', IPR Strategic Business Information Database, 14 Oct. Distributed electronically by Reuters (Business Briefing Select), 14 Oct. 1997.

IPR (1999a). 'Deficit hits 9.7% of 1999 budget', IPR Strategic Business Information Database, reporting from *Al-Hayat* (18 Feb). Distributed electronically by Reuters (Business Briefing Select), 22 Feb. 1999.

IPR (1999b). 'Slow GDP growth in 1999', IPR Strategic Business Information Database, reporting from *Al-Hayat* (18 Feb). Distributed electronically by Reuters (Business Briefing Select), 22 Feb. 1999.

Isa, Mariam (2001a). 'Saudi hands seen tied against media attacks', Reuters news service, 1 Nov.

———— (2001b). 'Saudi Arabia dampens hopes of quick WTO entry', Reuters news service, 4 Nov.

Islami, A. Reza S. and Rostam Mehraban Kavoussi (1984). *The Political Economy of Saudi Arabia.* Seattle, WA: Department of Near Eastern Languages and Civilization, University of Washington.

Jabbra, Joseph G. (1989). 'Bureaucracy and development in the Arab World', *Journal of Asian and African Studies*, 24 (1–2), 1–11.

Jafri, S. Husain M. (1989). *Origins and Development of Shi'a Islam.* Qum, Iran: Ansariyan Publications.

Jehl, Douglas (1996). 'U.S. military in Saudi Arabia digs into the sand', *New York Times*, 9 Nov., 3.

———— (2001a). 'Saudi princes assail U.S. media for linking kingdom to terrorism', *International Herald Tribune*, 21 Dec., 10.

———— (2001b). 'Saudis ignored fighters', *International Herald Tribune*, 28 Dec., 1.

Johnston, Philip and Sean O'Neill (2002). '1998 bomb suspects still in Britain', *Electronic Telegraph*, 30 Nov. http://www.portal.telegraph.co.uk/news/main.jhtml?xml= %2Fnews%2F2002%2F11%2F30%2Fwkenya430.xml&secureRefresh =true&_requestid=37960

Jury, Louise (1996). 'Tories charged with appeasing Saudi rulers', *Independent*, 5 Jan., 1.

Kalicki, Jan H. (1999). 'The US and the Gulf: Trade, investment and economy'. Transcript of address to Gulf '99 Conference, Abu Dhabi, 10 Mar.

USIA Washington File, 15 Mar. (Internet site of the US Information Agency).
http://www.usia.gov/regional/nea/mena/kala315.htm

Kanovsky, Eliyahu (1994). *The Economy of Saudi Arabia: Troubled Present, Grim Future* (WINEP Policy Paper no. 38). Washington, DC: The Washington Institute for Near East Policy.

Karl, Terry Lynn (1997). *The Paradox of Plenty: Oil Booms and Petro-States.* Berkeley and Los Angeles: University of California Press.

Kay, Shirley (1982). 'Social change in modern Saudi Arabia' in Tim Niblock, ed., *State, Society and Economy in Saudi Arabia.* London and Exeter: Croom Helm/Centre for Arab Gulf Studies.

Kechichian, Joseph K. (1986). 'The role of the ulama in the politics of an Islamic state: The case of Saudi Arabia', *International Journal of Middle East Studies*, 18, 53–71.

———— (1990). 'Islamic revivalism and change in Saudi Arabia: Juhayman al-'Utaybi's "letters" to the Saudi people', *The Muslim World*, 80 (1), (Jan.), 1–16.

———— (1999). 'Trends in Saudi national security', *The Middle East Journal*, 53 (2), (Spring), 232–53.

Kedourie, Elie (1987). *England and the Middle East: The Destruction of the Ottoman Empire 1914–1921*, 2nd edn. Boulder, CO: Westview Press.

Kelsey, Tim and Peter Koenig (1994a). 'Job fears kept Saudi report secret', *Independent*, 11 Oct., 2

———— (1994b). 'US firm "bribed" princes in $6bn helicopter deal', *Independent*, 11 Oct., 2

Kelso, Paul and David Pallister (2002). 'Britons tortured by Saudis in bombings inquiry fiasco', *Guardian Unlimited*, 30 Jan. Internet site of *The Guardian* and *Observer.*
http://www.guardian.co.uk/Archive/Article/0,4273,4345815,00.html

Kelso, Paul, David Pallister, Brian Whitaker, Richard Norton-Taylor and Andrew Osborn (2002). 'How friends who liked a drink were blamed for wave of anti-western terror', *Guardian Unlimited*, 30 Jan. Internet site of the *Guardian* and *Observer.*
http://www.guardian.co.uk/Archive/Article/0,4273,4345722,00.html

Kemp, Murray C. and Koji Shimomura (1999). 'The internationalization of the world economy and its implication for national welfare', *Review of International Economics*, 7 (1), 1–7.

Khashoggi, Jamal (2001a). 'Once again Ramadan gives Muslims something to lament', *Daily Star* (Beirut), 23 Nov., 6.

———— (2001b). 'United States and Saudi Arabia on the brink of parting ways after 60 years', *Daily Star* (Beirut), 12 Dec., 5.

———— (2002). 'Saudi Arabia gears up to act on poverty', *Daily Star* (Beirut), 30 Nov., R5.

Khazen, Jihad (1996). Interview in *Index on Censorship*, Feb. edn. Available online at: http://www.indexoncensorship.org/issue296/saudi. html

Kofman, Eleonore and Gillian Youngs (1996). *Globalization: Theory and Practice*. London: Pinter.

Kostiner, Joseph (1990). 'Transforming dualities: State formation in Saudi Arabia' in *Tribes and State Formation in the Middle East*, eds P.S. Khoury and J. Kostiner. Berkeley and Los Angeles: University of California Press.

—————— (1993). *The Making of Saudi Arabia, 1916-1936: From Chieftaincy to Monarchical State*. New York: Oxford University Press.

Krimly, Rayed (1999). 'The political economy of adjusted priorities: Declining oil revenues and Saudi fiscal policies', *The Middle East Journal*, 53 (2), (Spring), 254–67.

Kronemer, Alexander (1997). 'Inventing a working class in Saudi Arabia', *Monthly Labor Review*, 20 (5), May. Carried by Northern Light Technology LLC Internet news service: Special Collection (document ID: LW19970829010001725).

Lacey, Robert (1981). *The Kingdom*. London: Hutchinson.

Lackner, Helen (1978). *A House Built on Sand: A Political Economy of Saudi Arabia*. London: Ithaca Press.

Lancaster, John (1998). 'Saudi absolves Iran of 1996 bombing that killed 19 US soldiers', *Washington Post*, 23 May, A6.

Lapidus, Ira M. (1990). 'Tribes and state formation in Islamic history' in *Tribes and State Formation in the Middle East*, eds P.S. Khoury and J. Kostiner. Berkeley and Los Angeles: University of California Press.

Laurence, Michael (1999). 'Spending: Drowning in debt', *Business Review Weekly* (Aust.), 21 (32), 20 Aug.

Lawson, Kirsten (1999). 'Howard defends adviser's US posting' *Canberra Times*, 6 Dec., 1, 2.

Lerrick, Alison and Q. Javed Mian (1982). *Saudi Business and Labor Law: Its Interpretation and Application*. London: Graham & Trotman.

Liberty for the Muslim World (1993). 'The judiciary and human rights in Saudi Arabia. Special report on the occasion of the Second International Conference on Human Rights in Vienna, 14 to 25 June 1993', published by Liberty for the Muslim World (London). http://www.lmw.org/Saudi%20Judiciary.html (when active) (Liberty home page: http://www.lmw.org (when active))

Library of Congress (1992). *Saudi Arabia: A Country Study*, ed. Helen Chapin Metz. Washington DC: Federal Research Division, Library of Congress (Internet site).

http://lcweb2.loc.gov/cgi-bin/query/r?frd/cstdy:@field(DOCID+sa0047)

Lichfield, John (1996). 'Masari "ejected from own dissident group"', *Independent*, 7 Mar., 6.

Lindholm, Charles (1996). *The Islamic Middle East: An Historical Anthropology*. Oxford: Blackwell.

Lockwood, Christopher (1996). 'Shia backlash puts Saudi regime under new threat', *Electronic Telegraph*, 30 Aug.

http://www.telegraph.co.uk:80/et?ac=000148889415120&rtmo=qXtsqRX9&atmo=ttttlxLd&pg=/et/96/8/30/wsaud30.html

——— (1997). 'Anger over hajj deaths turns on House of Saud', *Electronic Telegraph*, 17 Apr.

http://www.telegraph.co.uk:80/et?ac=000148889415120&rtmo=0GRib20q&atmo=hhhhhhhe&pg=/et/97/4/17/wmecc17.html

Long, David E. (1991). 'Stability in Saudi Arabia', *Current History*, 90 (552), (Jan.), 9–13, 38.

——— (1996). 'A fight to follow Fahd?', *Middle East Insight*, 12 (4–5), (May–Aug.), 62–5.

Looney, Robert E. (1982). *Saudi Arabia's Development Potential*. Lexington, MA: Lexington Books.

——— (1990). *Economic Development in Saudi Arabia: Consequences of the Oil Price Decline*. Greenwich, CT: JAI Press.

Luciani, Giacomo (1987). 'Allocation v. production states: A theoretical framework' in H. Beblawi and G. Luciani, eds, *Nation, State and Integration in the Arab World*, vol. 2: *The Rentier State*. London: Croom Helm.

Macalister, Terry (2000). 'OPEC prepares to raise production', *Guardian Unlimited*, 29 Mar. Internet site of the *Guardian* and *Observer*.

http://www.guardianunlimited.co.uk/Archive/Article/0,4273,3979763,00.html

MacDonald, Fiona (2001). 'Kuwait's government must work harder to pass privatisation bill: economists', Agence France Presse news agency, 6 Dec.

MacFarquhar, Neil (2001). 'Bin Laden's popularity is a problem for Saudi rulers', *International Herald Tribune*, 6–7 Oct., 2.

——— (2002). 'Arab street view: Nothing new from an America that still doesn't understand', *International Herald Tribune*, 1 Feb., 4.

el-Mallakh, Ragaei (1982). *Saudi Arabia: Rush to Development*. London: Croom Helm.

Man, Morgan Charles Garnet (1966a). Letter ('confidential') to T. Frank Brenchley, Foreign Office (Arabian Dept), London, 8 Feb., no. BS1015/3(c); FO 371/185477.

Man, Morgan Charles Garnet (1966b). Letter ('confidential') to T. Frank Brenchley, Foreign Office (Arabian Dept), London, 30 Nov., no. BS1015/25; FO 371/185477.

Mani, A. (1998). 'Curricula enhancement at the higher educational institutions in Singapore'. Paper presented at the Riyadh Conference on Higher Education, 22–25 Feb.

Marshall, Katherine (1998). 'The Asian crisis: Social implications and the agenda ahead' in proceedings of the conference: *Social Implications of the Asian Financial Crisis* (Seoul, 29–31 July), eds Elizabeth Pyon and Hyehoon Lee (EDAP Joint Policy Studies, no. 9). Published by the Korea Development Institute.

Marwan, Khalil (1998). 'Saudis, too, take up the begging bowl', *Muslimedia International*, 16–31 Dec. Muslimedia Internet site archives.
http://www.muslimedia.com/archives/oaw98/saudbeg.htm

May, Barry (1998). 'Gulf Arabs end summit with oil cut pledge', Reuters news service, 9 Dec.

——— (1999). 'Oil price rise boosts Gulf privatisation prospects', Reuters news service, 5 Apr.

McKenna, Barrie (2000). 'Venezuela brings unity to OPEC', *The Globe and Mail* (Toronto), 30 Mar. Distributed electronically by Reuters (Business Briefing Select), 30 Mar.

MEED (1997a). 'Economy: In recovery after dose of intensive care' (*MEED* Special Report: Saudi Arabia), *Middle East Economic Digest*, 21 Mar. Carried by Northern Light Technology LLC Internet news service: Special Collection (document ID: SL19970508170011662). (NL home page: http://www.northernlight.com/)

MEED (1997b). 'Much reform talk, action is pending' (*MEED* Special Report: Saudi Arabia economy), *Middle East Economic Digest*, 15 Sept. Distributed electronically by Reuters (Business Briefing Select), 19 Sept.

MEED (2000). 'In brief: Al-Gosaibi addresses MEED conference', *Middle East Economic Digest*, 7 Apr. Distributed electronically by Reuters (Business Briefing Select), n.d.

The Middle East (1993a). 'Jobs for the boys', 225 (July), 25–8.

The Middle East (1993b). 'Something will turn up', 225 (July), 27.

The Middle East (1994). 'Sabic eyes the future', 238 (Oct.), 22–3.

The Middle East (1995a). 'Saudi Arabia sorts itself out', 242 (Feb), 19–22.

The Middle East (1995b). 'Privatising the business', 244 (Apr.), 24.

The Middle East (1995c). 'Gulf push towards privatisation', 246 (June), 30–1.

The Middle East (1996a). 'Slow but steady progress', 257 (June), 28–9.

The Middle East (1996b). 'Towards the year 2000', 258 (July/Aug.), 27–8.

Middle East Insight (1995). 'Saudi Arabia', Special Edition.

Middle East Monitor (1995). 'A worrisome consensus takes shape', 5 (3), Mar., 3–4.

Middle East Report (1993). 'Pride and prejudice in Saudi Arabia', (Nov.–Dec.), 18–20.

Mideast Mirror (1994). 'Government to revamp information policy', Saudi Arabia section, vol. 8, no. 152, 9 Aug..

Mideast Mirror (1995). 'Could Qatar's palace coup have a domino effect in the Gulf?', Qatar section, vol. 9, no. 123, 29 June.

Milne, Seumas and Ian Black (1996a). 'Arms bosses' secret plot', *Guardian Weekly*, 14 Jan., 10.

———— (1996b). 'UK bows to pressure over dissident', *Guardian Weekly*, 14 Jan., 1.

Mohamedi, Fareed (1993). 'The Saudi economy: A few years yet till doomsday', *Middle East Report*, Nov–Dec., 14–17.

Mohammed, Arshad (2001). 'US team heads to Saudi to discuss anti-terror work', Reuters news service, 6 Dec.

M2 Presswire (1997). 'Saudi Arabia Government—MWL reports billion dollar Saudi support', M2 Communications Ltd, 9 Sept. Distributed electronically by Reuters (Business Briefing Select), 9 Sept., 1997.

Muhammad, Omar Bakri (1997). 'The Saudi Family must pay blood money', Statement from the Al-Muhajiroun organisation (London), 21 Apr.

Muslimedia International (1996a). 'Saudi treachery, court scholars and American military occupation'. Extracts from *Subverting Islam: The Role Of Orientalist Centres*, by Dr Ahmad Ghorab, formerly of King Saud University, Riyadh. Muslimedia Internet site archives.

http://www.muslimedia.com/archives/special98/trechery.htm

(Muslimedia homepage: http://muslimedia.com/mainpage.htm)

Muslimedia International (1996b). 'Fahd's kingdom to become a full US colony', Muslimedia Internet site archives.

http://www.muslimedia.com/archives/oaw98/usbase.htm

Muzaffar, Chandra (1999). Interview by Nigel McCarthy. Report on post-Asian economic crisis Malaysian political economy, 'Dateline', SBS-TV (Aust.), 22 Sept.

Myers, Steven Lee (1997). 'At Saudi base, U.S. digs in, gingerly, for a longer stay', *New York Times*, 29 Dec., 1.

———— (1998). 'Standoff with Iraq: The military. U.S. forces ready to strike', *New York Times*, 4 Feb., 8.

Nando.net (1995). 'Now, stately cricket joins stadium disaster roll', Nando.net/Reuters, 26 Nov.

http://somerset.nando.net/newsroom/sports/oth/1995/oth/mor/feat/archive/112695/mor51596.html

al-Naqeeb, Khaldoun Hasan (1990). *Society and State in the Gulf and Arab Peninsula: A Different Perspective*, trans. L.M. Kenny. London: Routledge and the Centre for Arab Unity Studies.

Nebehay, Stephanie (2000). 'Saudi Arabia defends record at UN rights body', Reuters news service, 6 Apr.

Nehme, Michel G. (1994). 'Saudi development plans between capitalist and Islamic values', *Middle Eastern Studies*, 30 (3), 632–45.

New York Times (1980). 'Saudi prince is said to have made a fortune in business', 16 Apr., A8.

Niblock, Tim (1982). 'Social structure and the development of the Saudi Arabian political system' in Tim Niblock, ed., *State, Society and Economy in Saudi Arabia*. London and Exeter: Croom Helm/Centre for Arab Gulf Studies.

Norton-Taylor, Richard and David Pallister (1999). 'Millions in secret commissions paid out for Saudi arms deal', *Guardian Unlimited*, 4 Mar. Internet site of the *Guardian* and *Observer.*

http://www.guardian.co.uk/Archive/Article/0,4273,3831465,00.html

——— (2002). 'Secret report detailed violence', *Guardian Unlimited*, 31 Jan. Internet site of the *Guardian* and *Observer.*

http://www.guardian.co.uk/Archive/Article/0,4273,4346587,00.html

Nowshirvani, Vahid (1987). 'The yellow brick road: Self-sufficiency or self-enrichment in Saudi agriculture?', *Middle East Report*, Mar–Apr., 7–13.

Nuesse, Andrea (2001). 'Saudi Arabia sheds ambiguities', *Frankfurter Rundschau*/German Newspaper News Service, 22 Oct.

Olson, William J., ed. (1987). *US Strategic Interests in the Gulf Region*. Boulder, CO: Westview Press.

Omer, Mohammed Zayyan (1978). 'Modern Saudi history', Supplement to *Who's Who in Saudi Arabia 1978–79*. Jedda: Tihama.

Osama, Abdul Rahman (1987). *The Dilemma of Development in the Arabian Peninsula.* London: Croom Helm.

O'Sullivan, Edmund (1996). 'Crisis talks end, calm descends' (*MEED* Special Report: Saudi Arabia), *Middle East Economic Digest*, 8 Nov. Carried by Northern Light Technology LLC Internet news service: Special Collection (document ID: ZZ19970731030200687).

Ouattara, Alassane D. (1999). 'The political dimensions of economic reforms: Conditions for successful adjustment'. Transcript of keynote address, Berlin, 9 June. IMF Internet site.

http://www.imf.org/external/np/speeches/1999/061099.HTM

Pallister, David, Paul Kelso and Brian Whitaker (2002). 'Caught in Bin Laden's wave of terror', *Guardian Unlimited*, 31 Jan. Internet site of the *Guardian* and *Observer*.
http://www.guardian.co.uk/Archive/Article/0,4273,4346488,00.html

Palmer, Monte, Abdelrahman al-Hegelan, Mohammed Bushara Abdelrahman, Ali Leila and El Sayeed Yassin. (1989). 'Bureaucratic innovation and economic development in the Middle East: A study of Egypt, Saudi Arabia, and the Sudan', *Journal of Asian and African Studies*, 24 (1–2), 12–27.

Palmer, Monte, Ibrahim Fahad Alghofaily and Saud Mohammed Alnimir (1984). 'The behavioral correlates of rentier economies: A case study of Saudi Arabia' in Robert W. Stookey, ed., *The Arabian Peninsula: Zone of Ferment*. Stanford, CA: Hoover Institution Press, Stanford University.

Parker, Barry (2001a). 'Saudi Arabia at centre of gathering storm of terror accusations', Agence France Presse news agency, 14 Oct.

——— (2001b). 'Saudi Arabia hits back angrily at terror accusations', Agence France Presse news agency, 15 Oct.

Parssinen, Catherine (1980). 'The changing role of women' in *King Faisal and the Modernisation of Saudi Arabia*, ed. Willard A. Beling. London: Croom Helm.

Paul, Jim (1980). 'Insurrection at Mecca'. *Merip Reports*, 91 (Oct.), 3–4.

Perlez, Jane (2001). 'Saudis uncooperative, White House aides say', *International Herald Tribune*, 12 Oct., 5.

Peterson, John E. (1986). *Defending Arabia*. London: Croom Helm.

Philby, H. St. John B. (1922). *The Heart of Arabia: A Record of Travel and Exploration* (2 vols). London: Constable.

——— (1928). *Arabia of the Wahhabis*. London: Constable.

——— (1952). *Arabian Jubilee*. London: Robert Hale.

——— (1957). *Forty Years in the Wilderness*. London: Robert Hale.

——— (1964). *Arabian Oil Ventures*. Washington: Middle East Institute.

——— (1968). *Sa'udi Arabia*. Beirut: Librairie du Liban.

Pike, David (1992). 'Reforms begin as business bounces back' (*MEED* special report: Saudi Arabia), *Middle East Economic Digest*, 20 Mar., 9–16.

Pilkington, Edward and Paul Kelso (2002). 'Fear among expats as bomb kills banker', *Guardian Unlimited*, 21 June. Internet site of the *Guardian* and *Observer*.
http://www.guardian.co.uk/international/story/0,3604,741284,00.html

Pincus, Ward (2001). 'Anti-US sentiments run high at Friday prayers in Mideast', Associated Press, 26 Oct.

Piscatori, James P. (1983). 'Ideological politics in Sa'udi Arabia' in J.P. Piscatori, ed., *Islam in the Political Process*. Cambridge University Press.

Platt's (2000). 'OPEC majority revert to pre-March 1999 quota—delegates', *Platt's Commodity News*, 28 Mar. Distributed electronically by Reuters (Business Briefing Select), 28 Mar. 2000.

Power, Colin (1998). 'Higher education: Future vision'. Paper presented at the Riyadh Conference on Higher Education, 22–25 Feb.

Preisler, Ulf (1998). 'Saudi Arabia braces for Internet revolution', *Gulf Business*, 3 (8), Dec.

http://www.gulfbusiness.com/cgi-local/index.cgi?article=1&ID= 19&ww=on&pg=1

Presley, John R. (1984). *A Guide to the Saudi Arabian Economy*. London: Macmillan.

Pyon Elizabeth and Hyehoon Lee (1998). 'Miracle or mirage?' in proceedings of the conference: *Social Implications of the Asian Financial Crisis* (Seoul, 29–31 July), eds Elizabeth Pyon and Hyehoon Lee (EDAP Joint Policy Studies, no. 9). Published by the Korea Development Institute.

Quandt, William B. (1981). *Saudi Arabia in the 1980s: Foreign Policy, Security, and Oil*. Washington, DC: Brookings Institute.

Ramonet, Ignacio (1997). 'Disarming the markets', *Le Monde Diplomatique* (Internet edn), Dec.

http://www.monde-diplomatique.fr/md/en/1997/12/leader.html

al-Rasheed, Madawi (1996a). 'Saudi Arabia's Islamic opposition', *Current History*, 95 (597), (Jan.), 16–22.

——— (1996b). 'God, the King and the Nation: Political rhetoric in Saudi Arabia in the 1990s'. *The Middle East Journal*, 50 (3), (Summer), 359–71.

——— (1998). 'The Shi'a of Saudi Arabia: A minority in search of cultural authenticity', *British Journal of Middle Eastern Studies*, 25 (1), 121–38.

Rentz, George (1972). 'Wahhabism and Saudi Arabia' in Derek Hopwood, ed., *The Arabian Peninsula: Society and Politics*. London: Geo. Allen & Unwin.

Reporters sans Frontières (1999). 'The twenty enemies of the Internet', Press Release, 9 Aug.

http://www.rsf.fr/uk/alaune/ennemisweb.html

Reuters (1997a). 'Saudi to start bilateral WTO talks next year', Reuters news service, 5 Aug.

Reuters (1997b). 'King Fahd approves members of regional assemblies', Reuters news service, 6 Aug.

Reuters (1999a). 'Saudi's USB, SAMBA shareholders approve merger', Reuters Business News, 4 July.

Reuters (1999b). 'Saudi issues some $1.1 bln in bonds for contractors', Reuters news service, 1 Aug.

Reuters (2000a). 'Iran to work with OPEC despite rift, says state TV', Reuters news service, 29 Mar.

Reuters (2000b). 'Saudi says Amnesty report lacks objectivity', Reuters news service, 2 Apr.

Reuters (2000c). 'Gulf Arabs condemn Amnesty report on Saudi Arabia', Reuters news service, 9 Apr.

Reuters (2000d). 'Saudi, Iran finalise security pact details—diplomat', Reuters news service, 4 July.

Reuters (2001a). 'Saudi will not comromise faith to join WTO', Reuters news service, 4 Nov.

Reuters (2001b). 'Gulf War radicalised bin Laden—former spy chief', Reuters news service, 6 Nov.

Reuters (2001c). 'UK says terror acts could outlive bin Laden', Reuters news service, 6 Nov.

Reuters (2001d). 'Saudi minister warns teachers against extremism', Reuters news service, 8 Nov.

Reuters (2001e). 'Rights groups welcome to visit Saudi prisons—paper', Reuters news service, 5 Dec.

Reuters (2001f). 'US team heads to Saudi to discuss anti-terror work', Reuters news service, 6 Dec.

Reuters (2001g). 'OPEC will not cut output without non-OPEC deal', Reuters news service, 8 Dec.

Reuters (2001h). 'Saudi sees $12bln '02 budget gap, $6.6bln in '01', Reuters news service, 8 Dec.

Richards, Charles (1994). 'Islam finds cracks in Saudi rule', *Independent on Sunday*, 24 Apr., 13.

Richardson, Ian (1997). Text of original reports on BBC Arabic Television for publication in the *Independent* (UK) and *Al-Quds al-Arabi* (London).

Ricks, Thomas E. (2001). 'Defining the objective of U.S. fury: to defeat or annihilate Qaida?', *International Herald Tribune*, 14 Dec., 7.

Riyadh Daily (1997a). 'Al-Mohaya meets US Defense aide', 9 May. Distributed electronically by Reuters (Middle East News Briefs, article ref. no.: 001036184099), 29 May. 1997.

Riyadh Daily (1997b). 'GCC gearing up for WTO role', 19 Aug. Distributed electronically by Reuters (Business Briefing Select), 26 Aug. 1997.

Rose, David (1996a). 'Labour MP lashes captains of industry over "stifling" of Saudi dissident cleric', *Observer*, 7 Jan., 1.

——— (1996b). 'Arms and the man they had to silence', *Observer*, 7 Jan., 11.

Rossiter, Caleb (1995). Interview on 'Network Asia', ABC-PNN Newsradio (Aust.), 10 Aug.

Rowell, Andy (1999). 'Faceless in Seattle', *Guardian Unlimited*, 6 Oct. Internet site of the *Guardian* and *Observer*.

http://www.guardianunlimited.co.uk/Archive/Article/
  0,4273,3909384,00.html

Roy, Olivier (1998). 'Fundamentalists without a common cause', *Le Monde Diplomatique*, Oct. edn (*Guardian Weekly*, supplement), 2.

Royce, Knut (1991). 'Family feud, Saudi style', *The Nation*, 243 (23), 30 Dec., 844–6.

Rugh, William (1973). 'Emergence of a new middle class in Saudi Arabia', *The Middle East Journal*, 27 (1), 7–20.

Sachs, Jeffrey (1998). 'Global capitalism: Making it work', *The Economist*, 12 Sept., 19–23.

Saeed, Abdullah (1993). 'Islamic banking in practice: A critical look at the *murabaha* financing mechanism', *Journal of Arabic, Islamic and Middle Eastern Studies*, 1 (1), 59–79.

——— (1995). Islamic banking in practice: The case of Faisal Islamic Bank of Egypt', *Journal of Arabic, Islamic and Middle Eastern Studies*, 2 (1), 28–46.

——— (1996). *Islamic Banking and Interest: A Study of the Prohibition of Riba and its Contemporary Interpretation*. Leiden: E.J. Brill.

——— (1998). 'Idealism and pragmatism in Islamic banking: The application of *shari'ah* principles and adjustments', *Journal of Arabic, Islamic and Middle Eastern Studies*, 4 (2), 89–111.

Safran, Nadav (1985). *Saudi Arabia: The Ceaseless Quest for Security*. Cambridge, MA: The Belknap Press of Harvard University Press.

Salameh [Salamé], Ghassane (1980). 'Political power and the Saudi state', *Merip Reports*, 91, (5-22 Oct.).

Salamé, Ghassan (1989). 'Political power and the Saudi state' in Berch Berberoglu, ed., *Power and Stability in the Middle East*. London: Zed Books. [Revised and updated version of Salameh, 1980.]

SAMBA (1997). 'Outlook for the Saudi economy: Fall 1997', Saudi American Bank publication, 13 Nov.

SAMBA (1998a). 'Update on the Saudi economy: January 1998', Saudi American Bank briefing paper, 15 Jan.

SAMBA (1998b). 'Oil prices and the Saudi budget—1998', Saudi American Bank briefing paper, 24 Feb.

SAMBA (1998c). 'The Saudi economy—Feb. '98. Summary update', Saudi American Bank briefing paper, 3 Mar.

SAMBA (1998d). 'Gulf capital markets and family businesses', Chief Economist's seminar paper, Riyadh, 8 Mar.

SAMBA (1998e). 'The Saudi economy at end-1998', Saudi American Bank briefing paper, 27 Nov.

SAMBA (1998f). 'Saudi Arabia: Quest for economic opportunity', Saudi American Bank publication, Dec.

SAMBA (1998g). 'Saudi Arabia: A special report prepared by Saudi American Bank (SAMBA)' in *The 1998 Guide to Banking Services in the Middle East*. London: Euromoney Publications PLC.

SAMBA (1999). 'Saudi Arabia 1999 Budget: Analysis of the press reports', Saudi American Bank briefing paper, 25 Jan.

SAMBA (2000). 'Saudi Arabia's new foreign investment law', Samba Chief Economist's report, 25 Apr.

SAMBA (2001). 'The Saudi economy: 2000 performance, 2001 forecast', Saudi American Bank publication, Feb.

(Economy Watch, SAMBA Internet site: http://www.samba.com.sa/sindex.htm)

SAMBA (2002a). 'The Saudi economy in 2002', Saudi American Bank publication, Feb.

SAMBA (2002b). 'The Saudi economy at mid-year 2002', Saudi American Bank publication, Aug.

Saudi Arabia Index (2000a). 'Basic Law of Government (1992)'. University of Wuerzburg, Internet political resource on Saudi Arabia (4 July 2000 update).

http://www.uni-wuerzburg.de/law/sa00000_.html

Saudi Arabia Index (2000b). University of Wuerzburg, Internet political resource on Saudi Arabia (27 July 2000 update).

http://www.uni-wuerzburg.de/law/sa__indx.html

Saudi Gazette (1997a). 'Kingdom to be full member of WTO in 2002', 4 Aug. Distributed electronically by Reuters (Business Briefing Select), 8 Aug. 1997.

Saudi Gazette (1997b). 'Cabinet for expanding private sector role in national economy', 5 Aug. Distributed electronically by Reuters (Business Briefing Select), 13 Aug. 1997.

Saudi Gazette (1997c). 'Salman opens King Fahad Mosque', 9 Aug. Distributed electronically by Reuters (Business Briefing Select), 15 Aug. 1997.

Saudi Gazette (1999). 'US expert supports Saudi Arabia's WTO membership', 3 Dec. Distributed electronically by Reuters (Business Briefing Select), 16 Dec. 1999.

Saudi Gazette (2000). Abdullah tells Govt agencies to improve performance', 2 Apr. Distributed electronically by Reuters (Business Briefing Select), 7 Apr. 2000.

SBS-TV (2000). Report on illegal drug use in Kuwait, 'World News', SBS-TV (Aust.), 10 Apr.

Schleifer, S. Abdallah (1998). 'Media explosion in the Arab world: The pan-Arab satellite broadcasters', *Transnational Broadcasting Studies*, no. 1

(Fall). Electronic journal of the Adham Centre for Television Journalism, the American University in Cairo.

http://www.tbsjournal.com/Archives/Fall98/Articles1/Pan-Arab_ bcasters/pan-arab_bcasters.html

(*TBS* home page: http://www.tbsjournal.com/index.html)

Schmitt, Eric and James Dao (2001). 'A nation challenged: The air campaign. Use of pinpoint air power comes of age in new war', *New York Times*, 24 Dec., 1.

Schneider, Howard (2001a). 'Saudi missteps gave bin Laden time to build his Qaida network', *International Herald Tribune*, 16 Oct., 2.

———— (2001b). 'U.S. probe unraveling the Saudi connection', *International Herald Tribune*, 18 Oct., 3.

Schulze, Günther and Heinrich Ursprung (1999). 'Globalisation of the economy and the nation state', *The World Economy*, 22 (3), 295–352.

Sciolino, Elaine (2002). 'Saudi warns U.S. to respect Arafat', *International Herald Tribune*, 28 Jan., 1.

Shahin, Emad Eldin (1995). 'Salafiyah'. In *The Oxford Encyclopedia of the Modern Islamic World*, ed. John L. Esposito, vol. 3, 463–9. New York: Oxford University Press.

Shakespear, Capt. W.H.I. (n.d.). Quoted in memo from British Political Agent, Kuwait, to Civil Commission, Baghdad, 13 June 1920, no. 6317; L/P & S/10, 6499/1920, Pts 1, 2. Quoted in Gary Troeller (1976), *The Birth of Saudi Arabia: Britain and the Rise of the House of Sa'ud*. London: Frank Cass, p. 171.

Sharani, Khalid (1998). 'SABIC gears up for 21st century', *Saudi Gazette*, 29 Nov. Distributed electronically by Reuters (Business Briefing Select), 9 Dec. 1998.

Shiels, Duncan (1999). 'Oil prices surge after Nigerian unrest', Reuters Business News, 9 July.

Sick, Gary G. (1997). 'The coming crisis in the Persian Gulf' in Gary G. Sick and Lawrence G. Potter, eds, *The Persian Gulf at the Millennium: Essays in Politics, Economy, Security, and Religion*. New York: St. Martin's Press.

Sick, Gary G. and Lawrence G. Potter (1997). 'Introduction' in Gary G. Sick and Lawrence G. Potter, eds, *The Persian Gulf at the Millennium: Essays in Politics, Economy, Security, and Religion*. New York: St. Martin's Press.

Simons, Geoff (1998). *Saudi Arabia: The Shape of a Client Feudalism*. New York: St. Martin's Press.

Snoddy, Raymond and David Gardner (1996). 'BBC–Saudi TV row reveals raw spot', *Financial Times*, 10 Apr.

Sonn, Tamara (1990). *Between Qur'an and Crown: The Challenge of Political Legitimacy in the Arab World.* Boulder, CO: Westview Press.

South China Morning Post (1997). 'Saudi paper chiefs jailed', 15 Sept. Distributed electronically by Reuters (Business Briefing Select), 15 Sept. 1997.

Springborg, Patricia (1992). *Western Republicanism and the Oriental Prince.* Cambridge: Polity Press.

Springborg, Robert (1999). 'Political structural adjustment in Egypt: A precondition for rapid economic growth?' Paper presented at the 18th Annual Conference of the Australasian Middle East Studies Association, The University of Sydney, 23–24 July.

Steketee, Mike and Benjamin Haslem (2000). 'Call to halve tax cuts for rich', *The Australian*, 19 June, 1.

Stevens, Paul (1996). 'Oil prices: The start of an era?', *Energy Policy*, 24 (5), 391–402.

———— (1997). 'Increasing global dependence on Gulf oil: 'This year, next year, sometime, never?', *Energy Policy*, 25 (2), 135–142.

Stratfor.com (1999). 'The Saudi Succession'. Stratfor Special Report (0130 GMT, 990925), 25 Sept.

http://www.stratfor.com/MEAF/specialreports/special12.htm

(Stratfor.com home page: http://www.stratfor.com/)

Syed, Parveez (1997a). 'Saudi Haj fire killed and injured 11,500', Shanti RTV News, 20 Apr. Distributed by Middle East Realities (MER) electronic news service (e-mail delivery).

———— (1997b). 'Saudi haj fire victims blocked-in', Shanti RTV News, 24 Apr. Distributed by Middle East Realities (MER) electronic news service (e-mail delivery).

Tanzi, Vito (1998). 'Corruption around the world: Causes, consequences, scope and cures', *IMF Staff Papers*, 45 (4), (Dec.). Washington DC: International Monetary Fund.

Taubman, Philip (1980). 'US aides say corruption is threat to Saudi stability', *New York Times*, 16 Apr., 1.

Tibi, Basam (1990). 'The simultaneity of the unsimultaneous: Old tribes and imposed nation-states in the modern Middle East' in P.S. Khoury and J. Kostiner, eds, *Tribes and State Formation in the Middle East*. Berkeley and Los Angeles: University of California Press.

Transparency International (2002). Corruption Perceptions Index, 2002. Transparency International (Internet site).

http://www.transparency.org/pressreleases_archive/2002/
2002.08.28.cpi.en.html

Troeller, Gary (1976). *The Birth of Saudi Arabia: Britain and the Rise of the House of Sa'ud.* London: Frank Cass.

Tusa, John (1996). 'Death of a service', *Guardian*, 10 Apr., 15.

al-Tuwaim, Saud and Saqr al-Amri (2000). 'Seven Haj agent licenses cancelled', *Arab News*, 22 Mar. Distributed electronically by Reuters (Business Briefing Select), 28 Mar. 2000.

Tyler, Patrick E. (2001). 'Saudis uneasy over U.S. use of bases', *International Herald Tribune*, 25 Sept., 5.

UPI (1997). 'Saudi man says he quit Hezbollah', United Press International news agency, 5 Mar. Carried by Northern Light Technology LLC Internet news service: Special Collection (document ID: XX19970808280004268).

US State Department (2000). 'Country Reports on Human Rights Practices for 1999' (Saudi Arabia report). United States Department of State: Bureau of Democracy, Human Rights and Labor, 25 Feb.

http://www.state.gov/www/global/human_rights/1999_hrp_report/saudiara.html

(State Dept home page: http://www.state.gov/www/dept.html)

USA Today (1999). 'OPEC agrees to curb oil production' (Internet edn), 23 Mar.

http://www.usatoday.com/news/world/nwstue03.htm

Valinejad, Afshin (2001). 'Sultan swipes at Americans over Khobar bomb charges', *Daily Star* (Beirut), 23 June, 5. Associated Press news agency, 22 June.

Vicini, James (1997). 'US to drop charges against Saudi tied to bombing', Reuters news service, 8 Sept.

Victor, Peter (1996). 'BBC to investigate Saudi censorship', *Independent*, 10 Jan., 10.

Viorst, Milton (1996). 'The storm and the citadel', *Foreign Affairs*, 75 (1), (Jan./Feb.), 93–107.

Wall Street Journal (1981). 'Paying "commissions" to Saudi leaders is nothing new for some US concerns', 1 May, 23.

Wehr, Hans (1976). J.M. Cowan, ed., *A Dictionary of Modern Written Arabic*. Ithaca, NY: Spoken Language Services Inc.

Weiser, Benjamin (1998a). 'US asks British to deliver suspected Bin Laden aide', *New York Times*, 29 Sept., A10.

——— (1998b). 'Senior aide could implicate Bin Laden in terrorist acts', *New York Times*, 3 Dec., A11.

Whitaker, Brian (2000). 'Saudis claim victory in war for control of web', *Guardian Unlimited*, 11 May. Internet site of the *Guardian* and *Observer*.

http://www.guardianunlimited.co.uk/Archive/Article/0,4273,4016777,00.html

——— (2002). 'Saudis want 100 nationals held by US', *Guardian Unlimited*, 30 Jan. Internet site of the *Guardian* and *Observer*.

http://www.guardian.co.uk/Archive/Article/0,4273,4345753,00.html

Williams, Evan (2000). *The Trial of Anwar Ibrahim* (video documentary). 'Foreign Correspondent', ABC-TV (Aust.), 10 (14), 3 Oct.

Wilson, Peter W. and Douglas F. Graham (1994). *Saudi Arabia: The Coming Storm.* New York: M.E. Sharpe.

Winder, Richard Bayly (1965). *Saudi Arabia in the Nineteenth Century.* London: Macmillan.

Woollacott, Martin (1996). 'Crude deals that buy our silence', *Guardian Weekly,* 14 Jan., 10.

World Bank (1998). 'Saudi Arabia at a glance', World Bank (Internet site), 30 Sept.

(World Bank home page: http://www.worldbank.org/)

World Bank (1999). *World Development Report 1998/99: Knowledge for Development.* New York: Oxford University Press.

World Bank (2001a). *World Development Report 2000/2001: Attacking Poverty.* New York: Oxford University Press.

World Bank (2001b). 'Saudi Arabia data profile' (from World Development Indicators Database, July 2001), World Bank (Internet site).

(World Bank home page: http://www.worldbank.org/)

World Press Freedom Review (1997). Media information Internet site. Saudi Arabia, Middle East and North Africa section.

http://www.freemedia.at/archive97/saudiara.htm

World Press Freedom Review (1998). Media information Internet site. Saudi Arabia, Middle East and North Africa section.

http://www.freemedia.at/archive97/saudiara.htm

World Press Freedom Review (1999). Media information Internet site. Saudi Arabia, Middle East and North Africa section.

http://www.freemedia.at/archive97/saudiara.htm

Wright, Robin (1996). 'Iran braces to get blamed for bombing of US site', *Los Angeles Times,* 25 Dec., A4.

WTRG (2000). 'OPEC reaches agreement', WTRG Economics (Internet site).

http://www.wtrg.com/opec/OPEC2000/Springaggreement.html

Wynn, Lisa (1997). 'The romance of Tahliyya Street: Youth culture, commodities and the use of public space in Jiddah', *Middle East Report,* July–Sept., 30–1.

Zhdannikov, Dmitry and Patrick Lannin (2001). 'Russia to cut oil exports after OPEC pressure', Reuters news service, 5 Dec.

Ziadeh, Farhat J. (1995). 'Sunni schools of law' in John L. Esposito, ed., *The Oxford Encyclopedia of the Modern Islamic World,* vol. 2, 456–64. New York: Oxford University Press.

Zilo, Alexander (1998). Feature Interview with Alexander Zilo (President and Chief Executive Officer, Orbit Communications Corporation), *Transnational Broadcasting Studies*, no. 1 (Fall). Electronic journal of the Adham Centre for Television Journalism, the American University in Cairo.
http://www.tbsjournal.com/Archives/Fall98/Interviews1/A_Zilo/a_zilo.html

INDEX